Leading Change Through the Lens of Cultural Proficiency

Bruce

Thank you for
your caring and
support , the past
I hope the story and the
resources we've included
are of use to you as you
continue your work with
school leaders.
All the best to you and your family

3/22

Neil Myatt

Dedications

We, the authors, dedicate this book to Eaveston's Superintendent of Schools, who embodies visionary leadership, resilience, dedication, and commitment to education in the service of all students. Your personal humility and professional will shine through in the greatness of Eaveston School District.

We, the authors, dedicate this work to Eaveston School District's educators, staff, and community members, who open doors for their students while fighting the COVID-19 global pandemic and attendant social injustices. To my cousin Kristin; my daughters, Brynley and Hailee; and my husband, Daniel, who collectively exemplify hope, courage, and love.

—Jaime

To my husband, Pastor Samuel J. Casey, and my three amazing adult children, Samantha, Tamia, and Kourtny, for their love, support, and straight talk. And to school leaders everywhere who will take this guide and change the world, leaving it better than we found it.

—Tamika

To my friend and guiding light Randy Lindsey. Forty years ago we began a journey of love and caring, which has grown with every year. I am deeply grateful for your friendship.

—Keith

To Dawson Combs and Eli Harp, who are Delores and my great grandsons and embody our collective future.

—Randy

Leading Change Through the Lens of Cultural Proficiency

An Equitable Approach to Race and Social Class in Our Schools

Jaime E. Welborn

Tamika Casey

Keith T. Myatt

Randall B. Lindsey

FOR INFORMATION:

Corwin
A SAGE Company
2455 Teller Road
Thousand Oaks, California 91320
(800) 233-9936
www.corwin.com

SAGE Publications Ltd.
1 Oliver's Yard
55 City Road
London, EC1Y 1SP
United Kingdom

SAGE Publications India Pvt. Ltd.
B 1/I 1 Mohan Cooperative Industrial Area
Mathura Road, New Delhi 110 044
India

SAGE Publications Asia-Pacific Pte. Ltd.
18 Cross Street #10-10/11/12
China Square Central
Singapore 048423

President: Mike Soules

Associate Vice President and Editorial Director: Monica Eckman

Program Director and Publisher: Dan Alpert

Senior Content Development Editor: Lucas Schleicher

Associate Content Development Editor: Mia Rodriguez

Editorial Assistant: Natalie Delpino

Production Editor: Megha Negi

Copy Editor: QuADS Prepress Pvt. Ltd.

Typesetter: Hurix Digital

Cover Designer: Scott Van Atta

Marketing Manager: Sharon Pendergast

Library of Congress Cataloging-in-Publication Data

Names: Welborn, Jaime, author. | Casey, Tamika, author. | Myatt, Keith, author. | Lindsey, Randall B, author.

Title: Leading change through the lens of cultural proficiency : an equitable approach to race and social class in our schools / Jaime E. Welborn, Tamika Casey, Keith T. Myatt, Randall B Lindsey.

Description: Thousand Oaks, California : Corwin, [2022] | Includes bibliographical references and index.

Identifiers: LCCN 2021035685 | ISBN 9781071823699 (paperback) | ISBN 9781071823675 (epub) | ISBN 9781071823668 (epub) | ISBN 9781071823651 (ebook)

Subjects: LCSH: Multicultural education—Study and teaching—United States. | Educational equalization—United States. | Professional learning communities—United States. | Educational leadership—United States. | Professional learning communities—United States.

Classification: LCC LC1099 .W44 2022 | DDC 370.1170973—dc23/eng/20211006

LC record available at https://lccn.loc.gov/2021035685

This book is printed on acid-free paper.

21 22 23 24 25 10 9 8 7 6 5 4 3 2 1

Contents

3 THE INTERSECTIONALITY OF RACE AND
SOCIAL CLASS

PART III: COMMITMENT TO PLANNING, COLLABORATION, GROWTH, AND IMPROVEMENT 187

Foreword

"Where do we go from here: Chaos or Community"?

As I write this foreword, these words are pulsing through my entire body. These words serve as the title of Dr. Martin Luther King Jr.'s last book in 1967. Fifty four years later, this question is still relevant and I would suggest to a larger extent a more pressing question now than in 1967. In 1967 King was asking the reader to reflect on what type of nation we would be, post–Civil Rights Movement. In an effort to simplify the possibility ruminating on the said question until eternity; King suggested that we only have two options: chaos or community.

Like W. E. B. DuBois almost a half of century before when stating, "the problem of the twentieth century will be the problem of the color line", King was calling America to confront "the color line," to confront the history of segregation, discrimination, oppression and racism; without mixing words, King suggests that if we do not address America's racist past we will find ourselves in a chaotic country.

As I write this foreword, America is holding a collective breath as the world awaits the verdict in the Derek Chauvin trial, the officer charged with the death of George Floyd, and we ask, where do we go from here?

As I write this foreword, state legislators across the country have introduced bills limiting voting rights that will disproportionately affect Black, Brown, and working-class Americans, and we ask, where do we go from here?

As I write this foreword, our public school system is more segregated now than at the height of the Brown v. Board of Education era, and we ask, where do we go from here?

As I write this foreword, I am consciously aware that America has yet to deal with the issue of the color line and as such has failed to build the beloved community.

But we are here now, with the opportunity to revisit Dr. King's question. Which brings us to Dr. Jaime Welborn and co-authors' new book. This book is a continuation of Dr. King's question, Where do we go from here? And what a wonderful time to have this question resurface. If Dr. King asked the question, Dr. Welborn and co-authors are offering a sort of roadmap, specifically for educators to answer the question.

This roadmap allows the reader to take a personal journey to discover their unconscious and implicit bias and beliefs while contextualizing the said beliefs within the moral imperative of education. The authors have set very specific goals for this road trip: close education gaps, reduce disproportionate outcomes, and build professional capacity.

The authors offer very specific tools to school leadership on the process of deconstructing systemic oppression through the Cultural Proficiency Framework. A framework that moves us from chaos, cultural destructiveness, to community, Cultural Proficiency. The time is now, educational equity is not a moment but a movement.

Through case studies and school/district narratives, the authors show the reader that there is a larger movement of educators, activists, and community leaders who are choosing community over chaos.

The question we have to reckon with in education is precisely this—"Where do we go from here?"

Terry Harris, Ed.D.

TRAVEL GUIDE
Introduction

Create Your Map

- Plan your itinerary.
- What is your destination?
- What will it take to get there?
- What's the best route for us to take?
- What's a good first step?

Resources

- The most important resource is the people on the journey.
- In what ways will you consider their readiness for this trip?
- What supports will need to be in place for a successful trip?
- What roadblocks might you foresee?
- Time and money provide the ability to develop the capacity of the individuals within the organization, which then improves organization's readiness and ability to respond.

Mileage

- How will you keep track of your travels?
- How will you know if your planning is getting you closer to your destination?
- In what ways will you measure the growth of those engaged in the work?
- How will you measure the effectiveness of your leadership?

Check the Weather

- Your organization sits within other organizations and cultures. Any and all of these will affect your journey. Be aware and include all stakeholders in your travel plans and updates.
- Be prepared for any weather.

Travel Phrases

- All learning is based on vocabulary, which then affects understanding and eventually values and beliefs. Along with data and leadership, these lead to action.

You're the Driver

- As you engage in this work, be conscious of your own growth as a leader.
- Enjoy the processes, the challenges, and successes of building something of value to your organization.
- Establish your personal goals in these processes.

Preface

"Once you have traveled, the voyage never ends, but is played out over and over again in the quietest chambers. The mind can never break off from the journey" (Conroy, 1986). Imagine a journey that gives promise to thrive, promise to help others thrive, promise to help your organization thrive. We welcome you on this journey with the Cultural Proficiency Framework and assume if you have chosen this book, you are hopeful for a road map that will guide you and your organization to a renewed purpose leading to a destiny, filled with stops along the way, to continuous school improvement and success.

The purpose of this book is to provide district- and school-level administrators, teachers, counselors, and other educational leaders, including researchers and scholars, with a guidebook for beginning or continuing their personal journeys of Cultural Proficiency. By initiating, implementing, and sustaining systemic work through continuous improvement efforts toward equity, educators can lead their organizations to excellence using the Tools of Cultural Proficiency. This book, foundational to the work of Cultural Proficiency, is designed to support the shift of adult mindsets, leading to all students thriving in our school systems. A shifting of mindsets helps actualize the vision and mission statements intended to move our practices and policies toward student success for all. Before we delve into the rationale for this book, we ask *you as a leader* to consider the integration of the following goals into your educational practice as you utilize this guidebook.

> *Goal 1:* Narrow and close access and education outcome gaps.
>
> *Goal 2:* Reduce and eliminate disproportional outcomes based on student ability, language, discipline, behavior, and academic placement.
>
> *Goal 3:* Build professional capacity within the organization to grow and support large-scale change initiatives focused on access and equity for all students.

WHY IS THIS BOOK NEEDED? THE DESTINATION TO EQUITY AND ACCESS

The foundations of American schooling are rooted in a belief that educated children go to school "to develop in an orderly and sequential way into members of society," (Dewey, 1934, p. 1). Thus, it is expected that children grow up into better citizens who know the laws of the land. The purpose of our government and citizenry is to aspire to the vision of a democratic republic set forth in the Constitution.

Today's citizenry requires an understanding of how all citizens are served, or not, by our current education systems. Educators and their school systems' deficit-based thinking models foster endemic barriers such as systemic oppression, ignorance of the effects of policies on underserved students, and the corollaries of privilege and entitlement, which detour the goals of education and the reality of access and equity for all students. The continuation of such systems, practices, and policies reflects the values, behaviors, and aspirations of the most powerful groups (Apple & Beane, 1995; Darling-Hammond, 1995; R. B. Lindsey, Karns, & Myatt, 2010; B. L. Love, 2019; Sarason, 1990).

One of the most notable outcomes resulting from this detour is the *education debt* experienced by educators and society (Ladson-Billings, 2006). Education debt occurs in forms known to school personnel as access, opportunity, and achievement gaps among students of diverse racial backgrounds and various socioeconomic statuses. It has been the focus of research and goals of improvement across the United States since the *Coleman Report*, officially titled *Equality of Educational Opportunity*, was published in 1966 (Fullan, 2000; Jencks, Smith, Henry, Mary, Cohen, Gintis, Heyns, & Michelson, 1972; Ladson-Billings, 2006; Sarason, 1996). The continued marginalization of students from historically underserved races and social classes has perpetuated systemic oppression in the forms of inequity and predictable failure in our schools. Apple and Beane (1995) posited, "Like other progressive educators, those involved with democracy care deeply about young people, but they also understand that such caring requires them to stand firm against racism, injustice, centralized power, poverty, and other gross inequities in school and society" (p. 12).

Educational leadership literature has driven reform efforts to reduce educational gaps, and while some progress is noted, inequities and limited access for some children and youth still exist. In spite of efforts such as the *Coleman Report*, which served to inform the nation as a whole and educators in particular, inequities persist (Fullan, 2016; Marzano, Waters, & McNulty, 2005; Murphy & Datnow, 2003; Tucker, 2019). In response, culturally proficient educational leaders are advocates for lifelong learning with the intent to be increasingly effective in serving the educational needs of all cultural groups of students, including those from low-income and impoverished communities (D. B. Lindsey, Thousand, Jew, & Piowlski, 2018). Embracing the moral imperative of doing what is right for all students demands that we consider how race and social class interact to shape the multiple dimensions and experiences of students of color who also live in poverty in our school systems.

As cited in Moore-Berg and Karpinski (2018), this Intersectionality of race and social class is the frame for seeing how social problems affect all members of targeted groups in our school systems (Brannon, Higginbotham, & Henderson, 2017; Jussim, Coleman, & Lerch, 1987; Mattan, Kubota, & Cloutier, 2017; Plous & Williams, 1995; Richeson & Sommers, 2016; Tapia, 2010). We, as educators, are called to rise and prevent any individual from falling through the cracks of our multilayered school systems. The Tools of Cultural Proficiency lead us to acknowledge our own behaviors and values, as well as our schools' policies and practices, in understanding the educational implication of serving students identified with demographic Intersectionality of race and social class group membership.

This book was developed as a contribution to the research literature on serving historically marginalized groups of students. It provides you with a school district case study to replicate collecting and analyzing data about demographic groups of students, specifically those of color and low socioeconomic status, in ways that lead to increased success for you and the communities you serve. You are encouraged to engage in reflection and dialogue through professional conversations as you navigate this journey. Opportunities and invitations are included throughout the book to reflect and use multiple resources to have those conversations. We hope you will use this guidebook to make decisions that meet the needs of all groups of students in your school system. You will gain insight from school leaders' success stories and lessons learned, and you will be provided a conceptual framework to understand the Tools of Cultural Proficiency, as well as leadership frameworks to implement the work in schools.

KNOWLEDGE BASE AND NATURE OF CONTENT

The content for this inquiry-based book is situated within a case study of a P–12 school district in the United States. We begin with a discussion of the moral imperative (Fullan, 2004) as it applies to the work of Cultural Proficiency (Cross, Bazron, Dennis, & Isaacs, 1989, 1993; D. B. Lindsey et al., 2018), as well as the Intersectionality of race and social class in our schools (Crenshaw, 1989; Moore-Berg & Karpinski, 2018). This introduction sets a context for you to examine your assumptions and beliefs about people who are different from you and your work using the inside-out approach to change. You will be asked to reflect on your own response to difference and the responses of the organization you lead.

Additionally, we provide vignettes drawn from the research study, centered on parent and community engagement, leadership and implementation frameworks, and collaboration of professional learning communities, to be used as a backdrop for the narratives from the case study, specifically related to the theory of change and historical effects of the use of the Tools of Cultural Proficiency in the school district. To be precise, quantitative and qualitative data that include school climate and other relevant data (e.g., state annual performance ratings, student achievement scores, attendance rates) as well as experiences from various stakeholders' viewpoints are utilized as illustrations of organizational change processes using the Tools of

Cultural Proficiency. This book is intended to support you, as a school leader, in discovering and uncovering inequities in your school and in developing policies and practices that respond to the educational and social needs of all students.

Metaphorically, you will notice we use words related to travel infrastructure, such as *road*, *trip*, *highway*, *on-ramp*, and *merging*, throughout the book because we truly believe this work is a lifelong journey that can take you and the organization in which you work to new places. The formatting of the book encourages the use of inquiry-based learning to keep you engaged and traveling along the highway on your personal and professional journey. We warn you of *oncoming traffic*, *traffic jams*, *road blocks*, and *construction sites* in the coming days. The inquiry-based design will allow you to pull over for periodic reflection, dialogue, and action—a process we will refer to as the RDA process. A *traffic light* is used to signal the RDA process throughout the book. Each chapter will end with the RDA process and push you to use an asset-based approach to action, change, and transformation.

HOW CAN YOU USE THIS BOOK? A ROAD MAP TO THE HIGHWAY OF EQUITY AND ACCESS

We designed this book to make it easy to initiate and sustain the personal and organizational change processes on which you are about to embark. You can use this guidebook as a road map. The book is divided into three parts.

> Part I: School Leadership: Educational Debt, Race, Social Class, and Change
>
> Part II: The Framework of Cultural Proficiency
>
> Part III: Commitment to Planning, Collaboration, Growth, and Improvement

Part I: School Leadership: Educational Debt, Race, Social Class, and Change sets the context for you with a focus on educational leadership, the Intersectionality of race and social class in education, the historical underpinnings of educational reform and our current education debt (Ladson-Billings, 2006), the Cultural Proficiency Framework, and personal and organizational change.

We decided to open this book in a unique way that honors the rationale for the work of equity, access, and inclusion. We simply ask, "Why?" to both experienced school leaders and educational researchers and scholars. Chapter 1 asks you to begin your travel log with the RDA process, focusing on your *why*. You will be guided to address this important question: *What calls us as educators to act to achieve equity in our school districts, buildings, and classrooms?*

In Chapter 2 we begin with a discussion used for planning your journey, using research and the Cultural Proficiency Framework. This conceptual Cultural Proficiency Framework is vital to the understanding of the journey throughout this book, and we expect it will cause a shift in your thinking related to serving students in today's complex and diverse school settings. Additionally, this chapter introduces the research kernel for this endeavor, the study of a school district implementing the Tools of Cultural Proficiency to improve outcomes. This research has been published multiple times, and three publications are included in the Resources at the end of this book. In the development of this scholarly work, it became evident that the story behind the data needed to be shared. Chapter 2 ends with the context and rationale for our inquiry-based approach.

Chapter 3 provides a review of race and social class in education, including differential opportunity, access, achievement, and related educational gaps. We combine the conceptual frameworks of Intersectionality (Crenshaw, 1989) and Critical Race Theory to provide reasoning for this book's focus on race and social class related to educators, students and their families, and the community. Because this work of providing equity and access to students who have been historically underserved by our school system structures and the people who maintain the status quo is a call to action, we shift the latter part of Chapter 3 to reviewing and supporting the work that comes before us. If we really believe we can create schools where *all* students can achieve at high levels and truly thrive, it is not important what equity model is being used but rather that models of equity work are being used. The Cultural Proficiency Framework serves as a lens or road map to examine your personal attitudes, beliefs, and behaviors, as well as the practices and policies of your organization.

The contents of Chapter 4 are designed to encourage and guide you in preparation for leading individual and organizational change in your school system. We help you to examine school leadership and the role it plays in student achievement. As you progress through the story of Eaveston's working toward equity using the Tools of Cultural Proficiency, we encourage you to take some time to plan for and employ the following leadership behaviors and structures as guideposts to improvement:

- Meaningful leadership

- Professional learning structures

- Assessment

- Cultures of collaboration

- Teams

- Sustainability

In Part II: The Framework of Cultural Proficiency, your journey moves from conceptual to applicable in Chapters 5 through 8 with the introduction of additional elements to the book, including vignettes related to three themes from the research: (1) continuous school improvement, (2) family and community engagement, and (3) professional learning communities. Each chapter focuses on one of the Tools of Cultural Proficiency and includes details related to the use of that tool connected to the narrative of Eaveston School District.

Chapter 5: Overcoming Barriers to Cultural Proficiency

Chapter 6: The Guiding Principles of Cultural Proficiency

Chapter 7: The Cultural Proficiency Continuum

Chapter 8: The Essential Elements of Cultural Proficiency

In Chapter 5 you will investigate the tool *Overcoming Barriers to Cultural Proficiency* using an inquiry process. Barriers to Cultural Proficiency are personal, professional, and institutional impediments to moral and just service to a diverse society. Often, the Barriers are functions of deficit-based core values that, in effect, inform educator behaviors and school policies and practices. Connections will be made throughout by reading the case narrative and using examples and illustrations from Eaveston School District's journey. You will learn the strategies and resources employed by Eaveston's leaders during their work of acknowledging, identifying, and overcoming the Barriers to Cultural Proficiency.

Just as Chapter 5 allows you to investigate the Barriers to Cultural Proficiency, Chapter 6 does the opposite in guiding you to investigate the Guiding Principles of Cultural Proficiency using an inquiry process. The Guiding Principles serve as a moral framework of beliefs for conducting one's self and organization in an ethical manner. The Guiding Principles are referred to as asset-based core values to inform development of inclusive educator behaviors and school practices. The case study narrative from Eaveston School District in this chapter is presented for you to make connections and learn new strategies and resources that are useful in shifting leaders' mindsets from deficit to asset based.

Chapter 7 guides you to implement the most involved data collection process of the journey of Cultural Proficiency through personal and organizational change. It is at this point that transformation of systems is grounded. The Cultural Proficiency Continuum is the tool by which leaders can guide the people in their organizations to distinguish between discriminatory practices and those practices deemed inclusive. There is power in this chapter as individuals begin to see the reality of practices and policies that are closing doors on students in their system (i.e., district, school, classroom, etc.). As you navigate Eaveston's journey of collecting data along the Continuum, across all systems (i.e., human resources, discipline, curriculum, celebrations, instruction, professional learning, classroom management, etc.), this chapter allows you to make connections and generalizations about your own school system.

Chapter 8 pushes you to become fully involved in the inquiry processes of personal and organizational change through the use of the Essential Elements of Cultural Proficiency. This tool serves as a set of standards for personal and professional behaviors and values, and organizational policies and practices. Based on the data collected in Chapter 7, you will engage in an inquiry process to identify immediate and long-term goals for the organization and begin the transformation by assessing cultural knowledge, valuing diversity, managing the dynamics of difference, adapting to diversity, and institutionalizing the cultural knowledge. The case narrative from Eaveston School District is included for connecting and generalizing the use of the Essential Elements. Resources and learning strategies employed by Eaveston's leaders on their journey are included in the chapter. In short, this chapter is about change through improvement and growth.

Part III: Commitment to Planning, Collaboration, Growth, and Improvement includes Chapters 9 to 12, which shift from Eaveston's case narrative to a commitment to your planning, collaborating to implement, and sustaining the difficult, ongoing journey toward personal transformation and increased culturally proficient educational practice in your school organization. Chapter 9 has you return to the leadership concepts introduced in Chapter 4, as well as the challenges Eaveston's school leaders faced as they implemented this work. The purpose is to support leaders as they break down the barriers to access for students of various racial and social class backgrounds, especially those who are not thriving in their school systems. The final sections of the chapter focus on the challenge of availability of time and resources as well as sustaining the work to actualize the impact on students. This information provides insight for the dispersion patterns of professional learning initiatives regarding impact on students.

Chapter 10 includes a case narrative of the process of joining forces in collaboration and building the critical mass necessary to implement and sustain the work at the systemic level. We present the lessons learned by Eaveston School District's leaders as they implemented the work and recommendations for leadership during your journey, including words of encouragement as you embark on your journey and build the capacity and critical mass in your system. The lessons learned and recommendations developed from the research study focus on (a) diverse family and community engagement, (b) professional learning communities, and (c) continuous school improvement.

Chapter 11 narrows the focus on the commitment to learning, action planning, and ensuring equitable access and outcome opportunities for all students. In this chapter you will gain an understanding of the commitment necessary for sustained organizational change at the district level and school level. You will explore strategic planning, a plan for how to implement and sustain this work over time, and you will be provided with an equity action template that can be used as you learn and apply the Tools of Cultural Proficiency.

Chapter 12 focuses on ensuring equity for all students. Often when you finish a trip, you have the opportunity to reflect on it as a whole journey. While your journey is not complete, Chapter 12 includes three resources, developed in Eaveston, that have proven essential in institutionalizing the application of the Tools of Cultural Proficiency in all aspects of the district. Exploring these resources will help you look at your school or district journey as a whole.

OUR INVITATION: USING THE FEATURES OF THIS BOOK

We wanted to bring a new resource to you related to Cultural Proficiency that can be used to advance the knowledge and skills necessary to lead personal growth and improvement and transform organizations that disproportionately lift up students from various racial backgrounds and social classes, so that they thrive in our systems more than they have done historically. To do so, we bring many concepts, theories, and "moving parts" to you in this guidebook. We want it to be interactive for you, to be easy to navigate, and to prompt the same level of passion, commitment, and excitement about the moral purpose of education and helping *all* students thrive as it does for us, the authors. In this section we provide a conceptual framework for you to use that incorporates and details all the features in this book and the ways in which you can employ them in your journey.

Travel Guide. The first section of each chapter is a "travel guide" for you to use as you begin your journey. The travel guide provides you with key terms that will help in unifying your mission of educational reform by applying the Cultural Proficiency Framework. Building unity around a common language is essential to understanding this guidebook and implementing this work. The travel guide also helps prepare you for upcoming chapters in consideration of the weather, your resources, your mileage, and your planned journey.

Calibration. This section is present in each chapter and provides you with the topic of the chapter. It is used as a tool for leaders to "calibrate" before starting or continuing the journey. This section provides questions related to the topic to center yourself, giving thought about what you are about to learn or engage in regarding self and organization.

Vignettes. This feature is used in Chapters 5 to 8 to allow you to step into Eaveston's journey of Cultural Proficiency. The story line of the vignettes illustrates the connection of the day-to-day work for increasing equity and access to three themes that emerged from the triangulation of data gathered in the research study in Eaveston: (1) continuous school improvement, (2) family and community engagement, and (3) professional learning communities. The research vignettes help you make connections to the case narratives and content presented in Part III of the book.

Research. This feature is something new and has not been presented in such detail in previous Cultural Proficiency books. The research used in this book was gathered by one of the authors, Dr. Jaime E. Welborn, over the course of two years. The close relationship with the district work allowed Dr. Welborn to provide exclusive details related to action, change, milestones, setbacks, and the realities of doing this work. We organize the research so that you can make connections and generalizations between Eaveston's journey and that of your own organization.

Case Study Narratives, District/School Level. We use a consistent narrative from the case study of Eaveston School District to illustrate the organizational change process using the Tools of Cultural Proficiency. The narratives are built from the case study research conducted in Eaveston School District as its leaders took a systemic approach to organizational change in the implementation of the Cultural Proficiency Framework. The narratives include examples and illustrations from their district-level and school-level work.

Cultural Proficiency Framework. This feature of the book helps centralize the concept of Cultural Proficiency and the research. While all books on Cultural Proficiency blend this feature into the text, this book organizes the Framework as a tool in navigating Eaveston's journey. The intent is that school leaders can apply the Framework, specifically the four tools, in an organized way using resources, examples, and illustrations from the case study. The use of this feature helps you apply and deeply analyze the Intersectionality of race and social class in the context of this work.

Culturally Proficient Learning Strategies. We present culturally proficient learning strategies that appear in *Cultural Proficiency: A Manual for School Leaders*, fourth edition (R. B. Lindsey, Nuri-Robins, Terrell, & Lindsey, 2019) in addition to some new culturally proficient learning strategies. This feature is used to reinforce the concepts and strategies used by Eaveston School District in their journey toward Cultural Proficiency. Many of the learning strategies have been adapted to help leaders and educators on this journey keep the Intersectionality of race and social class as a centralized focus. You, the reader, can use these learning strategies to engage in the work within the district or school building.

QR Codes/Resources. This book brings a new feature not presented in the previous Cultural Proficiency books. There are QR codes presented throughout the book that bring in multiple resources, such as videos, blogs, web pages, podcasts, social media presentations, interviews, literature, printable documents that can be used to do the work, and so on. It is our hope that you will use these resources, some authored by us and some by our many talented colleagues, to enhance your understanding of the work of Cultural Proficiency and embark on this journey.

Inquiry-Based Approach and the RDA Process. Inquiry-based investigations and dialogic and reflective activities guide you to understand your own assumptions, know your own values as well as the core values of the organization related to equity issues, surface relevant data, and create change within your own practices and policies through learned lessons and action planning. The RDA process is used throughout the book to conclude each chapter and promote reflection, dialogue, and action toward change and transformation. The Culturally Proficient Coaching model helps you engage with others with the intent to raise awareness of the "cultural connections of students and their families and to be educationally responsive to the diverse groups" (D. B. Lindsey, Martinez, Lindsey, & Myatt, 2020).

OUR PASSION TRULY IS FOR ALL STUDENTS

The original research paper that led to this book was focused on two variables, race and social class, and the Intersectionality of these cultural identities, as they affect student outcomes in a P–12 district in America. As such, the data produced outcomes for those variables and the bulk of the topics in this book. More important, Eaveston's school leaders, in response to the district data, focused their efforts on the improvement of students identified by social class and race. Therefore, the focus of this book, which grew out of this research, is primarily on these variables.

We acknowledge that there are many other variables to consider when working with Cultural Proficiency in public schools in America. In fact, G. Howard (2014) identified lenses of difference that contribute to an individual's culture, such as gender, sexual orientation, ableness, religion, and so on. The history of legislating mandated programs to make up for past practice begins with Title IX in 1972, which prohibited federally funded institutions from discriminating against students based on their sex. This was most apparent in the development of women's sports programs in colleges and secondary schools. It is estimated that in 1972 there were about 295,000 female athletes, compared with about 2.6 million today. We encourage the continued focus on women and girls and their unique needs in schools.

Before 1961 children with disabilities were not educated in public schools in the United States. Parents of these identified children had to either educate them at home or pay for their education privately. The Education for All

Handicapped Children Act was passed in 1975, followed by the Individuals with Disabilities Education Act of 2004. This legislation continues to provide an education for all children in the least restrictive environments at the expense of the state—a remarkable achievement that students and their families still benefit from today. The tenets of Cultural Proficiency will continue to focus on the needs of all children, including those who are differently able (D. B. Lindsey et al., 2018).

Most recently, LGBTQ (lesbian, gay, bisexual, transgender, and queer) students have been provided equal protection of the laws and are shielded legally from harassment and bullying. Title IX, which bans discrimination on the basis of sex, further provides protection to LGBTQ students. Some states are providing further protections to students by including sexual orientation, gender identity, and gender expression. The inclusion and even acknowledgment of LGBTQ students provide many lessons of Cultural Proficiency, but these students are not a specific focus in these chapters.

There are two pieces of legislation that made a difference in America for every demographic group: (1) the No Child Left Behind Act of 2001 and (2) the Every Student Succeeds Act of 2015. Both mandate the collection of educational achievement data by demographic group. The No Child Left Behind Act also required that every teacher be highly qualified, which meant they had to be credentialed in the area they were teaching. This greatly improved instruction in schools in low-socioeconomic areas. But the pernicious achievement gaps still exist in predictable ways.

Our aim in this book is to share a genuine example of how the Tools of Cultural Proficiency worked for this district by focusing on these students. That does not diminish the continued need, and our passion, for serving all children and families in our school communities. To read more about our focus on and commitment to serving all students across diverse cultural identities and associated historic events, listed in the preceding three paragraphs, we invite you to consult Resource F at the end of this book.

So *buckle up, start your engines, and put that turn signal on!* You are about to embark on a journey, a voyage that never ends. It may play over and over again. It may have you sitting with your mind in the quietest of chambers. Once you begin, your mind will not be able to shift off the journey as you take yourself and your organization to new places. In the following chapters you will find a road map. Take some time to plan your journey so that you visit all the places, some more than once. It is important to know that you will need to go to all the places to meet all the people and gain all the cultural experiences through learning events that provide opportunities for you to use the Tools of Cultural Proficiency on your journey. This cyclical process will allow you to realize that Cultural Proficiency is not just a journey but the process by which we continuously improve and educate *all* students.

We are very grateful to Corwin for its ongoing interest in and support for our work. In particular, we continue to be fortunate in having Dan Alpert as our editor, advocate, and guide, and the support of Lucas Schleicher, our associate editor, who guides us through all the stages of production. The production team at Corwin is most impressive in their commitment to high standards throughout all phases of turning the manuscript into a book. Finally, we appreciate you for your interest in our schools, in issues related to diversity and equity, and for your commitment to our profession. Together we make progress toward the goal of our democracy becoming inclusive in word and deed.

Jaime E. Welborn, *St. Louis, Missouri*

Tamika Casey, *San Bernardino, California*

Keith T. Myatt, *Burbank, California*

Randall B. Lindsey, *Fallbrook, California*

Acknowledgments

PUBLISHER'S ACKNOWLEDGMENTS

Corwin gratefully acknowledges the contributions of the following reviewers:

Angela M. Mosley, EdD
Professor
John Tyler Community College
Midlothian, VA

Jeff Ronneberg
Superintendent
Spring Lake Park Schools
Minneapolis, MN

Dr. Louis Lim
Vice Principal
Richmond Green Secondary School
Richmond Hill, Ontario, Canada

Melanie S. Hedges
Art Teacher, NBCT
West Gate Elementary School
West Palm Beach, FL

Melissa Miller
Sixth-Grade Science Teacher
Farmington Middle School
Farmington, AR

Patricia Baker
School Board (retired educator)
Culpeper County Public Schools
Culpeper, VA

Renee Ponce-Nealon
Teacher
Petaluma City Schools
Petaluma, CA

Verenice Gutierrez
Director, Educational Equity & Access
Salt Lake City SD
Salt Lake City, UT

About the Authors

Jaime E. Welborn, PhD, currently serves as an assistant professor in education leadership at Saint Louis University in Missouri. She completed her PhD in educational leadership from Saint Louis University and has presented research that investigated the degree to which principals use and value culturally proficient educational practices at Harvard University and California State University. Prior to coming to Saint Louis University, she served as an elementary school assistant principal in West St. Louis County and as a middle school mathematics and language arts teacher and elementary school teacher in rural and metropolitan public schools in Illinois. Jaime's experiences in education have been in working with diverse student populations, and her work and other life experiences have contributed to her passion in using the Cultural Proficiency lens in education for increasing educational equity, social justice, and culturally proficient leadership. In 2018 she started a consulting business, JWE Education Consulting, LLC—DBA (doing business as) the Midwest Collaborative for Cultural Proficiency in Schools. She works with school organizations, helping educators examine their individual values and behaviors, as well as their organization's practices and policies, to implement and sustain the work of Cultural Proficiency through transformative action plans. She lives in St. Louis with her husband, Daniel, and two daughters, Brynley and Hailee.

You can contact Dr. Welborn at info@midwestccps.org; website: midwestc cps.org; Twitter: @welborn_jaime

Tamika Casey currently serves as a site administrator in San Bernardino City Unified School District and copastor of New Life Christian Church of Fontana. She has served in many capacities in education, including as a mainstream classroom teacher as well as a SANKOFA Culturally Responsive Demonstration Teacher, teaching coach, program specialist for the Department of Equity and Targeted Student Achievement, elementary principal, and instructor in the school leadership program in the College of Education at California State University, San Bernardino. She has served as a conference speaker and session facilitator. She is the founder and lead consultant of Casey Education Solutions. Her leadership is focused on developing and building the capacity of individuals and organizations to align stated values and principles with more equitable and culturally proficient practices. Tamika's faith and passion for developing relationships drive her to her ultimate aim to effect change in communities and the lives of scholars.

Email: tamikacasey@caseyedsolutions.com

 **Keith T. Myatt, EdD,** was a full-time instructor in the School Leadership Programs at California State University, Dominguez Hills, where developing school leaders dedicated to dismantling systems of oppression and focusing on Cultural Proficiency was at the heart of the program. Prior to that he was at the Los Angeles County Office of Education in Educational Leadership Services as a director in the California School Leadership Academy. He is coauthor of *Culturally Proficient Education: An Asset-Based Response to the Conditions of Poverty* (Corwin, 2010) and *Culturally Proficient Coaching: Supporting Educators to Create Equitable Schools* (Corwin, 2020). He has worked at the Museum of Tolerance, providing seminars for educators wishing to establish Cultural Proficiency as an element of their work and for educators supporting credential candidates with the Tools of Cultural Proficiency and Coaching. He has recently been working to implement the California Administrator Performance Assessment and is currently helping to develop an EdD program at Dominguez Hills dedicated to creating school systems focused on the success of each and every child.

 **Randall B. Lindsey** is Emeritus Professor at California State University, Los Angeles. He has served as a teacher, administrator, executive director of a nonprofit corporation, Interim Dean at California Lutheran University, Distinguished Educator in Residence at Pepperdine University, and chair of the Education Department at the University of Redlands. All of his experiences have been in working with diverse student populations, and his area of study is the behavior of White people in multicultural settings. He has a PhD in educational leadership from Georgia State University, MA in Teaching in history education from the University of Illinois, and BS in social science education from Western Illinois University. He has served as a junior high school and high school teacher and as an administrator in charge of school desegregation efforts. At California State University, Los Angeles he served as chair of the Division of Administration and Counseling and as director of the Regional Assistance Centers for Educational Equity, a regional race desegregation assistance center. He has coauthored several books and articles on applying the Cultural Proficiency Framework in various contexts.

Email:randallblindsey@gmail.com; website: CCPEP.org; Twitter: @RBLindsey41

PART I

School Leadership: Educational Debt, Race, Social Class, and Change

TRAVEL GUIDE
Start With "Why?"

Create Your Map

- Take stock of your heart and mind about why you are engaged in this work and if this is your organization's best chance of improving student achievement.
- Envision success to define the real work.
- Plan on how you will marshal the resources of your organization and others to engage in this work in this way.
- Gather data about what currently exists and why it got that way.

Resources

- Your school's vision and mission statements' inclusion of equity
- Others in the organization who see the inequities
- This book and the experiences of Eaveston School District and the authors
- Many, many other publications and research into social justice and equitable education
- The experience of other schools and districts

Mileage

- Disaggregated student achievement data
- Goals for student achievement
- Qualitative data from stakeholder groups about what's working and why

Check the Weather

- What structures do you currently have in place—i.e., leadership groups, community councils, parent groups—that would see the need for this work?
- What district policies support equitable student achievement?

Travel Phrases

- Cultural Proficiency tools
- Assets-based approach
- Inside-out approach
- Cultural informancy
- Cultural Proficiency
- Systemic transformative levers (STLs)

You're the Driver

- What has led you to Cultural Proficiency as a tool for improvement?
- Is this going to be part of your leadership legacy?
- How will you measure the effectiveness of your leadership efforts?

CHAPTER 1

Leading Equity Starts With "Why"

Finding your why will help you find your way.

A great leader's courage to fulfill his vision comes from passion, not position.

—John C. Maxwell (2015, 2021)

CALIBRATION

Think about planning your equity journey—a trip to a new destination filled with cultural informancy (possession of cross-cultural relationships that are authentic and trusting and allow for mutual learning and feedback, leading to personal growth) and equitable outcomes for all students. We usually have many questions when planning for a trip:

Where do we want to go?

Why do we want to go there?

Will the trip be worth the time, effort, and money?

How do we get there?

Who is going with us?

What do we need to take with us?

How will we prepare for the unexpected on the trip?

Before you begin this journey, we ask you to consider the most important question, *Why?* The intent of this chapter is to allow you time to reflect on why you chose this book and why we, the authors, chose the concepts that you will encounter as you read this book. We have organized this chapter to begin with you, and then we ask you to consider the foundational concepts of this book: school leadership, Cultural Proficiency, and race and social class. On the lines provided, take a moment to answer these *why* questions: *Why are you reading this book? Why are you interested in equity? Why are you called to do this work?*

_____

_____

_____

_____

_____

WHY YOU?

You may be thinking about the challenges your school system is facing, the racial and social class contexts, or the differences that exist among your stakeholders. You may be searching for ways to foster diversity and inclusion and move your system toward equity and access. Whatever the reason may be for your ponderance, we want you to take one step back and think about you. Yes, you!

Cultural Proficiency is a process that begins with us, not our students, their families, or our school community. We, as leaders, are often hardwired to put others first, ahead of ourselves. In this case change only occurs if individuals are willing to examine their own assumptions about themselves and spend time sorting through the differences that exist between them and the individuals with whom they work. This includes their colleagues, their students and their families, and the environment in which they coexist.

Cultural Proficiency is a personal journey. It is an inside-out approach providing opportunity for individuals to explore their own personal values, behaviors, and beliefs, serving as a model for individual transformation. Using this mindset, Cultural Proficiency is a paradigm shift that allows you as a leader to view those who are culturally different from you as an asset to your life rather than an opposing person who is different, threatening, or even untenable to work with in any setting. The management of self (Gay, 2000); self-examination and reflection (Anderson & Davis, 2012); personal and professional growth in exploring your own attitudes, beliefs, and practices related to race and cultural difference (G. Howard, 2006); beliefs and individual truths (Nelson & Guerra, 2014); and "Who I am and What I am" (Taliaferro, 2011, p. 1) provides a research foundation for answering the question "Why you?"

As you continue to ponder, *Why you,* we ask you to focus on leadership. You are a leader; you have been called to do this work. The intentionality of culturally proficient leadership requires educators to use the inside-out approach for serving all students. Defining and relying on one's own personal values and beliefs drive actions, including all physical and verbal behaviors. Educational leaders can have a vision of a culturally proficient district or school, but without intentional actions to build capacity and ensure a presence and involvement in the work, there will be little change or measurable progress.

In *The Culturally Proficient School: An Implementation Guide for School Leaders*, Randall B. Lindsey, Roberts, and CampbellJones (2005) wrote,

> Culturally competent school leaders understand that effective leadership in a diverse environment is about changing the manner in which we work with those who are culturally different from ourselves. Personal transformation that facilitates organizational change is the goal of cultural competence. (p. 79)

We ask you to think about the students in your school who are not thriving, be it academically, socially, physically, or emotionally. *Why you?* Without a doubt, those students need you! The moral imperative is our call to act by first transforming ourselves to understand the differences that exist and then managing those dynamics to adapt to diversity by changing the organization so each and every child in your system is thriving.

WHY DISTRICT AND SCHOOL LEADERSHIP?

As you embark on this journey, we hope you begin to think about your leadership and the team of educators who will contribute to this quest for change. Fullan (2003) wrote, "Moral purpose means acting with the intention of making a positive difference in the lives of employees, customers, and society as a whole" (p. 3). That is an insurmountable task if done alone. We want you to think about building capacity to start the work and sustain the work. With the right people on the bus, you will be able to start the work. School leadership will take you and your organization closer to actualizing the goals of transformation and replicable growth. You as the superintendent, central office administrator, building principal, or even department or grade-level chairs have the ability to use systemic transformative levers (STLs). These levers, such as curriculum, instruction, assessment, discipline, professional development, or hiring practices, serve as focus areas in which effective educators can leverage change in organizational policies and practices as well as individuals' values, beliefs, and behaviors. Figure 1.1 includes examples of focus areas considered STLs.

As cited in Block, Everson, and Guskey (1995), Berliner suggested the use of "big variables" when planning for school change. Big variables, attributes that make a school a school, exist in similar contexts as STLs. The inquiry process we will introduce to you in Chapter 2 will set you and your teams on a path to collect data and facts regarding big variables in school systems. The inquiry process will help in planning, implementing, and actualizing change in your educational policies and practices. These changes focus on school improvement and consider major attributes or factors of our systems such as assessment, expectations, curriculum, leadership, and community/parent involvement.

FIGURE 1.1 ● Systemic Transformative Levers

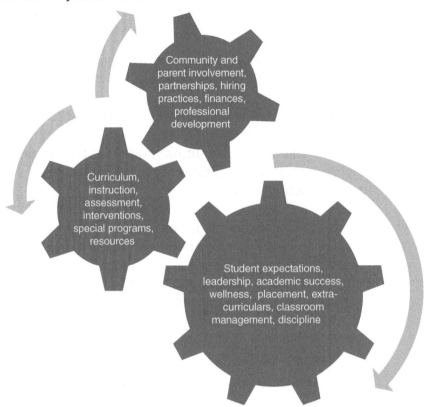

These attributes and factors of our system will be used as leverage points for change.

Those who hold administrative positions hold the power to use leverage leadership. Bambrick-Santoyo (2018) claimed that leaders have the ability to turn the lights on by *seeing it, naming it, and doing it.* He named seven levers to execute quality instruction and culture in school systems: (1) student culture, (2) staff culture, (3) managing school leadership teams, (4) data-driven instruction, (5) instructional planning, (6) observation and feedback, and (7) professional development. The work of Cultural Proficiency can be used to transform a school system into one where all students thrive and educational gaps are eliminated by increasing student achievement and well-being. The STLs can be used by district and school leaders during the journey of Cultural Proficiency to spur that change and open doors for students who have been historically underserved. We will continue to reference these levers throughout the book; however, we encourage you to focus on the essential step of planning and thinking about leading at the district and school levels to affect changes that last.

Ensuring that the work of Cultural Proficiency is being implemented at all levels in a school district or larger organization can establish lasting, systemic change results rather than the random acts of equity that check the box but do nothing for realizing outcomes. Singleton (2018) wrote, "Systemic equity transformation requires a shift in the organizational culture and climate of school systems and schools. That shift must flow from the highest-ranking leadership to and between staff in all divisions of the district" (p. 30). This makes the case for why leadership is necessary at the district and school levels during the implementation phases. If we are to see transformation and organizational change, we must see our highest-ranking leaders, namely superintendents and principals, *talking the talk* and *walking the walk*. Explicitly, this means participating in professional development that includes reflection and dialogic processes related to the work of Cultural Proficiency at the same time as their teachers and leaders. In fact, many of the school districts in which we have facilitated learning over the past several years preferred to train their leadership teams first before implementing the work of Cultural Proficiency at the classroom level. Nevertheless, school leaders' commitment to equity and excellence for all students is essential for long-term, systemic change.

WHY CULTURAL PROFICIENCY?

Based on our historical chronicle of education reform over the past half-century, we have had some positive trends of progress for student achievement, equality, access, inclusion, and, in some cases, equity. What we do not have yet are equitable outcomes for *all* students. We have not found that magic key yet. The work of leaders and educators across our country, up until this point, is to be commended; however, there is still work to be done.

SO WHY USE THE CULTURAL PROFICIENCY FRAMEWORK?

Detractors of the Framework tell the story of educators thinking that if we check the box, and thus use the Framework, we will someday be done with this reform effort. The truth is that this reform effort is here to stay and leaders who embark on this journey must accept that planning for sustainability, using the Cultural Proficiency Framework in their systems, is essential. It is planned change. Cultural Proficiency is a journey that will never be over. Nuri-Robins (2016) said, "It is important for teachers to understand that this isn't the latest educational Hershey Bar; it's something that has been around for a while and will be around for a while longer." She continued, "We can't know everything there is to know about everybody." We must continue to work every day, looking at all systems and using STLs to make changes for improved student outcomes.

Cultural Proficiency is a mindset developed by applying four tools of a framework to craft our schools' educational programs to be comparably effective with student populations across a wide spectrum of racial and social experiences. What all of our PreK–12 students have in common is the capacity and ability to learn. Our role as educators is to recognize our students' capacity to learn and to design and implement curriculum and instruction framed around the expectation that students can and will learn.

We want you to turn the pages to Chapter 2 of this book with confidence in your ability to lead positive, transformational change toward school improvement. The Cultural Proficiency Framework includes four inter-related tools, not strategies or techniques (Cross et al., 1989; R. B. Lindsey, Nuri-Robins, & Terrell, 2009). While we will cover the Cultural Proficiency Framework in detail in Chapter 2, we want to introduce you to this model or conceptual framework as you embark on this journey and consider your *Why*. Figure 1.2 shows the Tools of Cultural Proficiency and the ways in which they interact with and inform one another. The Cultural Proficiency Framework, along with additional information related to the Tools of Cultural Proficiency, can be found at The Center for Culturally Proficient Educational Practice website (ccpep.org). Image 1.1 provides access to this website.

CCPEP

The Tools of Cultural Proficiency, when applied strategically, can assist educational leaders in performing tasks such as developing and implementing school board policies, allocating resources, using assessment data, delivering curriculum and instruction, interacting with parents and community members, and planning and delivering professional development, with sustainability. We know from history that numerous school reform efforts have come and gone. Some have proven successful, while others have fallen flat. Fullan (2016) suggested,

> If a healthy respect for and mastery of the change process do not become a priority, even well-intentioned change initiatives will continue to wreak havoc among those who are on the firing line. Careful attention to a small number of key details during the change process can result in the experience of success, new commitments, and the excitement and energizing satisfaction of accomplishing something that is important. (p. 8)

As you continue to answer the question "Why Cultural Proficiency?" we want to emphasize certain keys for the success of any school improvement program: (a) understanding change, (b) improving relationships, (c) developing a shared meaning by knowledge creation and sharing, (d) capacity building with a focus on results, and (e) fulfilling the moral imperative (Fullan, 2001). Through reflection and dialogue, leaders who use the Tools of Cultural Proficiency can conceptualize and then actualize school change. In other words, we dream it, then we do it.

Following are additional details as to why Cultural Proficiency could and should be used as a means for educator and school improvement reform:

- It is an asset-based approach to equity work that allows leaders to focus on the positive aspects students and their families' cultures bring to the school system.

- It provides four tools for planning for change at all organizational levels (district, school, and classroom).

- It is based on a focus on *you*, which follows research on change.

FIGURE 1.2 ● The Culturally Proficient Framework

The Five Essential Elements of Cultural Competence

Serve as standards for personal, professional values and behavior, as well as organizational policies and practices

- **Assessing cultural knowledge**
- **Valuing diversity**
- **Managing the dynamics of difference**
- **Adapting to diversity**
- **Institutionalizing cultural knowledge**

The Cultural Proficiency Continuum portrays people and organizations who possess the knowledge, skills, and moral bearing to distinguish among equitable and inequitable practices as represented by different worldviews:

Informs

Unhealthy, unproductive, and inequitable policies, practices, and behaviors	Differing Worldviews	Healthy, productive, and equitable policies, practices, and behaviors
• Cultural destructiveness • Cultural incapacity • Cultural blindness	◄──►	• Cultural precompetence • Cultural competence • Cultural proficiency

Informs

Resolving the tension to do what is socially just within our diverse society leads people and organizations to view selves in terms productive and equitable.

Informs

Overcoming Barriers to Cultural Proficiency

Serve as personal, professional, and institutional impediments to moral and just service to a diverse society by:

- being resistant to change,
- being unaware of the need to adapt,
- not acknowledging systemic oppression, and
- benefiting from a sense of privilege and entitlement.

Ethical Tension

Guiding Principles of Cultural Proficiency

Provide a moral framework for conducting one's self and organization in an ethical fashion by believing the following:

- Culture is a predominant force in society.
- People are served in varying degrees by the dominant culture.
- People have individual and group identities.
- Diversity within cultures is vast and significant.
- Each cultural group has unique cultural needs.
- The best of both worlds enhances the capacity of all.
- The family, as defined by each culture, is the primary system of support in the education of children.
- School systems must recognize that marginalized populations have to be at least bicultural and that this status creates a distinct set of issues to which the system must be equipped to respond.
- Inherent in cross-cultural interactions are dynamics that must be acknowledged, adjusted to, and accepted.

Source: Adapted from R. B. Lindsey, Nuri-Robins, and Terrell (2009, p. 60).

- It is not a program to buy.

- Through inquiry-based learning, it allows leaders to focus on cultural identity differences, such as race and social class, in the context of continuous school improvement.

WHY RACE AND SOCIAL CLASS?

Research on the topic of culture presents many ideas and concepts related to race, ethnicity, social class, language, sexual orientation, ability, gender, age, and religion. In fact, culture has broadly been defined by a person's identity constructed of the aforementioned concepts, as well as one's beliefs, norms, customs, traditions, values, and behaviors (Bolman & Deal, 1997; Deal & Peters, 1991; Fraise & Brooks, 2015; Horsford, Grosland, & Gunn, 2011; Terrell & Lindsey, 2009).

Take a moment, and think about what you know related to race and social class in education. Parker's quote "The greatest educational challenge of our time is upon us," as cited in the foreword of Culturally Proficient Education (R. B. Lindsey et al., 2010, p. viii), embodies one of the most pernicious and intractable education research topics—inequity and opportunity in educational practice and policy. For decades, education researchers who focus on the inequities within school systems and structures have shown the persistence of depressed educational outcomes among students from lower social class and racialized backgrounds (Apple & Beane, 1995; Darling-Hammond, 1995; Freire, 1970; Hammond, 2015; G. Howard, 2006; Kozol, 2005; Ladson-Billings, 2006; Noguera, 2008). Differences among individuals from various racialized and social class backgrounds play an integral part in our society, thus affecting student achievement and well-being in all educational settings.

Race and social class are socially constructed. Race and social class are identifiable in ways that privilege some students and marginalize other students. Race and social class hold meaning and implications regarding the differential inputs and outputs of your students' experiences. Simply put, race and social class cannot be ignored!

The theoretical frameworks of race and poverty, covered in greater detail in Chapter 3, are critical to the understanding of our history and years of educational reform in ways that focus our future work in improving educational outcomes specifically for those who have been chronically underserved. We offer the Cultural Proficiency Framework and its attendant tools to lead your thoughts, beliefs, and behaviors, as well as your school organization's practices, procedures, and policies toward equity and demonstrable, continuous school improvement.

We, the authors, do not hold the belief that race and social class determine the success of an individual but merely that educational leaders should be aware of and be able to assess the ways in which the beliefs and values of individuals lead to behaviors that affect others. Consider this: Stakeholders in an organization enter a setting with their individual and shared history, beliefs, values, and patterns of behavior. These differences often give rise to culturally based conflicts in which the educators of the institution respond based on their experiences, beliefs, and values. Often, those responses are inadequate in that they unknowingly and unwittingly perpetuate a predictable failure for students who are culturally different from the dominant group. We want to make it clear that our belief is that all cultural identities and the intersectionality of cultural identities, for each and every student in our schools, are important. While we focus on the cultural identities of race and social class in this book, we recognize the importance of this work for opening doors for all students, including those of various national origins, ethnicities, genders, sexual orientations, religions/faiths, and abilities.

WHY DO WE EVEN HAVE TO CONSIDER OUR "WHY"?

We began this chapter with the question "Why you?" At that point you may have wondered, "Why should I ask *why*?" Simon Sinek introduced to the world of leadership, organizational learning, and development the importance of knowing our *why*. Put simply, *why do we do what we do?* Sinek (2009) provided needed and compelling provocations to help leaders understand and be able to articulate to self and others why we do what we do as leaders. No argument from us. In fact, full and total agreement. Sinek helped us understand the influence of *why* in the work of Cultural Proficiency:

> For values or guiding principles to be truly effective they have to be verbs. It's not "integrity," it's "always do the right thing." It's not "innovation," it's "look at the problem from a different angle." Articulating our values as verbs gives us a clear idea—we have a clear idea of how to act in any situation. (p. 53)

WHY ME? WHY US?

Too often in schools those championing the work of diversity and equity are challenged with a confrontive take on the *why* question. In those settings the *why* question often morphs into "Why do we have to do this work?"— followed by resistance masked with queries such as the following:

- "Are you serious? We did this a few years ago, but it had another name."

- Or "Are you saying there is something wrong with us? We don't need this training; as educators we are natural human relations people." And the variation: "It is the teachers and other educators who retired years ago yet are still with us."

- Or the venerable "Why us? It is [fill in the blank—the superintendent's cabinet, the 'suits' downtown, the restive parents) who could benefit from this training."

Yet leading Cultural Proficiency initiatives calls on us to be clear with ourselves as to why we are doing this work. It is only when we are clear within ourselves that we are positioned to serve as leaders for our colleagues and the communities served by our schools. This loops us back to the starting line: "Why do we even have to know our *why*?" Some might ask, "I know my subject matter craft, so why this other stuff?" It is our belief and experience that when educators believe they can educate all students, they do so. Students can learn, irrespective of the racial and social class demographics of educators in our schools or school districts.

You have been called to transform your system because of your leadership commitment to equity. Leaders play a vital role in the effectiveness of any school, having a significant impact on students' achievement and school culture (Augustine-Shaw, 2015). Leadership ranks second in effect size related to student achievement (Leithwood, Seashore-Louis, Anderson, & Wahlstrom, 2004). We encourage you to think about your relationships and experiences with race and social class, the moral imperative of education, and change.

WHY AN "INSIDE-OUT" JOURNEY?

As you proceed through this book, the phrase "inside-out journey" recurs in intentional fashion. Cultural Proficiency is a journey to better understand our values and beliefs, while simultaneously preparing to better understand the policies and practices of our schools and school districts in service to children and youth from diverse communities. Okay, let's pause for a moment.

You may be thinking that you are in a homogeneous community that reflects little or no racial, socioeconomic, gender, sexual orientation, or religious diversity and that there is no reason to believe that demographic change is imminent. You believe your children and youth will be fine. This may be true in the near term; however, there is a good chance your students will leave your community and venture into a fully diverse society. Also, communities change. Trends and indications across the United States and Canada lead us to believe that our communities are undergoing demographic changes, albeit slowly. As educators it is incumbent that we prepare ourselves and thereby the students in our schools to be able to function in diverse settings—schools, workplaces, neighborhoods.

So we are full circle in this first part of our Cultural Proficiency journey. It comes back to us. Being clear why we do the work of access and equity is important. The COVID-19 pandemic has laid bare the discrepancies in who is afflicted with the virus: disproportionately people of color, people from low-income communities, and the aged. It is more than coincidental that many children and youth of color and those from low-income communities are less successful in our schools. Our *why* is clear here—the gaps in data are unacceptable, untenable, and contemptible. Let us emphasize that we are referencing much more here than just student academic achievement scores and rates of discipline referrals. Until we see the day when we can say without a doubt, "All of our students are thriving" or "When students graduate from our system, they are prepared to navigate and be effective in diverse spaces," we as educators must be focused on creating systems, through continuous improvement and mindset growth, that show each child their worth through equitable, accessible, and inclusionary outcomes.

The question continues, "Why do we do this work? Why is this work even needed? Why do we even have to pose the 'why' question?" If we were visiting a friend's house for a pool party and we witnessed a child struggling in the pool and in danger of drowning, we would not ask, "Why lend aid to the child?" That said, wide swaths of society still resist equity and inclusivity that lend aid to those afflicted. Therefore, it is incumbent on us to be clear as to our values and commitment in fostering an inclusive, socially just experience for all children and youth in our schools.

 LOOKING IN THE REARVIEW MIRROR

Crafting a response to "Why do we do this work of access and equity?" is central to our success with students from a broad array of backgrounds and experiences. Cultural Proficiency entails a journey of continuous, endless learning and self-discovery. We learn about others—our colleagues, students, and communities—served by our schools. We learn of our reactions to racial and social communities different from our own.

Today, educators across the United States and Canada come together to guide our societies and help move them in the direction of becoming inclusive democracies. Posing the *Why* question can be fundamental to recognizing our central role in creating an inclusive democracy. We shift from believing *all students can learn* to believing that *we can learn to educate all students.*

ON TO OUR NEXT DESTINATION

The next chapter begins with a discussion of the moral imperative of education. Setting education as a moral imperative requires a "whatever it takes" mentality. Following this introduction, we provide the foundations of the research behind this book. This will include comprehensive descriptions of the Cultural Proficiency Framework and an introduction to Eaveston School District. The descriptive case study, completed during a two-year implementation of the Cultural Proficiency Framework, illustrates the organizational change process at the district and school levels using the Tools of Cultural Proficiency.

REFLECTION, DIALOGUE, AND ACTION PROCESS

REFLECTION • Dialogue • Action

What calls you as an educational leader to act to achieve equity in our school districts, buildings, and classrooms?

_____

_____

_____

_____

_____

Reflection • DIALOGUE • Action

Discuss the individual and collective reasons for engaging in the work of Cultural Proficiency with your team. Take note of your experiences while dialoguing with your colleagues.

_____

_____

_____

_____

_____

Reflection • Dialogue • ACTION

The strategy used here includes recommended actions to prepare you for creating your own culturally proficient leadership plan. We ask you to start with "Why?" Before reading Chapter 2, please take some time and complete your first travel log by answering the most important question: _Why are you taking this journey of Cultural Proficiency?_ Think personally and professionally.

_____

_____

_____

_____

_____

Travel Log

_____
_____
_____
_____
_____
_____
_____
_____
_____
_____
_____
_____
_____
_____
_____
_____
_____
_____
_____
_____
_____
_____
_____
_____
_____
_____
_____
_____
_____
_____
_____
_____
_____

TRAVEL GUIDE
Thinking and Planning Through Cultural Proficiency

Create Your Map

- Establish a context for using an inquiry-based approach for school change.
- Provide a rationale for using the Cultural Proficiency Framework for leading change.
- Begin to envision your cultural proficiency journey.

Resources

- The research in Resource B in this book
- The policies, procedures, and practices that represent culturally proficient principles in place in your organization
- The readiness of the people in your school community to continue, or begin, this work

Mileage

- Student achievement data
- Satisfaction or happiness surveys
- The history of systemic oppression in your school community
- Establishing ways to measure the success of your vision/mission statement(s)

Check the Weather

- What cultural groups exist in your community?
- In what ways do race and social class influence what your organization accomplishes and the ways it works?
- Who already sees the effects of race and social class and the cultural effects?

Travel Phrases

- Research-based case story
- Inquiry-based approach
- Systems thinking
- The Framework
- The Guiding Principles
- The Cultural Proficiency Continuum
- The Essential Elements
- Leader
- Moral imperative

You're the Driver

- How have you established a routine for your personal reflection?
- Determine the frontiers of what you can and cannot change.
- In what ways does your personal culture affect others?
- What is the principle that compels you to act at this time?
- In what ways will you walk your talk?

CHAPTER 2

The Cultural Proficiency Framework: Research and Planning

That all students and teachers benefit in terms of desirable goals, that the gap between high and low performers becomes less as the bar is raised, that ever-deeper goals are pursued, and that the culture of the school becomes so transformed that continuous improvement relative to the previous three components becomes built in.

—Michael Fullan (2003, p. 31)

It's not differences that divide us.

It's our judgments about each other that do.

—Margaret J. Wheatley (https://www.inspiringquotes .us/author/8821-margaret-j-wheatley)

CALIBRATION

Imagine being given a roadmap to meet the moral imperative of education—the imperative of leading change in education in a way that every single student is given a fair and substantive opportunity to not only learn but also thrive. As a leader in your district or school, we invite you to reflect on Fullan's quote to help center yourself in the context of this journey in which you are about to embark. The quote references the challenges of educational practice and policy, educational gaps, goals toward continuous school improvement, and culture. We ask you to draw yourself a bit closer in reflection of this quote related to the gaps between higher and lower performers in your school organization, be it at the district, school, or classroom level. Who is not thriving in your organization? To what degree does the current culture of your district or school support those students who are not thriving?

_____

_____

_____

_____

_____

ON-RAMP TO PLANNING, RESEARCH, AND CULTURAL PROFICIENCY

We invite you on this journey and provide you with a road map that guides your decisions and work so that students and teachers benefit, gaps narrow as expectations rise, goals become increasingly focused on results for historically underserved students, and transformation of the school culture creates an environment where continuous school improvement is embedded into the DNA of the school system. Equity is built into the systems, the places, and the people. Equity becomes "the way things are done around here."

The purpose of this chapter is twofold:

- To provide the context for using a case study and an inquiry-based approach to school change

- To provide a rationale for using the Cultural Proficiency Framework for leading that change

The context used throughout this book is a research-based case story, findings from the study, a model for inquiry, and an application of practice for use in your schools. District-level and school-level leaders like you can use the context to embark on your own journey and lead others in examining and changing educational practices for increased equitable access and outcomes for students, using the Framework of Cultural Proficiency. Throughout the book, you are given the opportunity to use reflection, dialogue, and action (RDA) processes to pace yourself and make progress throughout the implementation of this call to action.

This chapter introduces you to the case of Eaveston School District. A real district in the United States, the name *Eaveston* is pseudonymous, and the case is carried through each chapter of the book. We use this research-based application of the Cultural Proficiency Framework to provide a context for the road map that you may use to implement the work of Cultural Proficiency in your organization. This section in Chapter 2 includes a synopsis of the background, rationale, review of the literature, and methodology for the research study used to investigate Eaveston's implementation of their experiences with Cultural Proficiency. We provide thoughts around the importance of research-practice partnerships. Resource B, at the end of this book, contains the research case study publications.

Additionally, we introduce you to an inquiry-based learning model to help you in implementing your work. In this section, we review select inquiry-based models and then introduce one to guide your work, focusing on student outcomes using a systemic educational reform approach. The Cultural Proficiency journey is not for the faint of heart or for leaders looking to check the boxes of compliance. Simply put, this journey should be ongoing without end. The Cultural Proficiency pathway becomes the way in which you educate all students in your system and a lens for defining success.

If you are just beginning your journey toward Cultural Proficiency or have been on the highway for many years, we ask that you ponder the answers to the questions below before engaging and collaborating with others. The Cultural Proficiency journey is a personal one that begins with you. It is this deep understanding that will allow you to successfully lead change in your district or school. Take a moment to reflect on you.

- To what cultural groups do you belong? How does your culture affect others? How does your race and social class influence your work as a school leader? Who are you as a cultural being?

- What are examples of programs or practices in your organization that provide every child a fair and substantive opportunity to learn? What are your organization's areas of strength and areas of opportunity for growth?

- What is the principle that compels you to act? What is your moral imperative as a school leader?

_____

_____

_____

_____

_____

THE FRAMEWORK AND TOOLS OF CULTURAL PROFICIENCY

For this book one of the Cultural Proficiency authors summarized in very personal terms the societal realities of race and class. A few days after the slaying of Michael Brown in the St. Louis area in 2014, Raymond Terrell and Randall Lindsey were involved in deep discussion. This was not their first discussion on violence being visited on African Americans. During this discussion Raymond paused, took a deep breath thinking of his much-loved four-year-old grandnephew and asked the universe, "How do I tell an innocent, beautiful young Black child that people will not like him solely because of the color of his skin?" After a moment of silence, each recommitted to working with colleagues at all levels of education on ways to overcome the structural barriers of systemic oppression, the sense of privilege and entitlement that fuels individual and systemic resistance to change, and the need to adapt to the communities in their schools' service areas. Adapting to the communities in their schools' service areas means seeking out and building on the assets present in their cultures and neighborhoods as opposed to lamenting wistfully for the students who used to attend our schools or the students we wished were enrolled in our schools. To conceptualize the work referred to in the above story, we present the Conceptual Framework of Cultural Proficiency.

THE CULTURAL PROFICIENCY FRAMEWORK

The Tools of Cultural Proficiency are adapted from the work of Terry Cross and his associates (1989) and applied to the field of education. The term *tools* is used to communicate the processes and strategies used to guide educators' and related community members' reflections on their values and behaviors in ways that surface, examine, and seek to change unknown and often unacknowledged biases. Each tool is discrete and independent, yet they come together into a "framework" to guide personal and organizational change for ensuring that all demographic groups of students succeed in our schools. No hierarchy is implied or suggested among the tools as they function interdependently to guide individual educators' and all school members' actions. In Chapter 1 we provided the Cultural Proficiency Framework in Figure 1.2. Image 2.1 is a new graphic representation of the Cultural

Highway to Culturally Proficient Educational Practice

Overcoming	**Overcoming Barriers to Cultural Proficiency** Teams work to overcome barriers of Cultural Proficiency by understanding how those barriers inform all negative, unhealthy, and inequitable policies, practices and behaviors.
Relying	**Relying on Guiding Principles of Cultural Proficiency** Teams work to rely on the Guiding Principles by understanding how those beliefs inform all positive, healthy, and equitable policies, practices and behaviors.
Collecting	**Collecting Policy, Practice, and Behavior Data on the Cultural Proficiency Continuum** The Continuum helps teams identify policies, practices, and behaviors that produce inequities and deny access, and then create opportunities to change them.
Planning	**Planning for Change using the Essential Elements of Cultural Proficiency** The Essential Elements guide the team's actions and planning for increasing equity, access, and inclusion, so that all students thrive.

Proficiency Framework. In this representation we invite you to examine the role of teams as they apply the Tools of Cultural Proficiency on this highway to culturally proficient educational practice.

You may want to take another quick glance at The Center for Culturally Proficient Educational Practice website (ccpep.org) before reading the information that follows. Take the time to scan the QR code below to access this website from your device. You will find additional resources to help you on your journey.

THE TOOLS OF CULTURAL PROFICIENCY

Briefly, the tools are as follows.

OVERCOMING BARRIERS

This tool unlocks educator and school inactions. Learning about systemic oppression, privilege and entitlement, resistance to change, and adapting to the communities our schools serve is always an enlightening, if not challenging, experience for educators. The authors have had numerous occasions in recent years to pose the question that follows to educator colleagues in schools across the United States and Canada.

Do you believe that at some point in our country's history racism did exist?

The question is followed with this one:

Do you believe racism persists today?

Then, the authors pose the same questions for discrimination based on gender, sexual orientation and identity, social class, religious affiliation, English as a second language, or disability, among others, depending on the community. Almost uniformly, the first two rounds of questions are met with expressions such as these:

"Did" exist? Are they serious?

Never is there any equivocation about historical and current oppressions existing and persisting. Posing these somewhat naive questions creates the opportunity for observations such as this:

Then, if we can agree that people have been and are oppressed and marginalized by individual, political, and social forces, that means there are folks who benefit in ways they may not even recognize. Am I right?

The expressions that surface in the room serve to describe a sense of privilege and entitlement. With participant attention at hand, we proceed to the intended observation: *Once we become aware that such political, social, and economic forces exist and persist, then our responsibility is to respond in ways that provide equitable educational access and outcomes for all demographic groups of students in our schools.*

THE GUIDING PRINCIPLES OF CULTURAL PROFICIENCY

In juxtaposition to the negative core values embedded in the Barriers, the Guiding Principles serve to inform and to guide the development of inclusive educator values and behaviors, as well as inclusive school policies and practices. The nine Guiding Principles provide an opportunity to explicate the expressed "values" related to issues that emerge in serving diverse school communities. Consideration of the Guiding Principles allows educators and their schools to develop asset-based core values. These values serve and inform the development of healthy practices, policies, and behaviors that increase access to quality education for students and create conditions in which all students can thrive.

THE CULTURAL PROFICIENCY CONTINUUM

The six points of the Continuum describe educator values and behaviors and schools' policies and practices. Three points on the left are negative and three points on the right are positive. *Cultural Destructiveness*, *Cultural Incapacity*, and *Cultural Blindness* describe actions and practices that create hierarchies and separation. *Cultural Precompetence*, *Cultural Competence*, and *Cultural Proficiency* reflect the development of educator actions and school practices of inclusivity to meet the educational needs of all demographic groups of students.

THE ESSENTIAL ELEMENTS OF CULTURAL PROFICIENCY

Rubrics

The Essential Elements serve as actionable verbs, guiding the development of educator values and behaviors and school policies and practices to serve all students equitably. Located at the fifth point of the Continuum, *Cultural Competence,* the Essential Elements are derived from the Guiding Principles and are intended for here-and-now use. The sixth point of the Continuum, *Cultural Proficiency*, extends the Essential Elements in ways that are future focused on the changing demographics of the community and a commitment to lifelong learning.

For your reference, QR Code 2.2 includes several rubrics, organized by the Cultural Proficiency Continuum and the Essential Elements of Cultural Proficiency. You may download and use these rubrics to guide your consideration of topics including the following:

- Curriculum and instruction
- Parent and community outreach
- Educators' inclusion and support of English-learning students and their communities
- Professional learning
- Mentoring and leadership

The next section introduces you to the case story of Eaveston School District, as leaders in the district implemented the Cultural Proficiency Framework for leading organizational change.

A CASE STUDY: NARRATIVES AS ILLUSTRATIONS OF AN ORGANIZATIONAL CHANGE PROCESS USING THE TOOLS OF CULTURAL PROFICIENCY

A DEEPER LOOK: EAVESTON SCHOOL DISTRICT

Eaveston School District, a state and national award–winning district, is a diverse suburban, public P–12 school district in the United States. We, the authors, use a pseudonymous name, Eaveston, throughout the book to provide illustrations of an actual district implementing the Cultural Proficiency Framework. The name was changed to protect the identities of the school district and its employees, families, and community members, while maintaining efforts to gain reliable and valid findings from the case study research.

Eaveston was established as a place that fosters opportunities for children to learn, grow, and live as valuable members of the community. Although fewer than 10,000 students, Eaveston School District has multiple schools, serving students in grades P–12. The location of Eaveston School District is unique in its geographical and historical contexts. Positioned close to the county line that separates the urban center of a city and the suburban areas called the "county," Eaveston is situated in a corridor of numerous intersecting major interstate systems. Because Eaveston stands among many businesses and factories in a metropolitan county of more than 1 million people, the district receives approximately 90% of funds from local sources.

Most notably, Eaveston School District is rated as one of the most diverse school districts in the state. The student population represents 78 different countries, speaks 48 languages, and demographically is approximately 50% White, 30% African American/Black, 10% Hispanic, 5% multiracial, and 5% Asian. Intersectionality of cultural differences among Eaveston's students is at the heart of the Cultural Proficiency work in Eaveston School District, as nearly half of the district's students live at or below the U.S.-defined poverty line.

Central to the mission and core values of Eaveston School District is the focus on all students' opportunity to learn at high levels regardless of cultural identity. The district's asset-based core values guide the development and implementation of many practices and policies. Over the past two decades Eaveston has faced major geographical and economic challenges and changes in the larger community. These changes prompted increases in student body diversity, such as in culture, race, and social class; however, Eaveston leaders held fast to their belief that the diversity is a positive contribution to the values and assets of the school district.

In recent years Eaveston School District has been recognized as one of the best school districts in the state, according to state rankings. District leaders believe those rankings do not happen by chance. They happen because transformational leadership, focused on efforts of organizational change, transforms policies and practices to better serve Eaveston School District's students. District and school-level leaders believe their leadership actions have influenced the improvement in the district's accreditation status, student achievement indicators on state performance ratings, and demographic group achievement levels (i.e., subgroups disaggregated by race/ethnicity and free and reduced-price lunch status). Most important, they believe their leadership in embedding Cultural Proficiency in all aspects of the district and schools has led to shifts in educators' mindsets and changed conversations. In Chapter 4 you will read about the importance of teams, collaboration, and professional learning structures that aid in creating a culture where students feel like they belong.

EAVESTON'S WHY FOR CULTURAL PROFICIENCY

You may be pondering these questions:

Why is the work of Cultural Proficiency important?

How is the work being implemented in schools and school districts?

Case study methodology allows us to shape "why" and "how" questions and then answer them (Yin, 2018). Eaveston's mission is to ensure success for all learners, and leaders in Eaveston rely on their expressed core values of *diversity, knowledge, commitment, care, safety, learning, interdependence, contribution, strength, freedom,* and *success* to guide, develop, and implement their school improvement processes and programs to achieve the mission.

Block and colleagues (1995) summarized the importance of innovative school improvement programs as having a bold style and substance. While the Framework of Cultural Proficiency is not a program, it is a set of tools that allows for mindset shifts that lead to changes in educational policy and practice. Block et al. wrote,

> Each (successful school improvement programs) offers optimistic beliefs about learners, teachers, and schools—beliefs about all students' capacities to learn well, fast, and/or confidently; beliefs about all teachers' capacities to teach excellently, quickly, and or/humanely; and beliefs about all schools' capacities to educate effectively, efficiently, and/or invitingly. Each offers, too, an amalgam of ideas and techniques for realizing these beliefs, an amalgam that forms a scaffolding for the conduct of a particular school's curriculum-building, teaching, or testing affairs. This scaffolding is specific enough to suggest some general school reform/restructuring tasks, yet general enough to allow school leaders to accomplish these tasks in their own specific ways. (p. 4)

Now more than ever, school leaders are called to invest in school improvement programs, including professional learning that is *core, big, research-based,* and *institutionalized* (Block et al., 1995). These key elements of school improvement lead us to think about the possible outcomes of using the Tools of Cultural Proficiency in the current school reform landscape. The core of Cultural Proficiency allows educators to address issues of inequity in the classroom; the *big and research-based* elements of Cultural Proficiency allow educators to address issues of professional self-determination; and the *institutionalization* element of Cultural Proficiency allows educators to address inequities and professional self-determination over time (Block et al., 1995). So why did leaders in Eaveston commit to using the Framework for Cultural Proficiency? The rationale for selecting this Framework included the need to:

- systemically address opportunity and educational gaps among students based on demographics such as race, ethnicity, and social class (*core*);

- manage the dynamics of difference from the high level of cultural, racial/ethnic, and social class diversity (*core, big, research-based*);

- provide stakeholders in the district with tools to examine current implementation and outcomes of practices and policies and to make changes to those adversely affecting student success (*core, big, research-based, institutionalized*); and

- develop a common language around increasing school improvement efforts through opportunity, access, and equity while building capacity among all district stakeholders to initiate and sustain significant changes over time (*institutionalized*).

What leaders in Eaveston wanted was planned change (Everson, 1995). They wanted to improve by making reasoned, data-informed decisions about the actions they would take to create change, specifically increased equity, access, and opportunity in the district for all students, especially those who were not thriving in Eaveston. The question "Why Cultural Proficiency?" for Eaveston was easy to articulate: They wanted to see "the 'possibilities' for change available to school leaders as they clarify their school's problems and seek appropriate solutions to those problems" (Everson, 1995, p. 434).

FOR THE RESEARCHER/SCHOLAR COMMUNITY

There is always a space where the worlds of researchers, scholars, and practitioners collide. We know that researchers and practitioners cannot work in isolated silos. We need researchers to help uncover best practices for practitioners, and we need practitioners to inform research efforts toward continuous growth and improvement. Perhaps we should ponder the similarities in worldview of researchers and practitioners.

Creswell (2014) described a research worldview by identifying social constructivists as individuals who "seek understanding of the world in which they work and live" (p. 8). A constructivist researcher addresses the process of interactions among individuals and relies on the specific contexts in which people work and live to understand the historical settings and cultural identities of the individuals. Practitioners involved in this work lead in much the same way.

We ask you to think about your role as a researcher or scholar. Think about your understanding of self and how research can help others understand differing values and beliefs and how they influence daily decision-making and behaviors in schools. If we consider research in the name of students who are not thriving in our education systems, we lean on a transformative worldview of research.

As cited in Creswell (2014), Mertens (2010) suggested that research inquiry situated in a transformative worldview is connected to politics and political change agendas that confront social oppression at whatever levels it occurs. "Thus the research contains an action agenda for reform that may change lives of the participants, the institutions in which participants work and live, and the researcher's life (Creswell, 2014, p. 9). We ask you to consider in your planning how will you build partnerships with the research community.

PARTNERSHIPS: SCHOOL LEADERSHIP AND THE RESEARCH COMMUNITY

As you embark on this journey, we hope you begin to think about your relationship with either researchers and scholars or practitioners in school systems who will contribute to this quest for change. How can the research community support school leadership at district and school levels and vice versa?

There is a growing trend of research-practice partnerships (Penuel, Allen, Coburn, & Farrell, 2015). Partnerships between school leaders and the research community can take you, and the organizations you work with, closer to actualizing the goals of transformation and replicable growth. Research-practice partnerships are collaborations between practitioners and researchers that are organized to investigate problems of practice and provide solutions for improving schools and school districts over a long period of time (Coburn, Penuel, & Geil, 2013). As you read this book and navigate your own journey, we ask you to consider your own research-practice partnerships, like the one developed between the researcher and practitioners in Eaveston School District.

In Resource B, we provide a summary of the literature reviewed, methodology, findings, and conclusions of the case study conducted in Eaveston School District. This feature is something new that has not been presented in such detail in previous books on Cultural Proficiency. The research information used in this book was collected by one of the authors over the course of two years. Because of the close relationship with the district, the author provides exclusive details related to action, change, milestones, challenges, and the realities of doing this work. We present three QR codes that provide you with three published articles from the case study to further your reading beyond this book.

Welborn, J. E. (2019). Increasing equity, access, and inclusion through organizational change: A study of implementation and experiences surrounding a school district's journey towards culturally proficient educational practice. *Education Leadership Review*, 20(1), 167–189.

Welborn, J. E., & Lindsey, R. B. (2020). A descriptive study of the case of Eaveston School District: Core values from deficit-based to asset-based. *Journal of Leadership, Equity, and Research*, 6(1). https://journals.sfu.ca/cvj/index.php/cvj/article/view/73

Casey, T., & Welborn, J. E. (2020). Cultural proficiency as an advocacy tool to build a diverse workforce. *Leadership Magazine, March/April*. https://leadership.acsa.org/cultural-proficiency-as-an-advocacy-tool-to-build-

Now that you have an understanding of the conceptual framework of Cultural Proficiency and have been introduced to the case study of Eaveston School District, the next section will provide a context for using an inquiry-based approach to leading organizational change in your district or school.

INQUIRY: A GUIDE FOR LEADING ORGANIZATIONAL CHANGE TOWARD EQUITY, ACCESS, AND INCLUSION

We, the authors of this book, used an inquiry-based approach to the journey of Cultural Proficiency because we believe in Schwab's (1960) idea that individuals are able to learn by investigating problems and scenarios through social experiences. The work of continuous school improvement, as well as research, is conducted in much the same way. Bybee and Landes (1990) developed the 5E instructional model, which was used to design science lessons and is based on cognitive psychology, constructivist-learning theory, and best practices in science teaching. Bybee (1997) declared that "using this approach, students redefine, reorganize, elaborate, and change their initial concepts through self-reflection and interaction with their peers and their environment. Learners interpret objects and phenomena, and internalize those interpretations in terms of their current conceptual understanding" (p. 176). The work of Cultural Proficiency requires educators to use the same approach to redefine, reorganize, elaborate, and change their initial concepts through self-reflection and interaction with their peers and their environment. This precisely means changing their educational practice to be more culturally proficient.

Furthermore, appreciative inquiry, developed by Cooperrider and Whitney (2005), takes a positive, transformative approach to change. "Appreciative Inquiry offers a positive, strengths-based approach to organizational development and change management" (p. 1). This model is complementary to the Cultural Proficiency Framework because of its asset-based design. In the appreciative inquiry process, school leaders focus on *discovery, dreams, designs*, and *destiny*. The four phases of appreciative inquiry are described as follows:

1. *Discovery*: Mobilizing the whole system by engaging all stakeholders in the articulation of strengths and best practices—identifying "the best of what has been and what is"

2. *Dream*: Creating a clear, results-oriented vision in relation to discovered potential and in relation to questions of higher purpose, such as "What is the world calling us to become?"

3. *Design*: Creating possibility propositions of the ideal organization, articulating an organization design that people feel they can drawing on

4. *Destiny*: Strengthening the affirmative capability of the whole system, enabling it to build hope and sustain momentum for ongoing positive change and high performance

Table 2.1 includes the steps for each inquiry-based approach described above. While the words of action appear to be different in definition, there are similarities that exist. The most important conceptual learning to be gained from this table is how each approach relates to the work of Cultural Proficiency and involves using the Essential Elements of Cultural Proficiency

TABLE 2.1 ● The Essential Elements and Inquiry-Based Approaches to Change

ESSENTIAL ELEMENTS (CROSS ET AL., 1989; R. B. LINDSEY ET AL., 2019)	CULTURALLY PROFICIENT INQUIRY (R. B. LINDSEY, GRAHAM, WESTPHAL, & JEW, 2008)	APPRECIATIVE INQUIRY (COOPERRIDER & WHITNEY, 2005)	INQUIRY-BASED APPROACH (SCHWAB, 1960)	5E SCIENTIFIC INSTRUCTIONAL MODEL (BYBEE & LANDES, 1990)
Assessing cultural knowledge	Define the context. Establish the purpose. Define the scope.	Discovery	Ask	Engagement
Valuing diversity	Identify and select the inquiry participants.	Dream	Investigate	Exploration
Managing the dynamics of difference	Design the process.	Design	Create	Explanation
Adapting to diversity	Collect and analyze the data.	Design	Discuss	Elaboration
Institutionalizing cultural knowledge	Interpret and report the results.	Destiny	Reflect	Evaluation

through the RDA process. We invite you to consider how you will approach your inquiry-based journey to Cultural Proficiency.

LOOKING IN THE REARVIEW MIRROR

As we prepare to leave this destination, we must continue to look in our rearview mirrors with our newly discovered context for using a case study and an inquiry-based approach to school change, as well as the rationale for using the Cultural Proficiency Framework for leading that change. Once we cross over into our destinations of Chapters 5 through 8, you will continue to rely on the narratives of Eaveston School District as illustrations that can support the planning, implementation, and sustainability of the Cultural Proficiency Framework in your district or school.

ON TO OUR NEXT DESTINATION

Our next destination, Chapter 3, serves as a review of race and social class in education, including differential opportunity, access, and achievement, and related educational gaps. We introduce the term *Intersectionality* (Crenshaw, 1989) to provide reasoning for this book's focus on race and social class related to educators, students and their families, and the community. Because this work of providing equity and access to students who have been historically underserved by our school system structures and the people who maintain their status quo is a call to action, we shift the latter part of the chapter to Critical Race Theory and today's inequities.

REFLECTION, DIALOGUE, AND ACTION PROCESS

REFLECTION • Dialogue • Action

Before reading this chapter, what were your understandings and thoughts around Cultural Proficiency? School improvement work? Equity work? As a person and leader in an educational organization, what are you thinking now about this work? We have asked you to think about students who are not thriving in your buildings. To what degree have you been thinking about those students in the contexts of race/ethnicity and social class? How does what you have learned in this chapter influence your mindset and the lens through which you lead change in your school or district? Please use the following space to record your thoughts, observations, and questions.

_____

_____

_____

_____

_____

Reflection • DIALOGUE • Action

Following the opportunities to reflect on your learning and your thinking, we invite you to scan the QR codes below to hear from us, the authors, in the very first episode of our podcast, *Leading Through the Lens of Cultural Proficiency*. In this episode we tell our stories about our journeys of Cultural Proficiency to introduce the purpose and importance of the dialogue with others, seeking to understand others.

TELLING OUR STORIES

What might be some reasons why you are interested in the journey of Cultural Proficiency?

Use the lines below to record your new learning.

FACEBOOK
Join our Facebook page
to engage and dialogue
with others.

_____

_____

_____

_____

_____

Reflection • Dialogue • ACTION

Reflect on your school organization's mission statement. What do the words reflect? What values are identified in this statement? Is there something the organization's mission statement is missing? Write down your mission statement. What is the world calling you to become? What steps are necessary for you as the leader of your organization to take in order to accomplish this mission?

Examine the vision and goals of the school organization. Who is not thriving under this vision? Who is not able to meet these goals? If you are to lead change by asking all stakeholders to join you on this journey toward Cultural Proficiency, what pieces are missing that would be part of the ideal organization that you would propose/create?

Travel Log

_____

_____

_____

_____

_____

_____

_____

_____

_____

_____

_____

_____

_____

_____

_____

_____

_____

_____

_____

_____

_____

_____

_____

_____

_____

_____

_____

_____

_____

_____

_____

_____

_____

_____

TRAVEL GUIDE
Intersectionality of Race and Social Class

Create Your Map

- Develop background knowledge of the historical context of this work
- Examine local events with a cultural proficiency lens
- Understand the intersectionality of race and social class in your own context

Resources

- The positive intentions and work of the school community in which you work
- Chapter 3 resources for framing the issues related to inequality
- Race and social class are socially, not biologically, constructed

Mileage

- Gather data regarding the effects of the Intersectionality of race and social class on student achievement.
- What local events have affected the climate of your school community historically?

Check the Weather

- What events, nationally and locally, have influenced the gaps that exist in your schools and communities?
- How have these events shaped current attitudes, beliefs, and actions?
- How is local media helpful with these issues?

Travel Phrases

- Intersectionality
- Asset-based thinking
- Race
- Social class
- Critical Race Theory
- Oppression Olympics

You're the Driver

- In what ways do you make sense of the violence against citizens in America?
- How do you assist others in processing these events and issues?
- How are you keeping track of your growth as an equity leader?
- How do you become an equity leader?

CHAPTER 3

The Intersectionality of Race and Social Class

It is easy to say that every child deserves opportunity—regardless of race, disability, ZIP code, or family income. It is easy to say that we expect excellence from every child. However, it has been much more difficult to ensure that decisions connected to funding, policy, practice, and support translate into real access and opportunity for historically marginalized students.

—Monique M. Chism (2020)

When facts do not fit with the available frames, people have a difficult time incorporating new facts into their way of thinking about a problem. Without frames that allow you to see how social problems impact all the members of a targeted group, many will fall through the cracks of our movements, left to suffer in virtual isolation. It doesn't have to be this way!

—Kimberle Crenshaw (2016)

CALIBRATION

Take a few moments, and read the list of names and terms. Pause to consider each name and word. You may want to write notes to yourself as you consider each. Pause. Take your time with familiar terms. Do not spend time with names and terms you may not know or recognize.

George Floyd

Michael Brown

Breonna Taylor

1619

Slavery

Genocide

1776

Desegregation

1954

Integration

Hate-targeting Asian and Pacific Island Americans

Achievement gaps

Access and outcome gaps

Demographic profile of students in Advanced Placement (AP) classes

Demographic profile of students identified as "special education"

Parent and community involvement

Take a few more moments to write what you are thinking and feeling as you consider the names and terms. In reflecting on your consideration of the names and terms, what "sense" are you making of the ways in which the names and terms might relate to you as a person, as an educator?

_____

_____

_____

_____

_____

Please self-organize with colleagues to discuss the reflection activity. Listen to one another. Feel free to ask questions for clarification. Make every effort not to engage in debate or defense of responses. Listen to one another. Listen to self. Begin your conversations with breakthrough questions such as the following:

- What might be some of your thoughts and feelings as you read the terms?

- In what ways are you relating these terms to you as a person, as an educator?

- Given the value we have for diversity, how might our use of these terms affect the manner in which we approach the students we serve?

- What concepts and ideas do you have related to these terms that might be different from those with whom you work?

Take note of your experiences while dialoguing with • your colleagues.

_____

_____

_____

_____

_____

ON-RAMP TO THE INTERSECTIONALITY OF RACE AND SOCIAL CLASS

Cultural Proficiency is an interrelated set of tools set into a framework intended to guide us as educators working with colleagues to craft our schools' educational programs to be comparably effective with student populations across a wide spectrum of racial and social class experiences. When we, as educators, are culturally blind to the Intersectionality of students' cultural identities, we risk failing to help students thrive in the educational systems in which we work. Opportunity, access, and, consequently, achievement are denied. What all of our P-12 students have in common is the capacity and ability to learn. Our role as educators is to recognize our students' capacity to learn and to design and implement curriculum and instruction framed around the expectation that students can and will learn.

Students can learn, irrespective of the racial and social class demographics of our school or school district. The terms (names, events, trends) at the beginning of this section too often serve to contextualize, sometimes stigmatize, and marginalize our students. Such processes of exclusion are most often unintentional. However, it must be noted that the effects of intentional and unintentional marginalization feel the same to our students and their communities.

As an analogy, if while driving our automobile we turn a corner as a person steps into the crosswalk and (unintentionally) hit that person, the effect is little different from if we intended to hit them. They are still wounded and hurt.

Students come to our schools with vastly different experiences often due to the Intersectionality of their racial and social class identities. These experiences mold individuals' core values, perspectives, norms, and ways of behaving in the school culture, which sometimes produce dynamics of difference or conflict amid the vast and significant diversity. As you look back to your notes from the preceding reflection and dialogue processes, take note of your areas of being well-informed and areas of continued learning and growth. How might our consideration of race and social class inform the development of an asset-based mindset to guide educational practices that address and narrow educational gaps, and ultimately repay our educational debt?

A WORD ABOUT NOMENCLATURE: WORDS MATTER

Our U.S. society has been polarized since its very inception. From the beginning of European incursion into North America, our forebears quickly differentiated "us" and "them." Our history is replete with derogatory terms for others as well as adjectives selected to diminish and marginalize the "others." Table 3.1 displays the labels given for historically oppressed people.

What may be different today is that those of us who have not been directly affected or targeted are more aware of hate-filled incidents and violence in ways that one may not have paid attention to a generation ago. For historically targeted people, little has changed over time. Yes, modern media and communication platforms have brought public attention and scrutiny to this important issue in ways not previously known.

In our sophistication we have moved beyond "terms" to descriptors that serve to diminish. Intentionality is a nonissue. Subtlety is a nonissue too. Stereotypes and phrases that marginalize, whether intended or not, carry the same negative impact, much like microaggressions—those seemingly isolated events that are actually repeated frequently over time and egregious. In truth, negative impact affects the speaker as well as the targeted person or group of people.

In constructing this book as a contribution to the Cultural Proficiency body of work, the authors seized the opportunity to offer some terminology for readers to consider and to reflect about the possibility of bias in the use of terminology, depending on the views of the speaker or writer. In other words, the way we describe events carries importance for both the speaker and the targeted person.

TABLE 3.1 ● Labels for Historically Oppressed People

- Culturally inferior
- Minority
- Deficient
- Deprived
- Third World
- Poor
- Unskilled workers
- Different
- Disadvantaged
- Diverse
- Genetically inferior

Source: Adapted from R. B. Lindsey et al. (2019).

Examples from recent incidents publicized by the media include, but are not limited to, the following:

INCIDENT	TERMINOLOGY
January 6, 2021, event at U.S. Capitol	Insurrection or riot?
Trial following the death of George Floyd	George Floyd murder trial, Officer Derek Chauvin murder trial, or Derek Chauvin trial?
Death of George Floyd	Murder of Floyd or George Floyd's death?
Thirteen-year-old Adam Toledo shot and killed by a Chicago police officer investigating an incident of shots fired at 2:30 a.m.	Man or boy or "man-boy," as he was called?
Charlottesville, Virginia	Riots or protests?

REFLECTION • Dialogue • Action

- In what ways does this terminology carry importance or affect you?

- What might be some illustrations of bias terminology from the media that you would offer to this discussion?

- What might be some illustrations of bias terminology that you hear in your school or school district?

_____

_____

_____

_____

_____

THEORETICAL FRAMEWORKS

We have the capacity to develop our schools in ways that validate the cultures of all students, preschool through 12th grade, using a collection of theoretical frameworks that have been developed over the past 50 years. Twenty-first century education is an active, not passive, process. The historical contexts are essential too. The 1619 experience of enslaved Africans and the experiences of their descendants are very different from the experiences of Europeans who arrived on these shores, as sometimes indentured and often as immigrants, whose social status was not prescribed by skin color. The 1776 experiences with "All men are created equal" were not inclusive of native people, enslaved or free Africans, and women. The 1954 Supreme Court promise of vacating "separate but equal" has not been fully realized.

This book is about us, the educators in our schools. As we write this manuscript, each of the authors is in lockdown due to the coronavirus 2019 (COVID-19) pandemic and the recent civil unrest brought on by the seemingly racially motivated murders:

> *George Floyd*, whose tragedy unfolded in front of the world to see from their cell phones

> *Ahmaud Aubery*, whose killers were charged at the state level with murder and at the federal level with hate crime

> *Breonna Taylor*, whose killers were acquitted when the grand jury announced that no murder charges would be brought on the officers

So many others' lives have ended or been deeply affected by these tragedies that continue. Take a moment to reflect on your thoughts and feelings regarding these horrific, unfortunate events. Since this writing, what are similar occurrences of which you are aware?

Simultaneously, the spread of COVID-19, followed by misinformed comments spewed by prominent politicians and media pundits, has served to fuel expressions of hate and outright attacks on fellow citizens of Asian and Pacific Island heritage.

Issues of inequity are manifested in the daily news reporting that have long been in play among the Black, Asian, and Pacific Islander communities and other communities of color. Communities across the nation, including in Cleveland, Ohio, and parts of California, have doubled down and declared racism a public health crisis. Leaders in these communities took advantage of the open door to start the difficult conversations around race, social class, and issues of inequities. The collision of both a worldwide pandemic and national unrest brings an opportunity for our school communities to identify and confront persistent issues of inequity. The theoretical frameworks of *Intersectionality* and *Critical Race Theory* (CRT) and the conceptual framework of *Cultural Proficiency* are brought together in a way that addresses systemic issues of inequity.

CRT and Intersectionality inform Cultural Proficiency in ways that provide direction for educators and their school systems to address systemic, structural inequalities that foster oppression for some and privilege for others. Cross et al. (1989), in *Towards a Culturally Competent System of Care*, addressed issues of colorblindness endemic to the prevalent cultural competence models of that era. Recognizing the importance of CRT and Intersectionality, the authors of Cultural Proficiency have adapted Cross et al.'s work intended for social workers to the roles of educators and school systems serving the educational and developmental needs of the diverse communities of students in our P–12 schools (Arriaga, Stanley, & Lindsey, 2020; R. B. Lindsey et al., 2019). CRT and Intersectionality, having their origins in civil rights law, and cultural competence in social welfare, are brought together in ways that inform the Cultural Proficiency

Framework in service of children, youth, and their communities who have been and continue to be underserved in our schools.

INTERSECTIONALITY AND OPPRESSION: PAEAN TO CRENSHAW

Educational leadership has driven reform efforts to reduce educational gaps, and while some progress is noted, inequities and limited access for some individuals remain (Fullan, 2016; Marzano et al., 2005; Murphy & Datnow, 2003; Tucker, 2019). The difference is that culturally proficient educational leaders are advocates for their own lifelong learning with the intent to be increasingly effective in serving the educational needs of all cultural groups of students, including those from low-income and impoverished communities (D. B. Lindsey et al., 2018). The moral imperative of doing what is right demands we consider how race and social class interact to shape the multiple dimensions and experiences of many students of color, whom also may live in poverty.

This Intersectionality is the frame for seeing how social problems affect members of targeted groups in our school systems (Brannon et al., 2017; Jussim et al., 1987; Mattan et al., 2017; Plous & Williams, 1995; Richeson & Sommers, 2016; Tapia, 2010). We as educators are called to rise and prevent any individual from falling through the cracks. The Tools of Cultural Proficiency lead us to acknowledge our own behaviors and values, as well as our schools' policies and practices in understanding the educational implication of serving students identified with demographic intersectionality of race and social class group membership.

WHAT IS INTERSECTIONALITY?

In 1989, Kimberle Crenshaw coined the term *intersectionality*. "Intersectionality is a lens in which you can see where power comes and collides, where it interlocks and intersects" (Crenshaw, 2016). The purpose of *intersectionality* (Crenshaw, 1988), as theory, is to identify how overlapping categories of identity affect individuals and institutions and to take these relationships into account when working to promote social and political equity. This framework aims to identify how interlocking systems of power affect historically marginalized groups and focuses on the ideology of social identifiers—namely, race and social class. These identities are interlocking systems that do not exist in isolation.

To explain, Crenshaw (1989) suggested,

> Black women can experience discrimination in ways that are both similar to and different from those experienced by White women and Black men. Black women sometimes experience discrimination in ways similar to White women's experiences; sometimes they share similar experiences with Black men. Yet often, they experience double-discrimination—the combined effects of practices which

discriminate on the basis of race and on the basis of sex. And sometimes they experience discrimination as Black women—not the sum of race and sex discrimination, but as Black women. (p. 149)

We ask you to consider Crenshaw's definition of *Intersectionality* and apply it to the identities of the students and families you serve.

It is important to note that we human beings are not monolithic and that there are multiple facets to our individual and collective identities. People can be identified by, but not limited to, the following categories: religion, race, ethnicity, national origin, gender, sexual orientation, ableness, and social class. Consider your intersection(s) while on the journey to leading change through the lens of Cultural Proficiency.

You may think of an intersection as a place where two or more streets cross or intersect. Intersectionality is a framework that helps us understand how multiple forms of inequities cross in the experiences of marginalized individuals or groups. Intersectionality attends to socially constructed categories and their intersections with race in ways that analyze the power exerted by individuals and organizations in communicating with and listening to the diverse voices in any given community.

In the upcoming chapters, you will read about Eaveston School District as they push toward excellence and equity. We, as practitioners, can consider how the Intersectionality of race and social class presents barriers by nature of individuals' behaviors and beliefs, as well as the organization's policies and procedures. In this case, opportunities for growth can be actualized by relying on the Guiding Principles and using the Essential Elements of Cultural Proficiency to provide the "frame"—a frame for hope and action in valuing access, inclusion, and equity to close the opportunity and achievement gaps for our most vulnerable students at the crossroads of intersectionality. Intersectionality, as described by Crenshaw, and culturally proficient education practice are the "new facts" to incorporate in thinking about our current educational dilemmas.

WHAT IS CRITICAL RACE THEORY?

Beginning in the late 1970s and early 1980s, predominant legal scholars such as Derrick A. Bell Jr., Charles Lawrence, Richard Delgado, and Kimberle Crenshaw worked to develop the complex and multifaceted theoretical framework of CRT (Burrell-Craft, 2020). Based on delayed advancements in justice following the civil rights movement, the CRT movement attracted a group of activists and scholars engaged in studying and transforming the relationship among race, racism, and power (Delgado, 2017, p. 3).

With CRT becoming a highly politicized topic in the past couple of years, school leaders are grappling with these questions: How does this theory relate to our policies and practices? How can school leaders manage the dynamics of difference among school community stakeholders around this polarized topic? How should school leaders respond when asked about teaching CRT?

CRT is the view that *race*, instead of being biologically grounded and natural, is socially constructed and that *race*, as a socially constructed concept, functions as a means to maintain the interests of the White population who constructed it (Delgado, 2017). Some of the present-day conflict in opinion and resistance to CRT come from the identified seven tenets as cited by Burrell-Craft (2020):

1. Interest convergence (Bell, 1992)

2. Whiteness as a property (C. Harris, 1993)

3. Counterstorytelling (Delgado, 1989)

4. Critique of liberalism (Gotanda, 1991)

5. Intersectionality (Crenshaw, 1991)

6. Racial realism (Bell, 1992)

7. Social change (B. J. Love, 2004; Smith-Maddox & Solórzano, 2002).

CRT is a framework that offers researchers, practitioners, and policymakers a race-conscious approach to understanding racial inequality and structural racism and finding solutions that lead to greater justice for historically excluded and marginalized populations. In recent years researchers and scholars have added to the literature and social justice movements by expanding the tenets of CRT to Indigenous peoples, Latinx, Muslims and Arabs, Asians, LGBT community members, and people of color (Delgado, 2017). "Dynamic sub-disciplines, such as the Latino-critical movement, queer-crit (LGBT) studies, and an emerging Muslim community with a critical orientation challenge civil rights thinkers to reconsider the ways they conceptualize equality, civil rights, and national security" (Delgado, 2017, p. 113).

Proponents of CRT clearly state the prevalent cultural competence models employed in social work education since the 1990s and early 2000 failed to consider the structural inequality that has existed since the beginning of our countries (Abrams & Moio, 2009). Actually, we the authors of Cultural Proficiency books believe the Framework provides tools for educators to analyze the extent to which the power of our positions as educators and our school systems, often unwittingly, serves as a barrier to racial and other cultural groups of students getting equitable access in our schools and related organizations. Unrecognized barriers too easily serve as negative, unacknowledged core values in a school that allude that *some students can't learn due to their race or social class membership.* In brief, barriers, as core values, function as a negative mindset that "these students can't learn because of their culture" and/or "I am not going to put a lot of effort in educating these students." Let's be clear, these "core values" are not in print anywhere, yet they exist in the ways we talk and interact with our students, their parents and guardians, and their communities.

Recognizing and acknowledging the barriers that exist, in terms of which groups of students are the least successful in our schools, is an important step in the journey of Cultural Proficiency. Examination of the barriers that serve to resist change in people and their organizations is accompanied by analysis of the Guiding Principles that serve to influence educators' values and behaviors and schools' policies and practices. Culturally proficient educators and schools intentionally develop core values informed by the Guiding Principles. Such schools and educators believe that students' cultures are an asset on which to build educational experiences and that educators have the capacity to teach students from any cultural background.

The Guiding Principles, supported by the five Essential Elements, guide the behavior of educators and their schools in developing schools that serve students equitably. The Essential Elements of Cultural Competence guide school policies and practices and educator values and behaviors in service of students from all communities.

Just as Cultural Proficiency is an asset-based mindset that provides us with tools for critically examining our policies and practices with regard to the ways in which they are affecting students of various racial, ethnic, and social class backgrounds, CRT provides school leaders with a tool to "counter" deficit storytelling (Solorzano & Yosso, 2002). Moving forward, school leaders can speak of CRT as an academic framework that intently considers the impact of systemic racism, present in policies and practices, on students in our schools.

CURRICULUM DISTORTION–PRODUCED BARRIERS THROUGHOUT HISTORY

Let us continue with consideration of a prevalent curriculum distortion and its relationship to deficit storytelling (Solorzano & Yosso, 2002). Throughout his career, comedian and civil rights activist Dick Gregory famously probed the national psyches of the United States and Canada regarding race and racism. Frequently, as a stand-up comedian, Gregory posed the then revolutionary idea that Columbus did not *discover* America, after which he intoned, "How can you discover something that is not lost and is being used by millions of people?" Sit with that notion for a moment or two. In what way(s) does that observation affect you, your thoughts, and your feelings? Now, just think for another moment. Even today that fallacy is still taught as a historical "fact" in text materials and instruction in schools all over the North American continent.

Structural inequality and oppression begin at the most basic levels of our educational structures in ways that privilege White people and disadvantage all others. Ighodaro and Wiggan (2010) introduced the term *curriculum violence* as a means of describing the effect curriculum can have on students. Most important, the researchers considered intentionality to be immaterial. Intentional harm and unintentional harm have similar effects of marginalizing our students. It is important to note that our use of the term *curriculum* here is the total lifetime of experience students have from arrival at school to the time they leave campus (brick and mortar or virtual). The effect that curriculum violence has on all students and their educators is the material point.

White students can "see" themselves in a curriculum that looks like them and reflects a Eurocentric perspective. Students of color have fewer opportunities to participate in a curriculum that portrays or reflects themselves. Importantly, both groups of students experience "curriculum violence."

Both groups of students experience a curriculum that does not reflect an authentic history. Both groups of students experience a curriculum that does not reflect knowledge about the contrasting experiences of everyday living in today's communities. Both groups of students experience a curriculum that does not reflect people's historical and continuing struggles to gain unfettered access to the benefits of living in a democracy. White students are routinely validated by the curriculum they experience. Too often, students of color are rendered invisible or are marginalized in the curriculum. Across the United States and Canada, school communities are learning new ways of reaching and teaching students. When the "will" exists, finding "how" becomes a tactical issue.

Who is not thriving in your schools? Who is on the lower end of educational gaps in terms of academic success and discipline referrals? Who is reading below grade level? Who is being referred for the gifted program? Who is predominantly represented in books, resources, and artwork throughout the school? Who is being referred for special education services? Who is taking AP courses? As stated before, students do not exist as a monolith, but what did you notice about your answers? The data across the United States are too strong to ignore.

We do not use CRT to focus on individual people with prejudices or to create an idea of blame, shame, or guilt. After all, that would be the opposite of the culturally proficient mindset. Rather, CRT offers a lens by which school leaders can become lifelong learners and activists to critically examine the degree to which their systems' policies and practices are "opening doors" for all students toward equitable outcomes, especially those who have been historically marginalized. At this destination in your journey, we ask you to pause and consider what you have learned about CRT and apply it to the identities of the students and families you serve.

_____

_____

_____

_____

RACE AND SOCIAL CLASS IN EDUCATION

RACE AND EDUCATION

Race is a social construct that often gives rise to intergroup divisions in our society. All human beings are *Homo sapiens*, a biological construct. In the 19th century, the concept of race was created by Europeans in a way that characterized people by their physical features and used those differences to justify the evolution of a social power structure that demonstrated a preference for Europeans, often using the term *Caucasian* over groups of people who were different from them.

Educational opportunity has been inequitable throughout the history of the United States. For the past century and a quarter, our country's courts and legislators at all levels have wrestled with educational equity issues. The 1896, *Plessy v. Ferguson* U.S. Supreme Court decision supported prevailing Jim Crow laws that served to segregate Black and White students from each other in public schools. Though the expressed intent of *Plessy* was *separate but equal*, implementation of the laws led to government-sanctioned inequities. In the 1946 ruling of *Mendez v. Westminister* and the 1954 ruling of *Brown v. Board of Education*, the courts held separate but equal to have no place in public education and to be unconstitutional. While the 1960s and the decades since have brought integration movements and federal government–led reform efforts such as the Elementary and Secondary Education Act, the educational inequities and racial segregation in schools persist (Kozol, 1991, 2005; Ladson-Billings, 2009). The consequence of social and institutional resistance to legal and educational attempts at educational equity, educational disparities in access and outcome gaps between African American, Native American, and Latinx students, and their White and certain Asian American peers continue almost unabated (T. Howard, 2010).

SOCIAL CLASS AND EDUCATION

For those engaged in educational equity work, it is vital to approach social class or socioeconomic status with a lens of Intersectionality that combines, yet distinguishes, analyses of race and poverty. In 1989 Dr. Kimberle Crenshaw coined the term *Intersectionality* by the way in which individuals see where power comes, collides, interlocks, and intersects (Crenshaw, 2016). While Crenshaw directly discerned interlocking social identifiers of race and gender, it is important to note how interlocking systems of power affect historically underserved groups and focus on the ideology of social identifiers—namely, race and social class. Socioeconomic status is a distinct demographic group that intersects with other cultural identifications such as race, ethnicity, language, gender, sexual orientation, and ability (R. B. Lindsey et al., 2010). Often students living in poverty have different experiences in the world related to limited access to experiences and opportunities afforded many of their school-age peers.

A consequence of educators not being aware of their reactions leads to forms of deficit thinking where students are deemed not capable of higher forms of learning due to their socioeconomic living conditions. When such deficit thinking permeates educational practice, it becomes the norm when working with children, youth, and family members from low-income families. However, deficit thinking can give way to asset-based thinking and action when educators examine their own assumptions, beliefs, and behaviors; focus on relationships; and model resilience and promotion of self in the context of society (R. B. Lindsey et al., 2010).

POVERTY IN OUR COMMUNITIES AND SCHOOLS

"Of all the preposterous assumptions of humanity over humanity, nothing exceeds most of the criticisms made on the habits of the poor by the well-housed, well-warmed, and well-fed" (Melville, 2009, p. 6). In *Culturally Proficient Education*, R. B. Lindsey et al. (2010) used this quote as a chapter introductory epigraph to draw attention to a demographic group of students who are notably underserved in our society.

Historically underserved students, as referenced in the quote, are often targets of policies and practices that lead educators to behave, unknowingly and knowingly, in ways that regard these students' cultures as deficit, needing to be corrected and remediated. Deficit-based policies and practices communicate a low regard for students, their neighborhood communities, and their cultures. In such settings educators and their schools do not regard it as their personal, professional, or moral responsibility to respond to the communities they serve. Rather, adaptation is the responsibility and task of the community to learn the culture of schooling, as if they could only be dichotomous realities.

Given the complexities of cultures and demographic realities in current societies, socioeconomic status must be approached as a demographic group within our schools that intersects with, and yet is distinct from, the cultural groups of race, ethnicity, language acquisition, gender, and ableness (R. B. Lindsey et al., 2010, p. 12). Freire (1970) believed that the conditions of society, especially for the poor and the oppressed, were made by man and could be changed by man. Just as Freire did in his book *Pedagogy of the Oppressed*, we intend to bring hope and responsibility to your mind and work with this text. The educational issues of African American children and youth of low socioeconomic status, or living in poverty, are the focus of this book.

In contrast to the daily lived experiences of most of us who are educators, it is important to consider data provided by the Children's Defense Fund (2018) titled "Child Poverty in America 2018: National Analysis"—it reflects the intensity of poverty many of our students experience every day. The number of poor people in 2018 was 38.1 million, with a third of them being children. The number of children living in poverty was 11,869,173. Poverty was defined as a family of four with two children having an annual income below $25,465.

Children living in conditions of poverty have diminished access to health care and sufficient number of schools and are often in homes where parents/guardians are underemployed. Thomas and Fry (2020) reported, "In 2019, the year with the most recently available data, 14% of children under age 18, or 10.5 million children, were living in poverty, down from 22%, or 16.3 million, in 2010. All major racial and ethnic groups saw declines since 2010, but the greatest decreases were in the shares of Black and Hispanic children living in poverty." Table 3.2 illustrates the number and percentage of children living in poverty by racial/ethnic demographic group.

TABLE 3.2 ● Child Poverty by Race/Ethnicity Under Age 18, 2019

White	3,000,000	21.4%
Black	2,900,000	35.5%
Hispanic	3,900,000	40.7%
Asian	300,000	19.5%

Source: Thomas and Fry (2020).

The numbers and percentages are stark. As seen in Table 3.2, more than 11 million children and youth live in conditions of poverty. Black students are significantly overrepresented in the grim statistics of poverty. Posing poverty and race as distinct, intersecting demographic groups provides an opportunity for analyzing the extent to which schools seek out the cultural assets students bring to school as opposed to somewhat reflexively using terms and phrases that serve to diminish children and youth. We don't have to list the terms and phrases here; unfortunately, we all know them. We have heard them from colleagues and neighbors and, maybe sometimes, absentmindedly uttered them ourselves.

This book is about realized possibility. The content of this book rests on close study of the Eaveston School District, where race and poverty intersect. In the real world of schools centered in the racial and poverty realities shown in Table 3.1, some Eaveston school personnel have lived experiences markedly different from their students. Yet their students are progressing in ways that defy the deficit-laced norms of our society. The adults at Eaveston embrace their students as arriving at school each day and each year with assets on which to construct their learning experiences.

DEFICIT AND ASSET-BASED THINKING OF RACE AND SOCIAL CLASS

So what can we do once our students from various race and social class backgrounds arrive? Murphy (2009) indicated that educators must ensure programs are being used that specifically target marginalized students. In addition, educators would use strategies that can provide gains to all, but greater gains for those disadvantaged students. This is not meant to imply that there are programs and strategies that will solve the educational gaps with isolated use. Glenn Singleton (2018) referred to these as "random acts of equity."

We must examine the use of discussions related to the achievement gap in our districts and schools to ensure that affirmative language envelopes the goal. The goal cannot be to "fix" the students. That deficit mindset allows for the persistent inequitable outcomes. As defined above, achievement is a combination of opportunity, expectation, and input. The input category implies that educational leaders, at both the district level and the school level, are committed to continuous learning through high-quality literature on the issue; accepting of their responsibility and the urgency for closing the gap; committed to communication with all constituents, including parents and the outer community; and understanding of policies at the federal, state, and local levels. After all, school boards are composed of those members who have the power to influence school quality the most (Paige & Witty, 2010).

In the paragraphs above, the achievement gap highlights the disparities and inequitable outcomes between those children with opportunity and privilege and those who have been historically marginalized. But why does this persist in our schools with such highly educated people who enter their undergraduate degree program hoping to change the world?

It is most difficult to look inward and be constructively critical about your own practices as an educator, but it is essential. To answer the question, it is deficit-based thinking, and to be honest, sometimes we don't know what we don't know. Deficit-based thinking is often a result of beliefs and stereotypes with negative implications about non-White people, including those living in poverty. When deficit-based thinking is employed by educational professionals, knowingly or unknowingly, these negative beliefs about students and their families often lead to lower expectations, which leads to lower student achievement and reciprocal blame on the culture (Nelson & Guerra, 2014).

OPPORTUNITY, ACCESS, AND EDUCATIONAL GAPS

All who work in education know the complexities of student achievement and wellness, but seldom are they focused on the opportunity gap. These educators go to work every day to teach, inspire, mentor, and care for their students in the hope of seeing an increase of achievement level on the next assessment. But what is it that causes the educational gaps to persist? Prominent researchers identify the opportunity gap, which gives rise to the achievement gap (Conley & Darling-Hammond, 2013; Ladson-Billings, 2013; Milner, 2013).

WHAT IS OPPORTUNITY? HOW IS IT GIVEN? HOW IS IT WITHHELD?

Opportunity is a set of circumstances that make it possible to do something. When applied to school-age children, they enter our schools targeted by pre-arranged sets of circumstances, core values, beliefs, and norms—those who live in a small house in a rural community with two parents and enough income to adequately meet all the needs of the family; those who are being raised by a single parent on the 10th floor of a dilapidated apartment that has no air conditioning and enough food to have one meal per day; those who are in transition, often referred to as homeless; and those living in million-dollar homes with two parents who are doctors, and college savings accounts that are fully funded several years prior to college entry.

So if opportunity is the set of circumstances, how is it distributed? While we are all born into a set of circumstances or opportunities, it is inevitable that those sets of circumstances can change for the better or worse. At the young age of five, and sometimes earlier, school districts welcome students faced with a wide range of opportunities. What we as educators do from the moment they enter our schools and classrooms either "opens the door" to opportunity or "closes the door" to opportunity.

What we do matters because for the next 13 years, the educators in the school district are responsible for laying the grounds for opportunity and, hopefully, giving rise to a different set of circumstances. It is the administrators, teachers, and staff who can serve as "champions" for the children and can provide opportunities in the form of access to inclusive and enriching curricular and instruction experiences. Sure, these children navigate the world between home and school, but the opportunities that we provide to the youth of our nation while they are with us are essential to academic achievement and social well-being. Educators may view their role as an opportunity to "open doors" through embracing students' cultures as an asset.

WHAT DEFINES ACHIEVEMENT?

For many years we have verbalized the idea that all students can achieve at high levels. However, expressions of inclusivity vary widely across demographic groups when observed by race, ethnicity, social class, levels of English language acquisition, and special needs. The intersection of demographic groups presents students even more challenging school experiences.

The level to which educators have internalized belief in this statement varies, and it has changed over the course of the history of education in the United States. Students from minoritized groups, such as women, students of color, students with disabilities, students living in poverty, and those who do not speak English much, too often have not been educated with the same high expectations as their White middle-class counterparts. Unknowingly and knowingly, too many educators and their schools have yet to build student school experiences in ways that honor and build on students' cultures.

An "opportunity gap" sets the stage for achievement, setting certain standards for minoritized students. Educating 25 students placed on the continuum of the opportunity scale to the same level of achievement presents challenges, but it is essential to know that providing opportunity for all students to achieve at high levels is not defined as all students meeting the same standard at the same time in the same manner, particularly for historically underserved students. In sharp contrast, Cultural Proficiency is implemented in ways for educators to have success with students who have been historically underserved by the educational systems in our country. We must look inward to provide equity to those who have been denied access, barred from opportunity. We must be willing to pause and think about our own cultural identities and the ways in which those cultural identities, such as race and social class, are affecting student outcomes.

Too many students are not thriving; they are not well served; they need us! With our current demographic educational settings in education and as a nation, educators are called to their moral purpose. We must get this right!

How do we get it right? How can we "open the doors" for students to experience success in our systems? Achievement and wellness are keys to success. Achievement and wellness are progress toward a standard, whether it is academic, social-emotional, or health related. When expectations are high and relationships are strong, students will meet those expectations. Rita Pierson (2013) said, "Every kid needs a champion." It is the opportunity gap that determines the length of time children need to reach those expectations. Through racial equity and social class equity practices, culturally proficient educators can "open those doors" to success for these students so that our students of color and those living below the poverty line in our country are no longer underserved by our educational institutions. In summary, what defines achievement? We use an equation to define the relationship between opportunity, expectation, and input.

Opportunity + Expectation + Input = Achievement

It is clear that the indirect relationship of opportunity and input brings to the stage the concept of equity. Equality will not work in this equation, hence the misunderstanding and failure of some educational reform programs. Culturally proficient educators recognize their role in providing substantial, rich opportunities to those students who are not thriving. They know that assessing their own cultural knowledge, valuing diversity, and managing the dynamics of cultural differences in their classroom are essential for individual transformation and organizational change in systems where student achievement is low. Race and social class–related equitable policies, practices, and behaviors are essential for the achievement and wellness of our students. The gap remains the same if we remain the same.

HISTORICAL CONTEXT OF THE ACHIEVEMENT GAP: RACE AND SOCIAL CLASS DATA

In the 1960s the U.S. Department of Education instituted an assessment designed to collect data on academic achievement for students in reading and mathematics in designated grade levels. These data were compared "across age, gender, race/ethnicity, and time" (Ferguson, 2008). In the same decade *The Coleman Report* (Coleman, Campbell, Hobson, McPartland, Mood, Weinfeld, & York, 1966), officially titled *Equality of Educational Opportunity*, was published. Not only did sociologist James Coleman's report present the data regarding the first academic achievement comprehensive assessment in the United States, but it also highlighted the learning results of the achievement gap between White and Black students to the public for the first time in history.

> With some expectations—notably Oriental American—the average minority pupil scores distinctly lower on these tests at every level than the average White pupil. The minority pupils' scores are as much as one standard deviation below the majority pupils' scores for the 1st grade. At the 12th grade, results of tests in the same verbal and nonverbal skills show that, in every case, the minority scores are farther below the majority than are the 1st graders. For some groups, the relative decline is negligible: for others, it is large. (Coleman, Campbell, Hobson, McPartland, Mood, Weinfeld, & York, 1966, p. 21)

In his analysis of the achievement gap, Coleman discussed the relationships or correlations between the scores and schools.

> The schools do differ, however, in their relations to the various racial and ethnic groups. The average White student's achievement seems to be less affected by the strength or weakness of his school's facilities, curriculum, and teacher than is the average minority pupil's. To put it another way, the achievement of minority pupils depends more on the schools they attend than does the achievement of majority pupils. (Coleman et al., 1966, p. 22)

"The achievement gap is one of the most stubborn and pernicious manifestations of racial inequity in our country" (Chubb & Loveless, 2002, p. vii). This quote summarizes the focus of the inequities and disparities in education that have been present in public school education in the United States for decades. While it does exclusively mention racial inequities, we also acknowledge social class inequities.

Educators across the United States in urban, suburban, and rural communities sit in rooms and discuss the differences in data based on gender, socioeconomic status, race/ethnicity, ability, and disability as well. The achievement gap as defined by the U.S. Department of Education

(2009) is "a difference in scores that is statistically significant, meaning larger than the margin of error, between two groups of students" (p. 1). While there have been decreases in the achievement gap between White students and those who have been historically underserved, national legislation has attempted to mandate substantial closing of the educational gaps.

When we examine the history of one-room schoolhouses, the Supreme Court decision of *Brown v. Board of Education* (1954), and the authorization of the Elementary and Secondary Education Act (1965) and Every Child Success Act (2015), we can see that the design and practices of our school organization have failed some of our children. These children arrive in our schools with various levels of opportunity and privilege. For years educators fought for equality, as some still do, but equitable practices are necessary to mitigate the low levels of opportunity and privilege of some of our children so they can thrive.

Educational practitioners, including administrators, teachers, researchers, policymakers, and state and national legislators, recognize the achievement gap as one of the most important issues, but disparities in academic outcomes between African American, Native American, and Latinx students, and their White and certain Asian American peers persist (T. Howard, 2010, p. 120).

Achievement gaps equate to inequity. Gaps in grades, standardized test scores, high school graduation rates, dropout rates, placement in special education, placement in advanced courses, admittance rates to college and graduate and professional programs, and suspension and expulsion rates are among the many sources of data that prove educational inequities exist and are important to keep at the forefront of every school district's vision and mission.

Closing the educational gaps is complex. The goal of closing the achievement gap has persisted for decades in the United States. It has allowed for many federal education reforms and countless hours spent analyzing data, attending professional development workshops, and changing practices to meet students' needs. Lisa Delpit (2006), author of *Other People's Children*, wrote, "What should we be doing? The answers, I believe, lie not in a proliferation of new reform programs but in some basic understandings of who we are and how we are connected and disconnected from one another" (p. XXV). While the achievement gap has narrowed in the past 50 years and, essentially, higher expectations have allowed for higher achievement in all groups, still large gaps remain.

The answer, as Delpit (2006) discussed, a "basic understanding of who we are and how we are connected and disconnected from one another," points in all directions to using the Cultural Proficiency Framework as a way to educate today's youth. Educators and systems that look inward and work toward individual transformation and organizational change can close the gaps. Educational equity warriors must give students on the lower end of the student achievement and wellness spectrum an advantage if progress is to continue. "If closing the achievement gap means improving the learning of targeted students at a faster rate than for other students, then we need to disproportionately advantage these students" (Murphy, 2009, p. 11).

WHY EDUCATIONAL DEBT IS ASSET-BASED

Here we need to address Gloria Ladson Billings's call to end the use of the term *achievement gap*. Achievement gap uses deficit-based language because it blames students for their achievement scores. Ladson-Billings' term, *Education Debt*, known as the access/opportunity and achievement gaps between students of diverse races/ethnicities and socioeconomic statuses, has been the focus of research and goals for improvement across the United States since the *Coleman Report* was published in 1966 (Jencks et al., 1972; Ladson-Billings, 2006; Sarason, 1996).

The continuous oppression of underserving students from marginalized races and social classes has perpetuated inequity and predictable failure. Apple and Beane (1995) posited, "Like other progressive educators, those involved with democracy care deeply about young people, but they also understand that such caring requires them to stand firm against racism, injustice, centralized power, poverty, and other gross inequities in school and society" (p. 12). Using the Tools of Cultural Proficiency allows educators to stand firm against these inequities in school and society and repay the *Educational Debt*.

EQUITY BY WHATEVER MEANS IT TAKES

Those who study the history of the United States might find the work of equity and access motivated as a moral imperative to be incongruent with our authentic histories. Kendi (2019) reminded us that the enslavement of African people; the slavery and genocide of Native American, or First Nations, people; the social and political institutions of Jim Crow United States; and the resistance against desegregation and integration of schools were not lessened or defeated by moral suasion. Although moral purpose is noteworthy of our nation's social justice heroes, actually their efforts toward changing policies and practices that lead to observable and measurable impact on people's everyday lives is what was needed then and is certainly needed now. In education we are fortunate to be able to gauge, measure, and document over time the educational experiences of demographic groups of students.

The Cultural Proficiency Framework begins with a personal journey that invites educators to examine their own values and beliefs. In leadership positions this often informs policy and practice changes that constructively affect demographic groups of children and youth served by our schools. In some cases these new policies, practices, and structures may lead people to behave in different ways that lead to different outcomes for traditionally underserved groups. Within that process some resistors will change their beliefs and reexamine their values based on the new rules and evidence.

Fullan (2003) provided three criteria of moral purpose to inform our values, beliefs, and actions as well as the policies and practices of our schools:

- That all students and teachers benefit in terms of identified goals,

- That the gap between high and low performers becomes less as the bar for all is raised,

- That ever-deeper goals are pursued and that the culture of the school becomes so transformed that continuous improvement relative to the three components becomes built in. (p. 31)

Schools' policies and practices and educators' values and beliefs that guide their actions are central tenets of the Cultural Proficiency Framework and its attendant "tools." Culturally proficient educators are willing and able to recognize and identify systemic barriers that disproportionately impede students' equitable access to education. This includes educators' systemic barriers in terms of students' racial, economic, gender, and any other cultural groupings.

TODAY'S INEQUITIES

Issues of educational inequities have been brought to the fore by the COVID-19 pandemic in stark ways that now the general public cannot fail to see. It is now clear that access to digital learning is disproportionately available across social class communities. It is now abundantly clear that access to breakfast and lunch opportunities is disproportionately experienced among social class communities. It is now clear that educators are more likely to live in their middle-income communities than they might when serving low-income communities.

Amid these issues of disproportionality, an emerging theme that is not unclear is that the underserved, low-income communities are disproportionately populated by children of color, in particular African American children and youth. Sadly, these trends are not materially different from the descriptions chronicled in the *Coleman Report* (1966). Once again, the effects of poverty and racism are thrust onto the national psyche. As before, there are those attempting to explain away the disproportional experiences by using pathological terms to describe those targeted by racism and poverty.

Cultural Proficiency is not a panacea emanating from a mythical Mt. Olympus. Cultural Proficiency is a mindset that begins with the belief that children from all cultural and demographic groups have the capacity to learn. More important, adherents to culturally proficient practices believe that we the educators and, therefore, our schools have the capacity to learn how to educate each and every student who enters our schools. Learning is our lifelong professional commitment. Yes, we learn our craft. We also learn about ourselves in relation to the communities we serve. An analogy might be appropriate. We all prefer high-quality medical care. Each of us wants to be in the care of a medical practitioner having our best interests in mind.

In the modern era educational inequities have been documented, highlighted, and legislated many times since the 1954 U.S. Supreme Court decision *Brown v. Board of Education*. Yet the work continues. At the national and state levels, attention is being paid to equity in ways that provide opportunities for proactive educators willing to challenge their own and their schools' assumptions that hinder student access to equitable educational experiences and outcomes.

As we sit here this evening composing this passage, protestations against the murder of George Floyd are emerging in small and large communities across the United States and beyond. This is not a new occurrence. It is an illustration of curriculum violence as expressed in the lived experiences of many African American people made visible to the entire country. There will be those in the dominant group who will try to dismiss the grisliness of Mr. Floyd's death by indicating that "we don't know all the details. We don't know from watching the video what preceded the stopping of Mr. Floyd." True. However, what we do know is Mr. Floyd's murder is all too familiar to the experiences of many Blacks, Indigenous people, and people of color (BIPOC) in our society. An educational analogy is not too difficult to make. Too often, BIPOC students experience an educational environment that does not hear them say, "I can't breathe." Yes, the analogy is stark. It is meant to call our attention to the chronic, negative, often invisible experiences that African American students, in particular those from low-income settings, have in our schools.

It does not have to be that way. Creating an inclusive school environment that honors and embraces the racial and socioeconomic backgrounds of students as platforms on which to build their educational experiences begins with us educators being willing and able to probe and understand our biases. Becoming an effective educator begins with us. We are the central variable in the educator-student relationship. Race and social class are socially, not biologically, constructed. Since they are socially constructed, by definition race and social class can be deconstructed. Since the construction is within our societal agreements, we can choose to seek and embrace racial and social groups' practices as assets, not deficits.

EFFECTS ON STUDENTS, PARENTS, AND COMMUNITY

The foundations of education are rooted in a belief that educated children become better citizens. Although diversity holds great importance in democracy, too many schools in this country continue with systems, policies, and practices that largely reflect the values, behaviors, and aspirations of the most powerful groups (Apple & Beane, 1995; Darling-Hammond, 1995; Ravitch, 1985; Sarason, 1990). Systemic oppression, policy impacts on marginalized students, and privilege and entitlement limit educational outcomes and the reality of access and equity for all (R. B. Lindsey et al., 2010). The continuous oppression of students of different race, ethnicity, and social class has perpetuated inequities and educational performance deficits (Banks & Banks, 1995; Freire, 1970; Hammond, 2015; G. Howard, 2006; Kozol, 2005; Ladson-Billings, 2006; Noguera, 2008).

 LOOKING IN THE REARVIEW MIRROR

Chapter 3 served as a review of race and social class in education, including differential opportunity, access, achievement, and related educational gaps. We included the theoretical frameworks of Intersectionality and CRT to provide reasoning for this book's focus on race and social class related to educators, students and their families, and the community. If we really believe we can create schools where *all* students can achieve at high levels and truly thrive, it is not important what equity model is being used, but rather that models of equity work are being used. The Cultural Proficiency Framework serves as a lens or roadmap to examine your personal attitudes, beliefs, and behaviors, as well as the practices and policies of your organization that may be perpetuating the inequities of today. Take some time and listen to Episode 2 of the podcast, "Leading Through the Lens of Cultural Proficiency." Here you will hear conversations with the authors focused on school leadership, educational debt, and race and social class in education.

EPISODE 2

 ON TO OUR NEXT DESTINATION

In the next chapter, we ask you to take with you on this journey knowledge of the historical and conceptual reviews of educational inequities and reforms, the Intersectionality of race and social class, and the Cultural Proficiency Framework. As we grow closer to reading about Eaveston School District's journey of implementing Cultural Proficiency, we want to prepare you with some realities and "things you need to know" before you lead your school organization. Chapter 4 focuses on leadership. We designed this chapter to encourage and guide you to raise your awareness in the process of deconstructing systemic oppression that develops over time in our school systems. We will guide you to examine school leadership and the role it plays in student achievement. The historical review of educational reform bridges the application of school change and your current reality, and entices a mindset shift with Dilts's Model of Organizational Change and other leadership concepts.

REFLECTION, DIALOGUE, AND ACTION PROCESS

REFLECTION • Dialogue • Action

1. How does intersectionality manifest for the students your organization serves?

2. Think about your first experiences with individuals whose race and/or social class were different from yours. How did those experiences influence your current actions in leadership?

Reflection • **DIALOGUE** • Action

1. With your colleagues, discuss the differences in opportunity among your families and community.

2. In what ways are opportunity and access granted and denied for your students outside the school system and inside the school system?

Reflection • Dialogue • **ACTION**

1. Mobilize your efforts in discovering the strengths and best practices of the district, considering social class and racialized backgrounds.

2. Engage all stakeholders in this discovery process.

3. Identify those strengths and best practices. Be sure to consider the various social classes and race/ethnicity.

_____

_____

_____

_____

_____

Travel Log

_____
_____
_____
_____
_____
_____
_____
_____
_____
_____
_____
_____
_____
_____
_____
_____
_____
_____
_____
_____
_____
_____
_____
_____
_____
_____
_____
_____
_____
_____
_____

TRAVEL GUIDE
Individual and Organizational Change Leadership

Create Your Map

- Establish the *what* and *why* of this work.
- Create communication plans to reach every constituency.
- Determine how these changes will be systemic.

Resources

- Existing advisory and leadership structures
- Vision and mission of the district and schools
- Allocating time and money to build capacity
- Eaveston School District's story

Mileage

- Examine data from equity audits in your school and district.
- Create feedback loops to determine the effectiveness of leadership efforts.
- Create an influence map of all stakeholder groups.

Check the Weather

- What signs in your community indicate they are ready for this work?
- What is the scope of this work—citywide, districtwide, or school level?
- Is diversity tolerated, a goal, or valued? How do you know?

Travel Phrases

- Cultures of collaboration
- Inside-out work
- Dilts's Nested Levels of Organizational Change
- Manage the dynamics of difference

You're the Driver

- How are you preparing yourself and others to engage in this focused change?
- How will you communicate to many constituent groups the nature of inside-out work?
- How are you keeping track of your own inside-out journey?

CHAPTER 4

Individual and Organizational Change Leadership

Every system is perfectly designed to get the results it gets.

—W. Edwards Deming (n.d.)

CALIBRATION

We assume you are reading this book and are particularly interested in this chapter because you are preparing to lead others on a journey toward a more equitable and accessible educational system. Take a moment to reflect on W. Edwards Deming's quote above. Most likely, the school or district system that you are currently leading is designed to get the results it is getting. To what degree are you satisfied with those results?

We, the authors, have worked with numerous schools and school districts that have leaders, just like you, who want to see their systems rise to new levels of success and to open doors for students not thriving academically or socially. Change initiatives function at two levels:

1. Behaviors of the leaders displaying core values that are inclusive of students from all sectors of the community

2. The school system that lives into explicitly inclusive mission, vision, and core values statements

This is not a binary choice. Systemic change arises from the intertwining of personal and organizational continuous learning.

Perhaps you are apprehensive. You know you do not want to pull out of your garage, hit the highway, and immediately have a flat tire. Nor do you want those you are traveling with to be disappointed that you are trying to take them to the same "dead end" they have traveled to before. So what do you pack? What do you plan for? Before you read further, take a moment to list some of your leadership qualities and structures you believe you have in place to not only "do" this work but also implement it and sustain it by institutionalizing changes that open doors for your students.

_____

_____

_____

_____

_____

ON-RAMP TO LEADING THE CHANGE

The Eaveston School District study serves as a blueprint for equity-focused leaders guiding implementation of a change initiative. Leadership is about relationships, and the Eaveston story provides us with a way to determine how to build the capacity of leaders, implementers, and stakeholders to execute, improve, and maintain a focus on a Cultural Proficiency–informed equity plan. Such leadership intentionally guides systemic change to ensure equitable opportunities and outcomes for all students.

As you lead others in the change process using the Cultural Proficiency Framework, we ask you to lean on Fullan's (2016) words:

> There is no shortage of recommendations about how the ills of education should be rectified. But the remedies remain pie in the sky as long as competing "shoulds" fight it out without an understanding of how to get started and how to keep going. (p. 54)

These words serve as reminders of the importance of planned implementation and sustainability.

Eaveston leaders used data to set benchmarks that guided implementation of their equity plan. District leaders engaged colleagues and community members in the use of data to assess current practices and to monitor implementation of the equity plan, which ultimately led to success. Fullan (2016) emphasized building capacity, "The study of meaning has shifted emphasis in the past decade away from the examination of how to implement a given program or innovation to focus on how to build capacity for people to learn and innovate" (p. 54).

Any successful journey must attend to certain details. In Eaveston's case, the leadership behaviors were identified and practiced. It is helpful to explore the components of leaders' effective strategies to provide a framework, and possibly a deeper understanding, of why Eaveston School District was successful with the application of the Cultural Proficiency Framework in the implementation of their equity action plan. Figure 4.1 displays the

FIGURE 4.1 ● Leadership Components of Effective Equity Implementation and Sustainability

components of effective implementation and sustainability of the work of Cultural Proficiency.

These components are essential for planning for transformational change in your organization, be it at the district or school level. In the following section, we provide details of these components that you need to "pack" for your journey.

IDENTIFICATION

As we covered in great detail in Chapters 1 and 2, organizational leaders must establish the "what" and the "why" of innovation to implement it. Eaveston's leaders started with this "what" and their "why" by examining the quest for this work in the context of the district's core values and those values expressed in the school district's vision and mission statements. The identification of "what" and "why" is not done alone. Identifying an implementation team who held a high value for cultural diversity aided in fostering a process for organizational cultural changes within Eaveston School District.

The implementation team is to be composed of key stakeholders from across the school/district and community to influence and move implementation plans forward. Implementation is guided by team members' personal reflections and considerations of the questions below. It is important that team members follow their individual reflections by purposefully engaging with one another in ways that enable them to discuss their reflections and begin to develop a shared understanding of and commitment to the equity plan identified.

- What is the rationale for an equity change initiative in our school/district, and what do we hope to accomplish for our students and community?

- What data are we examining that convince us that this change initiative is needed?

- What changes will we need to make in our personnel and organizational policies, procedures, and practices?

- What resources will need to be organized and marshaled?

- What communication systems will be needed?

- What individual and organizational boosters (+) and barriers (–) might facilitate or impede implementation?

- In what ways do we measure the effectiveness of our leadership?

Furthermore, Fixen, Blasé, and Van Dyke (2019) in their work *Implementation Practice and Science* pose considerations for planned change:

- Meaningful leadership

- Professional learning structures

- Assessment

- Cultures of collaboration

- Teams

- Sustainability

MEANINGFUL LEADERSHIP

Anchoring ourselves in meaningful leadership involves putting ourselves on the line, disturbing the status quo, and surfacing hidden conflict (Heifetz & Linsky, 2017). Eaveston School District's superintendent knew that leading this work of Cultural Proficiency would require not only technical leadership skills but also value-centered leadership that would be adaptive along an unfolding professional learning journey for him, for his leadership team, and for every employee of the district. Culturally proficient leaders are mindful of the inside-out nature of the Cultural Proficiency journey. Leaders of the change initiative must be present in the phases of training, implementation, action planning, and progress monitoring to ensure sustainability. Culturally proficient leadership is a lifelong commitment to learning about self and the organization. Heifetz and Linsky (2017) posited,

> The roles we play in our organization, community, and private lives depend mainly on the expectations of people around us. The self relies on our capacity to witness and learn throughout our lives, to refine the core values that orient our decision—whether or not they conform to expectations. (p. 187)

Eaveston leaders, both formal and nonformal, were chosen and/or invited to participate in leading because of their roles in the district and community, as well as their effectiveness in modeling inclusive core values, learning strategies, and decision-making skills. They devised the policies, established the procedures, and initiated the practices that defined the course and principles of the equity initiative. Eaveston leaders have been guided through their willingness and ability to take a "balcony view" that embraced their leading organizational change initiative through meaningful use of these factors:

- *Policies* and *procedures* representing the official way things are to be done so there would be a unified effort across school sites in pursuit of equitable access and outcomes for all demographic groups of students

- *Practices*, being the implementation of procedures, the carrying out of the plan

- *Leadership teams*, organized and trained, to lead the equity-focused change initiative and to keep the organization responsive and moving forward through daily routines to ensure that equity would be central to the normal, everyday conversations in their schools and across the district

Implementing the Cultural Proficiency Framework in a meaningful way requires leaders to follow key developments as team members reflect on practice and engage in dialogue, seeking to understand one another with regard to planned policy, procedure, and practice changes. Through adaptive, meaningful leadership, leaders come to know and influence the context of policy, procedure, and practice changes to not only open doors for students but also escort historically marginalized students in such a way that they experience academic and social success (Arriaga & Lindsey, 2016; Fullan, 2003).

PROFESSIONAL LEARNING STRUCTURES

Resource management in a new initiative involves building the capacity of personnel to engage in the work of equity planning and implementation. McLaughlin and Talbert (1993) discussed the importance of professional learning structures: "The path to change in the classroom core lies within and through teachers' professional communities: learning communities which generate knowledge, craft new norms of practice, and sustain participants in their efforts to reflect, examine, experiment, and change" (p. 18). We would argue that the creation of professional learning structures should be well planned to include all district departments, schools, classrooms, content departments, grade levels, and stakeholders. Griffith, Ruan, Stepp, and Kimmel (2014) outlined a number of professional learning structures that we have taken to fit the context of applying the Tools of Cultural Proficiency, and that you might find useful in planning for your school organization's Cultural Proficiency journey:

- Participating in department-level or grade-level inquiry groups formed to solve a problem identified in data collected along the Cultural Proficiency Continuum

- Participating within and across grade levels discussing outcomes/insights related to policies, practices, and behaviors

- Embedding conversations of culturally proficient educational practices in all meetings (i.e., faculty meetings, leadership team meetings, department meetings, parent meetings, data team meetings, etc.)

- Designing professional development days when all school district employees have access to learn and grow using the Cultural Proficiency Framework

- Reading and responding to professional literature on Cultural Proficiency, equity, access, inclusion, and diversity-related topics

- Sharing written reflections

- Sharing results of new policies, practice, or behavior outcomes and impacts on colleagues, students, and their families

- Attending conferences and sharing results

Eaveston School District leaders created multiple levels of professional learning structures at the district, building, and classroom levels to embed the work of Cultural Proficiency in all aspects of the district. Careful planning is essential to ensure that teams have the resources they need, such as the time, funding, and expertise to lead discussions centered on equity, access, and inclusion and alignment with the district's direction for applying the Tools of Cultural Proficiency. Planning and implementation are guided by thoughtful questions such as the following:

- What do we currently have in place to develop the learning and capacity of the adults in the organization?

- In what ways might we improve the effectiveness of these structures?

- What is the current shared understanding of the equity plan?

- In what ways are members of the district to be engaged with the equity plan?

- What will it take to roll out the innovation to an entire district?

ASSESSMENT

Once the equity plan is launched, implementation team members monitor the progress of the implementation. We want you to be prepared that you, as the leader of this work, will receive questions on your journey such as the following:

How do we know this is working?

What evidence do you have that implementing this work will make a difference for our kids?

Have students' test scores increased or incidents of discipline referrals decreased?

What has changed?

Smith (2008) described the measurement of the change process:

It is a messy and unpredictable process. It is a journey, which often goes astray, takes a backward spin, or experiences natural ups and downs. Therefore, to move a school from Point A (where it is) to Point B (where it wants to go) is an incredible endeavor, especially if the change is substantial (rather than superficial), is sustained, and has meaning. (p. 30)

Perhaps the most important question Smith (2008) asked is about measuring the change, the distance from point A to point B: "How is it measured? Is it solution or outcome oriented?" (p. 40). The implementation team creates and distributes as appropriate periodic updates on progress to ensure that implementation is proceeding as intended with the intended equity-focused policies, procedures, and practices. Ensuring the fidelity of implementation strategies provides team members the benchmarks by which to assess and recalibrate the quality of the implementation strategies and the probability of attaining the desired results. A frequently used guiding question during implementation is "In what ways will we know when ___% of the innovations are being adopted and implemented with fidelity within our organization?"

It is important to remember that when you develop your equity action plan, your teams create goals based on relevant data and identify the assessment that will be used to monitor the distance from point A to point B.

- What do you want your school to look like?
- What do equity, access, and inclusion look like at point B?

We caution you on your path on this journey. Try to focus on teaching and learning for the students and adults in your school organization, and avoid focusing on student academic achievement by test scores alone.

Reeves (2009) wrote, "Too many school initiatives provide their chief feedback through annual test score reports—results that are almost never delivered until it's too late to reinforce or modify teachers' or leaders' behavior" (p. 90). This quote epitomizes the notion that all adults in our schools are responsible for embedding Cultural Proficiency in all aspects of a school organization to see changes that will endure in the journey toward increased equity, access, and inclusion for all students.

Our assessment of school change is about much more than test scores. Smith (2008) argued,

> Labeling school change as substantial means little if the change has not focused on teaching and learning—for the students and for the adults. Furthermore, if the improvement is limited to a few classrooms, we will not have change that is deep and broad. We cannot claim "better teaching" and meaningful learning without some evidence, some measurements. We will not move beyond today's results—as good as they might be—without creating a different belief system that values student achievement and growth. (p. 44)

While you will read in upcoming chapters about Eaveston's increase in student achievement, be mindful of the belief shifts in learning for the adults engaged in applying the Tools of Cultural Proficiency to their practices and behaviors. Pay close attention to the mindset shifts of educators responsible for changing policies and practices within the organization. Listen intently to the words of Eaveston's leaders as they describe the impact of this work. The Cultural Proficiency Committee in Eaveston used their equity action plan to monitor their distance from point A to point B as they used the Essential Elements of Cultural Proficiency to institutionalize a culture of continuous improvement and growth for the students and the adults.

CULTURES OF COLLABORATION

Leadership groups, by their very nature, involve spoken and unspoken rules for how members communicate. In our experience it is an even more important task for equity-focused initiatives to be intentional in developing commonly accepted communication and decision-making rules and guidelines. Donohoo and Velasco (2016) outlined the need to co-create norms for interactions and the art of navigating conflict:

> Norms are understood as the team's agreements for interpersonal interactions. . . . These norms are initially established to increase human and social capital by encouraging individual behaviors that contribute to team efficiency while simultaneously deterring behaviors that derail effective collaboration. (p. 89)

Eaveston's school leaders implementing the Cultural Proficiency Framework aimed to focus on shared decision-making, reflection, and dialogue on the impact of school policies and practices on their students and colleagues; a shared responsibility for learning, leading, and teaching; and the individual and collective impact on their colleagues (Donohoo & Velasco, 2016). They navigated conflict, while holding the value that conflict would promote opportunities for growth and change.

In Eaveston, leaders also relied on Garmston and Wellman's (1999) Seven Norms of Collaboration to guide team discussions:

1. Pausing

2. Paraphrasing

3. Probing

4. Putting ideas of the table

5. Paying attention to self and others

6. Presuming positive intentions

7. Pursuing a balance between advocacy and inquiry

Building this culture of collaboration helped build trust between and among group members as they applied the Tools of Cultural Proficiency in this work. Donohoo and Velasco (2016) wrote about the power of collaborative inquiry as a process that "provides a structure for educators to lead and learn together productively" (p. 3). Through these collaborative norms, educators in Eaveston developed leadership skills and professional capital for collaborating and engaging with others in reflection, dialogue, and action-related processes for changing the policies, practices, and behaviors in the district and individual schools that they discovered were not "opening doors" for students.

What was essential for Eaveston's Cultural Proficiency team was to build the capacity for all to do this work through an inside-out approach, develop a common language using the Cultural Proficiency Framework, promote a process based on inquiry or questioning, and ensure that there was a balance of collaboration among all stakeholders so that the change was not being driven in a top-down approach.

Wagner, Kegan, Lahey, Lemons, Garnier, Helsing, Howell, and Rasmussen (2006) posited,

> The work of reinventing schools and districts is not technical work that can be controlled by fiat from the top of the organization. Instead it is adaptive work that requires changes in people's heads, hearts, and actions. It requires all individuals in schools and districts to stay purposefully focused on the same work, be engaged in a thoughtful and deliberate manner, and work collaboratively toward common ends. Getting schools, districts, and the individuals within them to begin working in these new ways requires that leaders prepare the community and educators for the transformation and hard work ahead. (p. 138)

TEAMS

The implementation teams help others in the school/district execute implementation strategies and activities, measure progress, and develop effective communication structures to build the relationships necessary to monitor and implement the equity-focused innovation. DuFour, DuFour, Eaker, Many, and Mattos (2016) described the importance of teams: "The very reason any organization is established is to bring people together in an organized way to achieve a collective purpose that cannot be accomplished by working alone" (p. 75). The structure of your teams will depend on the resources that are available to your organization. Bambrick-Santoyo (2018) suggested that educational leaders look for reliability and receptiveness when selecting initial team members, as well as remember a 12:1 ratio, where there is one administrator to every 12 teachers or staff members.

As Eaveston School District built their initial team, they took these two ideas of reliability and receptiveness to heart. The Director of Learning, the person responsible for building the initial district-level team, considered the role of the school of origin, as well as the reliability and receptiveness of individuals to lead the efforts across the district.

SUSTAINABILITY

As you pack your bags for this journey, we want you to begin with the end in mind (Covey, 1989). Once the equity plan is under way, team members engage in reflective and dialogic processes to address questions such as the following:

- In what ways are we able to ensure that the intended organizational changes are systemic and not dependent on any one set of individuals in the present organization?

- Are we really changing the culture for the better, or are we just moving the castle in the aquarium? The fish might swim in a different pattern, but has there really been any systemic, cultural, enduring change?

Team members' discussing their responses to questions such as these serves to build cohesive teams dedicated to and focused on commitment to equity initiatives. Reeves (2009) posited,

> Implementing change requires focus, clarity, and monitoring—qualities that will place you among the very best change leaders in the world. Unfortunately, even superior accomplishments in focus, clarity, and monitoring are insufficient to sustain change. Indeed, most change efforts emphasize individual and organizational effectiveness—necessary but not sufficient conditions for sustainable change. (p. 123)

School leaders in Eaveston are focused on changes that extend past the immediate changes and look toward the bigger picture of all aspects of the school organization. Yes, it is important to get those "short-term wins," but "change leaders in schools know that we are engaged not only in the work of education but also in a complex enterprise of people, with all the human drama that accompanies personal pride and identity" (Reeves, 2009, p. 87). Creating that sustainable change requires leadership that goes beyond those temporary gains and focuses on the meaningful, lasting improvements (Hargreaves & Fink, 2004) to the organization's policies and practices and individuals' behaviors.

CULTURALLY PROFICIENT LEADERSHIP FOR SYSTEM TRANSFORMATION

Culturally proficient leaders consider systemic, transformational change as basic to improving and creating effective schools (Lezotte & Snyder, 2011; Sergiovanni, 1989). As they work to increase equity, and serve all, they must keep constant vigilance of self in their roles as change agents (Gay, 2000; G. Howard, 2006; Nelson & Guerra, 2014). The starting point for long-term, systemic change does not begin with changing the system or others around us. It is commenced by change within ourselves (Dilts, 1990; Fullan, 1997; Gardner, 2004; R. B. Lindsey et al., 2019).

Culturally proficient leaders place high value on well-planned change initiatives, designed to move the entire system into a continuous school improvement process. The change initiative must involve all levels of the school or district in planned systemic change designed to open doors for students who have been historically underserved and marginalized (Hargreaves & Fullan, 2012). So you might ask where do we start? We advocate planned, continuous school improvement that employs Dilts's (1990) Nested Levels of Organizational Change.

Take a moment, and read Table 4.1, Dilts's Nested Levels of Organizational Change. Note the intricacies and, at the same time, the familiarity of individual and organizational change. A key takeaway from Dilts's (1990) model is that at whatever level you introduce change, you can directly influence the levels below it. Leaders in Eaveston chose to initiate broad-based change by introducing it at the identity level, thereby setting in motion the ability to guide change through each and all layers of the district and its schools.

Dilts's (1990) model can guide leaders in transformational leadership efforts by locating leverage points for initiating change of policies, practices, and behaviors. Take note of the foundational level of initiating change at the identity level, the individual and the group. Culturally proficient leaders use the "inside-out" process of transformational change for the planning process and focus on "doing their own work first" before taking the work outside of the planning team. We present three questions you can use to guide your own learning and to engage others in the transformative personal

TABLE 4.1 ● Dilts's Nested Levels of Organizational Change

- **Identity:** The individual or group's sense of self
  Answers the questions: *Who are we?, or Who am I?*
  - **Belief System:** The individual or group's values, beliefs, and meanings
    Answers the question: *Why do we do what we do?*
    - **Capabilities:** The individual or group's meta cognitive and reflective skills available through consciousness and group member capabilities to use new knowledge, and skills
      Answers the question: *How will we develop and use the skills that we have?*
      - **Behaviors:** The individual or group's actions and reactions
        Answers the question: *In what specific behaviors will I or we engage?*
        - **Environment:** Basic physical surroundings, tools, materials, supplies, etc.
          Answers the questions: *What do we need to begin?*

Source: Bob Garmston; *The Adaptive School: Developing and Facilitating Groups Leadership Institute,* July 2004

change, and the school or district in transformational organizational change (Shields, 2010):

Who are we?

Are we who we say we are?

Why do we do what we do?

The role of a district leader is a critical component in both the implementation of the Cultural Proficiency Framework and the sustainability of embedding it in all aspects of the district or school. It is important to think about how you will lead others in your district or school through one of the most important steps in the equity transformation process. When acknowledging and overcoming the Barriers to Cultural Proficiency, leaders must keep in mind two equity-focused leadership roles:

1. Being present and involved in the work

2. Serving as a role model to school and community members while in this journey of learning (Welborn, 2019)

BEING PRESENT AND INVOLVED IN THE WORK

The intentionality of culturally proficient leadership requires educators to be mindful of the inside-out nature of the Cultural Proficiency journey. What this means is that you, as the leader, will need to ensure you are present in the phases of training, implementation, action planning, and progress monitoring to ensure sustainability. In our experience when district- and building-level leaders are not present and involved in the work, it is difficult to build capacity for a critical mass of those implementing the work, it is difficult to sustain, and, most of all, there are limited outcomes of increased equity, access, and inclusion (Welborn, 2019).

The journey of Cultural Proficiency includes the simultaneous intertwining of two paths. One path has school leaders developing personal values and beliefs that align with equity-focused, inclusive verbal and nonverbal behaviors. Educational leaders can offer a stated vision of a culturally proficient school or district, but without intentional actions guided by equity-based values and beliefs, there is little change or measurable progress. In the case of Eaveston School District, leaders have taken a stance on the importance of being present and involved in equity work, using the Cultural Proficiency Framework for building an organization of equity and excellence for its diverse student population (Welborn, 2019). A district administrator who has been involved extensively with the Cultural Proficiency Committee described her role thus:

> It's my job to work collaboratively with various components that we have in the teaching and learning department to find out what it is we can do to support administrators and teachers who ultimately support all of our learners. I always feel like it's important for me to be as involved as I can in learning, growing, and developing myself because if I can't talk the talk and understand the equity work using the Tools of Cultural Proficiency, then how can I support it? It's important that I'm there with them learning, especially on topics that maybe I'm not as proficient in myself.

A principal who believes strongly that every student in her school has their own story described her role of being present and involved in the work:

> I consider myself a Servant Leader. That's my role in this building. I want to be there for kids, teachers, parents, and the community. People have to see that my actions are demonstrating what's important to me, and it's an expectation that this is important to the staff because we, as a school community, have to engage and welcome all families, no matter where they're from or what language they speak. Families know we care about them as individuals. We take this very seriously, so that's what I want my presence to be on a daily basis.

In addition, Eaveston School District takes great pride in its family involvement. Valuing diversity on the Cultural Proficiency Committee is essential to the outcomes of the equity work focusing on goals to help Eaveston achieve its vision and mission (Welborn, 2019). A parent from one of Eaveston's elementary schools commented about his involvement regarding the vision of serving all students:

> My role is being as active in the work as possible: from the PTO to my children's academic and extracurricular activities and the Cultural

Proficiency Committee. My general practice in helping any cultural diversity situation is to be present because I feel people lack experience. This is what helps to build really true cross-cultural proficiency. It's an academic process of understanding history, but personal interaction and, actually, presence is probably where people become most proficient. Being an ethnic minority, I have life experience that isn't necessarily understood by the majority culture, so just being present and being active is a way I feel I can participate.

Effective culturally proficient leaders who are present and involved in the work embody the inside-out approach of transformational change. By focusing on core values, they are better able to identify personal and institutional barriers to access and achievement that have perpetuated inequitable outcomes for many students of color and those living in poverty (Welborn, 2019).

SERVING AS A ROLE MODEL FOR OTHERS ON THE CULTURAL PROFICIENCY JOURNEY

Change leadership and learning requires modeling, especially in the work of Cultural Proficiency.

> Leaders must lead by modeling the values and behaviors that represent collective goals. Role-based theories of leadership wrongly envision leaders who are empowered to ask or require others to do things they may not be willing or able to do. (Fullan, 2001, p. 130)

Eaveston School District's educators, who are deeply involved in leading the school district's work in applying the Tools of Cultural Proficiency, realize their role in modeling culturally proficient educational behaviors and practices while supporting others on the journey (Welborn, 2019). A principal described,

> I want to be a role model in the Cultural Proficiency work; I want to be that individual that is walking the talk, and my staff, students, families, and community members are able to see that we don't just go around saying, "Diversity is our strength." Honestly, I believe I want to show growth towards Cultural Proficiency in everything I do, in everything I say, every single day.

Acknowledging and overcoming the Barriers to Cultural Proficiency, and the manner in which these barriers perpetuate inequities and educational access and opportunity gaps, such as demographic differences in discipline rates, academic achievement, and placement into programs such as Advanced Placement, Gifted, and Special Education, is essential for leaders to serve as role models (Welborn, 2019).

Modeling continuous learning involving topics such as culture, diversity, equity, and access is a means to helping others acknowledge and overcome the Barriers to Cultural Proficiency. This is particularly our experience when encountering participants who are in denial—whether the denial results in passive or active resistance is immaterial. You will want to listen for comments such as "I just try to keep learning and talk with people in a way that we can start to see into others' experiences and perspectives a little better." One of the most difficult challenges in this work is the realization that everyone is on their own personal journey of Cultural Proficiency, some much further along on the Continuum than others. A type of comment to listen for is "I serve as a role model by being a reminder to all that we are all at different points on the Cultural Proficiency Continuum. My responsibility is to be calm and effective in conversations with others." Eaveston leaders noted that serving as a role model and supporting others on their journeys was vital for building the critical mass of consciousness in the district (Welborn, 2019).

Comments such as the following are indicative of what we have heard from educators in schools and districts with whom we have worked that serves to illustrate movement along the Continuum:

> We need to be cognizant that some staff members are not as comfortable with certain conversations related to culture as others. We have to find a way to try to make them feel comfortable. This work is urgent. I think our district is a model for the area in demonstrating an awareness of cultural diversity. We pride ourselves on being a community of support, and if we're not culturally proficient, then we're leaving people out.

In this case, the speaker is looking at things through an equity and diversity lens to see individual and organizational strengths and challenges and how they can continue on a path of continuous improvement. They want people to feel included. They want people to feel like this is a safe place, like this is a community. Effective educational leaders present a defined sense of self, others, and the ability to support others. Such leaders listen, learn, and create conditions for changing the way things are being done. These leaders seek and find ways to institutionalize cultural knowledge by creating systems and processes that enable students, teachers, administrators, and families to interact effectively in a variety of cultural settings (R. B. Lindsey et al., 2019).

FOUNDATIONAL LEADERSHIP RESEARCH ON THE CASE OF EAVESTON

The following paragraphs provide part of a review of literature, foundational to the research study, that investigated Eaveston School District's implementation of the Cultural Proficiency Framework. It was first published in *Education Leadership Review* (Welborn, 2019). We present this review of the literature in this format to draw your attention to what you will want to "pack" as you embark on your own journey of Cultural Proficiency.

The foundations of education are rooted in the belief that educated children become better citizens. Although diversity holds great importance in democracy, too many schools in this country continue with systems, policies, and practices that largely reflect the values, behaviors, and aspirations of the most powerful groups (Apple & Beane, 1995; Darling-Hammond, 1995; Ravitch, 1985; Sarason, 1990). Systemic oppression, policy impacts on marginalized students, and privilege and entitlement limit educational outcomes and the reality of access and equity for all (R. B. Lindsey et al., 2010). The continuous oppression of students of historically marginalized demographic groups—based on race, ethnicity, and social class—has perpetuated inequities and educational performance deficits (Banks & Banks, 1995; Freire, 1970; Hammond, 2015; G. Howard, 2006; Kozol, 2005; Ladson-Billings, 2006; Noguera, 2008).

Recently, scholars indicated that culturally proficient educational leaders are advocates for learning, with the intent to meet the needs of all students using an inside-out process. With the moral imperative, knowledge, and skills, effective educators examine their values, behaviors, and beliefs, as well as their organization's policies and practices (R. B. Lindsey et al., 2019). Thus, professional learning focusing on Cultural Proficiency is essential for educational leaders dedicated to serving all students.

THE IMPORTANCE OF EDUCATIONAL LEADERSHIP IN STUDENT ACHIEVEMENT: A LOOK AT THE LITERATURE

Research presents a correlation between school leadership and student achievement (Byrk & Schneider, 2002; DuFour & Mattos, 2013; Hallinger & Heck, 1996; Leithwood et al., 2004; Marks & Printy, 2003; Marzano et al., 2005). Fullan (2003) posited that the moral imperative of educational leadership is for leaders to introduce new elements into the setting, intended to influence behavior for the better, all while managing different interests, economic situations, cultural origins, religions, ethnicities, and races. Leaders are responsible for fostering social unity in our society of increasingly diverse students, families, and educators. Concurrently, leaders must maintain a focus on educational reform through continuous improvement efforts so all children of our nation are afforded the intended outcomes of public school. The correlates of effective school research (Edmonds & Frederiksen, 1978) identified the primary aim of public schools to reach the intended outcomes as teaching and learning (Lezotte & Snyder, 2011). Educational leaders' focus on teaching and learning is essential.

The moral imperative requires collective efficacy—combined efforts for making a difference in the lives of students, building relationships, and monitoring one's responsibility and contributions—in closing educational gaps. Research findings suggest that collective efficacy has strong correlative effects on student achievement (Donohoo, 2016; Eells, 2011; Goddard, Hoy, & Woolfolk Hoy, 2004; Hattie, 2012). Defined by Bandura (1997) as "a group's shared belief in its conjoint capability to organize and execute the courses of action required to produce given levels of attainment" (p. 477), collective efficacy influences the personal culture, how one thinks and behaves, and the school culture, which indirectly affects student achievement (Donohoo, Hattie, & Eells, 2018). Educational leaders play an integral role in building collective efficacy. Fullan (2001, 2003) suggested that the moral imperative involves leading cultural change that activates the passion and commitment of stakeholders, such as teachers and parents, to improve the learning of all students, which includes closing the achievement gap.

Building relationships is another critical factor in student achievement and school success (Milner, 2013). Educational leaders are expected to take risks toward leading change by assessing cultural knowledge and learning from one another, thus becoming more aware of the personal lives and interests of teachers, staff, and students and their families (Marzano et al., 2005; Wagner et al., 2006). In a meta-analysis, Marzano et al. (2005) identified relationships as a part of school leadership affecting the effectiveness of many other tasks and responsibilities completed at the school. The study identified behaviors and characteristics applicable to relationships between administrators, teachers, and their students and families, all of which influence school effectiveness and student achievement.

Because of the strong correlation between educational leadership and student achievement, educators who monitor their own responsibility and contributions in closing the educational gaps are essential. While the research on the effect size of school and environmental factors, as they relate to student achievement, is ongoing, it is greatly debated because there is no definitive answer for closing the educational gaps. Barton and Coley (2009) and Murphy (2009) have written extensively about educational gaps and declared that the solution is complex and cannot be managed by one focused effort. However, school leaders can contribute by ensuring that teaching is disproportionately advantaging students on the lower end of the educational gaps. Race and socioeconomic status are critical issues, and equitable learning outcomes can be actualized as leaders accept responsibility for performance and development of themselves, teachers' performance, and students' achievement and growth (Murphy, 2009). Overall, school leaders are responsible for promoting a collaborative culture and monitoring the collective impact of teaching on student achievement (Donohoo et al., 2018; Lezotte & Snyder, 2011).

EDUCATIONAL LEADERS AND ORGANIZATIONAL CHANGE TOWARD CONTINUOUS IMPROVEMENT

The educational system must change in one way or another, backward to intellectual and moral standards of a prescientific age or forward to the development of the possibilities of growing and expanding experience (Dewey, 1938). Educational leaders acknowledge change as inevitable and necessary for improvement in any school system. Each year, school leaders complete school improvement plans, providing a road map with the goal of increasing student achievement, thus changing the organization.

While well-planned initiatives are paramount, the process of involving stakeholders at the district and building levels, as well as families and community members, is equally valuable in developing a shared meaning in the continuous improvement process (Epstein & Associates, 2019; Lezotte & Snyder, 2011; Marks & Printy, 2003). Fullan (2016) further described stakeholder involvement in the change process as the shaping and reshaping of good ideas while building capacity and ownership among participants.

Moreover, Dilts's (1990) model of nested levels of learning provides further awareness of the importance of professional learning and collaboration necessary for organizational change and gains in student achievement. The five levels of organizational change identified by Dilts are (1) identity, (2) belief system, (3) capabilities, (4) behaviors, and (5) environment. It is vital for educational leaders to understand that change begins with identity, the individual's and/or group's sense of self, and one's own lived experiences, as Dewey (1938) noted.

The aforementioned literature review provides a summary of comprehensive consideration of the literature relative to the object of the study. The purpose of this study and research questions were designed to fill the gaps in the literature around outcomes related to the implementation and experiences surrounding a school district's journey toward culturally proficient educational practice and student achievement. While extensive literature exists regarding educational leadership, student achievement, and organizational change for school reform, there is little evidence of practical application for utilizing an equity framework at the school district level, namely the Cultural Proficiency Framework, to create organizational change and increase student achievement.

LOOKING IN THE REARVIEW MIRROR

As Deming wrote, "Every system is perfectly designed to get the results it gets" (https://deming.org/quotes/10141/). We know leadership influences that system design process. As you progress through the story of Eaveston's working toward equity using the Tools of Cultural Proficiency, look for these leadership behaviors and structures as guideposts to improvement. As the story of Eaveston unfolds, you can use these guideposts to develop your own implementation plan toward equity.

ON TO OUR NEXT DESTINATION

In the next chapter we hit the highway. You will begin learning about the Tools of Cultural Proficiency and how to apply them in your district or school for transformational change. In Chapter 5, you will investigate the Barriers to Cultural Proficiency using an inquiry process. The Barriers to Cultural Proficiency serve as personal, professional, and institutional impediments to moral and just service to a diverse society. Connections will be made throughout by reading the case narrative and using examples and illustrations from Eaveston School District's journey.

REFLECTION, DIALOGUE, AND ACTION PROCESS

REFLECTION • Dialogue • Action

1. As you scan the system that you are in, what do your results tell you about the current state of culturally proficient leadership?

2. In what ways has Dilts's (1990) model informed your plans for better outcomes for all students?

Reflection • DIALOGUE • Action

1. As you assemble or work with a leadership team, discuss the importance of Cultural Proficiency being an inside-out process. What does this mean to the members of the group?

2. In what ways will you hold yourselves accountable for the effective implementation of culturally proficient practices?

Reflection • Dialogue • ACTION

1. As you focus your efforts on Cultural Proficiency, what is the first step to set up predictable and effective communication structures that will educate and inform all stakeholders?

2. What implementation examples from Eaveston would be applicable to your initial efforts?

_____

_____

_____

_____

_____

_____

_____

_____

_____

_____

_____

_____

_____

Travel Log

PART II

The Framework of Cultural Proficiency

TRAVEL GUIDE
Overcoming Barriers to Cultural Proficiency

Create Your Map

- Use an understanding of the barriers to examine your own policies, practices, and procedures.
- Engage in an examination of why we are getting the results we are getting.
- Determine where our own entitlement and privilege affects student achievement.
- Develop plans to address the barriers.

Resources

- Board policies, district practices, and school procedures are rich with data regarding barriers to all students achieving.
- People in various parts of the organization are a resource for examining and improving school culture.
- The core values and beliefs of the organization guide this work of renewal.

Mileage

- Produce data regarding institutional and personal barriers.
- Establish a baseline for remediation.
- Collect qualitative and quantitative data regarding progress of the initiative, community responses, and student achievement. •
- Gather data about the effectiveness of your leadership.

Check the Weather

- Examining policies that represent barriers will require the cooperation of the district office, the board, and community partners.
- How will relationships be nurtured that will assist in the collection of these data across the organization?
- What community resources will inform this work?

Travel Phrases

- Identify, acknowledge, and overcome Barriers to Cultural Proficiency.
- Presumptions of privilege and entitlement
- Systems of oppression
- Unawareness of the need to adapt
- Resistance to change

You're the Driver

- How will you prepare yourself and those you work with to uncover and confront the barriers to student success that have been perpetuated in your organization?
- What assets do you bring to this work?
- What do you imagine will be some of your barriers to this work?
- In what ways do you hope to grow as a leader as you manage this process?

CHAPTER 5

Overcoming Barriers to Cultural Proficiency

STORIES FROM EAVESTON

This is a research-informed vignette developed from the researcher's lens and case study findings of Eaveston School District. It provides context for implementing the Cultural Proficiency Framework to identify, acknowledge, and overcome Barriers to Cultural Proficiency.

Eaveston School District's positive signature line, "ALL will learn," exudes its mission amid its proximity to a metropolitan city with racial and social class implications on governmental, political, and educational contexts. Over the past two decades, many events with racial and social class underpinnings have created divides among the regional community and have affected those living and attending Eaveston's schools. Eaveston's leaders recognize the historical effects of stress on teachers, students, and families of surrounding racial and social class inequities. A teacher reflected,

> This impacts our teachers and our students. We have spouses of police officers that work in our schools; we have students whose mothers and fathers are police officers; we have students who see their family members treated unfairly from social services. Eaveston is a strong community, bringing people together. Individuals' behaviors are present, valid, and important because of real people, our staff, our students, and our families' experiences in life.

Open conversations about relations between social service agencies, faith communities, and members of the Eaveston School District community, past historical events and racism are difficult. The encouraging news is, conversations are continuing in this school community through the Cultural Proficiency Committee. There is intentionality around creating brave and safe spaces for educators to be their true authentic selves. Although tears, anger, sadness, confusion, and other emotions come with this very real topic, Eaveston's leaders continue the conversations and acknowledge these issues as barriers that impede the organization, just as they do in any organization, across the United States and Canada. These barriers inform individuals' behaviors, as well as policies and practices in the organization, which, in some cases, prevent the fulfillment of the vision and mission of Eaveston of opening doors wide for all students to learn and thrive. The key to success in overcoming these barriers is continuous reflection and dialogue.

CALIBRATION

> Each time a man stands up for an ideal, or acts to improve the lot of others, or strikes out against injustice, he sends forth a tiny ripple of hope, and crossing each other from a million different centers of energy and daring, those ripples build a current that can sweep down the mightiest walls of oppression and resistance.
>
> —Robert Kennedy (1966, *Ripple of Hope* Speech)

Often, school leaders embark on a journey, an equity-focused journey, to begin the work necessary to increase access and improve educational outcomes for all students in their school districts or schools. Leaders understand equity and focus on the data to support why increasing equity is necessary. Many school leaders may have had little to no experience of how to initiate this important work or to sustain the work once it commences. We ask you to ponder these questions.

- *Why is beginning with understanding and identifying barriers so important?*

- *In what ways do school leaders utilize the tool, Overcoming Barriers to Cultural Proficiency, to embark on an equity-focused journey?*

- *In what ways will you explore the causes of inequitable outcomes in your school district? What will be your role as the school leader?*

- *Once barriers are identified, how will you and your team overcome them? How will you handle resistance to changes you propose?*

Take a moment and record your thinking.

_____

_____

_____

_____

_____

ON-RAMP TO OVERCOMING BARRIERS TO CULTURAL PROFICIENCY

The real values and beliefs of an organization are written on the hearts and minds of those associated with it; in this case the community and those who work in the schools. This chapter is designed to provide context for school leaders who are working to acknowledge and overcome Barriers to Cultural Proficiency. Take a moment and turn back to Chapter 2 ("The Cultural Proficiency Framework" section) to take a fresh look at the Cultural Proficiency Framework. In his seminal work, developing and advancing what is now presented as the Cultural Proficiency Framework, Cross et al. (1989) proposed Overcoming Barriers to Cultural Competence as fundamental for professionals and their institutions to be able to advance equitable outcomes for citizens. Cross's depiction of barriers serves as a category of barriers often found in organizations:

- The presumption of privilege and entitlement

- Systems of oppression

- Unawareness of the need to adapt

- Resistance to change

The case narrative of Eaveston School District provides examples of barriers acknowledged in the system and the ways in which Eaveston's leaders are working to overcome barriers to student progress and success. As a reminder, Barriers to Cultural Proficiency inform all unhealthy, unproductive, and inequitable policies, practices, and behaviors in our personal and professional lives. Take a moment to locate and find your school or district's mission, vision, and core value statements. Read and think about those words. Ask yourself, "To what extent do we live into and up to those statements? Where is the evidence that they guide our policies and behaviors? If we are falling short, what might be some impediments or barriers to progress?"

In effect, barriers too often serve as unannounced, stealth core values for some educators and some schools and districts. As the word *stealth* implies, barriers are covert or hidden values that, nevertheless, function as core values. Irrespective of stated core values or mission and vision statements that profess inclusiveness and value diversity, the not so subtle message is that *students cannot learn due to their cultural identities, such as their race or social class, or the neighborhoods in which they live.* Due to the apparent deficit nature of these core values, such statements do not exist on paper or on websites. Consequently, barriers inform the way the school functions and the level of respect that is accorded to the students, families, and community members, and their cultures, served by the school. In a most pernicious form some educators might express that *the students or community are not worth their best efforts.*

Culturally proficient educators, who value their students' cultural and community memberships, identify, acknowledge, and work to overcome barriers as presented in this chapter. Once informed, educators work with their colleagues and the members of the community being served to design and deliver an educational experience that welcomes all students in an inclusive manner. This is the work of Cultural Proficiency.

So let's jump into what may be an uncomfortable topic. If so, let us assure you that on building the knowledge and skills described in this chapter, you and your colleagues will be better prepared to take your students to high academic and social success. When you say, "All students will learn at high levels," you can lead with confidence, knowing that every student in your system will have the authentic opportunity to actualize this outcome through culturally proficient educational practice.

So how do you lead these efforts and apply this Tool of Cultural Proficiency? The key is to create systems and structures to facilitate conversations that acknowledge and overcome these barriers. When applied in this way, educators in the organization can identify areas of growth and then rely on the Essential Elements of Cultural Proficiency, covered in detail in Chapter 8, for transformational changes in practice that increase equity and access for students who are not thriving. Identifying, acknowledging, and overcoming barriers opens doors for all students.

You will notice we use three verbs to interact with Barriers to Cultural Proficiency in this chapter. Our intent is to provide a guide for you to apply this tool by sharing Eaveston School District's journey and using learning strategies when collaborating with your team. Identifying, acknowledging, and overcoming barriers is *the work*. Figure 5.1 outlines the process of applying the tool, using the three verbs: *identify*, *acknowledge*, and *overcome*.

FIGURE 5.1 ● Identifying, Acknowledging, and Overcoming Barriers

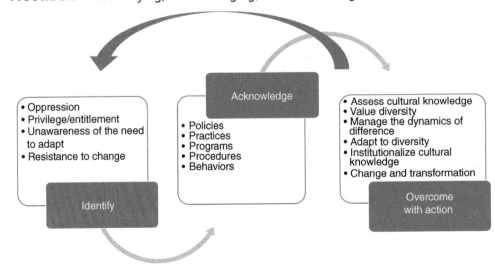

Take note of the Essential Elements in the box on the right. Overcoming Barriers to Cultural Proficiency requires school leaders to rely on these Essential Elements through five distinct actions. The intended outcome is organizational change and individual transformation. This chapter, infused with rich stories and voices from Eaveston School District, is organized using the three application verbs.

IDENTIFYING BARRIERS TO CULTURAL PROFICIENCY

The first tool educators utilize to initiate intentional, inclusive change for equitable educational access is to identify Barriers to Cultural Proficiency and then to make the personal and professional commitment to overcome them. Barriers are caveats that serve as organizational, professional, and personal obstructions to morally and socially just educator values, behaviors, and systemic policies and procedures. Incapacitating behaviors and underlying negative core values may not be apparent to educators themselves. It is our experience that too many educators become socialized into systems in such a way that low expectations are embraced as natural and normal, particularly when a relative disregard for the communities and cultures being served persists.

Identifying and acknowledging Barriers to Cultural Proficiency provide school leaders with a moral compass to discover and evaluate the magnitude of the damaging or marginalizing effects of the policies, practices, and behaviors informed by these barriers (R. B. Lindsey et al., 2019). Figure 5.2 displays the Barriers to Cultural Proficiency as they relate to the other Tools of Cultural Proficiency (Cross et al., 1989; R. B. Lindsey et al., 2019).

Subsequently, Table 5.1 is organized with explanations of each Barrier to Cultural Proficiency. Barriers to overcome include (a) systems of oppression, (b) a sense of privilege and entitlement, (c) unawareness of the need to adapt, and (d) resistance to change. When educational leaders focus on acknowledging and overcoming each barrier, the extent to which perceptions of race and social class inform unhealthy, unproductive, and inequitable policies, practices, and behaviors in a school system diminishes. Thus, school systems see an increase in equitable outcomes for students when culturally proficient educators lead the ongoing application of overcoming barriers in all aspects of the school organization, such as curriculum, instruction, and assessment practices; classroom management; fiscal management of resources; and hiring and retaining high-quality teachers who represent the students and community being served. This requires an understanding of, commitment to, and intentionality of creating space and time for professional learning communities to use reflection and dialogue focused on identifying barriers.

FIGURE 5.2 ● The Conceptual Framework for Culturally Proficient Practices

The Five Essential Elements of Cultural Competence

Serve as standards for personal, professional values and behavior, as well as organizational policies and practices

- **Assessing cultural knowledge**
- **Valuing diversity**
- **Managing the dynamics of difference**
- **Adapting to diversity**
- **Institutionalizing cultural knowledge**

The Cultural Proficiency Continuum portrays people and organizations who possess the knowledge, skills, and moral bearing to distinguish among equitable and inequitable practices as represented by different worldviews:

Informs

Unhealthy, unproductive, and inequitable policies, practices, and behaviors	Differing Worldviews	**Healthy, productive, and equitable policies, practices, and behaviors**
• Cultural destructiveness • Cultural incapacity • Cultural blindness	←→	• Cultural precompetence • Cultural competence • Cultural proficiency

Informs

Resolving the tension to do what is socially just within our diverse society leads people and organizations to view selves in terms productive and equitable.

Informs

Overcoming Barriers to Cultural Proficiency

Serve as personal, professional, and institutional impediments to moral and just service to a diverse society by:

- being resistant to change,
- being unaware of the need to adapt,
- not acknowledging systemic oppression, and
- benefiting from a sense of privilege and entitlement.

Ethical Tension

Guiding Principles of Cultural Proficiency

Provide a moral framework for conducting one's self and organization in an ethical fashion by believing the following:

- Culture is a predominant force in society.
- People are served in varying degrees by the dominant culture.
- People have individual and group identities.
- Diversity within cultures is vast and significant.
- Each cultural group has unique cultural needs.
- The best of both worlds enhances the capacity of all.
- The family, as defined by each culture, is the primary system of support in the education of children.
- School systems must recognize that marginalized populations have to be at least bicultural and that this status creates a distinct set of issues to which the system must be equipped to respond.
- Inherent in cross-cultural interactions are dynamics that must be acknowledged, adjusted to, and accepted.

Source: Adapted from R. B. Lindsey, Nuri-Robins, and Terrell (2009, p. 60).

TABLE 5.1 ● Barriers to Cultural Proficiency

Systems of oppression such as racism and classism are represented in systems and structures of organizations, as well as behaviors of individuals. Inequities persist in our systems, and historical data provide indications of the ill effects of such systems.
A sense of privilege and entitlement is when people believe they have acquired all of the personal achievements and societal benefits they have solely on the basis of their merit or character and do not feel the need to release or reorder the perquisites they have. They fail to acknowledge the extent to which their achievement, success, and benefits are based on their race and/or social class.
Unawareness of the need to adapt is when people fail to recognize the need to make personal or organizational changes in response to the racial or social class diversity among the people with whom they interact.
Resistance to change is manifested as organizations and individuals refuse to reflect and engage in dialogue with others around discriminatory policies and practices and unconscious biases. These policies, practices, and biases lead to discriminatory behaviors that perpetuate inequities for students. Whether negative perceptions of race or social class and related behaviors are intentional or unintentional, the effect on students is the same.

Source: Adapted from R. B. Lindsey et al. (2019).

REFLECTION • Dialogue • Action

Take a moment to think deeply about the Barriers to Cultural Proficiency. In what ways have you experienced or observed these barriers in your professional work? What examples of educational practices or individual behaviors can you identify related to oppression, racism, or classism? When have you heard adults in your organization saying something that represents one of the Barriers? In what ways have you experienced resistance to changing policies or practices in your organization? Record your thoughts.

_____

_____

_____

_____

_____

In the next section we take you on Eaveston's journey of Cultural Proficiency in applying the Tool of Overcoming Barriers to Cultural Proficiency. The road map for their journey includes the processes and learning strategies their leaders used throughout a two-year period to identify, acknowledge, and overcome Barriers to Cultural Proficiency.

Due to the interrelated nature of the Tools of Cultural Proficiency, the road map for you, just like for Eaveston, will not necessarily follow a linear path, where you continue to move down the same highway, in the same direction, at the same rate. We know there are multiple ways to arrive at a destination; sometimes we drive straight through, and sometimes we stop off at different places for various reasons. Sometimes, we revisit the same destination. Explicitly stated, we do not provide you with a step-by-step guide to apply this tool. As you read about Eaveston's journey, keep note of the processes and learning strategies that resonate with you and those you could envision leading while you guide your school organization on its journey of Cultural Proficiency by identifying, acknowledging, and overcoming barriers.

ACKNOWLEDGING AND OVERCOMING BARRIERS

This section describes the inquiry process Eaveston School District leaders used as an initial step in developing an equity plan to overcome Barriers to Cultural Proficiency. Cultural Proficiency is an inside-out journey. The extent to which district leaders engaged in this journey of self-discovery emphasizes the importance of the journey and the need to embed the work of Cultural Proficiency into all aspects of district planning and activities. Sustaining this work into the future requires school leaders to focus on building the capacity of a critical mass of educators who have adopted the mindset of applying the Tools of Cultural Proficiency to everything they do and say as people, and as employees, of the district. Community leaders use the Cultural Proficiency Framework to foster an inclusive mindset for implementing school policies and procedures by applying the tools proactively. Table 5.2 displays the guiding questions that Eaveston's leaders used to inform learning about and applying the Tool of Overcoming Barriers to Cultural Proficiency.

Eaveston's school leaders used select processes and learning strategies to help gain the answers to the guiding questions. The learning strategies were arranged in two parts:

1. Acknowledging barriers

2. Overcoming barriers

TABLE 5.2 ● Guiding Questions for Applying Overcoming Barriers to Cultural Proficiency

- Which demographic groups of students in Eaveston School District are not thriving or experiencing success?
- What data do we have to support the fact that students are not experiencing success?
- To what leverage areas (i.e., curriculum, instruction, discipline, hiring practices, programs, interventions) do the data relate?
- Given the value we have for "*all* to learn," what are we willing to change?
- What are we willing to do so that identified students experience success?
- What are the barriers to culturally proficient educational practice?
- What examples of systemic barriers in the district are precluding or preventing students from experiencing success related to the leverage areas?

CONTINUED STORIES FROM EAVESTON

This is a research-informed vignette developed from the researcher's lens and case study findings of Eaveston School District. The researcher-participant provides part of the backstory leading up to the decision of Eaveston's school leaders to fully commit to implementing the Cultural Proficiency Framework in all aspects of the district.

At the beginning of Eaveston's Cultural Proficiency journey, the former "social justice" committee convened after a change in district-level leadership led to reassigned roles and responsibilities among district and school leaders. In 2015, following the deaths of Tamir Rice, Philando Castile, and Michael Brown, district leaders decided that with national attention focused on the too frequent deaths of Black boys and men, as well as issues of systemic racism and intersections of social class tied to educational outcomes nationally, regionally, and locally, it was time for their schools to develop a formal process to acknowledge and overcome barriers such as systemic racism or classism that might exist in their schools. Eaveston's leaders were keen not to focus on law enforcement, social service agencies, or other external barriers but rather to turn attention inward to barriers within the school organization that could be transformed. They were most interested in targeting those existing educational disparities related to race and social class within the Eaveston School District, including the Intersectionality of other cultural identities such as language, ableness, sexual orientation, and gender identification.

During this time Eaveston's leaders worked with the Professional Development Services department of Corwin, the publisher of Cultural Proficiency literature. Corwin arranged to have two of the authors of Cultural Proficiency books, experienced in working with schools, provide an introduction and overview to the Cultural Proficiency Framework. The superintendent at the time had a strong sense of urgency around creating a school district with a culture that opened doors for students and engaged in continuous reflection and action toward change specifically related to racial contexts.

Prior to this work, some students in Eaveston's high school staged a walkout during the school day to demonstrate their belief that too little was being done nationally and locally to address discrimination and racism in its many forms. Two days after the walkout, the Cultural Proficiency Committee convened to continue plans for creating change in ways that ensure equitable access and outcomes for all students in Eaveston. The superintendent believed that assessing cultural knowledge was vital in launching the work. It was the superintendent's observation that the dynamics of difference with regard to race and social class among staff, students, and the district's culture would affect Eaveston's students and families, and in turn, those cultures would influence all educators as well as the educational outcomes in Eaveston.

By January of the following year, Eaveston had convened a group of more than 50 people to join the district's Cultural Proficiency Committee to launch the "Cultural Proficiency Journey Kick-Off." In the room were stakeholders including, but not limited to, parents, teachers, administrators, central office administrators, police officers, community leaders, and support staff, including administrative assistants, bus drivers, and the director of food services.

ACKNOWLEDGING BARRIERS TO CULTURAL PROFICIENCY

To overcome barriers, you start by acknowledging examples of implicit deficit-laden core values known as the impediments or Barriers to Cultural Proficiency. Eaveston's Cultural Proficiency Committee initially focused on acknowledging barriers internal to school policies and procedures that might be preventing historically underserved students from experiencing success in the district. Such internal barriers, often unrecognized and unintentional, give rise to unhealthy, unproductive, and inequitable policies, practices, and behaviors that impede access to education and prevent certain students from thriving in a school system. A cautionary word about "intent." If the effect of a policy or practice is negative, whether intentional or unintentional, harm is real.

The *Barriers to Cultural Proficiency* (R. B. Lindsey et al., 2019, p. 245) learning strategy was used to guide committee members through a process of acknowledging barriers within the school district that obstruct students from experiencing success in their classrooms, schools, and district. Committee members were asked to identify at least three examples of prevalent policies and/or practices under each of the following barriers:

- Systemic oppression

- Presumption of entitlement and unearned privilege

- Unawareness of the need to adapt

- Resistance to change

Table 5.3 provides opportunity for you to reflect on your own thinking and experiences and to dialogue with others to acknowledge examples of each barrier in your school district, school, or classroom.

Now that you have identified and acknowledged some of the barriers present in your school organization, take the time to read about Eaveston's process in acknowledging their barriers. Emergent findings from the research study are displayed in Tables 5.4 to 5.7. These findings represent examples of the barriers Eaveston leaders identified and acknowledged. The examples are organized by the Barriers to Cultural Proficiency as categorized initially by Cross et al. (1989): (a) systemic oppression, (b) unawareness of the need for educators to adapt to the diversity of the community being served, (c) a sense of privilege and entitlement, and (d) resistance to change (R. B. Lindsey et al., 2019).

Unfolding the Barriers to Cultural Proficiency as a means to embrace their historical negativity provided Eaveston's stakeholders the opportunity to study, embrace, and adapt to the inclusive Guiding Principles of Cultural

TABLE 5.3 ● Examples of Barriers to Cultural Proficiency

WHAT BARRIERS INTERNAL TO THE SCHOOL SYSTEM ARE IMPEDIMENTS TO STUDENTS THRIVING OR EXPERIENCING SUCCESS?
Examples of systemic oppression (racism, classism)
Presumption of unearned privilege or entitlement
Unawareness of the need to adapt
Resistance to change

Reflection • DIALOGUE • Action

Convene a group of colleagues to engage in dialogue about barriers internalized in your school policies and practices that obstruct or otherwise limit students' opportunities for academic and social success. As you think about your own practices and engage in dialogue with colleagues, take the time to consider your organization's practices, as well as the general climate in your school or district. Use Table 5.3 to guide you in acknowledging the barriers within your organization. As you acknowledge the barriers within your organization, keep in mind other group identities, such as national origin, language, or disability, that have been historically underserved or marginalized.

Proficiency. Tables 5.8 through 5.11 display the emergent findings from the case study related to the ways in which Eaveston's school leaders are working to overcome these Barriers to Cultural Proficiency.

Overcoming barriers help guide the district from being school-centric to being a community-centric district focused on the academic and social needs of Eaveston's diverse community. Chapter 6 includes the Guiding

TABLE 5.4 ● Eaveston School District's Acknowledgment of Systemic Oppression, a Barrier to Cultural Proficiency

- Policies—different norms, values, beliefs, behaviors are looked at as wrong (i.e., dress code and discipline efforts that result in disproportionate negative practices for students of color)
- A diverse student body in contrast to the school administration, faculty, and staff, who are predominately White, middle class, and female
- Differing feelings of belonging to the school (i.e., historical implications due to parents' childhood school experiences, teacher/administrator relationships with families, past experiences of families coming to school—discipline, IEP meetings, celebrations, student awards)
- Differing levels of support for family engagement (i.e., PTO, family attendance at events)
- Historical effects of stress between certain communities and social services nationally, regionally, and locally

Note: IEP, Individualized Education Program; PTO, parent-teacher organization.

TABLE 5.5 ● Eaveston School District's Acknowledgment of a Sense of Privilege and Entitlement, a Barrier to Cultural Proficiency

- Rejection of the term *privilege*
- Historical roles of teacher versus student as a power struggle
- Perspectives become some school members' reality in which community perspectives are often viewed as wrong

TABLE 5.6 ● Eaveston School District's Acknowledgment of Unawareness of the Need to Adapt, a Barrier to Cultural Proficiency

- Well-intended adults who desire to do the work but don't know how to initiate or sustain self-study
- Differences in norms, experiences, behaviors, and learning styles among educators and the community served give rise to culturally based misunderstandings that too often lead to mistrust
- Educators' lack of knowledge and experiences related to the community's history and experiences of being oppressed

TABLE 5.7 ● Eaveston School District's Acknowledgment of Resistance to Change, a Barrier to Cultural Proficiency

- Resistance to mandated Cultural Proficiency professional development
- Resistance/avoidance by some educators and staff members due to fear or discomfort in addressing issues related to cultural differences
- Resistance because some believe there has been little progress, change, or sustainability in prior equity work

TABLE 5.8 ● Eaveston School District's Actions for Overcoming Systemic Oppression

- Use disaggregated data, communicate clearly about who is being marginalized, left out, or denied access, then commit to action.
- Review/revise policies using the Culturally Proficient Policy Revision Framework.
- Review hiring practices through engagement with the Cultural Proficiency Committee.
- Extend and deepen restorative practices activities at school sites.
- Extend and deepen school and family involvement/engagement.
- Use cultural proficiency learning strategies to promote an asset-based approach to difference (i.e., managing conflict with our core values, guiding principles discussion starters, listening and hearing.

Source: R. B. Lindsey et al. (2009).

TABLE 5.9 ● Eaveston School District's Actions for Overcoming a Sense of Privilege and Entitlement

- Encourage family engagement strategies as a means for educators to gain healthy perspectives about the communities served by Eaveston School District
- Implement personalized learning and competency-based curricula that utilize research-based strategies and scaffolding to support students' realizing their full potential.
- Maintain high expectations, ensure discipline policies are equitable, expand the use of restorative practices.
- Honor individual stories of school members as well as community members.

TABLE 5.10 ● Eaveston School District's Actions for Overcoming Unawareness of the Need to Adapt

- Work continuously toward equity and understanding, appreciating, and respecting differences in cultures—targeted resources.
- Implement Eaveston's Personalized Learning Initiative.
- Maintain high expectations, assess needs, and focus on communication.

TABLE 5.11 ● Eaveston School District's Actions for Overcoming Resistance to Change

- Focus change on individuals' values and behaviors.
- Change the model and methods of professional development to focus on educator needs in responding to a diverse community.
- Utilize the professional learning strategies of reflection, dialogue, and action to build trust, empathy, and relationships in the professional development program.
- Provide opportunities for teachers and students to respond to contentious issues, to express feelings, and to support inclusive change processes.

Principles of Cultural Proficiency, aligned with descriptions of shifts under way in the district's policies and procedures as well as educators' values and behaviors. While Eaveston continues to work on overcoming the Barriers to Cultural Proficiency, the core of the work is focused on creating an environment where all staff, students, and their families feel heard and valued; examining their values and beliefs through reflection and dialogue; building trust among and between group members; and developing relational skills embedded in culturally proficient coaching (D. B. Lindsey et al., 2020).

OVERCOMING BARRIERS BY EXAMINING VALUES AND BELIEFS

One of the first learning strategies used during the Eaveston Cultural Proficiency Committee's "Kick-Off" event to begin the work of acknowledging and overcoming barriers was an adapted version of *Diversity Lifeline* (R. B. Lindsey et al., 2019, p. 199). Using this learning strategy, the participants were invited to think about their lives in relation to differences and experiences around cultural identities (race, ethnicity, national origin, gender, sexual orientation, social class, religion, native language, and ableness). Specifically, they were asked to recall their first experiences with people with cultural identities other than their own. The participants took several minutes to reflect on the many ways in which they have, over their lifetimes, experienced discussions about "other" cultural groups. In turn, they were invited to reflect on the ways in which their implicit and explicit biases may have been shaped as they were growing up.

Reflecting on biases provided the participants opportunity to connect their newly recognized and acknowledged biases collectively and to realize the ways in which those biases can become institutionalized into school systems' policies and practices. The insights gained from the strategy provided an opportunity to introduce a tool from the Cultural Proficiency Framework, Overcoming Barriers to Cultural Proficiency—systemic oppression, privilege and entitlement, unawareness of the need to adapt, and resistance to change.

To deepen and personalize the importance of core values to both educators and the communities being served by the Eaveston School District, members of the Cultural Proficiency Committee engaged in the learning strategy *Name 5 Things* (R. B. Lindsey et al., 2019, p. 201). In this learning strategy school leaders were asked to name five things that if taken from them, they would not be the same person they are today. Each participant, building on a core values learning strategy, discussed in Chapter 6, focused on their top five core values. As a facilitator read a hypothetical scenario, the committee members were asked to cross off the core values one at a time. The scenario and debriefing questions are presented in the following section.

As the hypothetical scenario played out, the group members felt like they were having to give up parts of who they are to participate in this learning strategy. In a manner of "planned redundancy," the group members returned to the question that guided this learning strategy: *Do our students have to leave part of who they are at the door because of oppression, privilege, entitlement, unawareness of the need to adapt, or resistance to change?*

REFLECTION • Dialogue • Action

Do students in your district, school, or classroom have to leave part of who they are at the door because of their race, ethnicity, language proficiency, socioeconomic condition, gender, sexual orientation, ability, or faith membership? To what degree do barriers of oppression, unawareness, privilege, entitlement, or resistance influence these experiences for students? On reflecting on those students' experiences, take a few moments to record your thinking and/or feelings.

_____

_____

_____

_____

_____

OVERCOMING BARRIERS BY BUILDING TRUST AND VALUING DIVERSITY

A culture of building trust and value for diversity are structures school leaders must create as they commit to overcoming Barriers to Cultural Proficiency. A key action to becoming a culturally proficient leader is to model trust and value for diversity. To acknowledge and overcome Barriers to Cultural Proficiency, Eaveston School District leaders worked to build trust among and between the group members. As mentioned earlier in this chapter, the Cultural Proficiency Committee was made up of 50 individuals from the school district and the community. The nature of the group brought individuals together from all schools, meaning most of the group members had never collaborated prior to joining this committee. Building trust in this diverse group was essential.

Your Name—Your Story (p. 310) was a learning strategy that was used to deepen trust among members of the Cultural Proficiency Committee (Table 5.12). The strategy was used to build relationships, trust, and capacity for conversations among the group, who would be facing difficult, challenging work ahead. This learning strategy allowed participants to find out more about those with whom they would be working, such as "a symbol that represents them," "a person who was instrumental in their decision to become an educator," and "names they had been called." This activity invited difference into the room to celebrate and encourage the presence of a variety of cultural groups of people in all activities throughout the day. The intentional

TABLE 5.12 ● Your Name—Your Story

One of your core values	Name	A person you would like to spend the day with
A person who was instrumental in your decision to become an educator	By what names others call you	A symbol that represents you

action of valuing diversity was used to introduce new and current members to one another.

Building trust is an ongoing process for Eaveston's Cultural Proficiency Committee. Other learning strategies were used to build trust among the group to enhance the ability of the committee to collaborate around issues of inequity in the district. *Introductory Grid* (R. B. Lindsey et al., 2019, p. 223) was used to help the group members become acquainted with one another and to orient the participants to differences and similarities with other people on the committee. *Strength Bombardment* (R. B. Lindsey et al., 2019, p. 221) was used to build a sense of being a team among the Cultural Proficiency Committee members through sharing personal stories and discovering similarities and differences. *What's in a Name* (R. B. Lindsey et al., 2019, p. 227) was used to demonstrate that people have strong feelings and interesting stories about their names.

Reflection ● DIALOGUE ● Action

Take a moment to reflect and record your thoughts, guided by the following questions: How will you build trust among your team members? How will you demonstrate value for diversity by engaging students in this process?

_____

_____

_____

_____

_____

OVERCOMING THE BARRIERS THROUGH CULTURALLY PROFICIENT COACHING

During Eaveston's Cultural Proficiency Committee work, members often spoke of disrupting the conversation, changing the narrative. Inevitably, when diversity is valued in a system, new voices emerge in the room with a variety of perspectives and experiences in life. New voices and differing experiences can lead to a clash of values and behaviors, which can provide leaders an opportunity to change conversations from "What is wrong with the kids?" to "What is it we can do differently?"

Using the breakthrough questions from *Culturally Proficient Coaching* (D. B. Lindsey et al., 2020) can lead to a deeper understanding of our roles as educators. Culturally proficient leaders are skilled in managing the dynamics of difference that often arise from a diversity of cultures coming together in support of school improvement processes. Rather than avoid or suppress the conflicts that arise in the workplace, effective leaders regard conflict as natural and normal in our personal and professional lives. Guiding colleagues to understand one another's viewpoints is important to valuing the diversity inherent in most school communities.

One of the concerns often expressed by the participants was "How do I respond when I hear something said by another adult in my school or see something being done that is culturally destructive?" For example, we have all heard expressions such as the following:

If their parents actually cared about education, those kids might be able to make something of themselves.

Why do I always end up with these kids in my class? They are never fed, always dirty, and never prepared for class. Their clothes are too little; they have holes in their shoes; they cannot even afford the school supplies. If mom were at home at night, this wouldn't be a problem.

I don't see color in my students. It's just not something I think about because I treat everyone the same. If you misbehave in my class, you get the consequences that come with it.

One of the goals of Eaveston School District's Cultural Proficiency Committee was to promote and support further Cultural Proficiency learning. In its second year of work with the committee, district leaders began to learn about Culturally Proficient Coaching (D. B. Lindsey et al., 2020). Culturally Proficient Coaching is a model that "intends for the person being coached to be aware of the cultural connections of students and their families and to be educationally responsive to the diverse student groups" (D. B. Lindsey et al., 2020, p. 4). This model of coaching was influenced by The Thinking Collaborative's Model of Cognitive Coaching (http://www.thinkingcollaborative.com), a model that encourages collaboration that influences policies, practices, and procedures focused on improving student achievement through improved instruction and reflective practice (Ellison & Hayes, 2003). The Model of Cognitive Coaching uses a combination of the Norms of Collaborative Work (Garmston & Wellman, 2016) and Five States of Mind (Costa & Garmston, 2015) to help coach educators in reflection and dialogue processes. See Tables 5.13 and 5.14.

Table 5.15 displays the mental model for Culturally Proficient Coaching. This map integrates coaching skills, the Five States of Mind, and culturally

TABLE 5.13 ● The Seven Norms of Collaborative Work

- **Pausing** before responding or asking a question allows think time.
- **Paraphrasing** helps members hear, clarify, organize, and better understand themselves and other group members.
- **Posing** questions helps to explore and specify thinking.
- **Placing ideas on the table** by naming them, specifically, enriches the conversation.
- **Paying attention to themselves and others** raises the level of consciousness for group members, as consideration and value are given to learning styles, languages, and multiple perspectives.
- **Presuming positive intentions** promotes meaningful and professional conversations.
- **Providing assessment data,** and identifying data that is still needed, provides a shared set of information.

Source: Adapted from Garmston and Wellman (2016).

TABLE 5.14 ● The Five States of Mind

FROM		TOWARD
An external locus of control	EFFICACY	An internal locus of control
Narrow, egocentric views	FLEXIBILITY	Broader and alternative perspectives
Vagueness and imprecision	CRAFTSMANSHIP	Specificity and elegance
Lack of awareness	CONSCIOUSNESS	Awareness of self and others
Isolation and separateness	INTERDEPENDENCE	Connection to and concern for the community

Source: Adapted from Costa, Arthur F., & Garmston, Robert J., *Cognitive Coaching: A Foundation of Renaissance Schools* (2nd ed.), © Christopher-Gordon Publishers, Inc. Used with permission.

TABLE 5.15 ● Mental Model of Culturally Proficient Coaching

			TO: TRANSFORMATION FOR EQUITY The focus is on our practice as a coach	
FROM: TOLERANCE FOR DIVERSITY The focus is on *them*				
Cultural Destructiveness, Incapacity & Blindness—Areas *of Unconscious & Conscious Incompetence characterized by:*	States of Mind present Opportunities for Coaching	*Cultural Precompetence*—Area *of Conscious Competence characterized by transitions:*	*Cultural Competence's Essential Elements & The States of Mind*—Area *of Conscious Competence characterized by:*	*Cultural Proficiency*—Area *of Unconscious Competence characterized by future focus:*
External locus of control	Efficacy	Emerging awareness of own skill and knowledge deficiencies	• Internal locus of control • Assessment of cultural knowledge	Commits to ongoing personal and organizational learning
Narrow, egocentric views	Flexibility	Openness to other ways of doing things	• Broader and alternative view of control • Value for diversity	Invites members of larger lay and professional communities to participate
Vagueness and imprecision	Craftsmanship	Willingness to focus on needs of demographic groups of students	• Specificity and elegance • Manage the dynamics of difference	Establishes a vision that is complete with assessable goals
Lack of awareness	Consciousness	Growing awareness of differential needs of community	• Awareness of self and others • Adapting to diversity	Continuously studies the community for demographic and economic shifts
Isolation and separateness	Interdependence	Willingness to work with others to meet own and school needs	• Connection to and concern for the community • Institutionalize cultural knowledge	Commits to professional development embedded in the cultural realities of the community

competent behaviors on the right side of the Cultural Proficiency Continuum. The map is intended to help you see how behaviors can migrate from tolerance for diversity to transformation for equity. With mindset shifts to inclusivity, facilitated the by use of culturally proficient coaching skills, educators transform their educational practices by action focused on equitable outcomes (D. B. Lindsey et al., 2020).

Epoch Cards

Additionally, in various learning strategies Eaveston's Cultural Proficiency Committee engaged in sessions that used brief case stories and discussion prompts from *Epoch Cards*.

That spring, the educators worked to identify the barriers present in each case story or embedded in culturally destructive comments on the Epoch Cards. After identifying the barriers, the committee members used the Seven Norms of Collaboration prompts to pause, paraphrase, pose a breakthrough question, and place ideas on the table to encourage a shift in mindsets.

Table 5.16 illustrates the differences between barrier questions and comments guided by *breakthrough questions*. One of the goals of Culturally Proficient Coaching is to use breakthrough questions that provide for continuous reflection and dialogue to promote a mindset shift about one's practice in service of all students, as opposed to shutting down, or blaming or attacking the person who used a barrier question or comment. The topic of the conversation is the barrier, or data, not the person or the person's beliefs.

School leaders in Eaveston realized the importance of utilizing Culturally Proficient Coaching to help overcome barriers to student success in the school. They recognized that if the Cultural Proficiency Committee understood and utilized the Seven Norms of Collaborative Work and Five States of Mind then they could develop the communication effectiveness of a team of educators. This team could model for others how to overcome barriers by changing mindsets to respond with breakthrough questions when difficult conversations arise.

TABLE 5.16 ● Differences Between Barrier Questions and Breakthrough Questions

Barriers questions/comments will	Breakthrough questions will
<ul><li>shut down thinking,</li><li>assign judgment,</li><li>focus on blame, and</li><li>attack or intimidate other members of the group.</li></ul>	<ul><li>encourage thoughtful responses,</li><li>redirect negative thinking toward positive responses,</li><li>invite flexibility,</li><li>generate "both-and" thinking,</li><li>consider others experiences and perspectives,</li><li>invite possibility and creative thinking,</li><li>value differences, and</li><li>create cognitive shifts in thinking.</li></ul>

🪞 LOOKING IN THE REARVIEW MIRROR

This chapter provided context for school leaders who are working to acknowledge and overcome Barriers to Cultural Proficiency. The case narrative of Eaveston School District provided examples of barriers acknowledged in the system and ways in which Eaveston's leaders are working to overcome barriers. As you prepare yourself to lead this work and apply the tool, Overcoming Barriers to Cultural Proficiency, focus on how you will help others identify, acknowledge, and overcome barriers present in your school or district. Examining values and beliefs, building trust, valuing diversity, and coaching will be essential to your plan.

🔍 ON TO OUR NEXT DESTINATION

In the next chapter, we guide you to investigate the Guiding Principles of Cultural Proficiency using an inquiry process. The Guiding Principles serve as a core values component of the Cultural Proficiency Framework of beliefs for conducting one's self and organization in an ethical manner. Just as the Barriers to Cultural Proficiency are deficit-based core values, the Guiding Principles are referred to as asset-based core values that inform development of inclusive educator behaviors and school organization's practices. The case study narrative from Eaveston School District in Chapter 6 is presented for you to make connections and learn new strategies and resources that are useful in shifting leaders' mindsets from deficit-based to asset-based. We provide opportunities for reflection and dialogue as you go deeper to investigate the Intersectionality of race of social class related to the Guiding Principles of Cultural Proficiency.

REFLECTION, DIALOGUE, AND ACTION PROCESS

REFLECTION • Dialogue • Action

You arrived at this point of the book most likely because you are a curious person who values learning. Give yourself the gift of a few moments of reflection to think and record your responses to the following prompts. Consider yourself as a school leader and your "inside-out" learning related to your personal values and behaviors in service of the racial and social class groups of students in your school or district. Then, apply the "inside-out" process to examine your school/district's policies and practices in responding to the racial and social classes of students served by your school.

Take a few moments to reflect on your understanding of the Barriers to Cultural Proficiency:

1. What internal barriers, personally and systemically, do you face in leading the work of Cultural Proficiency?

2. To what degree are you resistant to changing policies, practices, and behaviors?

3. What cultures do you feel you are unaware of to the degree that it affects your ability to work cross-culturally with them?

4. Record your thoughts on privilege and entitlement. In what ways do you have privilege? In what ways have you been denied privilege?

Reflection • DIALOGUE • Action

These are essential questions to help you dialogue with others as you apply the Tool of Overcoming Barriers to Cultural Proficiency:

1. What barriers to student learning exist within our school organization? How do we know?

2. What Barriers to Cultural Proficiency are present in our current situation? What unhealthy, unproductive, or inequitable behaviors are occurring? From whose perspective?

3. In what ways might we be demonstrating our unawareness of the need to adapt? Who would we talk with to find out?

4. In what ways do we as educators benefit from privilege or entitlement? Which students are succeeding, and why? How much of this has to do with our perception of them?

5. Among our students "not experiencing success," for which ones do we know the least about their culture?

6. What are the cultural identities of us as individual teachers, what is the culture of us as a group of teachers, and how do these affect your students "not experiencing success?"

7. How might we overcome these barriers?

Reflection • Dialogue • ACTION

These are essential questions to help you lead this work in your district or school through actions of acknowledging, identifying, and Overcoming Barriers to Cultural Proficiency:

1. Identify and acknowledge examples of policies and practices in your organization for each Barrier to Cultural Proficiency.

2. Assess your cultural knowledge regarding your own culture, the culture of your colleagues in your organization, the culture of your students and their families, and the barriers present in your educational practices and behaviors, as well as those present in your organization's policies and practices.

3. Create structures and processes, and lead others with strategies to identify, acknowledge, and overcome the Barriers to Cultural Proficiency.

Travel Log

_____

_____

_____

_____

_____

TRAVEL GUIDE
Guiding Principles of Cultural Proficiency

Create Your Map

- Use an inquiry process to determine individual and organizational values. How do they influence your daily actions?
- Learn about the Guiding Principles of Cultural Proficiency.
- Rely on the Guiding Principles to inform healthy, productive, or equitable practices, policies, and behaviors that open doors for students who are not thriving.

Resources

- What strategies were used in the Eaveston School District? How might they be adapted to your situation?
- What outreach has been done to stakeholder groups? What worked? What didn't? Who says so?

Mileage

- What gaps emerge in student achievement data? How might the lens of the Guiding Principles further refine these data?
- What gaps emerge as each group and culture are examined in your organization?
- Where is communication the strongest with stakeholder groups? Where is it lacking?

Check the Weather

- Where are the Guiding Principles already evident in your organization? Who thinks so?
- Which family and cultural groups are already identified?
- Where has friction existed in the past between cultures and groups in your organization?

Travel Phrases

- Culture is a predominant force
- Dominant culture
- Group identities
- Unique cultural needs
- Bicultural
- Cross-cultural interactions

You're the Driver

- How do I utilize the Guiding Principles of Cultural Proficiency to embark on an equity-focused journey with the goal of providing excellent instruction for all students?
- What are my core values and those of my district?
- What communication skills do I need to develop to engage in this work?

Relying on Our Inclusive Core Values: The Guiding Principles of Cultural Proficiency for Organizational Change

STORIES FROM EAVESTON

This a research-informed vignette developed from the researcher's lens and case study findings of Eaveston School District. It provides a context for implementing the Cultural Proficiency Framework by relying on the Guiding Principles of Cultural Proficiency to change policies, practices, and behaviors.

Eaveston School District, "a place to learn and grow," breeds a culture focused on tradition, community values, and growth. For many communities in Eaveston, schools that served students decades ago now serve those students' children and grandchildren. When you think about culture, it is usually expressed as "the way things are done around here" (Deal & Kennedy, 2000). During the years of change over the past two decades in the communities surrounding Eaveston, the school district has served as an anchor and a source of stability and pride for the community. Eaveston School District, once having near-unaccredited status from the state for failing in academics and other performance measures, is now nationally recognized for academic excellence in a diverse setting. Eaveston continues to grow and change. It must. More important, impact data collected from the administration, teachers, and staff following the two years of work applying the Cultural Proficiency Framework indicate deeper levels of understanding and mindset shifts, as well as changes in educational practices.

So when culture means "the way things are done around here," leaders and educators in Eaveston demonstrate their foundational value that its schools and educators will be responsive to their students' and their families' needs; they will change at their core and not sacrifice students' futures for what worked in the past. The Cultural Proficiency Committee, through reliance on the core values, the inclusive Guiding Principles of Cultural Proficiency, helped to focus the district's efforts on change related to the lack of diversity in hired certified teaching staff. "Culture" for Eaveston School District is centered on continuous school improvement through change. "Students must see themselves in their teachers and administrators, not exclusively in support staff" (Casey & Welborn, 2020).

Eaveston's expressed core values promote a foundational component of practice—what they actually do. This intentional alignment of the core values with behaviors and practices around recruiting, hiring, and retaining teachers of color in Eaveston sends the message to the school community that the district continually assesses their cultural knowledge related to student needs and instils a value for diversity in the workforce educating the students. A district-level administrator believes his role in building a community where unity among students, families, patrons, and staff fosters learning, responsibility, and appreciation of diversity is to recommend to the Board of Education the very best employees in the district who will help students achieve their goals. He reflected,

> The Eaveston human resource department strives to recommend the best bus drivers, custodians, music teachers, chemistry teachers, etc. we can find to support our students. It is our goal to have the district workforce be as representative as possible of our student demographics in all job classifications. While efforts are made to recruit a broad and diverse applicant pool, candidates need to have the appropriate teaching certification or have a pathway to obtain the appropriate certification. State certification can be an obstacle to diversifying the teaching staff.

Eaveston's human resource department worked with the Cultural Proficiency Committee to understand and rely on one Guiding Principle in particular, "People are served in varying degrees by the dominant culture." Recruitment practices changed in Eaveston. For all recruiting trips, both to local fairs and to Historically Black Colleges and Universities, leaders in the Human Resource Department now take teachers of color because they acknowledge that people are served in varying degrees by their own culture. Diversity at the table leads to diversity among the prospective teacher candidates who visit the table at these recruitment events. Overall, Eaveston School District leaders' reliance on the Guiding Principles of Cultural Proficiency equipped them with the ability to change practices and policies to express the culture and worldview that are backed by their actions that value diversity.

CALIBRATION

Success is to be measured not so much by the position that one has reached in life as by the obstacles which he has overcome while trying to succeed

—Booker T. Washington (1963, p. 19)

In the previous chapter you had the opportunity to examine the Barriers to Cultural Proficiency. Along your equity-focused journey, we asked you to acknowledge these barriers by naming examples that deny or minimize access and educational outcomes for students in your school or district. You may recall that barriers, as discussed in Chapter 5, too often function as de facto core values expressed as deficit views of students due to their race, ethnicity, socioeconomic status, language, religious affiliation, gender, or sexual orientation; the neighborhoods where they live; or some intersection of these demographic characteristics.

Deficit views range from low expectations of students' academic capabilities to maintenance of curricular and instructional programs in which images of people who look like the students are invisible. These views portray an unwillingness or inability to interact effectively with the communities in which the students live. Deficit-focused values are expressed in comments such as the following:

> *Given that neighborhood, they are fortunate to even be in school.*
>
> *I put it in the air around them; if they don't get it, it's not my problem*
>
> *Their parents don't care, so why should I?*

Now that you have engaged in reflective thinking, journaling, and dialoging with colleagues about the Barriers to Cultural Proficiency and the extent to which they are present in your practices, we invite you to shift your thinking to the Guiding Principles of Cultural Proficiency. Relying on these principles for developing a mindset for transformational change is key to opening doors to equitable opportunities for your students and increasing equity using the Cultural Proficiency Framework. We invite you to ponder on the answers to these questions before we delve into the Guiding Principles.

- Once you identify examples of the Guiding Principles in your district or school, how will you rely on them to advance equity?

- Why is examining practice and policy with the Guiding Principles so important?

- How do you, as the school leader, utilize the Guiding Principles of Cultural Proficiency to embark on an equity-focused journey with the goal of providing open access to all students? What are the core values of your district?

- What do your vision, mission, and values express about your belief in educating all students?

- Do your policies, practices, and procedures align with your expressed core values?

- In what ways can you acknowledge and celebrate your transformational policies, practices, and behaviors that promote equitable outcomes in the school district? What will be your role as the school leader?

- How will you build capacity for others in using the Guiding Principles to inform the evolution of inclusive, equity-focused core values to guide your district or school's practices and policies?

Take a moment, and record your thinking.

_____

_____

_____

_____

_____

ON-RAMP TO RELYING ON THE GUIDING PRINCIPLES OF CULTURAL PROFICIENCY

This chapter provides context for school leaders to rely on the Guiding Principles of Cultural Proficiency in developing mission and vision statements and inclusive core values within a framework for school improvement. The case narrative of Eaveston School District provides the expressions of core values and shifts in mindsets that inform the thinking and behaviors of Eaveston leaders' professional practice. The Guiding Principles of Cultural Proficiency are intended to inform the advancement of inclusive core values that, in turn, guide the development and implementation of healthy policies, practices, and behaviors in our personal and professional work. School leaders who facilitate conversations about core values using the Guiding Principles as a framework develop expressly inclusive mission, vision, and core value statements. Educators in the organization can identify those policies, practices, and behaviors that meet the academic and social needs of students from the asset-based core values.

THE GUIDING PRINCIPLES OF CULTURAL PROFICIENCY

One of the roles of a school leader is to uphold the expressed core values of the district by building a culture that serves all students (Fisher, Frey, & Pumpian, 2012). With this role comes difficult tasks such as incorporating the expressed values into the systems and structures of the school and holding people accountable for policies, practices, and procedures that are consistent with the vision, mission, and values of the organization (R. B. Lindsey et al., 2019). We ask you, "Do you do what you say you do?"

The Guiding Principles of Cultural Proficiency exist within the Cultural Proficiency Framework for examining the core values of your school or district. School leaders who learn to use the nine Guiding Principles of Cultural Proficiency experience success in transformational change by countering the pernicious effects of the Barriers to Cultural Proficiency. Reflection and dialogue focused on continuously acknowledging the Guiding Principles as core values inform changes in policies, practices, and behaviors from being tolerant of diversity to being transformative for the development of inclusive educator core values and behaviors as well as inclusive school and district policies and practices.

Figure 6.1 displays the Guiding Principles of Cultural Proficiency. Table 6.1 is organized to focus our attention, as leaders, on the roles race and social class play as informants of healthy, productive, and equitable policies, practices, and behaviors. Take a few moments to think about each Guiding Principle.

While reading each principle, take note of your personal reactions to each. Your levels of comfort and discomfort may be an indication of your receptivity to this work. Be authentic in your thoughts and feelings. Cultural Proficiency is a journey of self-discovery. Enjoy the ride—bumps in the road, hairpin turns, sluggish rush-hour traffic, all are natural and normal in the human condition. Self-awareness precedes actions in service of our diverse student population. If you see your student body as homogeneous, know that you are missing the diversity that is certainly present, and learning about that diversity should be a goal.

In the next section we take you on Eaveston's journey of Cultural Proficiency in applying the Guiding Principles of Cultural Proficiency. The road map for their journey includes the processes and learning strategies their leaders used throughout a two-year period to turn inward, examine their own core values, and rely on the Guiding Principles of Cultural Proficiency to increase equity and access through planned change. Due to the interrelated nature of the Tools of Cultural Proficiency, the road map for you, just as for Eaveston, will not necessarily follow the linear path as

FIGURE 6.1 ● The Conceptual Framework for Culturally Proficient Practices

The Essential Elements of Cultural Proficient Practices

Serve as standards for personal, professional values and behavior, as well as organizational policies and practices

- **Assessing cultural knowledge**
- **Valuing diversity**
- **Managing the dynamics of difference**
- **Adapting to diversity**
- **Institutionalizing cultural knowledge**

The Cultural Proficiency Continuum portrays people and organizations who possess the knowledge, skills, and moral bearing to distinguish among equitable and inequitable practices as represented by different worldviews:

Informs

Unhealthy, unproductive, inequitable policies, practices, and behaviors	Differing Worldviews	**Healthy, productive, equitable policies, practices, and behaviors**
• Cultural destructiveness • Cultural incapacity • Cultural blindness		• Cultural precompetence • Cultural competence • Cultural proficiency

Resolving the tension to do what is socially just within our diverse society leads people and organizations to view selves in terms productive and equitable.

Informs

Informs

Overcoming Barriers to Cultural Proficiency

Serve as personal, professional, and institutional impediments to moral and just service to a diverse society by:

- Being resistant to change,
- Being unaware of the need to adapt,
- Not acknowledging systemic oppression, and
- Benefiting from a sense of privilege and entitlement.

Ethical Tension

Guiding Principles of Cultural Proficiency

Provide a moral framework for conducting one's self and organization in an ethical fashion by believing the following:

- Culture is a predominant force in society.
- People are served in varying degrees by the dominant culture.
- People have individual and group identities.
- Diversity within cultures is vast and significant.
- Each cultural group has unique cultural needs.
- The best of both worlds enhances the capacity of all.
- The family, as defined by each culture, is the primary system of support in the education of children.
- School systems must recognize that marginalized populations have to be at least bicultural and that this status creates a distinct set of issues to which the system must be equipped to respond.
- Inherent in cross-cultural interactions are dynamics that must be acknowledged, adjusted to, and accepted.

Source: Adapted from R. B. Lindsey, Nuri-Robins, and Terrell (2009, p. 60).

TABLE 6.1 ● Guiding Principles of Cultural Proficiency

Culture is a predominant force in society.
Acknowledge culture as a predominant force in shaping behaviors, values, and institutions. Although you may be inclined to take offense at behaviors that differ from yours, remind yourself that they are not personal, they are cultural. Acknowledging that schools have many cultures represented is an important preliminary step to improvement.
People are served to varying degrees by the dominant culture.
What works well in organizations and in the community for you and others who are like you may work against members of other cultural groups. Failure to acknowledge this puts the burden for change on the nondominant groups. The curriculum in a school represents the dominant culture in the school; how students attain grade-level standards needs to be examined.
People have individual and group identities.
Although it is important to treat all people as individuals, it is also important to acknowledge their group identity. Actions must be taken with the awareness that the dignity of a person is not guaranteed unless the dignity of his or her culture is also acknowledged. What works well in one school may not work in another because of the mix of group identities.
Diversity within cultures is vast and significant.
Since diversity within cultures is as important as diversity among cultures, it is important to avoid thinking about cultural groups as monoliths. Often, because of the class differences in the United States, people have more in common across cultural lines than within them. Schools need to find data and establish relationships to learn about the differences within the differences in their schools.
Each cultural group has unique cultural needs.
Each cultural group has unique needs that cannot be met within the boundaries of the dominant culture. Expressions of one group's cultural identity do not imply disrespect for yours. Make room in your organization for several paths that lead to the same goal. Sharing what we learn about the needs of those in our school has to become a regular part of the school day.
The best of both worlds enhances the capacity of all.
Shifting the beliefs of adults working in the school to see diversity as an asset instead of a problem requires attention to school cultures and the building of relationships. Parents have to be fluent in the communication patterns of the school, as well as the communication patterns that exist within their community. They also have to know the cultural norms and expectations of the school, which may conflict with or be different from those in their community, their country of origin, or their cultural group. An understanding of the adults working in the school of what the parents have to add to the working culture of the school leads to enhancing the capacity of all.
The family, as defined by each culture, is the primary system of support in the education of children.
School leaders understand that the traditional nuclear family, comprising two parents and their children, and the way they understand and interact with the culture of the school is different from the way many nontraditional families understand and interact with the culture of the school. Schools must adapt to, support, and connect with families as defined by their culture. This includes being aware of how "father-daughter" events or asking students to interview their grandparents might be perceived.
School systems must recognize that marginalized populations have to be at least bicultural and that this status creates a distinct set of issues to which the system must be equipped to respond.
Culturally proficient educators are self-consciously aware of their own cultures and the culture of their schools. This is crucial knowledge because in addition to the cognitive curriculum, the cultural norms and expectations of the school must be taught as well. First, culturally proficient educators must assess and raise consciousness about their own individual and organizational cultures. Then, as they teach the cultural expectations of the school and classroom to all students and their families, educators must learn about the cultures of their students.
Inherent in cross-cultural interactions are dynamics that must be acknowledged, adjusted to, and accepted.
People who belong to groups that have a history of systemic oppression have heightened sensitivities regarding the societal privileges they do not receive and to the many unacknowledged slights and putdowns that they receive daily. These microaggressions are usually unnoticed by dominant group members and, when brought to their attention, are often dismissed as inconsequential. Time spent examining each individual's culture and how to understand other perspectives becomes a focus for professional development.

Source: Adapted from R. B. Lindsey et al. (2019).

laid out in this chapter. As you read Eaveston's story, keep note of the processes and learning strategies that resonate with you and those you could envision leading while you guide your school organization on its journey of Cultural Proficiency.

TURNING INWARD AND RELYING ON THE GUIDING PRINCIPLES OF CULTURAL PROFICIENCY

This section includes details related to the inquiry process Eaveston School District leaders used to turn inward and examine their own core values, as well as rely on the inclusive core values represented in the Guiding Principles of Cultural Proficiency. The goal from the initiation of this inquiry and application of the Cultural Proficiency Framework was to embed a value for the community being served as possessing cultural assets on which the children's education could be developed. Eaveston's leaders initiated and guided learning about the Guiding Principles of Cultural Proficiency in the inquiry process with three imperative questions. Table 6.2 displays the guiding questions.

Eaveston leaders selected learning strategies to help gain responses to the imperative questions. The learning strategies were arranged in two parts:

1. Turning inward to examine core values

2. Relying on the Guiding Principles

TABLE 6.2 ● Guiding Questions for Applying the Guiding Principles of Cultural Proficiency

What are our individual and organizational values? How do they influence our daily actions?
What are the Guiding Principles of Cultural Proficiency?
In what ways might the Guiding Principles help transform practices, policies, and behaviors that contribute to students not experiencing success related to the leverage areas?

CONTINUED VOICES FROM EAVESTON'S TRAINING SESSIONS

This section includes an example of a learning strategy implemented during a training session in Eaveston School District. The researcher-participant provides voices from the training session to help you conceptualize leading this work of applying the Guiding Principles of Cultural Proficiency.

Cultural Proficiency is a worldview, a mindset. One's worldview is an expression of core values, and when we examine our own values by looking inward, we gain an understanding of how those core values show up in our daily actions as educators. As you think about leading this work of Cultural Proficiency in Eaveston, I want you to think about this quote: "In order to be a great leader, you must clarify your values. In order to clarify your values, you must look inward" (Singh, 2018).

I have given you 52 value cards in an envelope. These cards have core values written on them. I would like you to begin by sorting them into three piles. First, a pile that is "most important to you." These are going to be the values that you absolutely cannot live without. The second pile should include those values that are important to you. Again, you could probably live without them, but you still think they are important to you. The third pile should include those core values that are not important to you at all.

The participants take approximately five minutes to sort through the cards.

Okay, now that you have them in three piles, I would like you to take your pile that is "not important to you" and those that are "somewhat important to you" and place them back in the envelope. Now you should only have those values that are most important to you. Take that pile, and I want you to sort them again into three piles: those that are "most important to you," "somewhat important to you," and "not important to you." I know this might seem difficult, but I want you to try to organize the core values you have left into those piles.

The participants take another five minutes to sort the remaining cards.

Now that you've sorted again, take your "most important to you" pile, and select five core values from the list. I want you to commit these to writing.

TURNING INWARD TO YOUR CORE VALUES

Eaveston School District's Cultural Proficiency Committee took to heart the focus on core values for both individuals and the organization, acknowledging Cultural Proficiency to be a worldview, a mindset. One's worldview is an expression of core values, and when you are brought together as a group of educators, your shared values represent your organizational culture (R. B. Lindsey et al., 2019). Eaveston's leaders engaged in two learning strategies to examine their core values as applied to the Guiding Principles of Cultural Proficiency. As described above, the first learning strategy Eaveston's Cultural Proficiency Committee engaged in was *Clarifying Our Values* (see Resource C at the end of this book). Committee members identified their top five values through the sort process, provided examples of how the values were reflected in their work life, and used reflection and dialogue to examine the influence these core values have on their educational beliefs and practices.

The importance of knowing your core values is recognizing that these core values form your mindset, which leads to your behaviors—what you say and do. Core values also help you to assess your behaviors and compare them with others' behaviors. These core values inform the biases you have regarding those who are different from you. Eaveston's leaders acknowledged that to adopt the mindset of Cultural Proficiency using the Guiding Principles, they first had to increase their awareness of their mindset toward difference. Therefore, it was essential to begin by looking inward.

REFLECTION • Dialogue • Action

Take some time to reflect on your core values. We encourage you to engage in the learning strategy *Clarifying Our Values* (see Resource C at the end of this book). Once you have identified your top five core values, commit them to writing. In what ways do these core values influence your beliefs, educational practices, and behaviors as an educator? Record your thoughts.

_____

_____

_____

_____

_____

_____

_____

_____

Another learning strategy the Cultural Proficiency Committee engaged in was *Examining Your Organizational Values* (R. B. Lindsey et al., 2019, p. 271). While this activity is intended to help identify barriers in organizations that are evidenced through the covert values of the school or district, this activity helped Eaveston's committee members focus on the interconnectedness of the Barriers to Cultural Proficiency and the Guiding Principles of Cultural Proficiency. Collectively, the Guiding Principles of Cultural Proficiency are a moral response to overcoming the Barriers to Cultural Proficiency.

Eaveston's Cultural Proficiency Committee members first identified the overt core values, those that are written and explicitly communicated on the district's website, comprehensive school improvement plan, and other documents. By examining such documents, including the defined vision, mission, and core values statements, the members identified the district's overt core values. Table 6.3 displays the district's overt core values.

Committee members reflected and engaged in dialogic conversations with colleagues regarding the ways in which these overt values are demonstrated in the district. Members provided examples of programming, supports available for students, the focus on personalized learning in the district, the "family" feeling of Eaveston School District, the commitment to the newly formed Cultural Proficiency Committee, and the continuous focus on student and employee success and wellness.

As the committee members shifted to covert values, they were asked to come up with words not included or claimed as core values that they believed guided many of the practices of Eaveston School District. Specifically, the facilitator asked the committee's members to critically review and reflect on their responses regarding unarticulated information, hidden curriculum implications, and the consequences for Eaveston's students and their families. Table 6.4 displays a snapshot of the covert values and beliefs on which the committee focused.

Following the discussion of examples of these covert values, the team took the time to assess the extent to which the district's expressed core values relate to the Guiding Principles. For example, the team discussed *hope* as a value that relates to the work of Cultural Proficiency. While it is not a covert value in the sense that it is hidden and informed by one of the Barriers

TABLE 6.3 ● Eaveston School District's Overt Core Values

Diversity	Knowledge	Commitment
Care	Safety	Learning
Interdependence	Contribution	Strength
Freedom	Success	

TABLE 6.4 ● Eaveston School District's Covert Values

HIDDEN VALUE	UNARTICULATED INFORMATION	CONSEQUENCES	IMPLICATIONS FOR CHANGE
Organizational value	Is there an unarticulated contradiction or addendum to this value?	What behaviors or practices do you see as a result of this value?	Given the value, what are the implications for culturally proficient behavior or practices?
Hope	We have hope unless you are not meeting our expectations.	Everyone does not receive fair and equitable treatment or resources.	We need to examine the Barriers to Cultural Proficiency we are creating for our students.
Curiosity	We encourage innovation and curiosity unless you try to change our practices or programs.	While we push toward personalized learning in the district, there are students who are not thriving.	We must model risk taking to become innovative in our thinking, problem solving, and development of practices and programs that will produce equitable outcomes.
Achievement	We are focused on student achievement unless it will require changing the way we have always taught.	Educational gaps, including achievement and discipline, persist in our district.	We must not only disaggregate data but also hold meaningful conversations around the data and implement interventions with fidelity for students who are not thriving.
Communication	We believe in effective communication but know that denied access and cumbersome processes for securing translators, or written and verbal communications in families' native languages exist.	Everyone does not receive equitable communication that can be understood. Students' ability to thrive decreases.	We need to examine the degree to which our students and families have access to district-, building-, and classroom-level communications.

to Cultural Proficiency, it is essential to Eaveston School District's students who are not thriving. As you think about applying this learning strategy with your teams, consider the powerful, transformative conversations that can occur when you examine the relationship between those understated values and the implications for creating change.

In an additional phase of this same learning strategy, members of the Cultural Proficiency Committee addressed the hidden curriculum and related core values that cause a negative impact, unlike hope. These conversations are more difficult but result in changing mindsets as you think about creating change for your school district. An example of one of the covert values from Eaveston is communication. Communication is an important core value, but there is unarticulated information about the ways in which certain families or groups of families receive communication or its lack thereof because of conflict or difference. This positive core value can produce some unintended consequences and further perpetuate inequities for certain students. It is important to use the Guiding Principles to reflect on and dialogue about the implications of policies and practices associated with the district's core value of communication. This is how the process of relying on the Guiding Principles is essential in creating change that will open doors for students.

Reflection • DIALOGUE • Action

Gather a group of your colleagues together, and engage in a conversation related to your district or school's overt and covert values.

Take some time to reflect on your organizational core values. What are examples of your overt values found in your vision, mission, and core values statements? These would be found on your website, in district documents, in your halls, and on your walls. What are your organizational values that are hidden? Are there unarticulated contradictions to these values? What consequences do your behaviors or practices have because of this covert value? Given the value we have for diversity and for all to succeed, what behaviors or practices might you change? Record your thoughts.

_____

_____

_____

_____

_____

_____

_____

_____

_____

RELYING ON THE GUIDING PRINCIPLES

This section provides details related to Eaveston School District's inquiry process using the essence of the Guiding Principles of Cultural Proficiency to make changes to policies, practices, and behaviors adapted to the diverse student and community population. The World Café (www.theworldcafe.com) is a learning strategy the Cultural Proficiency Committee used early in their training to unpack the language and make sense of the Guiding Principles of Cultural Proficiency. The committee members were organized into nine equal-sized groups and placed at a table with one of the Guiding Principles. The facilitator displayed a question and provided silent writing time for individuals to draw or write on the chart paper in relation to the Guiding Principle during each discussion round. Through a reading, reflection, and dialogue process, each group further contributed to each "Guiding Principle Poster" and enhanced their individual and group learning around the Guiding Principles of Cultural Proficiency. School leaders in Eaveston acknowledged the importance of reinforcing the principles and understanding how the identification and adoption of these beliefs could be translated into transforming current educational practices. Table 6.5 includes the questions for each round.

Opportunity for reflection and dialogue using this learning strategy was a beneficial outcome of taking the time to process each Guiding Principle and apply the principle to practice. Another learning strategy, *Guiding Principles discussion starters* (R. B. Lindsey et al., 2019, p. 263), was also used to continue learning and application of this tool. It is one thing to have knowledge, and it is another to apply it to practice. It is essential, as you embark on this journey with your team, to facilitate initial processing and understanding of the Guiding Principles of Cultural Proficiency. Ask questions such as the following:

> What will our district or school look like if we acknowledge culture?

> What doors might we be closing if we do not acknowledge the Guiding Principles in the formation of equity plans?

When school leaders and others in their schools make intentional shifts in thinking by acknowledging the Guiding Principles of Cultural Proficiency, it informs their professional practice in a way that increases access and opportunity for their students to succeed.

TABLE 6.5 ● The World Café Reflection Questions for Relying on the Guiding Principles

Round 1: What does this Guiding Principle mean to you as an educator?

Round 2: What is resonating with you about this Guiding Principle?

Round 3: What thoughts does this Guiding Principle evoke for you?

Round 4: What would be strategies/practices for responding to this principle?

Round 5: How does this Guiding Principle relate to your role as an educator?

Round 6: In what ways are you relating this Guiding Principle to your organization?

Round 7: What are your feelings related to this Guiding Principle?

Round 8: What are examples that illustrate your understanding of this principle?

Round 9: What issues might arise if this principle is not acknowledged?

REFLECTION • Dialogue • Action

Take some time to reflect on your understanding and acknowledgment of the fundamental nature of the Guiding Principles of Cultural Proficiency.

1. *Culture is a predominant force in society.* What does this Guiding Principle mean to you as an educator?

2. *People are served to varying degrees by the dominant culture.* What is resonating with you about this Guiding Principle?

3. *People have individual and group identities.* What thoughts does this Guiding Principle evoke for you?

4. *Diversity within cultures is vast and significant.* What would be strategies/practices for responding to this principle?

5. *Each cultural group has unique cultural needs.* How does this Guiding Principle relate to your role as an educator?

6. *The best of both worlds enhances the capacity of all.* In what ways are you relating this Guiding Principle to your organization?

7. *The family, as defined by each culture, is the primary system of support in the education of children.* What are your feelings related to this Guiding Principle?

8. *School systems must recognize that marginalized populations have to be at least bicultural and that this status creates a distinct set of issues to which the system must be equipped to respond.* What are examples that illustrate your understanding of this principle?

9. *Inherent in cross-cultural interactions are dynamics that must be acknowledged, adjusted to, and accepted.* What issues might arise if this principle is not acknowledged?

_____

_____

_____

_____

_____

_____

EAVESTON'S RELIANCE ON THE GUIDING PRINCIPLES

Now that you have read about Eaveston School District's process for implementing the Cultural Proficiency Framework, specifically relying on the Guiding Principles of Cultural Proficiency, we provide you with evidence from the research study that investigated Eaveston's application of the Guiding Principles. The emergent findings are reviewed in the following section and organized by the Guiding Principles. These findings identify and explain Eaveston School District's outcomes related to behaviors and practices informed by asset-based core values.

CULTURE IS A PREDOMINANT FORCE IN SOCIETY

Cultures of individual students, families, teachers, staff, and administrators are always present in Eaveston School District and function as a predominant force in society. This holds true for the culture of the district and the cultures present in individual schools. The cultures of individual educators and the organization's culture, as a whole, provide context for conversations that allow Eaveston's educators to apply the Guiding Principles to the change process.

As the Cultural Proficiency Committee led the work in the school district and in their respective school sites, they came to realize that certain cultures are more prevalent at school sites. For example, depending on the geographical location of the school, students come from both low income housing and half-million-dollar homes. Eaveston's educators rely on this core value knowing that culture is a predominant force in society, and it matters as they serve students from various racial and social class backgrounds. A principal reflected on the prevalence of her students' cultural identities, which feed her middle school from two elementary school sites:

> Our middle school, in terms of the district, is on the more diverse side. We bring in all students who live in one area that tends to be a lower social-economic area in relation to the other municipalities Eaveston School District serves. We have four municipalities that feed into our school. Because our students are diverse, we have to think about culture in everything we do.

Table 6.6 provides context to the referenced two elementary schools in Eaveston School District that feed into the middle school.

Just as members of the Cultural Proficiency Committee were aware that culture exists within individuals, the district, and individual school sites, they recognized that culture will bring in a dynamic of difference. This is what makes the work difficult but an ongoing process or journey. Eaveston School District leaders are committed to continuous conversations and training, both informally and formally, to promote growth and development related to cultural knowledge. Some schools in Eaveston refocused their professional learning communities to routinely acknowledge the degree to which the culture identities, especially race and social class, of students, families, and the educators themselves, as well as the collective culture of the school, are playing a role in decisions and outcomes related to academic programming. A district-level administrator reflected,

> We've been working on PBIS [Positive Behavioral Interventions and Supports] now for a number of years, to try to support positive interventions that spell out the expectations of our building so that we're making fewer assumptions

TABLE 6.6 ● Differences in the Student Demographics of Two Eaveston Elementary Schools

SCHOOL	FREE/ REDUCED-PRICE LUNCH	NUMBER OF STUDENTS	WHITE	BLACK	HISPANIC	OTHER
Elementary A	58%	746	30%	46%	13%	11%
Elementary B	25%	361	64%	16%	9%	11%

about what students are coming into the building with. We make our building clear places where people with different backgrounds and different values can understand how we hope to grow and learn together.

We review data, and we take a look at where our students currently are and, through our professional development, try to do some reading and learning to help us understand better the needs of those students, and that we're reaching out.

Another thing that I think is part of our culture is that I see teachers who go above and beyond to really connect with students and families. We try to get to know our students and get to know our families, and make those connections because so much of it is about personally connecting and understanding the needs of our students of color and students living in poverty.

We're also delving into personalized learning to try and find more ways to make not only that outreach more personal but also the experiences students have in the classroom and the language they learn, so that students can make more meaning of that learning.

Additionally, Eaveston School District leaders focused on building the critical mass of those who are committed to equity work, but they recognized that due to cultural values and behaviors, some were uncomfortable, some were critical, and some avoided the conversation all together. As Eaveston relied on the Guiding Principle "Culture is a predominant force in society," they acknowledged that the cultures of the individuals working on the Cultural Proficiency Committee, as well as those of other administration and staff members, exist and shape all behaviors in the institution. Culture is the way things are, and whether we are aware of its presence or not, culture is ever present.

PEOPLE ARE SERVED TO VARYING DEGREES BY THE DOMINANT CULTURE

Providing appropriate time to reflect and discuss the ways in which students of color and students of lower social class are served in the district was a key component of Eaveston School District's Cultural Proficiency Committee meetings. Committee members knew that what works well for Eaveston students in one school may work against students at another school. For example, the district offers many extracurricular activities that come with a cost. School sites with more students from lower social class families try to ensure that those costs are subsidized when possible so that those students have the same access as students who attend school sites with lower free/reduced-price school lunch rates.

Subsequently, what works well for some students in a school site may work against members of other cultural groups in the same school site. Using the Guiding Principles of Cultural Proficiency helped school leaders acknowledge those policies, practices, and behaviors that are serving students well but also recognize that failure to make such an acknowledgment puts the burden for change on one group, especially on students of color and of lower social class. In Eaveston's schools, staff members have focused on intentionally listening and learning from others from a different culture, whether that be based on racial or socioeconomic differences. They know this practice affects how they interact with students and staff on a daily basis. Listening is key in making sure no one feels left out and acknowledging other cultures. It is most important that staff recognize when students and staff are being affected in a negative way. The Cultural Proficiency Committee relied on reflective questions for members at each school site to identify the ways in which students are served in varying degrees by the dominant culture in their school sites. A teacher discussed the focus of relying on this Guiding Principle:

> Representing, honoring, and celebrating all cultures in our school is important for portraying positives in our school. The culture of the school should be about the students, but we have to be careful so that the culture is not damaging to our students.

A building-level leader reflected on the degree to which the district serves its students:

> I think our district is very supportive of cultural diversity, and they are very aware.

> Our district is looking at things through the diversity lens to see where our strengths are, where our weaknesses are, and how we can improve upon those weaknesses so that students can achieve. . . . They want people to feel included. They want people to feel like this is a safe place, like this is a community. We pride ourselves on being a community, and if we're not culturally proficient, then we're leaving students out.

The following questions were used as a guide to help Eaveston's district and school site administrators and staff think about how the culture of the school serves their students:

- What makes up the dominant culture in our school?

- What practices and behaviors are part of the dominant culture?

- Is it the culture of the teachers or the students we are putting forth?

- To what degree are our policies and practices serving the nondominant culture?

PEOPLE HAVE INDIVIDUAL AND GROUP IDENTITIES

Eaveston School District acknowledges that its students have individual identities and group identities. Because this Guiding Principle informs equitable practices, Eaveston's leaders and teachers are implementing personalized learning plans to help each child thrive and succeed in the learning environment, with a critical focus on individual identity. Through personalized learning initiatives in the district, teachers discover ways in which every child is unique, having their own strengths, ways of exploring the world, and ways of learning. Not every child learns at the same rate and in the same way. To help each child realize their full potential, staff members are committed to personalizing the learning to their needs and empowering each child to take charge of the journey. In Eaveston, personalization to accommodate the individual identities and group identities of the students refers to instruction paced to the learner's needs, tailored to learning preferences, and adapted to the specific interests of different learners. The learning objectives and content, as well as the method and pace, may vary from classroom to classroom because learners have voice and choice in their learning. Part of the success in increasing culturally proficient educational practices in Eaveston has been centered on this work.

Additionally, Eaveston's Cultural Proficiency Committee members relied on this Guiding Principle of people having individual and group identities by promoting conversations among the staff related to perceived group identities and behaviors of students of color, especially male students of color. The district adults learned about their own identities by engaging in culturally proficient learning strategies such as *Cultural Identities*, *Family Portrait*, *Diversity in Your Life*, and *Diversity Lifeline* (R. B. Lindsey et al., 2019) and focused their discussions on how their identities influence their behaviors as educators. A district administrator reflected on the approach used to acknowledge that male students of color have individual and group identities:

> *I know that we have talked a lot about our discipline data, and the fact that our discipline data is skewed much like many other school districts. It seems to be more heavily impacting students of color, especially boys, and that is something that we have looked at; we discuss, and we try to find ways to change.*

> *We have our policy; what can we do in our practices to make sure that we are being more equitable and really looking at the way we enact what we do? Because what is on paper and how we do it can look very different.*

> *I know trying to get to the root of some of those things like, with students, would some be better served if we could get them more connected or to build relationships, opportunities, and activities where we help kids get more connected, and help them feel more a part, and change our perceptions in the work that we do as staff members? Are there things we can do to influence that so that we're being more equitable? Aside from that, I think we try to have those pieces in place to support equity.*

DIVERSITY WITHIN CULTURES IS VAST AND SIGNIFICANT

Because Eaveston School District is one of the most diverse school districts in the state, leaders rely on the belief that diversity within cultures such as race, social class, and national origin is vast and significant. Leaders acknowledge that when educators make assumptions about students because of their race, social class, or family structure, damage is done, and doors are closed on students. As a district on the journey to Cultural Proficiency, Eaveston leaders are keenly aware of their recognized diversity in terms of race/ethnicity, socioeconomic status, and language. Eaveston focuses on students' individual stories, building relationships, increasing communication, and providing services and support related to that story. A school principal reflected on his belief related to student diversity being vast and significant that led to innovative changes in a competency-based learning model:

> We build a story for every kid, so how we approach this at our school is going back to the individual kid and the families. When you build a story with an understanding of where each kid is from and talk about different things with those families and with the child about his or her academics and where they want to go in life, there's the foundation within that piece. With the model that we are currently doing, we have a three-tiered system for the academics. And we utilize an assessment where kids come in, in grades 1 through 5; they're given assessments in the area of English language arts, or ELA, which is the reading and writing component, as well as with mathematics.

> We have a three-tiered system, and this system was built and designed to combat the mobility factor, where kids are moving from place to place and never have mastery within academic skill zones. Tier 1 is at or above grade-level expectations set by both state and by our school board. Tier 2 is one year below grade-level expectations to grade-level expectation, and Tier 3 is two or more years below grade-level expectations.

> What has happened with this is that kids are in control of their academic success. They can progress through the district's curriculum as fast as they can as long as they're hitting mastery. In doing so, both the state and Eaveston's School Board have asked roughly that a child will have gains academically of 12 months. What we're finding within this pilot is that we're having growth rates of anywhere between 14 to 18 months. A local university did come in and do a study. The results were overwhelmingly successful and positive in regard to our delivery model. It was a statistically significant difference of what we do compared to what another school in this district does in getting the results that we're getting. That's all despite race, mobility, free and reduced, poverty rates, everything on those lines because it's down to the actual individual child level.

Educators adapt their practices and behaviors as they rely on the core value that student diversity is vast and significant in Eaveston. Data revealed that the personalized learning initiative and the competency-based model, as described above, are leading to equitable outcomes. Change begins with this belief that diversity within and between cultures of students and educators is important.

EACH GROUP HAS UNIQUE CULTURAL NEEDS

Eaveston's educators rely on the core belief that each group of students has unique cultural needs that must be respected. While some educational practices are implemented to provide some uniformity among students, Eaveston's leaders provide opportunities for staff to engage in professional development and professional learning communities to learn about the unique cultural needs that individual students have. Conversations or professional learning events related to responding to students in transition (often referred to as "homeless"), in trauma-informed care, who are English language learners, or who have personalized learning that acknowledges different learning styles, cognitive styles, and ways of processing information are examples of how Eaveston worked to acknowledge and respond to students' unique cultural needs in a respectful and effective way. Events and conversations are intentionally used to teach members of the dominant group about differences.

Because the work of Cultural Proficiency in an inside-out process, understanding how culture is responsible for many of the outcomes is important in Eaveston School District. For example, during a school-level Cultural Proficiency meeting, the committee heard a presentation from the school counselor related to "students in transition." Historically, students in transition were considered or called "homeless." Through various conversations, a mindset shift occurred because educators realized the power of those words and the disrespectful, damaging effect they could have on a student who has absolutely no control over his or her living situation, while allowing many of the educators to keep their benefits and privileges as members of the dominant group in society who never have to think about "being in housing transition." By relying on this core belief of Cultural Proficiency and using the inside-out approach, Eaveston's educators were able to actualize mindset shifts and change language and practices to respond to the unique needs of a certain cultural group and, thus, become more respectful.

Additionally, Eaveston's leaders realized that students in the district have unique cultural needs that must be respected. Relying on this Guiding Principle led the district to develop culturally proficient practices and policies around learning to respect various groups. Prior to the global COVID-19 pandemic, a district administrator of curriculum in Eaveston had already been working at the state level on virtual learning for some of their students to address cultural needs. She reflected,

I have actually been working on a lot with the changes in virtual learning in the state. All students will now have the ability to have access to virtual learning at the cost of the district. I think that policies are written generally open to meet the needs of various groups. We have really worked because we are embracing personalized learning in Eaveston. We are trying to open up through policies in our district, with the support of the school board, allowing students to have multiple paths to achieving their learning, whether that be virtually or hands-on learning experiences outside of the building in the school day. So really, we're trying to find different ways to meet the needs of the students, having more alternative education programs for students who are not being successful in the traditional classroom setting. Those types of things, I think, are done through policy, and then roll into what happens in practice.

Eaveston's educators keep cultural needs as the focus of the conversation as they come together to talk about practice and policy. Disaggregated data by race and social class allow them to identify cultural needs that require change for students of certain cultural groups to succeed.

THE BEST OF BOTH WORLDS ENHANCES THE CAPACITY OF ALL

Eaveston School District leaders are committed to the belief that their district will operate optimally when diversity is viewed as a positive attribute for the district rather than an obstacle. Through Eaveston's core values of diversity and teamwork, Eaveston School District has experienced much success because of their own understanding of how their diversity is an important part of their story. For example, the collaborative nature of including multiple perspectives based on cultural identity differences such as race, social class, gender, and sexual orientation has enhanced the capacity of all students because of the intentional attempt to learn from the diversity that exists within the school system. A member of the district-level Cultural Proficiency Committee described her stance related to having the "best of both worlds" and the work necessary to enhance outcomes for all:

I try to do an even better job in my own work. Trying to observe more. Trying to learn more. Trying to have more conversations with people about even difficult issues. I've had to educate myself about some aspects of gang activity, but you need to be aware of it and how it presents, and what it might mean in one culture versus another.

I just try to keep learning, and try to not just use the buzzwords, but talk with people in a way that we, in a meeting, can start to see into somebody else's experience and perspective a little better. And knowing my go-to people. I have developed relationships with people who are very good at this, and sometimes if I need some perspective or if I'm confused by something or I might be disappointed in a student's work or something, or confused by their struggle, I can say, "Well, what do you think is going on here?" And I get a perspective that I think may be helpful.

So again, I think it comes back to understanding, and not being arrogant and saying, "Oh, I get it. This is what it is." Always learning and always thinking and always reevaluating and reconsidering our assumptions, and then trying to find a new way to work, always. This is a very progressive school in a lot of ways. I think it really does value relationships. The principal of the school always talks about, we build relationships, and I think it's very genuine. It's not just, anything goes, it's certainly not that. But it's trying to understand people better, and trying to know that when kids walk into this building, that we are a community, they are welcome, that much is expected of them, yes, but we're here for them, and that means everybody.

The commitment to everybody in this teacher's comments demonstrates the notion of having the best of both worlds, or various perspectives, enhance the capacity of Eaveston School District to open doors for all students.

Another example of how Eaveston School District leaders rely on the best of both worlds is that they provide avenues for continuous growth through reflection and dialogue where multiple perspectives are included for results that will serve each and every child in the district. Eaveston's CSIP (Comprehensive School Improvement Plan) Steering Committee is a prime example of the commitment to having diverse perspectives guide the planning for the next several years in the district. The committee, made up of family stakeholders (parents), teachers, administrators, Board of Education members, and staff, worked for months to develop a multiyear plan that would direct the overall improvement of the district's programming and services. Honoring the best of both worlds in this educational practice was essential in gaining perspectives on the focus areas of improvement in subgroup achievement scores, discipline rates, and overall whole-child wellness, all of which affect individuals differently across various racial, socioeconomic, and ableness cultural identities. A parent recalled a specific interaction with Eaveston's superintendent during this process:

I was volunteering at the school, and he (the superintendent) was really interesting. Somehow, he saw me from some meetings when I was early on, and he was really good at pointing that out. He was talking to me, and we began to talk about why I came to the district, and I talked about diversity. It seemed like he was really attuned to that being a really good aspect of Eaveston. It made me recognize that they are actually thinking about their diversity, not only as a positive, but as something that is part of Eaveston.

Additionally, Eaveston School District leaders worked extensively around increasing diversity in the workforce. They know it is critical for students of color to have teachers and administrators, not solely support staff, who look like them. Practices have changed over the years for enhancing the capacity of educating all students with equitable outcomes because of their reliance on "the best of both worlds." For example, the Human Resources department tracks and reports the number of teachers disaggregated by race each year. Procedures for recruitment have changed, such as who attends job fairs with administration. Teachers of color are present each time, and a list of questions was developed by the Cultural Proficiency Committee to help hire individuals who already have an awareness of what it takes to successfully educate students with complex, diverse backgrounds and experiences (see Resource 5D).

THE FAMILY, AS DEFINED BY EACH CULTURE, IS THE PRIMARY SYSTEM OF SUPPORT IN THE EDUCATION OF CHILDREN

One key asset of Eaveston School District has been the intentional development of a "community-centric" perspective to educate its students. The term *community-centric* is focused on the involvement of parents at the school in activities that meet the needs of their children, rather than involvement in activities structured by the school (Lawson, 2003). Because the family is the primary system of support in the education of children, Eaveston School District leaders understand the importance of connecting with and engaging families in those activities that will meet the basic needs of their children. For example, a principal discussed the services provided that follow the community-centric mindset:

> We strive to build relationships with the families as well. In doing so, we generate funds in multiple ways that we're able to assist families in times of need or crisis. The district also has a program for that as well. The programs that we have here, it could range from anything from going to a grocery store and buying gift cards, or going to a grocery store and paying for some different food items, medical bills, new glasses, shoes, clothing. We do have a food bank that is here. We partner with a local agency. That organization is so generous to our families that we basically touch anywhere between 60 to 70 kids a week with a take-home food package program.

Additionally, Eaveston School District leaders engage families by intentionally reaching out to increase the diversity, perspective, and participation of various cultures in committees and events. One of the core values related to family engagement is communication. Because of differing family structures, leaders work to keep families informed and connected through multiple modalities of communication, including those that are translated and/ or interpreted to address the diversity among families, in both communication and structure. For example, a teacher discussed her perspective on working with students with varying family structures:

> Understanding that our families vary in their composition, their membership, their unity, or disunity, that our families may be going through all kinds of changes. Those changes might be socioeconomic, they might be marital, they might even be gender identification of parents. At the same time that the families come to us with cultural values and experiences, that

some of which may be obvious and some of them will not be obvious. They may affect everything from the sense of how people communicate properly versus not, or what's an appropriate transition plan versus not, and those kinds of issues.

So to try to understand where a family is coming from, and know that in our society that families of certain groups that are marginalized often pay for that in terms of their socioeconomic security and stability and safe housing, and transportation. Just transportation alone. Make it possible for somebody to participate in the meeting some way. Find a way.

Effective partnerships between Eaveston School District and its families rely on school leaders understanding the Guiding Principle that all families have their own composition and that the school must be community centered. Eaveston's School-Community Relations department helps in organizing this for the district by providing timely two-way communication that supports Eaveston's mission, namely "All students will learn at high levels." Culturally proficient educational practices, such as intentionally choosing language to address and connect with families with diversity in mind or including an extensive "Family Resources" section in every edition of the monthly *Eaveston Highlights* newsletter, are imperative to keep the community-centered perspective and honor the partnerships with families from different socioeconomic, racial, or ethnic cultural groups.

THE SCHOOL SYSTEM MUST RECOGNIZE THAT MARGINALIZED POPULATIONS HAVE TO BE AT LEAST BICULTURAL AND THAT THIS STATUS CREATES A DISTINCT SET OF ISSUES TO WHICH THE SYSTEM MUST BE EQUIPPED TO RESPOND

Eaveston School District leaders rely on this Guiding Principle to respond to the needs of the students they serve. Underserved student populations, such as those related to race and social class, present opportunities for Eaveston's teachers and leaders to use reflection and dialogue to acknowledge the effects of the Intersectionality of cultural identities. The school system works to incorporate the knowledge of various cultural identities into practice and policy making. For example, there are various professional development opportunities for Eaveston's staff throughout the year that focus on diversity, trauma-informed systems of care, and culturally responsive practices. Professional development opportunities such as these have led to the implementation of programs and events that focus on the assets of student diversity and help respond to student needs. An elementary school principal reflected,

We want to bring the diverse cultures into our school. What we don't want to do is have children who do speak a different language as their native language

come to our school and just simply be indoctrinated. That is not our focus. We want them to come to Eaveston, and we want to learn as much about them and their families and their culture as they are learning from us. We want it to work both ways.

We do quite a bit with family inclusion and things like that. We have a Family English Night here. The families of Eaveston students can come to our school two nights a week, and there is a formal English class that they can take for free. They can bring their children with them because we know that is a difficult issue sometimes in the evening.

One of the most profound undertones of this Guiding Principle is that school systems are places where children are taught cultural norms and expectations, which vary from place to place. For example, students and their families learn to develop bicultural skills to navigate systems, as demonstrated in the previous principal's reflection. What is most important to highlight here is the knowledge leaders in Eaveston School District use to ensure that as students and families code-switch appropriately and as cultural expectations in their environments change, they engage in professional learning community work or smaller-group work to reflect on and discuss ways in which they can refrain from penalizing those who do not respond to the expected norms of Eaveston School District. This is where practice and policy come into play around classroom management, discipline, and restorative practices.

INHERENT IN CROSS-CULTURAL INTERACTIONS ARE DYNAMICS THAT MUST BE ACKNOWLEDGED, ADJUSTED TO, AND ACCEPTED

Eaveston's Cultural Proficiency Committee acknowledged early on in their implementation of the Cultural Proficiency Framework the importance of cross-cultural interactions and communication. They identified histories of systemic oppression and heightened sensitivity to unacknowledged slights or put-downs, often in the form of microaggressions, that the members themselves had received or had witnessed students receiving based on race and/or social class. A parent reflected,

There was a time I had to set a meeting with my child's teacher. My child complained that a teacher was "mean," and "that she treated Black kids different than White kids if they didn't turn their work in." As a parent, I talked to my child about how she felt. My child expressed she felt it was "unfair." I knew, as a parent, this could be a possible teachable moment for my child, me, and the teacher. I knew if I didn't say anything, the question I would ask myself was "How many other children would feel this way and their parents wouldn't have interest or awareness of how to inquire about it?" Through our effective communication, I focused on us being honest with ourselves about the type of environment being fostered for our children.

The reflection and dialogue that occur because of this communication in Eaveston are indicative of the awareness of the effects on Underserved populations. Race and social class are a part of the conversation because Eaveston's educators realize the demands the school system is placing on those students and their families. By working to increase their cultural knowledge, Eaveston's educators incorporate this awareness to inform changes in their classroom and school management practices and policies. Culturally proficient educators model self-reflection of the impact their cultural identities, core values, and practices have on their students.

 LOOKING IN THE REARVIEW MIRROR

This chapter provided context for school leaders who are working to rely on the asset-based, inclusive core values represented in the Guiding Principles of Cultural Proficiency. The case narrative of Eaveston School District provided examples of practices they have changed or are beginning to change due to their reliance on the Guiding Principles of Cultural Proficiency. As you prepare yourself to lead this work and apply this tool, focus on how you will help others turn inward and rely on the core values of themselves as individuals, and of the organization.

 ON TO OUR NEXT DESTINATION

In the next chapter we guide you to learn about and gain skills to apply the tool of the Cultural Proficiency Continuum using an inquiry process. Chapter 7 focuses on implementing the most involved data collection process of the journey of Cultural Proficiency through personal and organizational change. It is at this point where transformation of systems is grounded. The Cultural Proficiency Continuum is the tool with which leaders can guide the people in their organizations to distinguish between unhealthy practices and those practices deemed healthy. You will begin to see the reality of practices and policies that are closing doors on students in your system (i.e., district, school, classroom, etc.) as you navigate Eaveston's journey of collecting data along the Continuum, across all systems (i.e., human resources, discipline, curriculum, celebrations, instruction, professional learning, classroom management, etc.). This chapter allows you to make connections and generalizations about your own school system. We will guide you through an RDA process related to the Intersectionality of race and social class, again, in this chapter. Again, we will encourage you to look beyond race and social class into the Intersectionality of the other cultural identities of your students.

REFLECTION, DIALOGUE, AND ACTION PROCESS

REFLECTION • Dialogue • Action

These are essential questions to help you reflect on the application of the Guiding Principles of Cultural Proficiency:

1. What are your core values? How do they affect other people in your personal and professional life? How do your core values align with the core values of your district or school?

2. People have individual and group identities. What is your individual identity? What is your group identity? How do you know?

3. Think about a cultural identity to which you belong. What are the needs of this group? Diversity among cultures is vast and significant, and each cultural group has unique cultural needs. What would you say are some differences in the cultural identities to which you belong? Are there stereotypes that can lead people to act in ways that are culturally destructive, incapacitating, or blind?

Reflection • DIALOGUE • Action

These are essential questions to help you dialogue with others on the application of the Guiding Principles of Cultural Proficiency:

1. What are your school or school district's core values that support equitable learning outcomes for students?

2. What healthy behaviors are occurring in your situation? Which of the Guiding Principles of Cultural Proficiency are leading to healthy behaviors?

3. Look at your students who are "not experiencing success" this year.

   • What characteristics describe their culture?

   • With what groups do these students identify?

   • What characteristics of these students are different from the characteristics of others in the same cultural group?

   • What are the unique needs of these students?

4. In what ways is the family, as defined by these individual students' culture, the primary system of support in their education?

5. Describe how students who are "not experiencing success" have to be bicultural?

6. What must we, as educators, acknowledge about these students? Are there things we could consider adjusting or adapting to? What things can we accept? What things can we not accept?

Reflection • Dialogue • ACTION

These are essential questions to help you lead this work in your district or school through actions of relying on the Guiding Principles of Cultural Proficiency:

1. Identify your organization's overt and covert values. Discuss the ways in which the various cultural groups of students in your organization are affected by these overt and covert values. Cite specific examples of indications of inequities created from the practices and behaviors informed by those overt or covert values.

2. Provide examples from your organization of ways in which each Guiding Principle of Cultural Proficiency is acknowledged in the district and examples of when they are not acknowledged.

3. Engage other teams in your organization (school teams, grade-level teams, departments) to have the same discussions and/or engage in the learning strategies to apply the Guiding Principles to their relative policies, practices, and behaviors.

4. Find evidence in your existing documents of practices that align with the Guiding Principles.

Travel Log

_____
_____
_____
_____
_____
_____
_____
_____
_____
_____
_____
_____
_____
_____
_____
_____

TRAVEL GUIDE
The Continuum

Create Your Map

- Understand Continuum to develop language about difference and investigate the causes in your organization.
- Establish regular opportunities to discuss Continuum findings.
- Identify the Barriers and representation of the Essential Elements in your organization's policies, procedures, and practices.

Resources

- Those who are ready to engage in this work
- Models for this work
- Your work with the Barriers and the Continuum
- Table 7.1 and other resources from Chapter 7

Mileage

- Organizational data from the Continuum exercises
- Student academic success data
- Examine policies, procedures, and practices that contribute to the disparities discovered by using the Continuum.
- Gather data on the effectiveness of your implementation.

Check the Weather

- What is the current state of your district and community regarding cultural proficiency?
- Who's ready to work with the data from the Continuum exercises?
- Where has collaborative work in your district been successful? Why did it work?

Basic Travel Phrases

- Cultural Proficiency Continuum

Harmful	Helpful
- Destructiveness	- Precompetence
- Incapacity	- Competence
- Blindness	- Proficiency

You're the Driver

- Pay attention to your own inside-out journey.
- Celebrate success.
- Demonstrate use of the language and concepts in the Continuum in your daily work.

Telling Our Stories and Changing the Conversations: The Cultural Proficiency Continuum

STORIES FROM EAVESTON

This a research-informed vignette developed from the researcher's lens and case study findings of Eaveston School District. It provides context for implementing the Cultural Proficiency Framework to identify inequities, set goals to address the inequities, and leverage change.

On a cold morning in January, Eaveston's executive director, a principal, and a consultant from a local university entered a large room in Eaveston's Community Center. In just one hour 50 stakeholders would enter the room for a day of equity work using the Cultural Proficiency Framework. Eaveston's executive director had given much thought over the fall semester in preparation for this day. She knew that involving families and the community in this work was essential. Invited stakeholders had been carefully planned to include parents, members of the Board of Education, district and building administrators, and community members, including police officers, teachers, and support staff. Involving the wide array of stakeholders would help the district in the inquiry process of planned action toward change by helping others assess their cultural knowledge, including the culture of the district, and value for diversity by seeing their responses plotted along the Cultural Proficiency Continuum.

Just two years ago the district engaged in social justice work that left many angry, discouraged, "shut-down," and, quite frankly, skeptical of moving forward with any related work because of the painful experiences. Eaveston's executive director, the principal, the consultant, and the superintendent of the district planned each portion of the upcoming day very carefully, taking into consideration the risk of what one wrong move could lead to. This work could be over as quickly as it started. The goal for the new start of this equity work using the Cultural Proficiency Framework was systemic, long-term, continuous school improvement. The day began with reflection on Eaveston's mission: "So that ALL will learn at high levels."

Throughout the day there was a focus on telling stories and seeking to understand others. As soon as the members of this newly revised committee entered the space, they were asked to begin telling their stories. They were grouped in triads throughout the day to build relationships, gain trust, and prepare for the journey. The cornerstone of the day was to begin the journey of building a professional learning community that would lead to changes for students in Eaveston who were not thriving, the most vulnerable populations, the "at-risk" students, those who had been historically underserved, students of color, and those living in poverty. Involving various members from Eaveston's school community was intentional and necessary for building the capacity of others to do the work, by changing the conversation through storytelling and creating pathways for change through goal setting using the Cultural Proficiency Framework.

In the front of the room six posters were arranged from left to right: Cultural Destructiveness, Cultural Incapacity, Cultural Blindness, Cultural Precompetence, Cultural Competence, and Cultural Proficiency. The consultant from the local university, earlier in the day, had introduced the room to the Framework of Cultural Proficiency. The focus now was on using The Cultural Proficiency Continuum to collect data. Each piece of data referenced a policy, practice, or behavior of Eaveston School District and/or its employees. As the day progressed, the consultant led the group through each point on the Continuum, asking for additional pieces of data to tell a complete story. At the end of the day hundreds of color-coded sticky notes were arranged in front of the room. Members of the committee were asked to color code the sticky notes by their application to stakeholder groups of students, families/parents, the community, and staff. The committee left at the end of the day with the following question: What are your hopes and fears for future steps in Eaveston?

CALIBRATION

Only when we are brave enough to explore the darkness will we discover the infinite power of our light.

—Brene Brown (2012)

As we addressed in earlier chapters, Cultural Proficiency is an inside-out approach to effectively interact in cross-cultural settings. The Cultural Proficiency Framework provides educators a set of tools for use in leading their districts and schools to gather an array of data to guide personal and institutional development. A common misconception in this context is the confusion of the word *data*. Often when we hear the word *data*, we are looking for quantitative data related to state test scores, the number of discipline referrals, graduation rates, and so on. Applying the Barriers to Cultural Proficiency and Guiding Principles of Cultural Proficiency to current practice most often yields significant, often surprising, results. The Cultural Proficiency Continuum provides an organizational mechanism for qualitative data to be surfaced in ways that help educators tell their stories, using their authentic voices. Identified, reactive policies, practices, and behaviors are often laden with, heretofore invisible or barely visible, macroaggressions that are bold, blatant, offensive, and just plain wrong.

School leaders use the Cultural Proficiency Continuum to organize data generated from the study of the Barriers and Guiding Principles. The three points on the left side of the Continuum represent the Barriers and serve to highlight areas of growth for the district or school. Likewise, the right side of the Continuum includes three points informed by the Guiding Principles, which allow school leaders in progressive fashion to identify culturally competent policies, practices, and behaviors intended to "open doors for students."

Progression from *culturally precompetent* to *culturally competent* to *culturally proficient* occurs as intentional acts. Microaggressions can and do occur in educator behaviors and school practices at any point along the Continuum. Educators and schools progressing along the Continuum surface microaggressions as they occur, both as a means to protect those targeted by the intentional or unintentional microaggression and as a means of growth for the aggressor. As stated earlier in this book, the effect on targeted people, whether intended or not, is negative.

Culturally competent and proficient policies, practices, and behaviors are points to be celebrated as schools and individuals work toward transformational change. The goal of this work is increasing equity in access and outcomes for all students through transformational changes in educator behaviors, which, in turn, inform school policies and practices. You can use the Continuum as a means of identifying opportunities for growth and change that will make a difference for the most vulnerable, targeted, and historically underserved groups of students in your schools. As you read how Eaveston applied the Cultural Proficiency Continuum, pay close attention to how the data they surfaced was not related to academic test scores but rather the behaviors of the adults in the school system. We ask you to ponder how you might answer these questions for yourself and your school and district:

- *In what ways has this description of the Continuum added to your knowledge of the Tools of Cultural Proficiency?*

- *What policies, practices, and behaviors in your school or district need to be examined and changed to make a difference for all of your students?*

- *How can you, as the school leader, utilize the Cultural Proficiency Continuum to embark on an equity-focused journey with the goal of opening access to all students?*

- *In what ways can the Continuum serve as a useful tool as you explore evidence of inequitable outcomes in the school district?*

Take a moment, and record your thoughts and feelings about this topic.

_____

_____

_____

_____

ON-RAMP TO THE CULTURAL PROFICIENCY CONTINUUM

The intent of this chapter is to provide context for school leaders working with their educator colleagues to record evidence of both the Barriers and the Guiding Principles in their school organization's policies and practices, as well as individuals' behaviors along the Continuum. In a culturally proficient school district, educators are open to change and take advantage of opportunities to identify areas of needed change and growth, as well as celebrate the successes of those policies, practices, and behaviors that "open doors for students and allow students to thrive."

The case narrative of Eaveston School District provides examples from their use of the Cultural Proficiency Continuum. The Continuum served as a tool for Eaveston's Cultural Proficiency Committee members to identify and have language for healthy (positive and productive) and unhealthy (negative and unproductive) policies, practices, and behaviors. School leaders structured professional learning sessions to provide participants opportunities to individually *reflect* on the ways in which this study of the Continuum in the context of their individual practice was being informed.

Similarly, the professional learning sessions provided participants opportunities to *dialogue* with colleagues for the purpose of understanding their and others' often differing perspectives. Dialogic conversations gave rise to facilitated conversations to identify, acknowledge, and begin the process of overcoming systemic barriers that serve to impede equitable access and outcomes for chronically underserved students. Eaveston's Cultural Proficiency leaders used the Guiding Principles of Cultural Proficiency as core values in developing their equity plans for overcoming the barriers in ways that lead to transformational changes that increase equity and access for students who have not been well served. Again, the focus of collecting the data was to see the whole picture of Eaveston School District and provide a path for participants' minds to shift toward change.

In Chapter 7 we provide a road map for you to identify and locate along the Continuum policies, practices, and behaviors in your school system, be it district or school level. It is important to acknowledge these policies, practices, and behaviors at each of the six points of the Continuum. Data arrayed along the left side of the Continuum provide a glimpse of the work that lies before you and your colleagues. Data arrayed along the right side of the Continuum are informed by the Guiding Principles of Cultural Proficiency and are a result of effective educator behaviors and school policies and practices. In other words, data on the left side of the Continuum represent challenges ahead, and data on the right side of the Continuum reveal the extent of a base of effective work on which intentional actions can be constructed. Engaging in this activity of arraying honest, truthful data along the Continuum is intended to inform intentional change processes. The goal is to increase equity in access and outcomes for children and youth served by your school system.

Most likely, you have been anticipating this part of the book due to an interest in change intended to affect the educational access and outcomes of historically underserved students, disproportionately students of color and students living in poverty. Along your journey be sure to focus on all students. In what ways are your policies, practices, and behaviors affecting students with disabilities? Students who are Asian? Students who speak English as a second language? Students who are Muslim? Students who are Latinx? Students who are in housing transition (homeless)? Students who identify as nonbinary? Students who are gay, lesbian, or bisexual? We recommend a deep understanding of the Cultural Proficiency Continuum, informed by the Barriers and the Guiding Principles, to initiate change in your school system, driven by a collective desire to increase equitable educational access and outcomes for all students in your district. We have designed this chapter to guide your journey in developing a plan of action.

THE CULTURAL PROFICIENCY CONTINUUM

The Cultural Proficiency Continuum is a tool to provide language describing schools and districts' inequitable and equitable policies and practices, as well as school employees' unhealthy and healthy, or unproductive and productive values and behaviors. The Continuum serves as a tool to distinguish between healthy and unhealthy practices, as represented by committee members who may have different worldviews (R. B. Lindsey et al., 2019). Figure 7.1 displays the Continuum of Cultural Proficiency as it relates to the other Tools of Cultural Proficiency.

The Cultural Proficiency Continuum is designed to be used by educators to help assess their organization's policies and practices and individuals' behaviors deemed unhealthy and unproductive for students. As you undoubtedly know by now, in this book we focus on students of color and

FIGURE 7.1 ● The Conceptual Framework for Culturally Proficient Practices

---

The Essential Elements of Cultural Proficient Practices

Serve as standards for personal, professional values and behavior, as well as organizational policies and practices

- **Assessing cultural knowledge**
- **Valuing diversity**
- **Managing the dynamics of difference**
- **Adapting to diversity**
- **Institutionalizing cultural knowledge**

The Cultural Proficiency Continuum portrays people and organizations who possess the knowledge, skills, and moral bearing to distinguish among equitable and inequitable practices as represented by different worldviews:

Informs

Unhealthy, unproductive, inequitable policies, practices, and behaviors	Differing Worldviews	Healthy, productive, equitable policies, practices, and behaviors
• Cultural destructiveness • Cultural incapacity • Cultural blindness		• Cultural precompetence • Cultural competence • Cultural proficiency

Resolving the tension to do what is socially just within our diverse society leads people and organizations to view selves in terms productive and equitable.

Informs

Informs

Overcoming Barriers to Cultural Proficiency

Serve as personal, professional, and institutional impediments to moral and just service to a diverse society by:

- Being resistant to change,
- Being unaware of the need to adapt,
- Not acknowledging systemic oppression, and
- Benefiting from a sense of privilege and entitlement.

Ethical Tension

Guiding Principles of Cultural Proficiency

Provide a moral framework for conducting one's self and organization in an ethical fashion by believing the following:

- Culture is a predominant force in society.
- People are served in varying degrees by the dominant culture.
- People have individual and group identities.
- Diversity within cultures is vast and significant.
- Each cultural group has unique cultural needs.
- The best of both worlds enhances the capacity of all.
- The family, as defined by each culture, is the primary system of support in the education of children.
- School systems must recognize that marginalized populations have to be at least bicultural and that this status creates a distinct set of issues to which the system must be equipped to respond.
- Inherent in cross-cultural interactions are dynamics that must be acknowledged, adjusted to, and accepted.

Source: Adapted from R. B. Lindsey, Nuri-Robins, and Terrell (2009, p. 60).

those living in poverty, two groups of students historically underserved in our nation's schools.

It may be important to note at this point in your reading that the Continuum is never intended to be used as a "gotcha" game or evaluative in any way. Rather, an appropriate use of the Continuum is a means for gathering and arraying data in terms of the manner in which students at your school are regarded, from very negative to very positive. The first three points on the Continuum, *Cultural Destructiveness*, *Cultural Incapacity*, and *Cultural Blindness*, represent a deficit worldview, grounded in the Barriers to Cultural Proficiency. This deficit-based mindset toward difference holds little regard for students and their communities. The following three paragraphs include descriptions of the three points on the Continuum rooted in reactive change mandated for tolerance.

Cultural destructiveness—seeking to eliminate certain cultural groups' values and practices that may be different from the dominant, mainstream culture. In relation to this book culturally destructive policies, practices, and behaviors attempt to eliminate vestiges of the cultures of students of color and those living in poverty due to their racialized and social class identities.

Cultural incapacity—seeking to make the culture of others appear to be wrong based on a belief in the superiority of the dominant mainstream culture. Relative to this book culturally incapacitating policies, practices, and behaviors attempt to dismiss and demean the cultures of students of color and those living in poverty—that is, there is something wrong with them and their cultures that needs to be dismissed or corrected.

Cultural blindness—refusing to acknowledge the cultures of others by acting as if you do not see difference or do not recognize there are differences between and among cultures. Culturally blind policies, practices, and behaviors attempt to dismiss students of color and those living in poverty. Cultural blindness includes both an ability and a pretense to not see the differences that their racialized identity and social class bring into the school system.

On the opposite side of the Cultural Proficiency Continuum, equity-focused educators use the three points to assess their organization's policies and practices and individuals' behaviors that are deemed healthy and productive for students—namely, students of color and those living in poverty. These three points on the Continuum, *Cultural Precompetence*, *Cultural Competence*, and *Cultural Proficiency*, are based on an asset worldview because they are developed and implemented from the informant Guiding Principles of Cultural Proficiency. This asset-based mindset toward difference is grounded in proactive change toward transformation. The following three paragraphs include descriptions of the three points on the Continuum rooted in positive change with the goal of transformation.

Cultural Precompetence—being aware of what one does not know about the cultural identities of students from racial and socioeconomic cultures that are different from the dominant culture. Culturally precompetent policies, practices, and behaviors are a result of educators who possess an initial level of awareness of students of color and those living in poverty and who often respond inadequately or inappropriately to the dynamics of difference caused when schools are not prepared or willing to consider what students' racialized and social class identities bring into the school system.

Cultural Competence—viewing one's personal and organizational work as an interactive arrangement in which educators embrace the diverse settings served by the school. These educators intentionally engage with difference by assessing theirs culture and the culture of the organization, valuing diversity, managing the dynamics of difference, adapting to diversity, and institutionalizing cultural knowledge. Culturally competent policies, practices, and behaviors are a result of educators who intentionally engage with students of color and those living in poverty, viewing their racialized identities and social class as an asset to the school system.

Cultural Proficiency—educators and their schools making the commitment to lifelong learning for the purpose of being increasingly effective in serving the educational needs of diverse cultural groups, and holding the vision of what can be and committing to assessment that serves as a benchmark on the road to student success. These educators esteem and learn from others as a lifelong practice—a journey. In relationship to this book culturally proficient policies, practices, and behaviors are a result of knowing how to learn about and from individual and organizational cultures as they relate to students of color and those living in poverty. Culturally proficient educators intentionally and effectively interact in a variety of cultural settings, advocating for students of color and those living in poverty.

Table 7.1 displays the Cultural Proficiency Continuum with a focus on race and social class.

In the next section, we take you on Eaveston's journey of Cultural Proficiency in applying the Cultural Proficiency Continuum tool. The road map for their journey includes the processes and learning strategies their leaders used throughout a two-year period to collect and array their organization's data. Plotting their collective behaviors along the Continuum provided participants an opportunity to view their organizational leadership profile. With their leadership profile revealed to the leadership team, they were then ready to make choices in leadership that exhibited value and demonstrated inclusive and equitable leadership behaviors.

As we indicated in the previous two chapters, the road map for you, just like it was for Eaveston, will not necessarily follow a linear path. You may have a different travel plan for collecting data about your organization's policies, practices, and behaviors. This chapter is organized with field notes, Eaveston's voices, Eaveston's outcomes, and learning strategies. As you read Eaveston's journey, take note of the processes and learning strategies that resonate with you and those you could envision leading while you guide your school organization on its Cultural Proficiency journey by collecting and plotting data along the Cultural Proficiency Continuum.

TABLE 7.1 ● Race and Social Class Cultural Proficiency Continuum

CULTURAL PROFICIENCY					
CULTURAL DESTRUCTIVENESS	**CULTURAL INCAPACITY**	**CULTURAL BLINDNESS**	**CULTURAL PRECOMPETENCE**	**CULTURAL COMPETENCE**	**CULTURAL PROFICIENCY**
Eliminates others based on race and/or social class	Demeans others or attempts to disempower them based on race and/or social class	Dismisses others or does not recognize that there are differences in race and/or social class	Responds inadequately with self-awareness of limitations while interacting with others of different race and/or social class	Engages with others of different race and/or social class by assessing cultural knowledge, valuing diversity, managing the dynamics of difference, adapting to diversity, and institutionalizing cultural knowledge	Esteems, advocates for, and learns from others of different race and/or social class as a lifelong practice

Source: Adapted from Nuri-Robins, Lindsey, Lindsey, and Terrell (2012).

REFLECTION • Dialogue • Action

Take a moment, and think deeply about the six points along the Cultural Proficiency Continuum from Table 7.1. How might you use this Continuum to identify inequitable and equitable policies and practices in your own organization? Take a moment to think about three or four of your own leadership behaviors in the past month, those things you say and do. Where do you believe those behaviors fit on the Continuum? Record your thinking.

_____

_____

_____

_____

_____

EAVESTON'S VOICES

The Cultural Proficiency Continuum provides a powerful tool that can be used to guide transformational change. This section includes the inquiry process Eaveston leaders used to identify policies, practices, and behaviors along the six points of the Continuum, from *Culturally Destructive* to *Culturally Proficient*. The use of this tool emphasized the importance of the journey and the need to embed the work of Cultural Proficiency into all aspects of the district. Reading this section will help you understand exactly what Eaveston School District did to apply the Continuum. The process is described in five phases of using the Continuum of Cultural Proficiency to

- collect data,

- identify emergent themes,

- set goals,

- celebrate culturally competent practices and policies, and

- leverage change.

The committee members guided their learning about use of the Cultural Proficiency Continuum in the inquiry process with one essential question. Table 7.2 displays the guiding question.

TABLE 7.2 ● Guiding Question for Applying the Cultural Proficiency Continuum

GUIDING QUESTION FOR APPLYING THE CULTURAL PROFICIENCY CONTINUUM
What are examples of your own policies, practices, and behaviors that are informed by the Barriers and by the Guiding Principles?

The following sections include the learning strategies used to help obtain the answers to the essential question.

USING THE CONTINUUM TO COLLECT DATA

Applying the Cultural Proficiency Continuum to uncover and examine prevalent policies, practices, and behaviors began for the Eaveston Cultural Proficiency Committee during the first meeting in January. Members of the committee engaged in the learning strategy *Going Deeper With the Continuum* (R. B. Lindsey, 2019, p. 275). Six posters were arranged on a large wall in the meeting space from left to right: *Cultural Destructiveness*, *Cultural Incapacity*, *Cultural Blindness*, *Cultural Precompetence*, *Cultural Competence*, and *Cultural Proficiency*. In this data collection process the participants referenced policies and practices of Eaveston School District and/or individuals' behaviors along each point on the Continuum. Specifically for behaviors, the group generated examples of negative and positive comments about students and actions of educators they have experienced in Eaveston. The committee members color coded the sticky notes by their application to stakeholder groups, including students, families/the community, and staff, to ensure a focus on looking at impact across all stakeholder groups.

The meeting's facilitator addressed each point on the Continuum, one at a time, giving examples of each to increase thinking around correct placement of the policies, practices, and behaviors. Table 7.3 displays the six points of the Continuum and the progression of terms from least tolerant to transformative.

TABLE 7.3 ● Progression on the Cultural Proficiency Continuum

REACTIVE CHANGE MANDATED FOR TOLERANCE		
Destructiveness	**Incapacity**	**Blindness**
Hostility/negativity	Dismissive/blaming	Pretending not to see or unable to see cultural differences
PROACTIVE CHANGE CHOSEN FOR TRANSFORMATION		
Precompetence	**Competence**	**Proficiency**
Beginning to know what we don't know	Doing and speaking up	Advocacy for social justice

The following paragraphs display examples of policies, practices, and behaviors along each point on the Continuum that the Cultural Proficiency Committee members used to generate their own examples.

CULTURAL DESTRUCTIVENESS: SEE THE DIFFERENCE, AND ELIMINATE IT

- Elimination of curriculum topics

- "I don't want those kids in my class/school."

- "There is no such thing as autism."

- Physical or verbal abuse

- "They don't value education." (CampbellJones, CampbellJones, & Lindsey, 2010)

CULTURAL INCAPACITY: SEE THE DIFFERENCE, AND MAKE IT WRONG

- Questioning qualifications

- Mispronouncing unfamiliar names, making fun of names, or laughing at names

- Mocking with an accent or behavior

- Institutionalizing low expectations by tracking students

- "His behavior is too bad for him to learn anything."

- "Their parents don't care; why should I?" (CampbellJones et al., 2010)

CULTURAL BLINDNESS: SEE THE DIFFERENCE, AND PRETEND LIKE YOU DON'T

- Diversity/equity training separate from professional development

- Ignoring access/achievement gaps

- "Really, I don't see color; I treat all kids the same."

- "I teach it in many ways, and they should learn it."

- "Don't be so sensitive. I was just kidding."

- Always using whole-group instruction with no differentiation (CampbellJones et al., 2010)

CULTURAL PRECOMPETENCE: SEE THE DIFFERENCE, AND RESPOND INADEQUATELY OR INAPPROPRIATELY

- Short-term professional development is event based, not data driven.

- Episodic events such as Women's History Month, Black History Month, International Night

- Begin to recognize issues of disproportionality, such as gifted student identification, discipline data, membership of certain clubs

- "We are trying to teach the kids who used to go to school here."

- Reading a book or attending a presentation about an ethnicity different from your own to learn about your students (CampbellJones et al., 2010)

CULTURAL COMPETENCE: SEE THE DIFFERENCE, AND UNDERSTAND THE DIFFERENCE THAT DIFFERENCE MAKES

- Students and visitors can see images like and different from them.

- School is using disaggregated data to drive decision-making.

- Access data are gathered and analyzed for developing strategies for inclusion, including but not limited to gifted children, advanced placements, and sports.

- "I notice voices of our families who practice Islam are not present. We cannot make a decision until we engage them."

- Differentiating instruction or assessment to effectively support all learners (CampbellJones et al., 2010)

CULTURAL PROFICIENCY: SEE THE DIFFERENCE, AND RESPOND POSITIVELY, INCLUSIVELY

- Advocacy for social justice; doing what's right for students

- Lifelong learning about self and others

- Realization that Cultural Proficiency is a "process"

- "I'm starting to seek conversations and learn about how people who self-identify as other than the dominant group may react to me because of my dominant group self-identification."

- Learning how to surface, examine, challenge, and change (if necessary) personal and organizational behaviors, policies, and practices (CampbellJones et al., 2010)

FIGURE 7.2 ● Continuum Data Collection

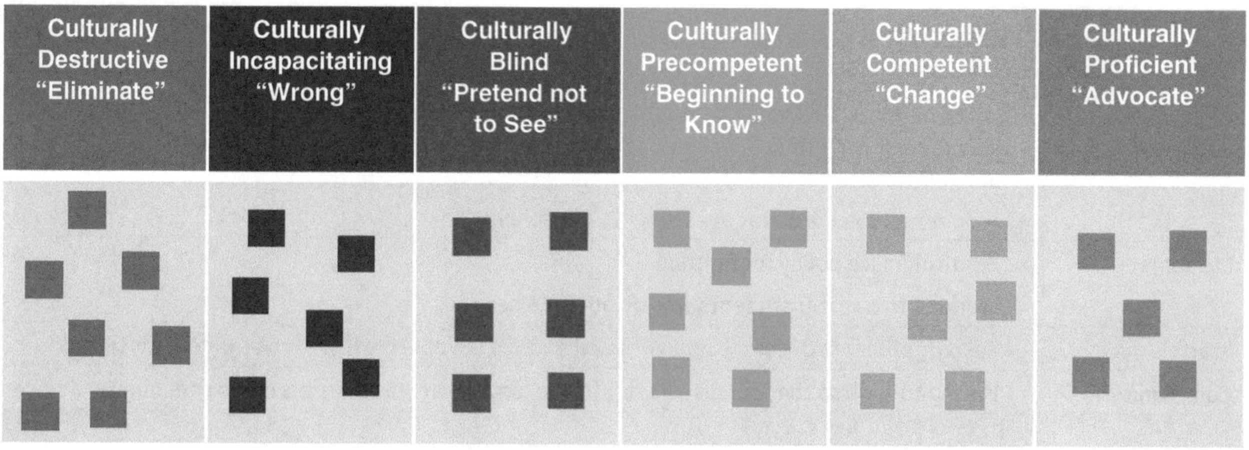

Culturally Destructive "Eliminate"	Culturally Incapacitating "Wrong"	Culturally Blind "Pretend not to See"	Culturally Precompetent "Beginning to Know"	Culturally Competent "Change"	Culturally Proficient "Advocate"

At the end of the learning strategy, hundreds of color-coded sticky notes were arranged at the front of the room along the Continuum. Figure 7.2 provides a picture of what this learning strategy looks like. Committee members debriefed the activity by reflecting on the following questions:

- *What did you notice as you wrote the comments?*

- *What did you notice as you read the other comments?*

- *What did you feel, think, or wonder about the comments or the process?*

- *What does this say about you?*

- *What does this say about Eaveston School District?*

The following section includes a sample of Eaveston's data collected along the Continuum, as shown in Table 7.4. Each part of the table provides data samples referencing each stakeholder group as well as each point on the Continuum.

USING THE CONTINUUM TO IDENTIFY EMERGENT THEMES

In the second phase of applying the Continuum of Cultural Proficiency, the members of the Cultural Proficiency Committee engaged in a *gallery walk* with the data on policies, practices, and behaviors gathered at the first committee meeting three months earlier. The gallery walk guided the participants with questions to encourage thinking around the emergent themes of the data:

- *What do you notice about the policies, practices, and behaviors listed?*

- *What themes emerged from the data or "stand out"?*

- *Which policies, practices, and behaviors are missing?*

TABLE 7.4 ● Data Samples From the Cultural Proficiency Continuum

STAKEHOLDER GROUP	ORGANIZATIONAL POLICIES AND PRACTICES AND INDIVIDUAL BEHAVIORS
CULTURAL DESTRUCTIVENESS	
Parents/family	• IEP practices/meetings—teachers/administrators who speak down to parents; they don't assume positive intentions first • Assumptions made about our students' households
Students	• Zero-tolerance policy for fighting • Working to transfer students who do not fit in here
Staff	• Sending students of color to the office when they are upset; a trip to the office leads to OSS
Community	• Having to work so that our district doesn't become what "that" area is in the community
CULTURAL INCAPACITY	
Parents/family	• "That student is parentally disabled." • "That acorn doesn't fall far from the tree." • Blaming parents for low expectations for schoolwork at home, resulting in failure of students
Students	• Discipline ISS/OSS/detentions data (Black boys with disabilities vs. White girls without disability) • Students' lack of online access—assignments not able to be done
Staff	• Staff attitude: "Cultural Competency/Proficiency is ELL's job; does not apply to other staff" • Lack of diversity in staffing/hiring • Do our staff members "look" like the culture we serve? Not all cultures are represented • Cultural Proficiency conversations—staff members *shut down* and refuse to talk about intolerance! • Staff deny any need for Cultural Proficiency training
Community	• Response to civil unrest based on racial division • Limited staff visibility in the community
CULTURAL BLINDNESS	
Parents/family	• Ignoring how home culture affects student ability to navigate Eaveston's culture
Students	• Discipline referrals—treating all students "the same" • Referring to all students who speak Spanish as hailing from Mexico
Staff	• Does our interview process allow for other cultures to shine? Are we promoting in a way that attracts all cultures? • Limiting times to meet with parents/families to school hours; ignoring working families' needs
Community	• A shift to exclusive electronic communication
CULTURAL PRECOMPETENCE	
Parents/family	• Enrollment procedures for proof of residency
Students	• Students are involved in the community • Does our curriculum (including diverse representation) come across clearly, positively, and accurately to students? • Attempts to disaggregate data regarding discipline (race, gender, social class, ability)
Staff	• We could do a better job of increasing PD for support staff • "Playing polite" when staff offends other staff
Community	• Holding PD in the community

(Continued)

TABLE 7.4 ● (Continued)

CULTURAL COMPETENCE	
Parents/family	• Having an available translator at all events/meetings to increase families' ability to communicate with the school
Students	• Teaching kids to decide what they want to think and believe rather than be told
Staff	• Administration is creating a long-term plan for equity PD, not just haphazard planning and presentations • Special education teachers and staff are viewed as part of the Eaveston teachers and staff, not separate (inclusive culture)
Community	• Partnering with local experts around Cultural Proficiency, equity, restorative practices, trauma-informed care • Inviting all stakeholders to be part of the Cultural Proficiency Committee
CULTURAL PROFICIENCY	
Parents/family	• Eaveston attracts a diverse group of families; families want to bring their children to attend "the most diverse school district in the state"
Students	• Ensuring student voices are heard as a catalyst for staff learning PD and personal growth
Staff	• A small but mighty group learning how to examine practices, policies, and procedures that are harmful to students in Eaveston
Community	• Intentionally find diverse mentor/business partnerships • Buildings such as the swimming pool are open for community groups to use • Using community connections for diversity of speakers/presentations • Taste of Eaveston

Note: IEP, Individualized Education Program; ISS, in-school suspension; OSS, out-of-school suspension; PD, professional development; ELL, English language learner.

REFLECTION • Dialogue • Action

Think about things you have heard or witnessed in your organization. What is an example of something you have heard that is culturally destructive (it attempts to eliminate another person's behaviors or values that are culturally different from those of the group)? What is an example of something you have heard or witnessed that is culturally incapacitating (it intends to make the other person feel their cultural identity is wrong)? What is an example of something you have heard or witnessed that is culturally blind (it attempts to pretend the cultural difference does not matter)? Record your thoughts.

_____

_____

_____

_____

_____

Committee members were encouraged to add additional policies, practices, and behaviors they noticed were missing. Following the gallery walk, the committee formed *listening triads* (R. B. Lindsey et al, 2019, p. 254) and had time to reflect on and discuss what they noticed, what stood out or emerged, and what was missing. The listening triads provided an opportunity for all voices to be heard, and then the committee held a whole-group discussion regarding the discussions in the listening triads to prepare for the next phase of using the Cultural Proficiency Continuum—setting goals.

Additionally, Eaveston's Cultural Proficiency Committee members took the emergent themes from the points on the left side of the Continuum identified in the second phase of the work and used the learning strategy *The World Café* (http://www.theworldcafe.com) to further analyze the data before narrowing the focus down to three emergent themes. Regarding the need to improve, the themes were too powerful to ignore and were believed to help students of color, those living in poverty, and/or some intersection of the two identities to thrive. In the World Café, the committee members focused on targeting policies, practices, and/or behaviors listed as areas of growth that would make the most difference in Eaveston. The committee members worked in seven groups, seated at tables around the room, each focused on a different emergent theme, and were asked these questions:

- *Using examples of policies, practices, and behaviors, what are the needed areas of growth?*

- *If the needed areas of growth become areas of Cultural Proficiency, what will that look like, sound like, be like?*

- *What action steps are necessary for the needed areas of growth to become areas of Cultural Proficiency?*

- *What role(s) will each stakeholder group play in the journey of moving the needed areas of growth into areas of Cultural Proficiency?*

For a designated time, the participants wrote notes on their own framework and also shared ideas in response to the question/prompt provided for the round on chart paper.

Table 7.5 displays the framework used to guide the learning strategy and allow the committee members to think deeply about each policy, practice, and behavior identified. Please note that the strategic transformative levers (STLs) are the focus areas that emerged from the data collection on the Cultural Proficiency Continuum for Eaveston School District. We encourage you to use this framework once you and your team have collected data along the Continuum.

Following this learning strategy, intended to promote additional reflection and dialogue around the policies, practices, and behaviors identified as areas of growth, Eaveston's committee moved into the final work with the Continuum regarding the setting of equity goals for the committee and district.

TABLE 7.5 ● Strategic Transformative Levers Framework

STRATEGIC TRANSFORMATIVE LEVERS (FROM EMERGENT THEMES IN THE DATA)	WHAT ARE THE NEEDED AREAS OF GROWTH IN THE DATA?	IF THE NEEDED AREAS OF GROWTH BECOME AREAS OF CULTURAL PROFICIENCY, WHAT WILL THAT LOOK LIKE, SOUND LIKE, BE LIKE?	WHAT ACTION STEPS WOULD BE NECESSARY FOR THE NEEDED AREAS OF GROWTH TO BECOME AREAS OF CULTURAL PROFICIENCY?	WHAT ROLE(S) WILL EACH STAKEHOLDER PLAY IN THE JOURNEY OF MOVING THE AREAS OF GROWTH TO AREAS OF CULTURAL PROFICIENCY?
Professional learning				
Communication				
Curriculum and resources				
Classroom management discipline				
HR/hiring practices				
Family and community partnerships				
Special education services				
Other				

Note: HR, human resources.

USING THE CONTINUUM TO SET GOALS

In the stages of applying the Cultural Proficiency Continuum to set goals for the district, Eaveston's leaders used the data collected on the Continuum to think about the changes that could be implemented to adapt to diversity and institutionalize cultural knowledge across the district. These actions for transformational change were intended to "open doors for students" in Eaveston, thus allowing students from racialized and social class backgrounds, as well as other intersections of cultural identity, to thrive in the school system.

In choosing the goals each committee member selected the most important policies, practices, and behaviors to target for transformational change. The committee members conducted a final gallery walk in which they placed their dots beside a policy, practice, and/or behavior they believed to be the most important. At the end of the session, the leadership team for the committee moved pieces of data with dots to another wall in the room and grouped them by theme.

Three themes emerged from this learning strategy for Eaveston School District:

1. Professional learning around the Cultural Proficiency Framework

2. Classroom management/discipline

3. Staff diversity

Eaveston's themes are discussed in further detail in the next chapter as school leaders applied the Essential Elements of Cultural Proficiency tool to adapt to diversity and institutionalize change. These three themes became the STLs that the committee members believed could be most impactful for the district. These levers were noted by the Committee as the most urgent issues to examine and change. The three themes are identified by the following goals:

1. *Reduce disparities in discipline:* Support and grow restorative justice practices, evaluate current practices and data to eliminate inequities, and provide strategies for improving classroom management and relationships.

2. *Promote and support further Cultural Proficiency training:* Provide further opportunities for more Cultural Proficiency work for staff, find resources to help staff understand personal bias, and support more Cultural Proficiency training for all staff across the district.

3. *Support and grow staff diversity:* Attend/host recruitment efforts in diverse communities and seek/support diverse candidates.

USING THE CONTINUUM TO LEVERAGE CHANGE

Culturally proficient leaders know how to institutionalize cultural knowledge in the systems in order to leverage change that is transformative to the system. These changes create pathways leading to "opening of doors" for students from racialized and lower social class backgrounds, and the intersection of the two. By applying the Cultural Proficiency Continuum, Eaveston's school leaders built the case for leveraging change by identifying and making public prevalent policies, practices, and behaviors along the six points of the Continuum. One of the first steps in leveraging change is to identify those areas of needed growth and have data to support the identified need. As described earlier in this chapter, Eaveston's Cultural Proficiency Committee engaged in multiple learning strategies to identify their three themes and to set goals intended to attain equitable educational outcomes for all Eaveston students. Table 7.6 displays all the themes that emerged from the data collection along the Continuum, with examples for each theme.

The Cultural Proficiency Continuum allowed Eaveston's Cultural Proficiency Committee members to see where "doors were closed" for students and where they were "open." Those closed doors provided avenues to leverage change. Once the three goals were set, the action planning around these goals began the following school year.

The most important step in this process is to focus on how practice and policy are connected. When examining practices, culturally proficient leaders also examine policy. Table 7.7 displays questions to help guide this process and leverage change for policies and practices on the Cultural Proficiency Continuum.

TABLE 7.6 ● Destructive, Incapacitating, and Blind Data Themes

DESTRUCTIVE, INCAPACITATING, AND BLIND DATA THEMES	
Discipline	"Instead of having an in-school suspension room, what if we had a de-escalation or mindfulness room? Are we utilizing restorative justice practices?" "We must work on the subconscious bias toward Black males; don't create power conflict with Black males."
Hiring practices	"Our hiring practices do not appear to promote all cultures."
Lack of knowledge and skills in working with differences	"Our staff must begin to see color." "Find more ways to engage staff in Cultural Proficiency training."
Supporting families	"Our language must honor parents and not make assumptions that they don't value their children's education." "Find creative ways to involve families who lack the resources to do so; don't blame families for this problem."

TABLE 7.7 ● Questions to Leverage Changes in Policy and Practice

CONTINUUM	POLICIES	PRACTICES
Cultural Destructiveness	Does this policy use language that attempts to eliminate any group of students, staff, families, or community members? Given our value for diversity, what might be some ways we can adapt the language in this policy to be less culturally destructive? What practices are associated with this policy?	Does this practice attempt to eliminate any group of students, staff, families, or community members based on their cultural identity? Given a change in policy, how might we adapt our practices to diversity and institutionalize cultural knowledge so that students, staff, families, and/or community members are not eliminated?
Cultural Incapacity	Does this policy use language that is demeaning to any group of students, staff, families, or community members or attempt to prove their culture is wrong? Given our value for diversity, what might be some ways we can adapt the language in this policy to be less culturally incapacitating? What practices are associated with this policy?	Does this practice demean any group of students, staff, families, or community members or attempt to prove them wrong based on their cultural identity? Given a change in policy, how might we adapt our practices to diversity and institutionalize cultural knowledge so that students, staff, families, and/or community members are not demeaned?
Cultural Blindness	Does this policy use language that pretends not to recognize the differences among any group of students, staff, families, or community members? Given our value for diversity, what might be some ways we can adapt the language in this policy to be less culturally blind? What practices are associated with this policy?	Does this practice pretend not to recognize cultural differences among any group of students, staff, families, or community members? Given a change in policy, how might we adapt our practices to diversity and institutionalize cultural knowledge so that students, staff, families, and/or community members are "not recognized"?

USING THE CONTINUUM TO CELEBRATE AREAS OF CULTURALLY COMPETENT POLICY AND PRACTICE

Just as the Cultural Proficiency Framework serves as a veritable road map of four interrelated sets of tools to guide this most important work, the Continuum provides us with a vehicle to learn about dead ends, wrong turns, and detours. By setting the goal for our journey to visit places along the Continuum that celebrate culturally competent policies and practices, we are on the "highway" that leads to equity, access, and inclusion for all students, especially those who have been historically marginalized because of their race, socioeconomic status, and/or other cultural identity intersections.

Eaveston School District's Cultural Proficiency Committee found it important to use the Cultural Proficiency Continuum to examine their institutional policies, practices, as well as the values behaviors of individuals employed in Eaveston. In doing so, they were able to target areas of needed change and to celebrate areas of strength. In completing this process of identifying areas of concern and then building on the many strengths of the district, many of which were once adapted to better serve the changing population of students in Eaveston School District, policy and practice themes emerged along the Continuum. The culturally competent areas for policy in the district related to student achievement, diversity, high expectations, continuous improvement, and needs-based programming. Similarly, the emergent themes for culturally competent practices related to innovative strategies and programs, professional learning, and communication and collective family and community involvement.

POLICY

R. B. Lindsey et al. (2010) described culturally proficient policy development with two components for school leaders to consider. First, educational leaders should consider supporting values and policies by deeply pondering the Guiding Principles and Essential Elements of Cultural Proficiency. By examining personal and organizational values in this process, stakeholders improved the language in some of their policies to address barriers that may be obstructing the lived mission of the school district. Second, Eaveston's school leaders intentionally engaged in reflection and dialogue around policies to ensure that the language is written to promote action, monitoring, and continuous improvement.

Throughout the Cultural Proficiency journey in the district, educators, family members, and community members regularly come to the table to discuss the status and outcomes of policies and measurable plans of action. The creation of goals and action steps is important for ensuring that all students in Eaveston learn in a safe and productive environment without barriers to each child realizing their potential and experiencing high levels of achievement and success during their time in the district.

Overall, school board members and school leaders in Eaveston School District are committed to prioritizing efforts focused on the big picture through the comprehensive school improvement plan. As written on the school board's web page,

> The Eaveston School District Board of Education is dedicated to providing personalized educational opportunities for all students. In order to accomplish this goal, it is essential school district employees, families, and community partners collaborate around the district's vision toward educational excellence.

PRACTICE

A number of culturally competent practices emerged from the descriptive case research study of Eaveston School District (Welborn, 2019). Table 7.8 displays the emergent themes from the data collection and quotes from Eaveston's leaders to support each theme.

The following themes emerged among the practices:

1. Innovative strategies and programs

2. Professional learning

3. Communication and collective family and community involvement

Eaveston's school leaders work each day to provide opportunities and experiences to the children attending their schools. They have an understanding that challenges caused by differences in race, social class, and other cultural

TABLE 7.8 ● Precompetent, Competent, and Proficient Data Themes

PRECOMPETENT, COMPETENT, AND PROFICIENT DATA THEMES	
Resources to support families	"The most important thing we do is build relationships so we have a better understanding of what the needs truly are."
Community partnerships	"Our success is founded on the open and respectful relationship we've established with our community."
Support for Eaveston's staff (PD and PLC)	"The district is providing an opportunity to come together for a hefty investment of work time and resources to educate people at different levels and capacities throughout the district. Bringing people together is powerful."
Programs for students	"We offer programs and services that challenge, inspire, and motivate students to do their very best. Our personalized learning, alternative education, special education, gifted education, and extracurricular programs help in meeting the needs of all of our students in Eaveston."
Diversity with curriculum, events, artifacts	"We are one of the most diverse districts in our state. Our walls and buildings represent the diversity in our district. Students can see themselves."

Note: PD, professional development; PLC, professional learning community.

identifiers require a mindset to treat each child individually, accurately assess needs, and develop programs accordingly. One elementary principal who leads in a building that piloted a competency-based learning model for the district described the mental model his staff holds about individual students:

> The staff I have has a mental model that they're lucky that they get to work with the kids here. Our motto is "Think different, learn different, and teach different." They go to where the individual child is instead of an old school, traditional model of fitting a kid into a program that already exists. We need to adapt differently to the product coming into our schools from a public school standpoint. Every child is different, and everybody has their own story. We take that and build from that to make our community better.

Eaveston School District has taken the competency-based learning model and expanded it into a personalized learning initiative to provide equitable opportunities for its students. District leaders took the comprehensive school improvement plan and updated it to include the following task: "Design a competency-based, personalized learning environment in preschool through 12th grades that leads students to be ready for high school course content and, ultimately, success after graduation."

To do so, the district outlined innovative strategies and programs in the school improvement plan to meet all students' needs, such as a five-year personalized learning plan (Welborn, 2019).

Professional learning opportunities available to administration, faculty, and staff is another theme related to culturally competent educational practice. There are frequent opportunities for professional learning provided to Eaveston's educators related to student achievement, trauma-informed responsiveness, restorative practices, social-emotional learning, and equity. District leaders worked to ensure that professional learning related to equity is a priority by allocating time and resources to build capacity and embed the work of Cultural Proficiency in all aspects of the district.

Specifically, school leaders, at all levels, are working to increase professional learning and skills in utilizing the Tools of Cultural Proficiency to increase the effectiveness of school district personnel. Professional learning related to Cultural Proficiency occurs regularly among the district's Cultural Proficiency Committee members; in individual schools among groups of administrators, teachers, staff, and parents; in new teacher trainings; and in integrated, district-hosted events such as the Fall Professional Development Day and Spring Rally, where edcamp-style professional development is available to all employees of the school district (Welborn, 2019).

Communication and involvement with families and community members is also a strength and area of culturally competent practices. Eaveston School District's leaders recognize the importance of having families, students, and community members involved in committees that affect student learning. Due to the value for diversity in the district, all groups of stakeholders are regularly invited to participate on committees such as the Strategic Planning Committee and the Cultural Proficiency Committee. While involvement does not look the same for all families in Eaveston, school leaders are attentive to the needs of families and try to get to know them so they can forge toward greater understanding and better partnerships. Overall, there is much to celebrate concerning Eaveston's Cultural Proficiency journey regarding changes in policies and practices (Welborn, 2019).

LOOKING IN THE REARVIEW MIRROR

This chapter provided a context for gaining skills and knowledge for applying the Cultural Proficiency Continuum. By using the Continuum to collect data, identify emergent themes, set goals, leverage change, and celebrate culturally competent policies and practices already in place, school leaders can guide organizations through transformational change. The Cultural Proficiency Continuum is a tool with which leaders can guide the people in their organizations to distinguish between unhealthy practices and those practices deemed healthy, which expose the reality of practices and policies that are closing doors on students in their systems (i.e., district, school, classroom, etc.).

ON TO OUR NEXT DESTINATION

In the next chapter we guide you to investigate the Essential Elements of Cultural Proficiency using an inquiry process. This tool serves as a set of standards for personal and professional behaviors and values, and organizational policies and practices. Based on data collected in Chapter 7, you will engage in an inquiry process to identify immediate and long-term goals for the organization and begin the transformation by assessing cultural knowledge, valuing diversity, managing the dynamics of difference, adapting to diversity, and institutionalizing the cultural knowledge. The case narrative from Eaveston School District is included for connecting with one district's use of the Essential Elements. The resources and learning strategies used during this portion of Eaveston's journey are included in the chapter. Just as in Chapters 5–7, you will engage with the RDA process to examine the Intersectionality of race and social class. In short, this chapter is about change through improvement and growth.

REFLECTION, DIALOGUE, AND ACTION PROCESS

REFLECTION • Dialogue • Action

These are essential questions to help you reflect on the application of the Continuum of Cultural Proficiency:

1. What examples do you have for unhealthy and healthy policies, practices, behaviors, and language used by you and your colleagues? Where do they align on the Continuum?

2. What are some situations in which you know that current practices and policies are not working for students? Do you know how to respond?

Reflection • DIALOGUE • Action

These are essential questions to help you dialogue with others on the application of the Continuum of Cultural Proficiency:

1. In your leadership group explore how the Cultural Proficiency Continuum helps clarify what is and what could be in your school. Chart and share the results.

2. Examine your achievement data, and surface a group of students who are not achieving adequately. Gather more data regarding the causes, and use the Continuum to categorize your results. In what ways was this helpful?

3. As you look at this group's achievement data and the Continuum data, in what ways can you move to an assets approach versus a deficit approach in your thinking?

4. In what ways might we learn more about the culture of these students to "open the door" for them?

Reflection • Dialogue • ACTION

These are essential questions to help you lead this work in your district or school through actions of relying on the Cultural Proficiency Continuum:

1. Use sticky notes to represent the six points along the Cultural Proficiency Continuum related to your organization. Narrow the focus in providing examples of policies, practices, and behaviors along the Continuum of topics such as assessment, instruction, curriculum, parent and family partnerships, and so on.

2. After engaging in the dialogue above, what actions can you take immediately? What actions might require more time to engage more people in the effort? Develop your action plan.

Travel Log

_____

_____

_____

_____

_____

_____

_____

_____

_____

_____

_____

_____

_____

_____

_____

_____

_____

_____

_____

_____

_____

_____

_____

_____

_____

_____

_____

TRAVEL GUIDE
The Essential Elements

Create Your Map

- Examine and commit to your vision and mission.
- Focus district and school efforts on the Essential Elements.
- Develop action plans for filling the gaps between the vision/mission and the existing data.
- Examine and celebrate the results of your efforts.

Resources

- Allocated money for professional learning time
- Stakeholder communities that will share and discuss their experiences with your organization
- Existing structures that have developed visions and plans for the organization

Mileage

- Gather data on what you know about other cultures.
- Gather data on the effectiveness of current conflict resolution policies, procedures, and practices.
- Discover historical events that have helped shape the current culture in your organization.

Check the Weather

- In what ways are the Essential Elements evident in your communities?
- Who is ready to examine their values and beliefs related to the Elements? Who's close? Who's not?
- What has historically been a source of misunderstandings and disagreements?

Travel Phrases

- *Assessing* cultural knowledge: Claim your differences.
- *Valuing* diversity: Name the differences.
- *Managing* the dynamics of difference: Frame the conflicts caused by differences.
- *Adapting* to diversity: Change to make a difference.
- *Institutionalizing* the cultural knowledge: Train about the differences.
- Breakthrough questions
- Cultural knowledge

You're the Driver

- Determine to discover what's important to each stakeholder group in your school community.
- Develop relationships that will help you to learn and understand the values, beliefs, and customs of each group.
- In what ways can you institutionalize your work so that when you leave it doesn't leave with you?
- Find ways to incorporate the Essential Elements into your daily leadership practice.

Committing to Standards of Equity-Focused Change Through Improvement and Growth With the Essential Elements

---

STORIES FROM EAVESTON

This is a research-informed vignette developed from the researcher's lens and case study findings of Eaveston School District. It provides context for implementing the Cultural Proficiency Framework to commit to standards of equity-focused change.

At this stage of implementing the Cultural Proficiency Framework in Eaveston School District, the Superintendent convened the district's Board of Education and Cabinet to discuss plans for increasing the Cultural Proficiency work in the district. The goal had been to embed the work of Cultural Proficiency into all aspects of the district. The Cultural Proficiency Committee was tasked to lead the work. Following the initial talks with the Board of Education and Cabinet members to increase funds for work related to diversity, equity, and Cultural Proficiency, the Superintendent addressed the leaders of the committee:

> We have really taken time to build our vocabulary around the action verbs of the Essential Elements of Cultural Proficiency. We have experts for each of those actions: assessing cultural knowledge, valuing diversity, managing the dynamics of difference, adapting to diversity, and institutionalizing cultural knowledge. We need to be intentional in integrating the Essential Elements into our professional practice.

I would like to look at starting with our CSIP (Comprehensive School Improvement Plan). We have three goals that encompass what we mean by "all aspects" of the district. I would like to call all CSIP committee members, maybe even consider opening up the CSIP committee to additional members based on the current national climate, to examine the goals of our CSIP under the Cultural Proficiency Framework. Since our CSIP Committee includes representatives from all buildings, families, and the community, this will allow us to hold ourselves accountable to apply the equity and access lens to everything we do, which can lead to attaining our vision "So that all students learn at high levels."

Additionally, I would like to consider the institutionalization of the Cultural Proficiency work in the district. We have worked for the past couple of years with three goals related to the Cultural Proficiency Committee:

1. *Increasing Cultural Proficiency training for all employees in the district*

2. *Reducing disparities in discipline*

3. *Increasing staff diversity in Eaveston*

I would like to develop consistent, monthly strategic planning and action meetings for each school in Eaveston by working with our principals. I would like to take our three Cultural Proficiency Committee goals, add a leverage point of family/community engagement, and think through how we might use the Essential Elements of Cultural Proficiency to develop plans for each school based upon our Comprehensive School Improvement Plan goals. It is important we take these next steps as part of the institutionalization process, as it is foundational to our policies, procedures, and practices. We have to do our own work, and move these identified levers, to improve student outcomes for all of our students in Eaveston.

CALIBRATION

You see, the challenges we face will not be solved with one meeting in one night. Change will not come if we wait for some other person or if we wait for some other time. We are the ones we've been waiting for. We are the change that we seek. We are the hope of those boys who have so little, who've been told that they cannot have what they dream, that they cannot be what they imagine. Yes, they can.

—Barack Obama (2008)

Fight for the things that you care about, but do it in a way that will lead others to join you.

—Ruth Bader Ginsburg (Vagianos, 2015)

ON-RAMP TO THE ESSENTIAL ELEMENTS OF CULTURAL PROFICIENCY

Effective school leaders believe in the power of change. Change results from the efforts of school leaders who challenge practices and policies that marginalize students and, thereby, exacerbate educational access and achievement gaps. Deep change is often a result of transformational leadership. Culturally proficient leaders understand the Framework of Cultural Proficiency, how barriers inform and form unhealthy policies, practices, and behaviors and, conversely, the way the Guiding Principles inform healthy policies, practices, and behaviors. Adapting to an asset-based mindset allows leaders to see and hear evidence of change in their organizations, see and hear change within themselves, and see and hear change when they work with those who are culturally different from themselves.

Importantly, leaders of equity and access initiatives realize that leading diverse school organizations requires the commitment and modeling of being engaged in their own personal work. As you will recall from previous chapters, a leader's personal journey begins by using the Guiding Principles of Cultural Proficiency as an "inside-out" exploration of their own values and behaviors, as well as their school's expressed core values and vision/mission statements. We encourage you to go back to Table 6.1. The consequence of this personal and institutional reflection is the development of inclusive core values that guide the development of policies and practices designed to serve the academic and social needs of students from all demographic and cultural groups.

Equipped with specific and inclusive core values, culturally proficient school leaders use the Essential Elements of Cultural Proficiency to facilitate change in organizations' policies and practices and in employees' behaviors. The five Essential Elements serve as standards to guide continuous improvement in educators' practices and their schools' willingness and ability to develop policies and practices to guide the education of all students to high levels. Intentional, planned use of the Essential Elements leads to actions that

1. allow doors to be open to students who have been historically underserved or discriminated against, such as some students of color and students living in poverty, and

2. allow educators to find their on-ramp to the Cultural Proficiency highway to begin and continue their own journey of Cultural Proficiency, in which their values and behaviors transform from tolerance for diversity to transformation for equity.

Take a moment, and think about the epigraph at the beginning of this chapter from Barack Obama's 2008 speech on Super Tuesday before he was elected the 44th president of the United States in November of that year. In this chapter you are invited as a school leader to think about leadership actions and intentional, planned change in ways you may never have considered. First, calibrate and return to the "why" question:

• Why are you engaged in this work at this level? Who is not thriving in your schools? Who is thriving, and why?

• Have students of color, students living in poverty, or students of other historically underserved groups been implicitly or explicitly told during their education that they cannot have what they dream or become what they imagine?

- What messages are the policies, procedures, and practices in your organization sending?

- What might be some of the goals for your school that could be crafted to address persistent inequities?

- What are some action steps that could be taken this week that would be transformational toward your goal of planned change for these students?

- What might be some actions you can implement this semester, this year?

- What will Cultural Proficiency look like in your district or building?

Record your thoughts.

_____

_____

_____

_____

_____

THE ESSENTIAL ELEMENTS OF CULTURAL PROFICIENCY

The Essential Elements of Cultural Proficiency are an interdependent set of standards that are distinguished by five action verbs to create change in school policies and practices, and individuals' behaviors. It is important to note that these standards are initiated at the *Cultural Competence* point on the Cultural Proficiency Continuum. Figure 8.1 features an arrow indicating where those practices inform the Essential Elements of culturally proficient practice. With practice in applying the Essential Elements, you will begin to develop culturally proficient policies, practices, and behaviors that align with the inclusive core values of your district or school, as discussed in Chapter 6.

Table 8.1 provides definitions and descriptions of each Essential Element. It is important to note that while the Essential Elements are used to address issues of equity with respect to all cultural identities, as you will recall, the focus of this book remains on race and social class.

Eaveston leaders used the Essential Elements in their inquiry process to focus on the goals identified from the emergent themes from the Continuum data presented in Table 7.4. Reading this section will help

FIGURE 8.1 ● The Conceptual Framework for Culturally Proficient Practices

The Five Essential Elements of Cultural Competence

Serve as standards for personal, professional values and behavior, as well as organizational policies and practices

- **Assessing cultural knowledge**
- **Valuing diversity**
- **Managing the dynamics of difference**
- **Adapting to diversity**
- **Institutionalizing cultural knowledge**

The Cultural Proficiency Continuum portrays people and organizations who possess the knowledge, skills, and moral bearing to distinguish among equitable and inequitable practices as represented by different worldviews:

Informs

Unhealthy, unproductive, and inequitable policies, practices, and behaviors	Differing Worldviews	Healthy, productive, and equitable policies, practices, and behaviors
- Cultural destructiveness - Cultural incapacity - Cultural blindness		- Cultural precompetence - Cultural competence - Cultural proficiency

Resolving the tension to do what is socially just within our diverse society leads people and organizations to view selves in terms productive and equitable.

Informs   Informs

Overcoming Barriers to Cultural Proficiency

Serve as personal, professional, and institutional impediments to moral and just service to a diverse society by:

- Being resistant to change,
- Being unaware of the need to adapt,
- Not acknowledging systemic oppression, and
- Benefiting from a sense of privilege and entitlement.

Ethical Tension

Guiding Principles of Cultural Proficiency

Provide a moral framework for conducting one's self and organization in an ethical fashion by believing the following:

- Culture is a predominant force in society.
- People are served in varying degrees by the dominant culture.
- People have individual and group identities.
- Diversity within cultures is vast and significant.
- Each cultural group has unique cultural needs.
- The best of both worlds enhances the capacity of all.
- The family, as defined by each culture, is the primary system of support in the education of children.
- School systems must recognize that marginalized populations have to be at least bicultural and that this status creates a distinct set of issues to which the system must be equipped to respond.
- Inherent in cross-cultural interactions are dynamics that must be acknowledged, adjusted to, and accepted.

Source: Adapted from R. B. Lindsey, Nuri-Robins, and Terrell (2009, p. 60).

TABLE 8.1 ● The Five Essential Elements of Cultural Proficiency

1. *Assessing cultural knowledge: Claim your differences.*
• Recognize how your race and social class affect others.
• Describe the complexities of race and social class norms of your school or district.
• Understand how the culture of your school or district affects others in various racial and social class groups in various ways.
2. *Valuing diversity: Name the differences.*
• Celebrate and encourage the presence of people from a variety of racial and social class backgrounds in all activities.
• Recognize racial and social class differences as diversity rather than an inappropriate response to the environment.
• Accept that each culture informed by race and social class finds some values and behaviors more important than others.
3. *Managing the dynamics of difference: Frame the conflicts caused by differences.*
• Learn effective strategies for resolving conflict, particularly among people whose racial and social class backgrounds and values are different.
• Understand the effect that historic distrust has on present-day interactions.
• Realize that you may misjudge the actions of others of different race or social class based on learned expectations.
4. *Adapting to diversity: Change to make a difference.*
• Change the way things are done to acknowledge the complexity of racial and social class differences among the staff, educators, and community.
• Develop skills for intercultural communication related to race and social class.
• Institutionalize cultural interventions for the conflicts and confusion caused by the dynamics of difference in race and social class.
5. *Institutionalizing cultural knowledge: Train about the differences.*
• Incorporate cultural knowledge into the mainstream of the organization.
• Drive changes in the systems of the organization.
• For staff development and education, integrate into your systems information and skills that enable all to interact effectively in a variety of intercultural situations.
• Teach the origins of stereotypes and prejudices.

Source: Adapted from R. B. Lindsey et al. (2019).

REFLECTION ● Dialogue ● Action

Take a moment, and think deeply about the five action verbs associated with the Essential Elements of Cultural Proficiency. In what ways have you *assessed* cultural knowledge, *valued* diversity, *managed* the dynamics of difference, *adapted* to diversity, or *institutionalized* cultural knowledge in your own organization? Record your thoughts.

_____

_____

_____

_____

_____

you understand the precise steps Eaveston School District took to apply the Essential Elements in the creation of their Cultural Proficiency action plan. Eaveston deepened their inquiry process through learning about the Essential Elements of Cultural Proficiency in deep consideration of several essential questions. Table 8.2 displays the guiding questions.

Eaveston School District leaders used selected processes and learning strategies to help gain the answers to the guiding questions. The processes and learning strategies employed are organized around five purposes of applying the Essential Elements:

1. To learn about the change process

2. To conduct self-assessments for leading this work

3. To support change through dialogue

4. To develop a strategic action plan

5. To monitor progress toward equity goals

The inquiry process is cyclical, therefore the learning strategies Eaveston School District leaders used with this tool do not imply a sequential order. Rather, they are interactive and mutually supportive in implementing the work of Cultural Proficiency. As you continue your reading, we encourage you to think about the order in which you will engage your team with the learning strategies.

USING THE ESSENTIAL ELEMENTS TO LEARN ABOUT THE CHANGE PROCESS

Eaveston's Cultural Proficiency Committee members first engaged in a learning strategy, *Jigsaw of the Essential Elements of Cultural Proficiency* (p. 327), as they used the Essential Elements to learn about the change process. The objective was to create a team of experts on each Essential Element among the Cultural Proficiency Committee to examine various systemic transformative levers in the district (i.e., curriculum, instruction, programs,

TABLE 8.2 ● Guiding Questions for Applying the Essential Elements of Cultural Proficiency

• Given the value we have for "*all* students to learn at high levels," how might we adapt our behavior, policies, procedures, and practices to open doors for our students who are not thriving socially or academically?
• What are five recommended actions for changing our behaviors, policies, procedures, and practices to open doors so our all of our students may thrive?
• What actions are we implementing for improving our practices related to the STLs and goals we set? To what degree are these actions causing students to experience success? What data do we have to support the successes?
• In what ways did we change our policies, procedures, and behaviors? How do the planned changes aligned with the Cultural Proficiency Framework support our planning for sustaining the work in the next school year?

Note: STLs, systemic transformative levers.

professional development). Each team examined the committee's three goals, outlined in Chapter 7, through the lens of one particular action of the Essential Elements.

First, the members of the committee were invited to join their Cultural Proficiency learning "family," comprising five members per group. Additionally, consideration was given to ensure that each group reflected the teacher, staff, and administrator roles in Eaveston, as well as the location of work, such as central office or a specific department or school. Each person in the group selected an Essential Element and read descriptions from various articles provided. While reading the articles, the participants identified three or four most important points from each source.

In the second phase of learning about the Essential Elements, the Cultural Proficiency Committee members reorganized themselves by their Essential Element as an expert group and created a poster representing shared learning about their Essential Element. The first step in this learning strategy was to check their understanding of the Essential Element with the other members in the group. Next, the groups identified key ideas they would share on the poster and created a visual or symbol on the poster to represent the Essential Element. Image 8.1 shown below, which includes a sample of the posters created to represent each Essential Element. Eaveston's Cultural Proficiency Committee members used these posters to aid in their understanding of the Essential Elements before applying them in the development of the equity action plan.

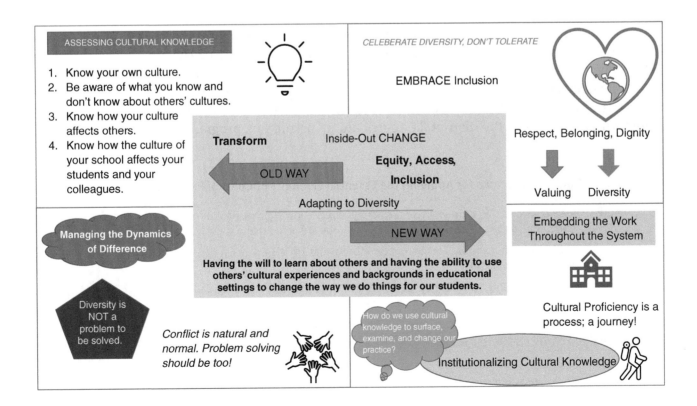

Another learning strategy Eaveston's Cultural Proficiency Committee used to deepen their learning about the Essential Elements was *Using the Essential Elements* (p. 329). This learning strategy was selected to reinforce and deepen efficacy with the Essential Elements and begin the process of translating the concepts into individual behaviors and organizational practice. During this learning strategy, the members of the committee rejoined their "expert" groups to examine each Essential Element in depth. Each group was asked to describe the behaviors of an individual or the practices of the school relative to their Essential Element and to record the group members' responses. The groups shared their findings to enrich the discussion and promote reflection and dialogue. The questions in Table 8.3 were used by each group to guide their conversations (R. B. Lindsey et al., 2019).

TABLE 8.3 ● Guiding Questions to Deepen Efficacy With the Essential Elements

ESSENTIAL ELEMENT	QUESTIONS	EXAMPLES OF INDIVIDUAL BEHAVIORS OR PRACTICES IN YOUR ORGANIZATION
Assessing cultural knowledge	What are the unwritten rules in your school? How do you describe your own culture? How does your school provide for a variety of learning styles?	
Valuing diversity	How would you describe the diversity in your current professional setting? How do you react to the term *valuing diversity*? How do you and your colleagues frame conversations about learners?	
Managing the dynamics of difference	How do you handle conflict in the classroom? In the school? Among the adults? What skills do you possess to handle conflict? Describe situations of cross-cultural conflict that may be based on historic distrust.	
Adapting to diversity	How have you recently adapted to the needs of a new member? How has your organization recently adapted to the needs of new members? Describe examples of inclusive language and inclusive materials. How do you teach your clients about the organization's need to adapt to diverse cultures?	
Institutionalizing cultural knowledge	What do you currently know about the cultural groups in your organization and among your clients? What more would you like to know about those cultures? How do you and your colleagues learn about these cultural groups?	

USING THE ESSENTIAL ELEMENTS FOR SELF-ASSESSMENT

In addition to using the Essential Elements to learn about the change process, Eaveston School District leaders used the Essential Elements at the district and building levels for self-assessment in leading this work. They engaged in the learning strategy *Cultural Competence Self-Assessment* (p. 330). The purpose of this learning strategy was to provide a baseline of information and a starting point for conversation about becoming a culturally proficient leader, regardless of role, in Eaveston School District. The self-assessment provides key questions that educators can use to explore practices aligned with the Essential Elements of Cultural Proficiency. For example, the self-assessment has participants circle the number that best reflects the frequency with which they assess cultural knowledge, from 1 to 5 (1 = *rarely*, 2 = *seldom*, 3 = *sometimes*, 4 = *often*, 5 = *usually*). Providing the committee members an opportunity to take this self-assessment allowed them to gain an understanding of the frequency of their actions according to each Essential Element.

USING THE ESSENTIAL ELEMENTS TO SUPPORT CHANGE THROUGH DIALOGUE

School leaders used the Essential Elements to support change through dialogue. In Chapter 5 we introduced breakthrough questions as a strategy for overcoming the Barriers to Cultural Proficiency. Eaveston's Cultural Proficiency Committee members practiced formulating breakthrough questions to help them respond by managing the dynamics of difference and communicating in the diverse school community they serve. Before you explore the construction of breakthrough questions using the Essential Elements, we encourage you to look back and refamiliarize yourself with the Culturally Proficient Coaching model in Chapter 5. Figure 8.2 displays the flow of Culturally Proficient Coaching.

The Cultural Proficiency Committee worked with barrier-laden statements related to each one of the goals identified for its work (see the chart displayed

FIGURE 8.2 ● Flow of Culturally Proficient Coaching

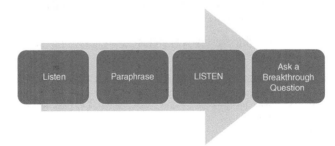

in Table 8.4). Each statement was collected when the committee engaged in the data collection process on the Continuum of Cultural Proficiency. Group members formulated breakthrough questions through the reflection and dialogue process for how they would respond as the committee members responsible for disrupting culturally destructive, incapacitating, or blind comments regarding the three goals for equity.

So how do you construct a breakthrough question? Eaveston School District leaders constructed breakthrough questions using the model of Culturally Proficient Coaching (D. B. Lindsey et al., 2020). Table 8.5 displays what breakthrough questions should include.

TABLE 8.4 ● Examples From Your Organization

BARRIER QUESTIONS/ COMMENTS	ESSENTIAL ELEMENTS OF CULTURAL PROFICIENCY	BREAKTHROUGH QUESTIONS
She keeps missing whole days to participate in the district's Cultural Proficiency Committee. . . . I'm sure they are "really" getting somewhere with this work.	Valuing diversity Adapting to diversity	Given the value and investment the district is making in equity, what might be some ways in which we can partner to adapt our classroom while I am gone?
This school district doesn't value diversity, I mean look at the teaching staff. They have ways of "not" hiring teachers of color.	Valuing diversity Adapting to diversity	In what ways might we collaborate in demonstrating a value for diversity and adapt our hiring practices?
There's nothing we can really do about the discipline data here. Do they really want us to lower expectations to stop referring them?	Managing the dynamics of difference Assessing cultural knowledge	Given those circumstances, what might be some ways we can assess our cultural knowledge and manage the dynamics of difference to get the outcomes we want for our students?

TABLE 8.5 ● Breakthrough Question Components

Culturally proficient breakthrough questions use the following:
- One or more of the Essential Elements
- Exploratory and plural language
- Positive intentionality
- Language to mediate thinking toward a specific action and/or goal
- Language that redirects thinking from certainty to curiosity and possibility, from knowing to not being sure you know

Table 8.6 provides a template with examples for you to construct break-through questions.

TABLE 8.6 ● Breakthrough Question Template

BARRIER QUESTIONS AND/OR COMMENTS	PRELUDE/CONTEXT	EXPLORATORY LANGUAGE AND PLURAL FORM TO NAME THE CONTENT	ESSENTIAL ELEMENTS ACTION VERB	REDIRECTED TOWARD ACTION AND/OR GOAL
If those families would have moved somewhere else besides our attendance area, we would have seen an increase in our test scores.	Given the core values of equity and diversity . . .	. . . what might be some resources we can access to better . . .	. . . demonstrate our value for diversity . . .	. . . so we can reach (y)our student achievement goals?
Why does the conversation always have to be about race?	Given the racial and cultural diversity of our students and families, . . .	. . . in what ways might our conversations about race and culture, as they are related to our community, . . .	. . . inform us in assessing cultural knowledge . . .	. . . to support all students' achieving at higher levels than ever before?
Since we know some kids can't do the work, why do they have to be in "inclusion" classes? Can't special classes (ability grouping) serve them better?	Given the value and respect we have for all students' ability to learn at high levels, . . .	. . . how might we differentiate our instruction practices . . .	. . . in managing the dynamics of difference . . .	. . . to support all learners in the same space?
Why do our administrators want us to do this new equity work in grade-level teams? Why can't they just implement better discipline policies with kids and parents?	Given the vision and mission of our school district, . . .	. . . what might be some ways we can . . .	. . . adapt to the diversity of our students . . .	. . . to ensure that students in our grade levels experience success both academically and behaviorally?
Before we begin this work and use all these resources and time, how do we know this equity stuff will work? When will we ever have enough time?	Given our value for best practices, in what ways might we explore schools like ours, with kids and families like ours, that are being successful?	In what ways might we explore schools like ours and . . .	. . . institutionalize cultural knowledge . . .	. . . to effectively use our time and resources, and monitor our progress to ensure our students' equitable outcomes?

Reflection • DIALOGUE • Action

Take some time to engage in reflection and dialogue with your colleagues to practice using the Essential Elements of Cultural Proficiency with examples from your own organization.

* What might be an area within your organization that you would like to see greater movement toward culturally proficient practice?

* What barrier comment(s)/questions(s) might you anticipate hearing?

* What might be some breakthrough question(s) in response to the barrier comments(s)/question(s)?

Record your examples in Table 8.7.

TABLE 8.7 ● Formulating Your Own Breakthrough Questions

BARRIER QUESTIONS/ COMMENTS	ESSENTIAL ELEMENTS OF CULTURAL PROFICIENCY	BREAKTHROUGH QUESTIONS

THE ESSENTIAL ELEMENTS GUIDE DEVELOPMENT OF A TRANSFORMATIONAL EQUITY ACTION PLAN

In Chapter 7 we introduced to you three main goals that the Cultural Proficiency Committee identified. We wish to repeat them here in Table 8.8 so you can understand how these three goals became part of the larger initiative to embed Cultural Proficiency into all aspects of Eaveston School District.

Eaveston School District leaders used the Essential Elements to develop a transformational equity action plan using the Culturally Proficient

Inquiry for Action Plan (p. 222). On the following pages you will notice the plan is organized and aligned with Eaveston's Cultural Proficiency goals. This is a reminder that these goals were developed from the learning strategies and processes used in applying the Tools of Cultural Proficiency. In Eaveston School District, since those goals were first set, the Cultural Proficiency Committee, along with the Superintendent's Cabinet, have worked to implement the action steps and strategies to achieve each goal. Table 8.9 displays Eaveston's Cultural Proficiency Inquiry for Action Plan.

TABLE 8.8 ● Eaveston Cultural Proficiency Committee's Equity Goals

Goal 1. Reduce disparities in discipline: Support and grow restorative justice practices, evaluate current practices and data to eliminate inequities, and provide strategies for improving classroom management and relationships.
Goal 2. Promote and support further Cultural Proficiency training: Provide further opportunities for more Cultural Proficiency work for staff, find resources to help staff understand personal bias, and support more Cultural Proficiency training for all staff across the district.
Goal 3. Support and grow staff diversity: Attend/host recruitment efforts in diverse communities. Seek/support diverse candidates.

TABLE 8.9 ● Eaveston School District's Cultural Proficiency Inquiry for Action Plan

Our district vision: "That *all* students will learn at high levels . . ."
School Improvement goals: Eaveston students will demonstrate significant improvement in their understanding and application of state academic standards Eaveston educators will develop and implement building-level school improvement plans to meet the needs of Eaveston's students and address educational gaps. Eaveston educators will develop a plan that addresses critical issues in the broader context of the district such as funding, enrollment, staffing, and safety.
Overt values: Diversity, knowledge, commitment, care, safety, learning, interdependence, contribution, strength, freedom, success *Covert values:* Communication, creativity, curiosity, teamwork, growth, hope, quality, innovation, achievement, service *Data sources:* Emergent themes from data Student achievement data Discipline data Diversity in staff data Climate survey data

Goal 1
Reduce Disparities in Discipline
Assessing cultural knowledge: Build relationships with students and families to understand cultural differences and meet their needs.
Valuing diversity: Engage students and families, when possible, in decision-making processes. Make changes to practices based on climate survey data.
Managing the dynamics of difference: Provide opportunities for administration and staff to engage in dialogue about discipline data and related practices.
Adapting to diversity: Review and revise policies related to discipline. Make changes to programs and supports related to classroom management and discipline.
Institutionalizing cultural knowledge: Build partnerships, and increase professional development for all staff to examine biases, increase cultural knowledge, and reduce gaps in discipline data by demographic group.
Goal 2
Promote and Support Cultural Proficiency Training
Assessing cultural knowledge: Increase opportunities for Eaveston's employees to participate in learning strategies and events that focus on increasing self-awareness and understanding of others.
Valuing diversity: Collect data around the diversity of the Cultural Proficiency Committee, as well as other committees at the district and building levels.
Managing the dynamics of difference: Create safe spaces for staff to talk about differences at the district, building, and grade/department levels.
Adapting to diversity: Increase funding and resources for Cultural Proficiency across the district.
Institutionalizing cultural knowledge: Create plans for embedding the work of Cultural Proficiency in all aspects of the school district (building plans, curriculum, ELL, reading specialists, librarians, human resources, programs, events, communications, CSIP).
Goal 3
Support and Grow Staff Diversity
Assessing cultural knowledge: Analyze and increase transparency by communication of data related to recruitment and hiring of staff in comparison with student demographics.
Valuing diversity: Increase diversity of staff, parents, and students involved in the recruiting and hiring processes.
Managing the dynamics of difference: Use the gaps identified between data of staff and students to make informed decisions in choosing the best candidate with the highest qualifications to meet students' needs.
Adapting to diversity: Change recruitment practices and increase programming to grow staff diversity.
Institutionalizing cultural knowledge: Build working relationships to support and grow staff diversity within Eaveston's Human Resources department, Cultural Proficiency Committee, and building principals.

Note: CSIP, Comprehensive School Improvement Plan; ELL, English language learner.

USING THE ESSENTIAL ELEMENTS TO MONITOR PROGRESS TOWARD EQUITY GOALS

Eaveston's Cultural Proficiency Committee monitored their progress on intended changes guided by their use of the Essential Elements of Cultural Proficiency to attain their goals and intended outcomes. For each of the three goals the following sections describe the outcomes and changes Eaveston realized due to their diligent work.

GOAL 1: REDUCE DISPARITIES IN DISCIPLINE

Eaveston School District leaders, like many administrators across the United States, focus on disaggregating their discipline data by race, gender, and disability. A focus of this work has been to reduce the gaps among and across these demographic groups. Eaveston's educators understand the importance of responsibility, as a counterpart and support to academic achievement and overall student success. As we work toward our goal of reducing the amount of disparity in student discipline data when disaggregated by race, gender, economic, and ability status, we center student and staff responsibility alongside student success. Table 8.10 displays numbers that show the risk of out-of-school suspension by race, gender, and disability status. The data come from the public 2015–2016 Civil Rights Data Collection for all students in Eaveston, grades K–12. These data are part of a larger study conducted on all out-of-school suspension data for districts in the metropolitan area. Reference and citations to the actual study are not presented here because of the protection of the school district, represented in this book by the name Eaveston School District.

Eaveston's goal to reduce disparities in discipline includes supporting and growing restorative justice practices, evaluating current practices and data to eliminate inequities, and providing strategies for improving classroom management and relationships.

TABLE 8.10 ● Eaveston's Discipline Data (2015–2016) by Race, Gender, Ability

STATUS	TIMES MORE LIKELY	DESCRIPTION
Race	2.7	Black students were 2.7 times more likely to receive OSS than males.
Gender	2.2	Males were 2.2 times more likely to receive OSS than females.
Ability	2.7	Students with a disability were 2.7 times more likely to receive OSS than students without a disability.

Note: Source is not included to protect the actual school district represented by Eaveston School District. OSS, out-of-school suspension.

Table 8.11 displays Eaveston's benchmark progress toward the goal of reducing disparities in discipline for each of the Essential Elements.

TABLE 8.11 ● Eaveston's Benchmark Progress Toward Reducing Disparities in Discipline

***Assessing culture*: Leaders and educators focus on building relationships to enhance the ability to gain a better understanding of each individual child and his or her family structure, experiences, and needs.**
Principal: *One of the most important things we do with all students is build relationships. We get to know them and their families, so then we have a better understanding of what the needs truly are. We have families from some cultures where they are very proud, and they don't want to state a need. But the more we get to know them, the more we can help, whether that's in a very small way or in a bigger way. We just want to make sure we are able to provide any assistance that they might need. It is just getting to know kids and their families.*
Special education teacher: *We work to find new ways of thinking. With families, understanding that our families vary in their composition, their membership, their unity, our disunity, that our families may be going through all kinds of changes. Those changes may be socioeconomic, marital, gender identification. In building relationships it's important to know that families come to us with cultural values and experiences, that some of which may be obvious and some of which will not be obvious. So we try to understand where a family is coming from, how that in our society families of certain groups that are marginalized often pay for that in terms of their socioeconomic security.*
Central office administrator: *I can think of a number of different places where students have had different wants and needs and teachers have responded in ways, but beyond that I feel like it's a lot of personal connection. It's a lot of trying to get connected with families and being able to understand students' needs, hear what they bring to the classroom and not assuming every student comes in as a blank slate. Every student comes in with a wealth of experiences, and knowledge, and talents, and getting to know all those pieces is really important to moving forward and meeting them where they are.*
***Valuing diversity*: Leaders intentionally invite families and community members to be part of activities and decision-making groups. Parents and students are asked for their perceptions of the school's culture and practices through a climate survey.**
Principal: *While I think we do a good job, I think we need more feedback from families as far as what they need, what we can do, or what their expectations are when they move into the district, before we even get to know them.*
Parent: *My role in this work is to be as active as possible. I'm active in the PTO, and I'm active, obviously, through my children's activities, whether it be academic activities or sports. My general practice in helping in any cultural diversity situation is to be present because what I feel like is people lack experiences, [which] is what helps to build really true cross Cultural Proficiency. It's an academic process of understanding history, but personal interaction and presence is probably where people become most proficient.*
Parent: *Being an ethnic minority, I have life experience that isn't necessarily understood by the majority culture, or even other minority culture, and so just be present and being in activities is a way I feel like I can participate in structural ways by including my perception of the school's culture and practices.*
***Managing the dynamics of difference*: Eaveston School District leaders focus on helping others recognize differences as diversity rather than inappropriate responses to the environment (i.e., discipline, communication, dress, learning styles; meet them where they are, not where the school is).**
Teacher: *With discipline policies, I think that it might be more that the teachers are not handling discipline situations to the best of their ability or they have yet to learn how to better handle it based upon differences in culture. I think we need to have conversations about how to deal with students, that their cultural norms are not your cultural norms, and that those differences in behavior do not mean they are wrong.*
Principal: *I'm fortunate to be in Eaveston, and that the district is progressive. They are not reactionary. There is a freedom that's given to us to have the opportunity to go and meet the needs of students and families where they are. It's about each individual kid and each individual family having their own story. Culture, race, socioeconomic [status] are not barriers here because everybody has their own story, and we take that and we build from that and make our community a better spot for all.*

(Continued)

TABLE 8.11 ● (Continued)

Special education teacher: *Working in an informed, careful, interculturally competent way, clinical skills that include careful, research-based consideration of language and culture differences as they might impact communication, and honoring those linguistic differences, not confusing those differences with disability or disorder. So in other words, if someone speaks or expresses themselves differently, that difference needs to be studied carefully in terms of, does it respect the cultural difference, and not simply presented as wrong.*
Teacher: *Being mindful of that [the diversity in Eaveston] is something that I think is a practical necessity in day-to-day work. The students themselves speak and communicate and dress, and move down the corridor very differently from one another. They might do and say things differently. They might approach a learning task very differently depending on their prior knowledge, their values, and their past experiences with school and life. Their own interests and their aspirations, their goals for transition vary significantly depending on their personal interests, cultural values, and experiences.*
Adapting to diversity: Policies, programs, and practices are reviewed, revised, and implemented based on cultural knowledge to ensure high expectations and rigorous standards. Leaders analyze demographic data to recognize how the misalignment of the student population and educator population in terms of race, gender, age, and socioeconomic status results in various outcomes, including academic and behavioral (intended outcomes vs. reality of outcomes for students).
Teacher: *I think it might be more that some teachers are not handling discipline situations to the best of their abilities, specifically with our African American boys, or they have yet to learn how to better handle it. I think it's at the teacher level where we really need to have conversations about how to deal with students, that their cultural norms are not our cultural norms.*
Building administrator: *Our policies need to be that way, and our programs need to be that way. This work is constantly evolving, constantly changing, constantly growing in our understanding, and that every day we get new kids, and we need to be prepared to be accepting and inclusive.*
Central office administrator: *Because the district is so diverse, that it is something that schools are working on to enhance teachers' skills, staff skills, students' skills on how to respect and treat differences.*
Building administrator: *For us, for probably every school in America, we have issues with our Black students, particularly our Black boys being disciplined and consequences at just a greater number than any other race and gender. And so the diversity is when I look in our halls and I see very diverse crowds, but I also see students that are misunderstood in a lot of ways by teachers and sometimes by administrators because a majority of our staff is White. A majority of our staff grew up middle class. And so the adults in the building versus the students in the building are living different lives. We also have White students who are poor, that our staff doesn't necessarily understand the struggles that those students are going through, whether they are poor, minority, or both. We have a very compassionate staff, but I think anytime you've not lived that life, it can be difficult to understand where the student is coming from.*
Institutionalizing cultural knowledge: Leaders increased opportunities for staff to examine barriers related to historical contexts, prejudices, and stereotypes. Experts and local community partnerships in the field of discipline trained staff on restorative practices, trauma-informed care, racial bias, and anti-bias.
Teacher: *We have a social worker in the building and a counselor. We've received trauma-informed training at the district level. We have a program for our teenage students with emotional or behavioral areas that need work. We have a space in our building where students can go and it's a quiet room. We have counselors that work with our students. For our students living in poverty I think our focus is on feeding and meeting the basic needs of our students, making sure they have winter coats, making sure they are fed. It changes the way we have conversations when we talk about a student and the discipline that they need. We have to take into account that all students are the not the same; their home isn't the same; the way they might be handling trauma might not be the same.*

Note: PTO, parent-teacher organization.

At the time of publication of this book, Eaveston School District leaders had provided additional training opportunities to support the implementation and sustainability of the Cultural Proficiency work across the district:

- The school district has developed a student responsibility framework that outlines how staff will support students to make responsible behavior choices. When implemented properly, the Framework helps schools to proactively identify and meet student needs when they arise. Key components of the Framework include Multi-Tiered Systems of Support for behavioral and social-emotional needs, problem-solving teams, and universal behavior screening in all of our K–8 schools.

- Eaveston added new social-emotional support specialist positions to support the growing need for ongoing therapeutic support and intervention for elementary-age students. These staff members also support staff in learning how best to meet the needs of students who may struggle with dysregulation as a result of trauma, disability status, or other factors through staff professional development and/or individual coaching. Also, the district has partnered with a community organization for the past three years to train staff and develop school-specific trauma plans that center each school's unique needs.

- An early-warning system in grades 6–12 helps staff to proactively identify students who are struggling in the areas of academics, behavior, and attendance. School teams are provided with support on how best to utilize these data to design interventions to meet and address student needs.

- Eaveston administrators engage in group discussions throughout the school year regarding student behavior guidelines, current discipline trends/patterns, and how best to support student growth in areas of concern. This includes a school-based approach to restorative practices implementation and the use of behavior refocus rooms and de-escalation strategies to support students in making positive behavior choices.

GOAL 2: PROMOTE AND SUPPORT FURTHER CULTURAL PROFICIENCY TRAINING

Eaveston School District leaders applied the Essential Elements of Cultural Proficiency to guide the creation of action strategies to help the district in meeting the goal of promoting and supporting further Cultural Proficiency training to involve all employees of the district. The Eaveston case study provides illustrations of the extent to which the work of the Cultural Proficiency Committee has provided continuing opportunities for more Cultural Proficiency professional learning for staff. The professional learning opportunities serve to help staff understand personal bias in ways that increase the ability to apply the Tools of Cultural Proficiency to all aspects of the school district by examining the impact policies, practices, and behaviors have on students. The changes are organized by the action-oriented Essential Elements and supported by quotes from Eaveston School District leaders. Table 8.12 displays the benchmark progress toward the goal of promoting and supporting further Cultural Proficiency training across the district for each of the Essential Elements.

TABLE 8.12 ● Eaveston's Benchmark Progress Toward Promoting and Supporting Further Cultural Proficiency Training

***Assessing cultural knowledge*: Leaders and educators participate in learning strategies and events that focus on increasing self-awareness and understanding of others.**
Central office administrator: *I feel like it's very important for me to be as involved as I can in learning, growing, and developing myself because if I can't talk the talk and understand it, then how can I support it? I've always valued the fact that it's important that I'm there with the Cultural Proficiency Committee members learning, especially on topics that maybe I'm not as proficient in myself.*
Principal: *The more PD the better because we just don't know what we don't know. We have had PD in working with groups of educators from other countries who were training at a local university and part of a Boeing group. We did some PD for us on that to help the teachers to understand and be more comfortable and welcoming and understanding of the cultural needs of the families and students.*
Teacher: *I learned very quickly in this Cultural Proficiency training that I needed this training, that I had bias, that I had prejudice, that I was unfair with my implementation of discipline, and that I viewed students whose cultural norms were different than mine . . . as disrespectful and wrong, so I was very appreciative that I received training early on related to asset-based mindsets.*
Parent: *I would say that the highlight and foundation of what the district stands for as far as being culturally sensitive, culturally sound, to me, that is the pillar of the district. Everyone is invited to participate in the committee, and then from there we're getting best practices. And then we are having honest conversations about things that are considered maybe barriers for us personally and professionally and how those barriers are preventing us from really being culturally sensitive or culturally aware for our learners.*
***Valuing diversity*: Professional learning opportunities bring a diverse community together at the district and building levels focused on understanding one's own values and experiences as well as others' perspectives and experiences. Discussions have shifted in ways that now recognize students who are not being served and thus not valued.**
Principal: *We have lots of professional development opportunities from early release days to full days, to monthly staff meetings. On a weekly basis within our master schedule, I've built in common plan periods for every grade level, which also ties into vertical teaming, so that multiple grade levels can meet at the same time on a monthly basis. One of the things that we do talk about is patterns such as mobility changes, demographic changes, academic needs, social and emotional needs, and trauma-informed practices. We've spent a lot of time looking at that, and lots of awareness in regards to watching for things that are out of the ordinary and changes in behavior.*
Teacher: *I've had the opportunity to participate in part of a district training day. I think that is something that the district is aware of the need to continue to develop and grow strength in how to address some issues with Cultural Proficiency. Eaveston wants to make sure that there is an understanding of cultures, cultural needs, develop an appreciation for those cultures, and respect for those cultures.*
Teacher: *Because Eaveston is so diverse, diversity among attendees in trainings is something that schools are working on to enhance teacher skills, staff skills, and students' skills on how to respect and treat differences while ensuring that all students' needs are being met.*
***Managing the dynamics of difference*: Eaveston School District leaders promote and facilitate difficult conversations that cause discomfort in district-level, building-level, and grade-level groups. From the Board of Education, to administration, to teachers, families, and students, they are talking about diversity.**
Teacher: *I feel like part of the work is the work I do on myself, making myself more aware and just continuing to challenge myself to learn more because then I can challenge others to do the same. With that being said, I've struggled with this because I don't know how to necessarily lead that change yet. My role in this work is to ensure that it doesn't go away; that it's a continued focus and to help people understand that this isn't just a one-shot program, that this is constantly evolving, constantly changing, constantly growing in our own understanding, and that every day we get new kids. We need to be prepared to be accepting and inclusive.*
Central office admin: *We (district administrators) engage in group discussions throughout the school year regarding diversity in our district.*

Adapting to diversity: Leaders are invested in using the Cultural Proficiency Framework at the district level to build the capacity of educators to break down barriers and promote equitable outcomes where all learn in Eaveston. Increases in budget funds and resources were approved by the Board of Education to promote and support embedding Cultural Proficiency in all aspects of the district's ongoing professional learning.
Teacher: *The Cultural Diversity Committee alone was mindblowing for me. It's easy to say, "Oh yeah, we're going to do these things, and it's one of our pillars." But to actually see it in action, to me, that speaks volumes. It means it shows the seriousness, the dedication to learning, and actually embracing the diversity we have within the Eaveston area.*
Institutionalizing cultural knowledge: The district- and building-level leaders sponsor professional learning opportunities related to equity, diversity, and Cultural Proficiency to transform self and the organization. Eaveston is committed to sustainable, equity-based diversity training using the Tools of Cultural Proficiency to identify and remove the barriers to achievement and promote successful academic and social outcomes.
Central office administrator: *Cultural Proficiency Committee members are aware of the need to continue to develop and grow in how to address some issues using the Tools of Cultural Proficiency and ensuring there is an understanding of cultures, developing an appreciation for cultures, and respect for cultures.*

Note: PD, professional development.

At the time this book was published, Eaveston School District leaders had provided additional training opportunities to support the implementation and sustainability of the Cultural Proficiency work across the district.

- The Cultural Proficiency Committee of approximately 50 stakeholders across the district continues to meet at least four full days per year.

- Principals are receiving training to help embed the work of Cultural Proficiency at the building level. Principals are working to create their own goals and plans of action to increase equity, access, and inclusion in the academic and social experiences of their faculty, staff, and students.

- Teachers newly hired in the district receive two days' introduction to Cultural Proficiency with an emphasis on instruction and classroom management.

- Librarians participated in two half-days of an introduction to Cultural Proficiency focused on library resources and practices. The focus of their work is revising their existing actionable items to include three equity goals related to instruction and achievement, collection standards and practices, and community outreach, relationships, and networking.

- The Comprehensive School Improvement Team is to examine the existing CSIP for the district and apply the Tools of Cultural Proficiency to policies, practices, and procedures related to achieving the goal of the CSIP.

- All reading specialists and English language learner teachers participate in an introduction to Cultural Proficiency focused on examining their classroom practices.

- The Social Studies department is working toward a curriculum revision. In this process they will use the Tools of Cultural Proficiency to examine their practices and behaviors around curriculum, instruction, and assessment. The focus of their work is creating a curriculum that includes civic responsibility, which is not a part of the state curriculum.

- The Cultural Proficiency Committee is working to create a resource center on the district's website related to the work of Cultural Proficiency. This resource center will be available to the public.

- The Cultural Proficiency Committee has planned multiple events for learning about Cultural Proficiency and celebrating diversity at the district and building levels.

- Additional training sessions are offered throughout the year to teachers and support staff who have not had a chance to attend previously offered opportunities. Members of the Cultural Proficiency Committee are now facilitating this work.

GOAL 3: SUPPORT AND GROW STAFF DIVERSITY

Eaveston School District leaders applied the Essential Elements of Cultural Proficiency to create action strategies that would help the district meet the goal of supporting and growing staff diversity. Table 8.13 presents evidence from the case study in Eaveston regarding the degree to which the Cultural Proficiency Committee in partnership with the Human Resources department has attended and hosted recruitment efforts in diverse communities to seek and support diverse candidates. The changes and progress are organized by the action-oriented Essential Elements and supported by quotes from Eaveston School District leaders. Table 8.13 displays the benchmark progress toward the goal of supporting and growing staff diversity.

TABLE 8.13 ● Eaveston's Benchmark Progress Toward Supporting and Growing Staff Diversity

Assessing cultural knowledge: Eaveston recognizes its homogeneous district employee population and acknowledges the conflict produced from these differences that requires additional needed training (i.e., trauma-informed care, restorative practices, Cultural Proficiency).
Teacher: *As an employee I had never had the opportunity to see data broken down of race and gender, as I did when our Assistant Superintendent of HR came in and worked with the us in the Cultural Proficiency Committee towards our goal of increasing diversity among the staff. Our students have to see themselves in their teachers.*
Teacher: *I think I have a very important role as a classroom teacher. We think classroom teacher, "Oh, they don't lead." To me it extends beyond the four walls of my room sometimes. For some kiddos they look for a familiar face like me. My little African American females, "Oh my goodness, there is Ms. Johnson. When I grow up I want to be a teacher just like her."*
Valuing diversity: Eaveston involves students, staff, parents, and community members to get various perspectives, events, and celebrations and, most important, in the recruiting and hiring processes.
Parent: *My experience in the school district as a parent has been really good. I have always felt like there have been good interactions between myself and the administration. I have always had good access, and they communicate really well.*

Parent: *I think the school reaches out to families in a lot of ways to communicate. I think their understanding of diversity is in the way they communicate with families. I don't ever feel like they pass over my head being a minority, and I feel like if I have an issue or a question, they would listen and address it. I was volunteering at one of our high school football games in the concession stand. The Superintendent, himself, approached me, and mentioned that he had seen me at a lot of events. He talked to me about why I came to the district, and we talked a lot about diversity. He seemed like he was really in tune to diversity being an asset for Eaveston.*
Managing the dynamics of difference: The HR department and administrators in Eaveston are committed to managing the difference in student demographics and teacher demographics by recruiting, hiring, and promoting people who think and act differently.
Central office administrator: *We are working on an educational assistance program for our support staff who want to get a teacher certification. We also realize the importance of educating our high school students about the career path for becoming a teacher. There's so much talk about the problem and the challenges, but how do we get from talking about it to action? We have to talk to kids about their experiences here in Eaveston.*
Central office administrator: *We have different groups of students, different populations that have grown, and students have expressed an interest in having something related to their needs. Our staff has been really responsive to that. For instance, we have a Jewish Student Union, Muslim Student Association, Gender Sexuality Alliance (Gay/Straight Alliance), Triple A (African American Achievers), and International Club. We have groups of students who reach out to teachers and say, "I'd really like this opportunity" and teachers saying, "Yeah, let's do this. I'll be your sponsor."*
Adapting to diversity: Teachers of color now attend and participate in the recruiting process at job fairs and events. The Cultural Proficiency Committee developed a list of interview questions for administrators to use when interviewing all teacher candidates to ensure a lens of Cultural Proficiency.
Central office administrator: *For all recruiting trips, both to local fairs and to Historically Black College and Universities, we take teachers of color because they acknowledge that people are served by varying degrees of their own cultures and diversity at the table will lead to diversity in those prospective teacher candidates who visit the table.*
Central office administrator: *The Eaveston Human Resources department strives to recommend the best bus drivers, custodians, music teachers, chemistry teachers, etc. we can find to support our students. It is our goal to have the district workforce be as representative as possible of our student demographics in all job classifications. While efforts are made to recruit a broad and diverse applicant pool, candidates need to have the appropriate teaching certification or have a pathway to obtain the appropriate certification. State certification can be an obstacle to diversifying the teaching staff.*
Institutionalizing cultural knowledge: The HR department works intentionally with the Cultural Proficiency Committee and building-level leaders to increase the workforce, including commitment of funding, staff, and time, and a culturally proficient lens of practice.
Central office administrator: *The district Human Resources department has the option of prehiring teachers of color identified at district recruitment events and then sending the candidates to sites for interviews; creates a guest teacher pipeline where district substitutes go through an onboarding process and extensive training in hopes of recruiting them to become future classroom teachers; engages in university partnerships; and has instituted a "Grow Your Own" initiative, which has doubled the efforts for increasing teachers of color.*

Note: HR, Human Resources.

At the time this book was published, Eaveston School School District leaders from the Human Resources department had met with Eaveston's Cultural Proficiency Committee to examine the barriers that were informing practices, policies, and behaviors related to the lack of staff diversity in Eaveston. Since it was the most diverse school district in the state, Eaveston School District leaders knew it was important to reflect and dialogue about the barriers to these areas of growth, incorporate cultural knowledge into the mainstream of the organization, and integrate systems knowledge and skills that would enable all to interact effectively in a variety of intercultural situations related to the human resources process of recruiting, hiring, and retaining a diverse staff. The goal was to propose, establish, and implement policies from a culturally proficient perspective; model culturally proficient inclusive practices and behaviors related to recruiting, hiring, and retaining a diverse staff; and create and support professional learning teams.

The Human Resources team met with the Cultural Proficiency Committee and presented local, state, and national data related to teacher graduates from institutions by race. Opportunity was provided for the members of the committee to use Padlet (padlet.com) to voice their opinions, provide feedback on current policies and procedures, and make suggestions for meeting the goal. Figure 8.3 includes some of the Padlet information gathered.

It is important to note that these changes to practices within the Human Resources have led Eaveston School District to see an increase in the diversity of newly hired staff. Nearly 13% of newly hired certified staff are teachers or administrators from demographic groups that were underrepresented prior to their efforts. Support staff from these groups now represent 50% of the new support staff hired since Eaveston School District leaders in the Human Resources department began meeting with the Cultural Proficiency Committee. These transformational changes are leading to increased institutionalization of cultural knowledge as these new hires, both certified and support staff, are being hired to have lasting impacts on Eaveston's students.

FIGURE 8.3 ● Feedback and Suggestions From the Cultural Proficiency Committee

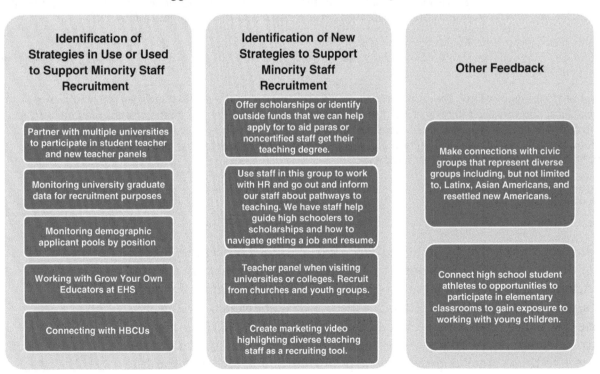

Note: Eaveston High School, Education & Human Studies; HBCUs, Historically Black Colleges and Universities; HR, Human Resources.

Leaders in Eaveston realize that it is simply not enough to hire a diverse support staff. Students from all demographic groups must see themselves in their teachers.

LOOKING IN THE REARVIEW MIRROR

This chapter provided a context for school leaders to use the Essential Elements to identify immediate and long-term goals for the organization and begin the transformation by assessing cultural knowledge, valuing diversity, managing the dynamics of difference, adapting to diversity, and institutionalizing the cultural knowledge. Culturally proficient leaders use the Essential Elements to learn about the change process, conduct self-assessment for leading this work, support change through dialogue, develop a transformational equity action plan, and monitor progress toward equity goals.

ON TO OUR NEXT DESTINATION

The next chapter extends your thinking by relying on asset-based core values to commit to strategic planning and implementation strategies around professional learning communities, family and community involvement, and continuous school improvement. The purpose is to support leaders as they break down the barriers to access for students of various racial and social class backgrounds, especially those who are not thriving in their school systems. We intend for you to focus on the three emergent themes from the research, thinking through the lens of the Intersectionality of race and social class, and make plans for change in the organization. Be sure to listen to Episode 3 of the podcast *Leading Through the Lens of Cultural Proficiency*. Here, you will hear the authors discuss some of the work they have facilitated to support school districts and schools in implementing and sustaining the application of the Tools of Cultural Proficiency.

EPISODE 3

REFLECTION, DIALOGUE, AND ACTION PROCESS

REFLECTION • Dialogue • Action

We include these essential questions to help you reflect on how you might apply the Essential Elements of Cultural Proficiency to your individual practice:

1. Have we, as a group, determined what a successful student can do at each grade level? In what ways have we committed to those goals?

2. How do we demonstrate not just tolerance but a true appreciation for the diverse children and adults in our schools?

3. In what ways have we adapted our practices, curriculum, and methods to accommodate those differences?

4. What rules do we have for dealing with conflicts and differing perspectives?

Reflection • DIALOGUE • Action

These are essential questions to help you dialogue with others on the application of the Essential Elements of Cultural Proficiency:

1. Using the Essential Elements of Cultural Proficiency—verbs for action (*assess*, *value*, *manage*, *adapt*, and *institutionalize*)—what actions will you and your team commit to?

2. In what ways can we assess how our culture is responsible for the varying levels of student success?

3. In what ways can we demonstrate tolerance, respect, and value for the cultural differences of our students who are "not experiencing success?"

4. What might be some effective strategies we can use to manage the conflicts that may arise when addressing issues of equity?

5. In what ways might we adapt to the differences represented by the varied cultures in our school?

6. What (knowledge, skills, resources) do we wish to share with others based on our reflection and dialogue for helping our students who are not experiencing success?

Reflection • Dialogue • ACTION

These are essential questions to help you lead this work in your district or school through actions of using the Essential Elements for transformational change through equity action planning.

1. Develop a working plan to examine your current practices through the lens of the five Essential Elements.

2. Determine the gaps between current practices and culturally proficient practices as defined by the Essential Elements. Create a plan of action to close those gaps.

3. Take the self-assessment.

4. Think of a barrier question or comment related to oppression, racism, or classism. Use the template and examples in Table 8.7 to help construct a breakthrough question.

Travel Log

_____

_____

_____

_____

_____

_____

PART III

Commitment to Planning, Collaboration, Growth, and Improvement

TRAVEL GUIDE
Implementation Challenges

Create Your Map

- Collect and marshal your resources, both personal and organizational, to engage in this work.
- Determine the outside resources that will be necessary to focus on Cultural Proficiency.
- Coordinate with the community in creating action plans.
- Determine ways to ensure this work will endure past your tenure.

Resources

- The relationships among the stakeholders can create a powerful new culture focused on Cultural Proficiency.
- The existing learning structures that can be focused on equity and social justice
- The newfound successes in this work

Mileage

- Determine the ways to measure qualitative shifts in attitude, values, and beliefs.
- Graph all of the events and initiatives currently in place at your school or district.

Check the Weather

- Who's ready to engage in this work? Who will support it? Who will choose not to engage? Who will oppose it?
- What is the history and general opinion of this work in your organization?

Travel Phrases

- Barriers to implementation
- Time and resources
- Building site-specific capacity for impact

You're the Driver

- In what ways do you make a habit of reflecting?
- How have you developed and improved your listening and questioning skills?
- Determine ways to ensure this work will endure past your tenure.
- In what ways will your expertise as a teacher be useful in this work?

CHAPTER 9

Implementation: Planning for Challenges Along the Journey

CALIBRATION

Effective approaches to managing change call for combining and balancing factors that do not apparently go together—simultaneous simplicity—complexity, loose-ness-tightness, strong leadership—user participation, bottom-up-top-down-ness, fidelity—adaptivity, and evaluation—nonevaluation. To put it positively, the more factors supporting implementation, the more change in practice will be accomplished.

—Michael Fullan (2016, p. 68)

How do you herd cats? . . . You tilt the floor. You point everyone in the right direction, not just through words but through action and through intent.

Maddie Grant on SocialFish (https://web.archive.org/
web/20100827143814/www.socialfish.org/2010/03/evolving-
into-a-social-organization-ceo.html)

ON-RAMP TO CHALLENGES OF IMPLEMENTATION AND SUSTAINABILITY

Implementing the Cultural Proficiency Framework and sustaining it to create organizational changes that illuminate equitable outcomes for students require that educational leaders honor individual stories through continued learning in varied, diverse, and inclusive professional learning communities. The central focus of equity work in every professional learning community is continuous improvement for student learning and well-being. Equity-focused professional learning is essential for implementing and sustaining the work of Cultural Proficiency, but as a process it does not come without its challenges.

We emphasize the work of Cultural Proficiency as a journey dedicated to life-long learning and continuous growth and change. Reflection and dialogue create the on-ramps to the highway of culturally proficient educational practice. Reflection provides opportunity for us to explore our own core values and behaviors relative to people different from ourselves. Dialogue allows us to hear about and learn from those who are different from us in their core values, beliefs, and experiences. As you near the end of this book and are preparing for your own implementation and journey toward Cultural Proficiency, we ask you to ponder the questions and prompts that follow based on the content we first introduced to you in Chapter 4 on topics of leadership. Take a moment, and record your thoughts in the space provided.

Identification: How do you define your "what" and "why" for engaging in this implementation process?

Meaningful leadership: What practices, policies, and procedures have you reflected on that are relevant to your quest to increase equity, access, and inclusion in your district/school?

Professional learning structures: What professional learning structures do you have in place to implement this work?

Assessment: As you implement this work, in what ways will you assess your progress?

Culture of collaboration: How would you describe the current norms of your culture of collaboration among your leadership team members? To what degree will these norms be revisited/revised in an ongoing manner as you implement this work?

Teams: How might you build the capacity of your existing leadership teams to implement this transformational work?

Sustainability: As you guide your district/school through the initial implementation of the Cultural Proficiency Framework, what structures and people will you have in place to sustain this work over time?

_____

_____

_____

_____

_____

This chapter includes the findings and conclusions drawn from the research study that investigated Eaveston School District's implementation of the Cultural Proficiency Framework (Welborn, 2019). The following sections are organized to include the challenges Eaveston's leaders faced during their work of implementing the Cultural Proficiency Framework and sustaining it over time. Three challenges are offered for you to consider as you continue this journey toward increased equity, access, and inclusion in your school organization. As you read, be sure to consider how you might use the leadership concepts we asked you to "pack" for your journey to overcome challenges such as those encountered by Eaveston School District.

PREPARING FOR THE CHALLENGES OF THE JOURNEY

District and school leaders face many challenges with educational change. Fullan (2016) cautioned, "To be fair, stimulating, coordinating, and sustaining 'coherent' development across many schools is exceedingly difficult because it requires balancing top-down and bottom-up forces" (p. 182). This section describes the challenges Eaveston's leaders faced during their work of implementing the Cultural Proficiency Framework. Three themes emerged from the interview and observational data, which illuminated similar contexts within meetings and professional learning events in the district: (1) barriers to implementing equity-focused initiatives, (2) availability of time and resources, and (3) building site-specific capacity to implement and sustain the equity work across the district (Welborn, 2019). As you read through the challenges Eaveston's leaders faced, think about the degree to which these challenges may manifest for you and what you might do to balance the "top-down and bottom-up forces" in your organization that cause these challenges as you implement and sustain the quest toward building a culturally proficient district or school.

BARRIERS TO IMPLEMENTING EQUITY-FOCUSED INITIATIVES

Educational leaders and stakeholders in Eaveston School District acknowledged the barriers to becoming a culturally proficient organization. In Chapter 5 we outlined Eaveston's use of one tool, *Overcoming the Barriers to Cultural Proficiency*. The research findings revealed that Eaveston's Cultural Proficiency Committee, particularly district-level administration, identified, acknowledged, and took preliminary steps toward overcoming the barriers to implementing and sustaining equity-focused initiatives—namely, systems of oppression, a sense of privilege and entitlement, unawareness of the need to adapt, and resistance to change. Research participants specifically discussed two of these barriers they encountered—unawareness of the need to adapt and resistance to change. One committee member commented,

> Some people resent these events; the idea of going to do what we chose to do and continuing to go back to the idea would be something that people would find offensive, not very attractive or worthless. They

would be quick to dismiss it. So I'm thinking about those folks who come from a different opinion, a different way of looking at the world, and talking about these issues. I'm thinking, how can we come back to the idea of the basic tools of trying to understand each other better?

A principal added,

> I think in terms of our building, there's a group of teachers that support addressing differences. I think most teachers don't want to be in an awkward or uncomfortable situation and don't want to cause a divide. Everyone just wants to be status quo, and no one wants to bring something up. . . . It's kind of the same mentality in the workplace. No one wants to say something or call someone out or address something because you don't want to have that awkward interaction in the workplace.

A building-level leader spoke to the individual's unawareness of the need to adapt:

> I think, generally, our teachers have a real desire to help students and to connect with students. They want to be culturally proficient, but they're not necessarily sure where they're not. They don't know what they don't know, and that can be challenging because it can cause situations to escalate that probably don't need to escalate between teachers and students.

An inherent and anticipated barrier to a smooth implementation of the Cultural Proficiency Framework and its attendant reading and self-study was based in historical mistrust formed from a previous social justice training conducted in the district. Likewise, abundant historical, social, and racial segregation contexts intrinsic to Eaveston's metropolitan area were acknowledged as barriers to Eaveston's work using the Cultural Proficiency Framework. School district leaders, in planning for intentional work to reduce disparities and gaps across the district, recognized as important that this "work of Cultural Proficiency" could not be viewed as the latest, greatest initiative, nor could they afford for it to create harm and hurt for Eaveston's staff like the social justice training had done. By relying on the Guiding Principles of Cultural Proficiency and the district's core values, district leaders built foundational levels of trust among the Cultural Proficiency Committee members and honored all voices on the Cultural Proficiency Committee through reflection, dialogue, and action (Welborn, 2019).

Trust was built by using the culturally proficient learning strategies described in previous chapters, consistently scheduling and conducting meetings that provided opportunities for reflection and dialogue, and providing district-level administrative support in engaging a diverse group of stakeholders as learners. An inclusive learning environment fostered establishing and working toward the goal of continuous equity-related school improvement. "Trust is a product of vulnerability that grows over time and requires work, attention, and full engagement" (Brown, 2012, p. 53). The research participants who were interviewed discussed the limitations experienced in the previous social justice training, in contrast to the trust growing among the Cultural Proficiency Committee members.

> When I came into the district, there wasn't a whole lot being done in terms of Cultural Proficiency. In the first two years there was more of push toward social justice. That didn't go well in our particular building. I'm not sure that it was presented in a way that people expected or appreciated. I think people resented the principal because, in their opinion, it was being forced on them, although it was really a districtwide effort.

An administrator added,

> I attended a social justice training, an overnight experience with all the new administrators and many established administrators, and early on I was impressed. It was very intense and important conversation early on, which was sort of unique because I didn't really know anyone yet in the district. I spent some time really talking with a lot of people about some of my personal experiences, outlooks, and hopes for kids.

> I had a group of teachers, who had done some social justice training as well and hoped to implement some of that through professional development. We had some successes, and we had some challenges as we were trying to do a lot of intense work in short professional development periods. . . . Sometimes that was challenging because those who were not familiar with the work sometimes felt like we were just barely scratching the surface. Some of those people persisted in working with that cause, and some slipped away and supported students in other ways.

A district-level administrator noted the trust among members of the Cultural Proficiency Committee:

> I was very impressed with the training going on and what I observed, people's willingness to open up, share their experiences, and be willing to have some tough discussions. I think that the district is moving forward with having those tough discussions and finding ways to take that work and expand it, yet respecting that balance of also not pulling in, not forcing it on people, which then could actually deteriorate the work that's being done by people who are passionate about it. It's about building trust and finding that balance.

AVAILABILITY OF TIME AND RESOURCES

Eaveston School District leaders acknowledge that time and resources were part of the challenge of implementing the work of Cultural Proficiency. In one year district leaders increased the time and resources (e.g., supplies, media/book resources, consultants, partnerships) necessary to conduct professional development days. Funding for capital expenditures was increased for high-priority needs, specifically a budget line item for the Cultural Proficiency work to be conducted in the first year. An increase in funds for this work would help cover the substitute teachers, resources, and professional services necessary to create evidence-based professional learning opportunities for Eaveston's staff. Eaveston school leaders serving on the Cultural Proficiency Committee felt that having sufficient time and resources would lead to implementing this work in a way that would lead to the most impactful changes. A district-level administrator reflected,

> My role is to work collaboratively with various components that we have at the district level to find out what it is we can do to support this process, whether it is using funds for training the Cultural Proficiency Committee, purchasing resources to support learning, or increasing funding for additional professional learning opportunities.

During the time frame of the case study, the district committee utilized four, full-day professional learning experiences during each of the two years, which required approximately 30 substitute teachers in each session. The school site committees utilized grade-level time twice a month for professional learning and dialogue related to equity, access, inclusion, and student achievement (Welborn & Lindsey, 2020).

Although the challenges of the COVID-19 pandemic were not recorded due to the conclusion of the research study occurring prior to the pandemic, time and resources have become even more of a challenge now in implementing this work, with increased time needed for administrators and teachers to plan for safety measures and continued effective learning in virtual settings plus major cuts to professional development budgets. Time and resources are always a factor in guiding organizational change. Culturally proficient leaders are dedicated to overcoming equity challenges brought on by time and fiscal constraints, yet they strive to avoid presenting them as insurmountable barriers. Time and fiscal limitations are real-world considerations to be acknowledged within educational practice.

Eaveston's educators are clear that this work is challenging, and that it is a journey. With the right people in leadership positions, the priority will remain to utilize the existing time and resources to build capacity and embed Cultural Proficiency in all aspects of Eaveston School District. Leaders want to ensure that there is an understanding that this work is here to stay; Cultural Proficiency is not going to be a place in which the district arrives but the ongoing journey of educating Eaveston's youth (Welborn & Lindsey, 2020).

Reflection • Dialogue • ACTION

Use the space below to describe the time, resources, and money you can allocate for equity-focused professional learning. In what ways might you plan for using these funds?

_____

_____

_____

_____

_____

BUILDING SITE-SPECIFIC CAPACITY FOR IMPACT

Change initiatives require school leaders to be forward thinking in how implementation will move from district level to school level, to classroom level, to student learning outcomes. Another challenge of implementing and sustaining the work in applying the Tools of Cultural Proficiency in a systematic way is the ability to build site-specific capacity that affects students. Eaveston School District leaders discovered along the journey that it is one thing to implementing training sessions—for example, the Cultural Proficiency Committee engaged in learning together, new teachers were trained to apply the Tools of Cultural Proficiency, and even support staff had training. However, it is another thing to institutionalize this work at the building level and classroom level. How could the Cultural Proficiency Committee take their learning and have it affect student outcomes in the classroom?

Prominent researchers claim that building capacity among those in a system is vital in implementing change and sustaining the work for continuous improvement (Lambert, 1998; Reeves, 2009; Stringer, 2013). Absence of proactive thinking about how you will build site-specific capacity for professional learning on the application and use of the Cultural Proficiency Framework at the school level or classroom level runs the risk of precluding sustainability. Eaveston School District's leaders realized early in their journey the need to plan for building site-specific capacity, starting with the principals.

We, as professional learning trainers, have witnessed pertinent attempts in the initial implementation of the work of Cultural Proficiency. Building the capacity of leaders at the district level and school level is vital in sustaining the work for a long period of time during which you can realize the attainment of the goals of increasing student success and closing learning gaps. Planned change using the Cultural Proficiency Framework is not any different. The real question is about impact. Scollay and Everson (1985) wrote, "There are some basic realities of planned change efforts operating in real world settings which mediate against establishing a direct cause and effect link between school development efforts and student learning even under the best of circumstances" (p. 202).

We do not want to discourage the journey of implementing the work of Cultural Proficiency; rather, we want you to proceed, taking into consideration the duration of this journey. Scollay and Everson (1985) created a graphic that outlined the tracing pattern of intended impact of a typical development program for building-level school personnel. With permission, we adapted the original graphic to apply to planned change using the Cultural Proficiency Framework. Understanding Figure 9.1 as you plan for change in your district will lead you on the highway of equity in relation to building site-specific capacity among your administrators, teachers, and staff. The ultimate goal of implementing and sustaining the Cultural Proficiency Framework is to improve student achievement and well-being by reducing inequities and closing educational gaps. The operational goal of the work is to change the on-site behavior of individuals in the school district and the policies, practices, procedures, and programs that perpetuate inequitable outcomes for students.

As you build capacity from the district level to the building level, it is important that you take the time to process the realities of how the Tools of Cultural Proficiency work in this model of planned change and affect dispersion. The Barriers to Cultural Proficiency will function as detours and blockades on your journey to positive change. You and your team will need to rely on the Guiding Principles to overcome those Barriers. The Continuum will help you visualize the impact realities during each level of change, and the Essential Elements of Cultural Proficiency will guide you to actions for change at each level. Action is required on multiple levels using the Essential Elements to reach both the ultimate and the operational goals of the work.

FIGURE 9.1 ● Dispersion Pattern of the Potential Impact of The Cultural Proficiency Framework

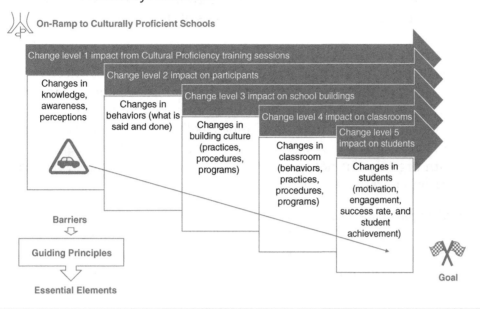

Source: Adapted from Scollay, Susan J. & Everson, Susan Toft. (1985). Measuring school improvement: A few experientially based words of caution. *Urban Review, 17*(3), 201–209.

Figure 9.1 presents the dispersion pattern of the potential impact of training-based development, which is important for you to consider as you embark on this implementation journey of Cultural Proficiency. Scollay and Everson (1985) wrote that the very best leadership teams and plans of action for change "cannot assume that all which is presented is understood, accepted, and internalized" (p. 204). Culturally proficient leaders also recognize "that the environment of development activities is rarely the same as that of the daily context of the school" (p. 204).

> And most basically, because the content and practice of school development are several levels of change and several spheres of activity away from the target of concern, their impact—both potential and real—is weakened through dispersion before having a chance to reach that target. (p. 204)

As you continue to process Figure 9.1, we ask you to keep in mind these realities from Scollay and Everson's (1985) work:

1. Even under optimal circumstances, significantly less than 100% of the content of a staff development program is understood, incorporated, and used by program participants.

2. At any given time, a professional development program is only one of a myriad of factors influencing the knowledge, perceptions, beliefs, behaviors, and daily lives of its participants.

3. Any content transferred from the program to the participants is only one of a myriad of factors determining what happens in the individual buildings and classrooms of those participants. (p. 204)

The participants in the Eaveston study discussed the challenge of balancing the urgency of spreading the equity work beyond the district's Cultural Proficiency Committee and throughout the district. We know many school decisions are made at the site level, which means that different organizational cultures, people, practices, values, beliefs, and behaviors exist. The district's progress is challenged by having to implement professional learning with urgency but not in a way that causes an increase in resistance, protest, and unrest within the larger school system and its community.

Interview participants from the research study held views that a "top-down" or a "one-size-fits-all" decision on the logistics of implementation would lead to no progress, and maybe even destruction of the progress gained over the past two years. A principal commented,

We have a committee of several teachers at our school that have stepped up to help us with implementing Cultural Proficiency. I think, ultimately, when I was in the teacher's seat and you have administrators talking at you, that's much different than when your colleagues are talking to you. . . . I just think it's going to be so much more meaningful coming from their colleagues and not from administrators. Oftentimes, teachers just assume that we "have to do this" because it is coming out of the district office.

Since the conclusion of the research study, Eaveston School District leaders are planning for training all school principals using the Cultural Proficiency Framework and discussing the next steps in building capacity for each site in the district. Future plans include creating school-site Cultural Proficiency plans of action, using the Framework for curriculum writing, increasing

---

REFLECTION • Dialogue • Action

How might you build site-based capacity for implementing and sustaining the work of Cultural Proficiency? Record your thoughts.

_____

_____

_____

_____

_____

collaboration of professional learning communities in each building, and aligning the district and school improvement goals to culturally proficient, equity-related goals. Overall, the impact for students depends on school leaders' ability to build this capacity and account for the dispersion patterns of the impact in the system. In the chapter that follows are Eaveston leaders' recommendations for systemically implementing and sustaining the Cultural Proficiency Framework.

LOOKING IN THE REARVIEW MIRROR

It is essential that school leaders plan for engaging all stakeholders in this journey, including families and the community, in various professional learning community opportunities for continuous school improvement, which encompasses the mindsets and well-being of both students and adults in the school system. This chapter included three challenges that Eaveston School District leaders faced as they implemented the Cultural Proficiency Framework: (1) barriers to Cultural Proficiency, (2) availability of time and resources, and (3) building site-specific capacity for impact.

ON TO OUR NEXT DESTINATION

Chapter 10 focuses on the lessons learned as Eaveston School District leaders implemented and began sustaining the work of Cultural Proficiency over time. These lessons learned are presented as recommendations for you as you plan for implementing and sustaining this work in your district or school. These lessons focus on the tenets of diverse family and community engagement, professional learning communities, and continuous school improvement, turned into opportunities for continuous growth and improvement in the mindsets of Eaveston's educators, as well as the increased equity and access identified in student outcomes.

REFLECTION, DIALOGUE, AND ACTION PROCESS

REFLECTION • Dialogue • Action

1. As you consider the challenges listed in this chapter,
   - barriers to Cultural Proficiency,
   - availability of time and resources, and
   - building site-specific capacity for impact,

   what work do you need to do as a school leader before implementing this work of Cultural Proficiency in your organization?

2. How have you experienced the realities of professional development or training in light of the dispersion patterns presented in this chapter?

Reflection • DIALOGUE • Action

1. Gather your team together, and discuss the realities of the three challenges presented in this chapter. How might your team overcome these obstacles?

2. Discuss with your colleagues the implications of Figure 9.1, Dispersion Pattern of the Potential Impact of the Cultural Proficiency Framework. How might you use this figure to help in your planning efforts for implementation and sustainability?

Reflection • Dialogue • ACTION

Create a preliminary plan for action considering your team, professional learning structures, budget, resources, calendar, culture of collaboration, and leaders.

_____

_____

_____

_____

_____

Travel Log

_____

_____

_____

_____

_____

_____

_____

_____

_____

_____

_____

_____

_____

_____

_____

_____

_____

_____

_____

_____

_____

_____

_____

_____

_____

_____

_____

_____

_____

TRAVEL GUIDE
Lessons Learned and Recommendations for School Leaders

Create Your Map

- Determine how all action plans emerge from and are informed by the Tools for Cultural Proficiency.
- Monitor the implementation of the throughout the organization.
- Determine how each stakeholder group is experiencing the implementation.

Resources

- The relationships forged through communication with all stakeholders
- Allocation of money and time to build capacity
- Building an understanding of the Tools of Cultural Proficiency

Mileage

- Data that emerge from the action plan
- Data on the effectiveness of leadership
- Disaggregated data on student achievement
- Data on stakeholder engagement
- Data gathered based on the Guiding Principles and the Essential Elements Monitoring how the work is moving through the organization

Check the Weather

- How have you ensured the participation of every stakeholder group?
- How are you representing the Essential Elements in this work?
- In what ways are policies, procedures, and practices helpful, or not, in sustaining this work?
- Which issues are technical, and which are going to require creating new values and beliefs?

Travel Phrases

- Sustainability
- Action planning
- Critical mass
- Continuous improvement
- Professional learning communities
- Adaptive leadership

You're the Driver

- What opportunities are there to improve relationships in this endeavor?
- How are you as the leader demonstrating the Guiding Principles?
- How are you and the people seeing themselves differently in this work?

CHAPTER 10

Lessons Learned and Recommendations for School Leaders

CALIBRATION

I think we first have to start with individuals. Each person, each one of us has a responsibility to learn as much as we can about the truth of who we are and be willing to speak that truth loudly and often. If we relegate ourselves to simply repeating the same narratives we have honed over the years, no progress can be possible.

—Terrence Roberts (2018)

ON-RAMP TO RECOMMENDATIONS FOR SCHOOL LEADERS

As you apply the Tools of Cultural Proficiency, embedding the Cultural Proficiency Framework in all aspects of your district or building, we encourage you to take some time to prepare for the journey ahead. Reflect on the words of Dr. Terrence Roberts above as you prepare to lead this journey in your district or school. What narratives have been honed over the years about your district or school? This journey will be difficult at times, but transformational and adaptive leadership, coupled with reliance on your district's vision, mission, and core values, will lead you on a path to implementing culturally proficient educational policies and practices, rooted in value for diversity and equity for all of your students. Progress will be made. In the case of Eaveston School District, school leaders learned three lessons in the early implementation phases of their journey. These lessons learned turned into opportunities to strengthen their leadership for continuous growth and improvement toward equity, inclusion, and access for all.

The intentionality of embracing value for diversity in a district's organizational change for equity-based policies and practices supports diverse perspectives for decision-making purposes. Consequently, the willingness and ability to engage in dialogue to acknowledge and overcome the barriers to culturally proficient educational policies, practices, and behaviors increase. School leaders focused on embedding equity work in all aspects of policy and practice can create systems in the district that build the capacity for continuous school improvement through a collaborative culture focused on student achievement (Lezotte & Snyder, 2011).

As D. B. Lindsey, Jungwirth, Pahl, and Lindsey (2009) described, culturally proficient learning communities provide for a deep sense of commitment and provide avenues of clarity and intentionality for acknowledging and overcoming the barriers and challenges throughout the school system. Clark-Louque, Lindsey, Quezada, and Jew (2019) discussed a framework for family, school, and community engagement: "Inclusive school leaders foster a partnering culture in which families, schools, and communities cultivate an environment that supports adults engaged in effective relationship building, goal achievement, and equitable collaboration in support of students" (p. 21).

The following sections include three recommendations derived from the study of Eaveston School District's journey toward becoming a culturally proficient school district. The case study of their implementation of the Tools of Cultural Proficiency for transformational change resulted in three emergent themes for school leaders to focus on as they embed this work in all aspects of this district (Welborn, 2019):

1. Diverse family and community engagement

2. Professional learning communities

3. Continuous school improvement

We present these emergent themes as recommendations for you as you lead this journey of implementing the Cultural Proficiency Framework for increasing equitable policies and practices in your district or school.

DIVERSE FAMILY AND COMMUNITY ENGAGEMENT

Recommendation 1: Build the capacity of all stakeholders in the district community by inviting diverse family and community perspectives to help identify barriers, focus on core values, create goals and action plans for changing inequitable policies, practices, and behaviors.

Eaveston's school leaders rely on the predominant role that relationships between the school, families, and the community play in efforts to maximize school effectiveness. We recommend that you begin to think of yourself as a change agent to build the capacity of all stakeholders in the district to implement and sustain the work of Cultural Proficiency. As educational leaders consider systemic, transformative organizational change to improve outcomes and create effective schools (Lezotte & Synder, 2011; Sergiovanni, 1989), increase equity, and serve all, they must keep constant vigilance of self in their role as change agents (Gay, 2000; G. Howard, 2006; Nelson & Guerra, 2014). Change agents focused on equity and access make intentional decisions to reform policies and practices that negatively affect families, students, and community members, especially those from historically underserved backgrounds (R. B. Lindsey et al., 2019). However, they never enter the space of decision-making alone.

Think about the Guiding Principle of Cultural Proficiency "The family, as defined by each culture, is the primary system of support in the education of children." Just as this Guiding Principle accentuates the importance of the family structure and the school's responsibility in a child's development, your ability to engage the community and build partnerships plays an important role in socializing youth and ensuring students' success (Epstein & Associates, 2019). The work of Epstein and Associates (2019) leads us to think about the types of partnerships we have with our families and parents. These include communicating, volunteering, learning at home, decision-making, and collaborating with the community.

> Because the importance of these multiple influences is well documented, schools need to attend to school, family, and community contexts and develop programs and practices that enable parents and community partners to help students reach school goals for high achievement and other measures of school success. (p. 43)

R. B. Lindsey et al. (2019) claimed the foundation of Cultural Proficiency is that families and the community are the heart of the school. Often, educators think of parents and families as something that must be invited into the school. What would it take for us to build the capacity of our families and community to do this work together? The Guiding Principles of Cultural Proficiency really do surface our assumptions and shape our beliefs and values, which ultimately lead to our behaviors. Therefore, we must be intentional in equity-focused work.

Culturally proficient school leaders, who promote the success of students, identify school-community partnerships as essential in supporting additional human, material, and financial resources for the school. For example, The Eaveston Community Action Team is a partnership between Eaveston School District and local charities, governmental agencies, religious organizations, businesses, and community members. This partnership provides opportunities for Eaveston to address the diverse life challenges of students and their families by working together to find and implement solutions (Welborn, 2019). Other partnerships with families and the community are intended to nurture students' social, emotional, physical, and intellectual development, including connections between schools and community individuals, organizations, and businesses (Epstein & Associates, 2019). Culturally proficient leaders collaborate in building a strong foundation of school-community partnerships and utilize their resources to provide appropriate education for all students (Welborn, 2019).

Reflection and dialogue are key components of equity work, especially as it relates to removing barriers and changing policies, practices, and behaviors. Clark-Louque et al. (2019) found that "opportunity/access and achievement gaps are challenges that must bring educators, parents, families, and community members together in committed partnerships" (p. 50). Examining the gaps present in student demographic data and engaging in reflection and dialogue practices with administration, staff, families, and the community are essential to changing hearts and minds in ways that embrace the community being served.

Eaveston's leaders led change processes through the use of the communication techniques of reflection and dialogue to embrace the Tools of Cultural Proficiency. Family and community members, representing the diversity of students in the district, partnered in conversation from the very beginning of the Cultural Proficiency Committee. Members of the district's Cultural Proficiency Committee utilized the committee to address areas of needed improvement in the district that were the most urgent. Involving families and community members in these discussions was key to the success of the committee.

An example of utilizing community resources is bringing experts to facilitate conversations about restorative practices and strategies for managing students facing trauma. These are two ways the district is progressing toward making gains in one of the goals related to discipline disparities. A middle school assistant principal who participated in the Cultural Proficiency professional learning, shared this learning as a reflection on his practice:

> We have identified that our Black students, particularly our Black boys, are being disciplined at a greater number than any other race and gender. I take a lot of pride in our staff for learning how to change with our students. Just the other day we had a situation where lots of things were going wrong with student behavior and discipline. All of a sudden, I had four students in my office. Each one of the four sat down with the teacher(s) and talked with them; it was a one-on-one conversation using restorative practices, where there was respect coming from both parties. What could have turned into teachers writing four referrals, turned into repairing relationships and everyone walking away happy and ready to start again the next day in class.

Educational leaders ensure value for diversity by inviting community members into the school who represent the diversity of the community's population based on race/ethnicity, age, sexual orientation, social class, language(s), and ability. "Valuing families' diverse backgrounds, respecting their cultural capital, and acknowledging their funds of knowledge when initiating policies and programs increases positive structure, systemic, and sustainable change" (Clark-Louque et al., 2019, p. 56). Our recommendation to you is to develop the capacity of stakeholders in the district community to identify and overcome barriers and to create goals and action plans for identifying and changing extant inequitable policies, practices, and behaviors.

PROFESSIONAL LEARNING COMMUNITIES

Recommendation 2: Develop a common language around the Cultural Proficiency Framework to intentionally embed the work of reflection, dialogue, and change and to promote access and equity for all students through various professional learning communities.

Eaveston's educational leaders focused on increasing equity, inclusion, and access for its students in the district by providing collaboration opportunities through professional learning communities. DuFour et al. (2016) cited the importance of professional learning communities that focus on a collaborative culture and a sense of collective responsibility in schools. The purpose of building professional learning communities around the work of Cultural Proficiency in Eaveston was to develop a common language in the district while embedding the Cultural Proficiency Framework into the daily process of educating Eaveston students.

Professional learning communities, groups of teachers, staff, and administrators, are typically organized by grade level or content area and meet regularly to collectively analyze student learning evidence to inform common efforts toward continuous school improvement (DuFour et al., 2016). The three big ideas that drive the work of a professional learning community are:

1. a focus on learning,
2. a collaborative culture and collective responsibility, and
3. a results orientation.

As you think about building professional learning communities around the work of Cultural Proficiency, these three big ideas run parallel with the Essential Elements of Cultural Proficiency. Table 10.1 displays this parallel.

TABLE 10.1 ● Professional Learning Communities' Big Ideas and Essential Elements

Focus on learning	*Assess culture:*
	As a team, analyze the depth of knowledge you share about the cultures of the district, school, educators, students, and their families, including the impact each culture has on the members of each group.
	Value diversity:
	Create opportunities for the team to learn from others who are culturally different from them.
	Institutionalize cultural knowledge:
	Commit to lifelong learning about culture and the role it plays in educating your students.
Collaborative culture and collective responsibility	*Value diversity:*
	Include diverse perspectives when analyzing data that will be used for informed decision-making.
	Manage the dynamics of difference:
	Develop an appreciation for the diversity in the group.
	Develop trust among group members by responding in a culturally competent way to issues that arise.
Results orientation	*Adapt to diversity:*
	Adopt new policies and practices that support equity, access, and inclusion.
	Change behaviors that are culturally destructive, incapacitating, or blind.
	Institutionalize cultural knowledge: Use levers to drive changes into the systems at the district, building, and classroom levels.

Eaveston's school leaders recognized the role professional learning communities would play in adapting to diversity and institutionalizing cultural knowledge, focused on making changes that result in greater involvement of the diverse communities served by the school or district. A team of educators, inclusive of administrators, teachers, counselors, and staff, participated with family and community members in professional learning communities to engage in reflection and dialogue strategies to explore and share learning about their own behaviors and practices that may be perpetuating unintended outcomes. Intentional use of reflective strategies provided opportunity for each participant to explore and share insights on their values and behaviors with regard to cultural groups different from their own.

An important component of reflective learning strategies was planning sufficient time for participants to share insights. Sharing of different experiences and beliefs contributed to an enhanced willingness and ability to share, learn about, and appreciate cultural differences. Eaveston's Cultural Proficiency Committee members used the camaraderie that evolved from sharing of reflections in a way that prepared them to engage in dialogue for the purpose of laying plans for inclusive policies and practices necessary for the district to become an inclusive, culturally proficient school district. The focus on transforming policies, practices, and procedures related to those unintended outcomes, such as disparities in discipline and discrepancies or gaps in achievement among racial or socioeconomic groups, allowed the actualization of continuous school improvement to become a reality (Welborn, 2019).

Findings from the case study of Eaveston's implementation of the Cultural Proficiency Framework included a description of the many opportunities for staff members to collaborate and share knowledge and skills about relevant topics, such as restorative practices, trauma-informed care, social-emotional learning, personalized learning, and Cultural Proficiency. Eaveston's leaders expressly delegated autonomy in the ways the Cultural Proficiency Framework would be applied across buildings, departments, and grade levels.

Some trainings were required. For example, Eaveston's newly hired teachers and staff engaged in reflection and dialogue in a two-day introductory session related to the Tools of Cultural Proficiency. Throughout the year, the district offered training sessions in which they attempted to build capacity to use the Framework through introductory sessions for those who had not been able to participate in the district's Cultural Proficiency Committee or in buildings where it was being implemented. One middle school teacher reflected on her professional learning at Eaveston:

> We engage in professional development about students of trauma, understanding Cultural Proficiency, and how that affects your discipline and how it affects how you communicate with students. We have professional development on making sure that what's present in our literature and books is reflective of a variety of cultures. We get Cultural Proficiency training from a lot of different angles. We have speakers and small groups. We have someone come in and talk to us about it, and we have tried to have staff members talk to staff members about it. We have had it districtwide and buildingwide. We have it every year, and multiple times it is offered.

Additionally, district administrators realized the importance of being involved in the district-level professional learning events and utilizing the Tools in their discussions with the Board of Education, families, and community members (Welborn, 2019). A district administrator commented,

> I feel like it is very important for me to be as involved as I can in learning and growing and developing myself because if I can't talk the talk and understand it, then how can I support it? So, I've always valued the fact that it's important that I'm there with them learning, especially on topics that I'm not proficient in myself. When we are talking about setting up the next day of the Cultural Proficiency work, I said, "Hey, I'd really like to make sure this is a day that I can be there all day," because I really want to hear the conversations and be part of that. It helps me understand what I can do to support the principal and the teachers that are ultimately going to support the learners.

Margaret Wheatley (2002) encouraged educators to develop "more harmonious and satisfying relationships" in their school organizations and personal lives by stepping out of the known and certain and relying on one another to increase their learning. When we consider the moral purpose of education and the fundamental ideas of student achievement, building relationships with others in professional learning communities deepens the commitment to planned or intentional change in policies, practices, and behaviors. The Cultural Proficiency Framework is an inside-out approach that can provide opportunities for reflection and dialogue to help educators learn about their own assumptions of self, others, and the organization. Using this approach with an action-based mindset for change, educators are guided to increase their cultural knowledge in professional learning communities and adapt to diversity by changing their personal values and behaviors and the organization's policies and practices in a way that maximizes student learning and deepens the commitment to continuous improvement through equity, access, and inclusion (D. B. Lindsey et al., 2009).

CONTINUOUS SCHOOL IMPROVEMENT

Recommendation 3: Align the district's strategic plan, professional learning, and policy review with the mission and core values of the district. Embed Cultural Proficiency in every aspect of the district while focusing on continuous school improvement toward student achievement.

Continuous improvement is taken very seriously by leaders in Eaveston School District. It is central to how school administrators lead the district toward high levels of school success that considers both academics and the social-emotional development of students. Fundamental to their continuous school improvement plan, otherwise known as the district's strategic plan, is the focus on *diversity, knowledge, commitment, care, learning, freedom,* and *success,* the overtly expressed core values of Eaveston School District. More important, the goals of the strategic plan include accountability measures for continuous improvement through the mission and vision, "That all students will learn at high levels."

Eaveston's school leaders have been involved in the work of Cultural Proficiency since the first conversation. The Assistant Superintendent of Curriculum and Instruction, serving as the Superintendent of Schools at the time of this book's publication, initiated the work in the district; however, this work is led by an Executive Director of Education. In the second year of the work, the Superintendent's cabinet members realized the importance of being more involved in the work. The district-level Cultural Proficiency Committee began to schedule all meetings around the Superintendent and the Assistant Superintendent's schedules to ensure they are present and more involved in the work.

As the work continued, conversations were pursued about the ways in which the work of the district-level Cultural Proficiency Committee would be institutionalized in the buildings. During the second year of work the leaders of the Cultural Proficiency Committee led the group through future event planning by dividing the group per school building in the district. One of the pitfalls in this initial design was that some buildings had no administration representation on the committee; therefore, they often felt a lack of support for the events they had planned for their buildings. They learned about the important role principals would play in leading the work in individual schools.

LOOKING IN THE REARVIEW MIRROR

This chapter presented three recommendations derived from the research study of Eaveston School District's implementation of the Cultural Proficiency Framework and its attendant tools. These recommendations were a focus on diverse family and community engagement, professional learning communities, and continuous school improvement. It is essential that school leaders plan for engaging all stakeholders in this journey, including families and the community, in various professional learning community opportunities for continuous school improvement.

ON TO OUR NEXT DESTINATION

Your next stop on the journey narrows the focus on the commitment to transformational equity action planning. In this chapter you will gain an understanding of the commitment necessary for sustained organizational change at the district level and school level. You will explore strategic planning, a plan for how to implement and sustain this work over time, and you will use an equity action template as you learn and apply the Tools of Cultural Proficiency.

REFLECTION, DIALOGUE, AND ACTION PROCESS

REFLECTION • Dialogue • Action

As you consider the recommendations drawn from the conclusions of the research findings in Eaveston School District, what might be your next steps as a school leader for launching the Cultural Proficiency Framework in your organization? How will you adapt the Eaveston plan to work in your own organization?

Reflection • **DIALOGUE** • Action

With your leadership team discuss the professional learning community's big ideas and Essential Elements of Cultural Proficiency as recommended in Table 10.1. Record your preliminary thinking around these recommended actions.

Reflection • Dialogue • ACTION

Build the capacity of all stakeholders in the district community by inviting family and community members, representing diverse experiences and perspectives, to help identify barriers, focus on core values, and create goals and action plans for changing inequitable policies, practices, and behaviors.

_____

_____

_____

_____

_____

Travel Log

_____

_____

_____

_____

_____

_____

_____

_____

_____

_____

_____

_____

_____

_____

_____

_____

_____

_____

_____

_____

_____

_____

_____

_____

_____

_____

_____

_____

_____

TRAVEL GUIDE
The Essential Elements

Create Your Map

- Establish a strategic plan for this work.
- Implement and sustain the work of Cultural Proficiency.
- Assess and regularly communicate progress.
- Monitor the allocation of resources and success of the work.
- Determine the level of commitment to this work.

Resources

- An understanding of the Tools of Cultural Proficiency and how they can be applied to your own organization
- The firm belief that people are doing the best job they can in the systems they are in
- The collective history of the organization and those who remember it
- Time, people, money to support the planning and implementation

Mileage

- Data needed to establish a strategic plan
- Data on the readiness of people to adapt to this initiative
- Systems to monitor progress on the initiative, on leadership, and on how people are adapting to the new changes
- Data on the readiness of the organization to take on this work

Check the Weather

- What is the history of strategic planning in your organization?
- What policies, practices, and procedures currently support Cultural Proficiency principles?
- Which leaders are already implementing Cultural Proficiency principles?
- What do you need to stop doing?

Travel Phrases

- Strategic plan
- Cultural Proficiency Framework
- Allocation of assets
- Collaborative structures
- Tipping point

You're the Driver

- In what ways are you using this initiative to deepen the relationships in your organization?
- How will you include all the adults in your Community in implementing Cultural Proficiency in their lives and work?
- How will you support those who long for the old way of doing things?

CHAPTER 11

Implementation and Sustainability: Commitment to Action Planning

CALIBRATION

We all carry worlds in our heads, and those worlds are decidedly different. We educators set out to teach, but how can we reach the worlds of others when we don't even know they exist? Indeed, many of us don't even realize that our own worlds exist only in our heads and in the cultural institutions we have built to support them.

What are we really doing to better educate poor children and children of color?

What should we be doing? The answers, I believe, lie not in a proliferation of new reform programs but in some basic understandings of who we are and how we are connected and disconnected from one another.

—Lisa Delpit (2006, p. XXV)

School leaders recognize that commitment toward continuous improvement is key in transforming systems to serve all students—especially students of color and those from lower social class backgrounds, who have been historically underserved. We pose questions to guide your thinking for becoming a leader who uses the Cultural Proficiency Framework both as your personal leadership guide for honing inclusive values and behaviors as well as a system's guide for ensuring inclusive policies and practices in your school or district. Take a few moments to mull over the questions in the paragraphs that follow, then use the space provided below to record your thinking. These initial thoughts may well inform the development of your equity action plan.

What will it take for you to successfully implement and sustain the work of Cultural Proficiency to transform your system in a way that all students are served in an equitable fashion?

Your responses will guide your commitment to learning, collaboration, action planning, and measuring progress to ensure equity. The time is now; ensuring equitable outcomes for all students is essential. As you prepare to lead your district or school toward equity for all, we invite you to reflect on what you have learned from reading this book:

- In what ways have you identified what you want to accomplish and why it is important to you, other stakeholders, and emerges from the vision/mission of your school?

- In what ways do your current policies, procedures, and practices help or hinder you in this work?

- In what ways do the assets of time, money, human capital, and the capacity of your organization to do this work need to change?

- In what ways will you assess not only progress toward equity but also the effectiveness and perceptions of your leaders?

- In what ways do you plan to align your strategic action plan to the vision, mission, and core values of your organization?

- What collaboration structures will you use to build and implement for this work at district and building levels?

- To what extent are the leaders in your district or school prepared?

- Do leaders at site levels and district levels know their roles in this work?

- To what degree will there be resistance to change?

- How will you support those who benefit and still want the previous practices?

- What time and resources are available for this work?

- What work might you need to do internally to lead the implementation of the Cultural Proficiency Framework as a culturally proficient leader?

- How will you build the critical mass in your district or school to ensure equity for students of color and/or lower social class?

Use the space below to record your thinking.

_____

_____

_____

ON-RAMP TO A COMMITMENT TO LEARNING, PLANNING, AND ENSURING EQUITY

This chapter focuses on the commitment to action embodied as the moral imperative of providing equitable access and outcome opportunities for all students. In this chapter you will review the leadership actions of the Eaveston leadership team and how the leadership at your school can examine and influence the culture of the school to engage in this work.

The case narrative in this chapter serves to illustrate the process for forging collaborations within the school community as well as with the community served by the school or district. Building relationships is needed for having the critical mass necessary to implement and sustain the work at systemic levels, whether school or district. You will deepen your understanding of the components of successful engagement and the implementation processes necessary when creating a leadership action plan for personal growth and improvement, as well as for organizational change.

Developing your leadership action plan is guided by the use of the Tools of Cultural Proficiency, with particular focus on the use of the Essential Elements of Cultural Proficiency. In the chapter that follows, we invite you to learn from our Eaveston colleagues and to use their story as encouragement as you embark on your journey and build the critical mass in your system. New destinations await!

COMMITMENT TO LEARNING AND ACTION PLANNING

A commitment to personal and systems learning and planning is key to providing for successful social and academic outcomes for students. When considering the leadership responsibilities in implementing and sustaining the work of Cultural Proficiency, we lead by modeling a commitment to learning from others, learning about others, and learning and planning together. This multipart strategy for transformational change in your organization involves strategic planning for how you will initiate, implement, and sustain professional learning using the tools embedded in the Cultural Proficiency Framework. Building and deepening relationship are foundational to this work.

A strategic plan will guide the implementation and sustainability of the equity-focused work of Cultural Proficiency, while the transformational action plan will guide the evaluation of progress toward equity-related goals and student outcomes. The following section includes details and graphics to guide you on your journey of Cultural Proficiency. Your journey will lead to the development of a long-term strategic plan for guiding systemic efforts of action planning in your school organization.

STRATEGIC PLANNING FOR IMPLEMENTATION AND SUSTAINABILITY

The importance of strategic planning cannot be understated. Strategic planning must not be random or haphazard. The process used by Eaveston is comprehensive and is recommended for your consideration in that it helps school organizations develop a plan that connects the needs of the organization, fully informed by students' social and academic strengths and needs, and is accompanied by a description of the resources needed. Strategic plans are important in that they establish priorities. The strategic plan format used serves as a big picture for implementing, evaluating, and sustaining the use of the Cultural Proficiency Framework in your district or school as a means for addressing equity, access, and inclusion issues for the next three to five years.

Figure 11.1 displays a sample three- to five-year strategic plan for implementing, evaluating, and sustaining the Cultural Proficiency Framework in the district. In your district or school most likely you would modify this strategic plan to suit your school organization's needs, continuous school improvement goals, and available resources. In this model year 1 focuses on implementation and evaluation at the district level and suggests a deliverable outcome of an equity action plan. In year 2 the focus is on implementation and evaluation at the building level, with continuation of planning at the district level and a focus on emergent themes for systemic transformative leverage points such as curriculum, instruction, classroom management/discipline, hiring practices, and so on. In years 3–5 the focus is on sustainment and evaluation of progress on the goals defined in the action plan.

Table 11.1 displays the goals and strategies for implementing, evaluating, and sustaining the Cultural Proficiency Framework. The constant vision of Eaveston's Superintendent of Schools was to embed the Cultural Proficiency Framework into all aspects of the district's operation. The Cultural Proficiency Committee realized that setting goals and monitoring the effectiveness of the strategies were essential but, more important, the strategies are and must be integral to the district's comprehensive school improvement plan. Table 11.1 also includes the five broad goals of Cultural Proficiency professional learning sessions, thus applying the Essential Elements of Cultural Proficiency to leverage points for designing, implementing, and sustaining change:

1. Student learning outcomes
2. Professional learning for all school members

FIGURE 11.1 ● Three- to Five-Year Strategic Plan

Implementing, Evaluating, and Sustaining the Work of Cultural Proficiency
School District Level

Implementation Evaluation Year 1	Implementation Evaluation Year 2	Sustainability Evaluation Years 3–5
Strategies 1. Form and train a district leadership team. 2. Train all building-and district-level leaders. 3. Offer "Introduction to Cultural Proficiency" training to others (i.e., interested teachers, support staff, counselors, etc.).	**Strategies** 1. Continue to train the district leadership team. 2. Evaluate progress toward equity goals. 3. Form and train building-level leadership teams. 4. Offer "Introduction to Cultural Proficiency" training to others (i.e., interested teachers, support staff, counselors, etc.).	**Strategies** 1. Monitor district-level transformational action plan, and revise as necessary. 2. Train district-and building-level committees to use Culturally Proficient Coaching. 3. Evaluate progress toward equity goals. 4. Implement PLC focus plans in buildings (by department or grade level).
Deliverables 1. A developed capacity of leaders to increase equity, access, and inclusion for your students 2. Data (practices, policies, and behaviors) collection from the Continuum 3. Emergent themes (areas of inequity) 4. Transformational action plan	**Deliverables** 1. A developed capacity of leaders to increase equity, access, and inclusion for your students 2. Transformational action plan for 3–5 years 3. Subcommittees developed for implementing and evaluating progress toward equity goals	**Deliverables** 1. A developed capacity of leaders to increase equity, access, and inclusion for your students 2. Actualized progress toward goals 3. Plan for implementation years 6–10

Expected Outcomes for School Implementation Teams

View Cultural Proficiency as a shared journey for educating the youth in our schools
Experience Cultural Proficiency as personal and professional work
Use the Cultural Proficiency Framework as a guide in addressing equity and access gap issues
Use the Tools of Cultural Proficiency to build professional capital for changing conversations
Increase equity, access, and inclusion for all students in our schools

Note: PLC, professional learning community.

TABLE 11.1 ● Goals and Strategies: Implementing, Evaluating, and Sustaining the Cultural Proficiency Framework

GOAL 1	GOAL 2	GOAL 3	GOAL 4	GOAL 5
Learning	Professional development	Continuous school improvement and data-based decisions	Family and community engagement	Equity, access, and inclusion
View Cultural Proficiency as a shared journey for educating the youth in our schools	Experience Cultural Proficiency as personal and professional work	Use the Cultural Proficiency Framework as a guide in addressing equity and access gap issues	Use the Tools of Cultural Proficiency to build professional capital for changing conversations	Increase equity, access, and inclusion for *all* students in our schools
Key performance measures will be established for all goals and strategies to monitor and report progress				
Strategies aligned to Goal 1	Strategies aligned to Goal 2	Strategies aligned to Goal 3	Strategies aligned to Goal 4	Strategies aligned to Goal 5

3. Continuous school improvement and data-based decisions

4. Family and community engagement

5. Equity, access, and inclusion

In some ways strategic planning using Cultural Proficiency works much like a comprehensive school improvement plan. In Eaveston the Superintendent made plans for principals to become more involved in learning the power of the Cultural Proficiency Framework, with its attendant tools, to help align an equity-focused process to the existing school improvement planning process. At the time of publication of this book, all building principals and assistant principals were receiving training in the application of the Tools of Cultural Proficiency so they could lead the work in their buildings by setting goals to help increase equitable outcomes for all students.

A word of caution! It cannot be overemphasized how imperative it is for you to consider your plan for professional learning opportunities, tailored to the needs of district administration, school building leadership teams, teachers, and support staff. As you plan, think about who will be trained first. How will training be rolled out to administrators, teachers, and support staff?

Culturally proficient educational leaders, committed to building knowledge around the diversity of their students, rely on the Guiding Principles of Cultural Proficiency to inform district core values fundamental to promoting equitable and inclusive practices and policies (R. B. Lindsey et al., 2019). As Eaveston's educators lead efforts to examine current policies and practices through professional learning communities, the Guiding Principles aid in the actualization of the deep work necessary to promote changes to policies and practices to make them increasingly accessible and inclusionary, leading to equitable educational outcomes. A vision to embed the work of Cultural Proficiency in all aspects of the district will help align the comprehensive school improvement plan goals with the goals informed through the use of the Cultural Proficiency Framework. It is important to remember that this level of strategic planning, including the development of goals, is required for implementing the Cultural Proficiency Framework in a manner that fosters inclusive and equitable policies. In the next section we provide a template for transformational action planning.

TRANSFORMATIONAL ACTION PLANNING

Transformational leadership focuses on leading an organization to maximize effectiveness related to achieving an organizational vision. In Eaveston School District that vision was captured in the phrase "That *all students* will learn at high levels." Once you have your strategic plan laid out for how you will initiate, implement, and sustain the work of Cultural Proficiency, you will have developed a plan for when smaller professional learning communities within your organization will collect data, set goals and strategies for achieving those goals, and monitor progress toward sustainability.

For example, Eaveston School District's Cultural Proficiency Committee developed a transformational equity action plan using the template in Table 11.2. You may consider how smaller teams will develop their own transformational equity action plans—such as schools; district departments, such as Transportation, Curriculum and Instruction, Food Service, or Athletics; or content departments, such as Mathematics, Social Science, Science, or Language Arts; or grade-level departments, such as third grade or high school.

Using the transformational equity action plan, your teams will set action goals using data they collect on the Continuum of Cultural Proficiency. Refer back to the learning strategies used in Chapter 7. After goals are chosen, the plan will formalize proposed actions to achieve the goals. Do not forget to align your actions using the Essential Elements of Cultural Proficiency. Refer back to Chapter 8. In addition, those teams will identify how to measure progress and success toward the goals, persons responsible, the date by which they will be achieved, and your actual outcomes. Resource G at the end of this book includes Eaveston's transformational equity action plan with strategies for each Essential Element.

 LOOKING IN THE REARVIEW MIRROR

This chapter focused on the commitment to action planning to ensure equitable access and outcome opportunities for all students. The commitment you demonstrate as a school leader will provide a path for organizational change at the district level and school level. Strategic planning is essential in planning for how to implement and sustain this work over time, as well as developing a transformational equity action plan to increase equity, access, and inclusion for all students.

TABLE 11.2 ● Transformational Equity Action Plan

SCHOOL/DISTRICT:

OUR DISTRICT/SCHOOL VISION:

OUR DISTRICT/SCHOOL MISSION:

Goals	Culturally Proficient Actions	Success Measure(s)	Person(s) Responsible	Date by Which to Be Achieved	Actual Outcomes

• What goals do we need to address to achieve outcome?
 	
• Is the goal written using SMART criteria (see below)?
 	
• To what extent does the goal align with current vision and mission statements? Do the vision and/or mission statements need to be revisited or revised to better align with culturally proficient values?
	• List actions chronologically.
	
	• Include preparation (e.g., funding) and implementation actions.
	
	• Include actions for the following:
	
	  - Assessing cultural knowledge and the current reality
	  - Valuing diversity
	  - Managing the dynamics of diversity
	  - Adapting to diversity
	  - Institutionalizing cultural knowledge
		"We will know we are successful if/when . . ."
		
		• What is measured?
		• Who will measure?
		• When do we measure?			

OUTCOME: CRITICAL QUESTION FOR INQUIRY: What do we want to know that will address gaps of inequity? What data will we need?					
Goal One:	Actions to Achieve Goal One:	Success Measure(s):	Person(s) Responsible:	Date:	Outcomes:
Goal Two:	Actions to Achieve Goal Two:	Success Measure(s):	Person(s) Responsible:	Date:	Outcomes:
OUTCOME: SKILLS: What skills and capacity will we need for culturally proficient inquiry?					
Goal One:	Actions to Achieve Goal One:	Success Measure(s):	Person(s) Responsible:	Date:	Outcomes:
Goal Two:	Actions to Achieve Goal Two:	Success Measure(s):	Person(s) Responsible:	Date:	Outcomes:

OUTCOME: INCENTIVES: What incentives might we use to engage people in culturally proficient inquiry and practice? What goals do we need to reach this outcome?

	Actions to Achieve Goal	Success Measure(s)	Person(s) Responsible / Date	Outcomes
Goal One:	Actions to Achieve Goal One:	Success Measure(s):	Person(s) Responsible: / Date:	Outcomes:
Goal Two:	Actions to Achieve Goal Two:	Success Measure(s):	Person(s) Responsible: / Date:	Outcomes

OUTCOME: RESOURCES: How might we orchestrate technical, material, organizational, and human resources for culturally proficient practice? What goals do we need to reach this outcome?

	Actions to Achieve Goal	Success Measure(s)	Person(s) Responsible / Date	Outcomes
Goal One:	Actions to Achieve Goal One:	Success Measure(s):	Person(s) Responsible: / Date:	Outcomes:
Goal Two:	Actions to Achieve Goal Two:	Success Measure(s):	Person(s) Responsible: / Date:	Outcomes:

SMART Goals:

Specific = Who, what, when, where, which, why?

Measurable = Concrete criteria for measuring success: How much, how many, how will we know?

Attainable = What do we need to be successful? What knowledge, skills, attitudes, and/or resources do we need to develop to attain the goal?

Realistic = Is our goal high enough, and are we willing to work hard enough to reach it?

Timely & Tangible = What is our sense of urgency? Do we have a timeline with short- and long-term actions to achieve the goal? Can we picture the outcome? Do we know when we have reached the goal?

ON TO OUR NEXT DESTINATION

In the final chapter of this book, we focus on ensuring equity for all students. Often when you finish a trip, you have the opportunity to reflect on it as a whole journey. While your journey is not complete, Chapter 12 includes three resources, developed in Eaveston, that have proven essential in institutionalizing the application of the Tools of Cultural Proficiency in all aspects of the district. Exploring these resources will help you look at your school or district journey as a whole.

REFLECTION, DIALOGUE, AND ACTION PROCESS

REFLECTION • Dialogue • Action

As you consider developing your strategic plan, how will you communicate the "what" and the "why" of an equity-focused initiative in your school or district? How might you leverage current policies, practices, and procedures to reach your goals? What professional learning structures are in place, and how can they be focused on this initiative? What metrics will you keep track of to determine the progress of the initiative and also the effectiveness of your leadership team(s)?

Reflection • DIALOGUE • Action

Gather together with your team, analyze, and discuss Eaveston School District's three- to five-year strategic plan. How might your plan be organized for implementing, evaluating, and sustaining the work of Cultural Proficiency in your district?

Reflection • Dialogue • ACTION

Using the transformational equity action plan in Table 11.2, set goals from the data you collected using the Continuum of Cultural Proficiency; then, use the Essential Elements of Cultural Proficiency to define the action steps your team will take to achieve those goals of increased equity, access, and inclusion.

_____

_____

_____

_____

_____

Travel Log

_____

_____

_____

_____

_____

_____

_____

_____

_____

_____

_____

_____

_____

_____

_____

_____

_____

_____

_____

_____

_____

_____

_____

_____

_____

_____

_____

_____

_____

_____

TRAVEL GUIDE
Sustainability: Commitment to Ensuring Equitable Outcomes

Create Your Map

- Sustain the work past the current administration.
- How will each piece of paper you generate reflect and guide the work of equity?
- Assess and regularly communicate progress.
- Determine other resources that will support this equity work.
- Build a sustainability plan of action.

Resources

- A commitment by the community to the betterment of their schools
- The understanding that the students of today are our future citizens
- The ability to nurture and develop the leaders of tomorrow
- The collective love for students and their futures

Mileage

- Establish markers of progress to determine when you're getting closer to your goals.
- Monitor the building toward critical mass.
- Measure the moral commitment of this work.

Check the Weather

- Building on the story of the district and inventing its future
- What is collective vision for the future of the school, the district, the city, the state?
- Who represents the future?
- Who represents the initiatives of the past?

Travel Phrases

- Equitable outcomes
- Moral commitment
- Invent your future
- Plan for sustainability
- Systemic change

You're the Driver

- How will you demonstrate your commitment to advocating for all students?
- In what ways will this work help you improve your best self?
- What will you do to see the work continues after you leave?
- Examine not just what we do but why we do it

CHAPTER 12

Sustainability: Commitment to Ensuring Equitable Outcomes

CALIBRATION

If a significant amount of the organization's leadership team has a robust under-standing of educational equity, a sense of urgency, experiences creating or elimi-nating policies, systems, or practices that impact the experiences, outcomes, and access to resources for students from previously excluded groups, and if they consistently align their words and actions related to equity, your organization is proficient in this area.

—Fields (2021, p. 103)

ON-RAMP TO ENSURING EQUITABLE OUTCOMES

When you think about creating a culturally proficient school system that ensures equitable outcomes for all students regardless of cultural iden-tity intersections, it is essential that school leaders, especially superinten-dents and principals, take responsibility for the journey. Create your map, know the travel phrases, and check the weather, your mileage, and your resources. You are the driver. You must make sense of this journey in the context of your school district or school, as a whole system, if you are to sustain this journey.

As you commit to ensuring equitable outcomes for all students, we want to leave you with three last narratives from Eaveston School District. These narratives introduce three resources, developed in Eaveston, that have proven essential in institutionalizing the application of the Tools of Cultural

Proficiency in all aspects of the district. As you read the sections that follow, we encourage you to reflect on these questions:

1. In what ways will you embed the work of Cultural Proficiency in all aspects of your district or school using the organizational chart or already existing school improvement plan in your district or school? How might you use a model similar to the Districtwide Model for Raising Equity in Figure 12.1?

2. How will you use the *Culturally Proficient Policy and Practice Review* in Figure 12.2 to sustain the implementation of applying the Tools of Cultural Proficiency in examining the impact of policies and practices on your students and staff?

3. In what ways will you lead change through the levels of impact introduced to you in Figure 9.1? Level 5 in the dispersion pattern represents the impact of professional learning related to Cultural Proficiency on student outcomes. How might you use the building Cultural Proficiency Annual Cycle of Continuous Improvement to help teams embed the work of Cultural Proficiency in their everyday classroom practices in Figure 12.3?

Your journey-will be uniquely different from that of other educators, schools, and school districts. Think of this chapter as the part of your journey similar to crossing a body of water between two landforms connected by a bridge. Imagine driving from one destination, across the bridge, to another destination. Pause and look down at the water beneath the bridge. It may seem to be moving fast, sometimes with rough waters, but continue to lead change, ensuring equity, access, and inclusion in your organization as you move to your next destination, by keeping that mile-high view.

EPISODE 4

DISTRICTWIDE MODEL TO EMBED CULTURAL PROFICIENCY IN ALL ASPECTS OF THE DISTRICT

As Eaveston's Superintendent worked to embed Cultural Proficiency in all aspects of the organization, he knew there had to be a connection to existing structures, which included the Comprehensive School Improvement Plan (CSIP), which was developed in 2018 and would be implemented until 2023. In taking the work that the Cultural Proficiency Committee had built on in the past two years, the Superintendent called on the assistant superintendents, executive directors, building principals, and university consultant to discuss how the three goals of the Cultural Proficiency Committee would be connected to the CSIP goals. Figure 12.1 displays the *Districtwide Model For Raising Equity* by embedding Cultural Proficiency in all aspects of the organization.

The developed action plan, with embedded strategies for achieving the goals of the Cultural Proficiency Committee, was linked with the strategies set forth in the CSIP. The blue arrows in the diagram represent the flow of how each set of goals are interconnected. Table 12.1 displays a deeper

FIGURE 12.1 ● District-Wide Model for Raising Equity

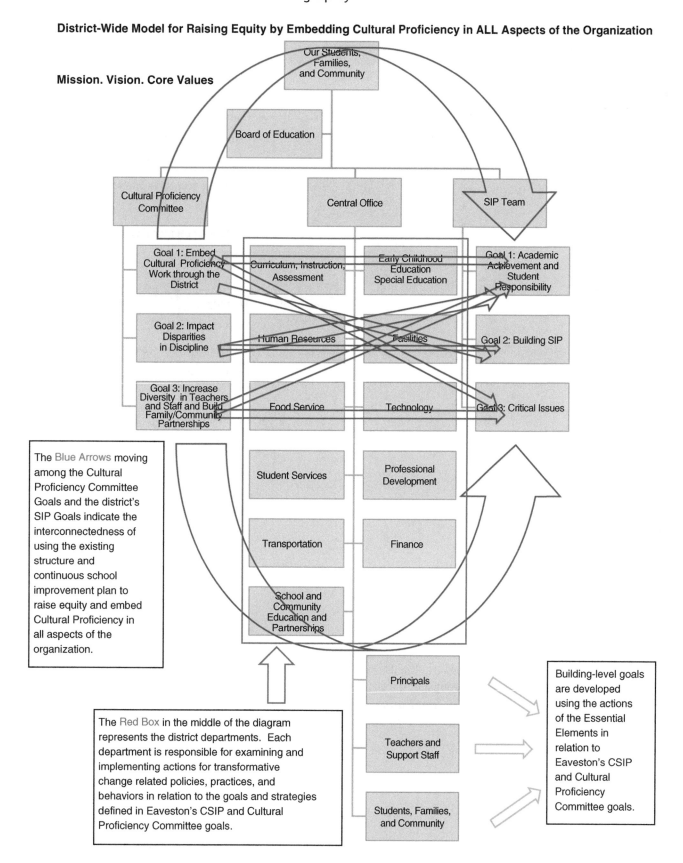

District-Wide Model for Raising Equity by Embedding Cultural Proficiency in ALL Aspects of the Organization

Mission. Vision. Core Values

Our Students, Families, and Community

Board of Education

Cultural Proficiency Committee

Central Office

SIP Team

Goal 1: Embed Cultural Proficiency Work through the District

Curriculum, Instruction, Assessment

Early Childhood Education Special Education

Goal 1: Academic Achievement and Student Responsibility

Goal 2: Impact Disparities in Discipline

Human Resources

Facilities

Goal 2: Building SIP

Goal 3: Increase Diversity in Teachers and Staff and Build Family/Community Partnerships

Food Service

Technology

Goal 3: Critical Issues

Student Services

Professional Development

Transportation

Finance

School and Community Education and Partnerships

The Blue Arrows moving among the Cultural Proficiency Committee Goals and the district's SIP Goals indicate the interconnectedness of using the existing structure and continuous school improvement plan to raise equity and embed Cultural Proficiency in all aspects of the organization.

Principals

Teachers and Support Staff

Students, Families, and Community

The Red Box in the middle of the diagram represents the district departments. Each department is responsible for examining and implementing actions for transformative change related policies, practices, and behaviors in relation to the goals and strategies defined in Eaveston's CSIP and Cultural Proficiency Committee goals.

Building-level goals are developed using the actions of the Essential Elements in relation to Eaveston's CSIP and Cultural Proficiency Committee goals.

TABLE 12.1 ● Relationship Between CSIP Plans and Cultural Proficiency Goals

CSIP GOAL	CULTURAL PROFICIENCY GOAL(S)	STRATEGIC TRANSFORMATIVE LEVERS (PROBLEMS OF PRACTICE)
State academic achievement and student responsibility	1. Embed Cultural Proficiency throughout the district. 2. Reduce disparities in discipline. 3. Increase staff diversity, and build diverse family/community partnerships.	• Tiers I, II, and III instruction and interventions • Community programs • Discipline • Responsible citizens • Response to intervention • Equity • Career and technical education • Staffing supports • School climate • Therapy • Data • Technology resources • Online learning • Title I • Communication • Professional development • Trauma-informed care • Transitional programs • Whole-child focus • Social-emotional learning supports • Summer camp • Before- and after-school academic supports • Sports • Extracurricular activities
Building school improvement plans	1. Embed Cultural Proficiency throughout the district. 2. Reduce disparities in discipline.	• Building structure • Instruction • School climate • Professional development • Professional learning communities • Student responsibility • Valuing diversity • Evidence-based practice • Personalized learning

Critical issues	1. Embed Cultural Proficiency throughout the district. 2. Increase staff diversity, and build diverse family/community partnerships.	• Safety • Funding • District staffing • Technology • Current economy • Current social climate • Title I • Health • Wellness

Note: CSIP, Comprehensive School Improvement Plan.

connection between the two goal sets. While all of these leverage points are listed, it is important to note that applying the Tools of Cultural Proficiency to examine practices, policies, and behaviors related to each problem of practice and work toward change takes years. As you begin to think through all aspects of your organization, think about where you would start if this list is like yours.

CULTURAL PROFICIENCY: POLICY TO PRACTICE

School leadership is key in implementing policy through procedures and practice in the organization. Policy review is an ongoing, district-level process. The procedures and practices consume many collaborative conversations among district and building leaders, but how well do those conversations examine the degree to which they serve students?

Eaveston leaders learned that changing policies to be intentionally inclusive was only the first, albeit very important, step. As policies were revised and new policies created, discussions about the procedures and practices to roll out the new and revised policies involved many collaborative conversations among district and building leaders. These conversations led to examining the degree to which both past policies and new, emergent policies serve(d) students. It became necessary to take a deep dive to consider the degree to which current policies were effective or not. Such study would be guided by deep understanding of both the Guiding Principles and the Essential Elements of the Cultural Proficiency Framework.

The purpose of the *Culturally Proficient Policy and Practice Review* is to provide a framework for educators to examine school district policies and practices to identify those that are unproductive, unhealthy, and/or inequitable for students. The review is not to be used as an evaluative tool. In your commitment to ensuring equitable outcomes and sustaining this work for years to come, use the following questions and steps to complete a culturally proficient policy and practice review.

Another important process for sustaining this work and ensuring equitable outcomes includes continuous improvement efforts toward increasingly culturally proficient educational practices and policy development using the Tools of Cultural Proficiency that constitute the Framework. Figure 12.2 is the *Culturally Proficient Practice and Policy Review*. Using this review provides school leaders the ability to engage with the Tools of Cultural Proficiency with the purpose of reviewing and revising school board policies and working with stakeholders in professional learning communities to change the related practices. Specifically, the Continuum of Cultural Proficiency is essential to the review as it provides a way for all stakeholders to have a voice in what is most needed for all students to learn and achieve at high levels (R. B. Lindsey et al., 2019).

FIGURE 12.2 ● Culturally Proficient Policy and Practice Review

Policy	
Procedure cross-references	
Law cross-references	
District-level application	

CULTURALLY DESTRUCTIVE	CULTURALLY INCAPACITATING	CULTURALLY BLIND	CULTURALLY PRECOMPETENT	CULTURALLY COMPETENT	CULTURALLY PROFICIENT
The practices and/or behaviors attempt to eliminate groups of individuals based on cultural identity differences, such as race or social class.	The practices and/or behaviors demean groups of individuals based on cultural identity differences such as race or social class. The practices and/or behaviors prompt belief in the superiority of one's culture and disempower the other group.	The practices and/or behaviors intentionally or unintentionally dismiss cultural differences, such as race or social class. The practices and/or behaviors lead others to believe that cultural differences do not matter or cannot be seen.	The practices and/or behaviors inadequately respond to the dynamics of difference between individuals' cultural identities, such as race or social class.	The practices and/or behaviors address differences between individuals' cultural identities, such as race or social class, and the organization's culture. They take into consideration value for diversity, managing the dynamics of difference, adapting to diversity, and institutionalizing cultural knowledge.	The practices and/or behaviors address a commitment to advocating for individuals with varying cultural identities, such as race and social class, who have been underserved by the organization.

Using the professional learning strategies of personal reflection and dialogue with colleagues, use the space below to record your feelings and thoughts about continuous school improvement.

1. What practices and behaviors are related to the named policy?

2. What practices and behaviors align with the descriptions of precompetent, competent, and proficient?

3. What practices and behaviors align with the descriptions of destructive, incapacitating, and blind?

4. For the policies, practices, and behaviors aligned with the descriptions of destructive, incapacitating, or blind, what barriers (R. B. Lindsey et al., 2019) are overtly or covertly present?

   - Presumption of privilege or entitlement
   - Unawareness of the need to adapt
   - Systemic oppression—racism, sexism, classism
   - Resistance to change

5. In what ways must the Guiding Principles (R. B. Lindsey et al., 2019) as core beliefs be internalized for the policies, practices, and behaviors rated destructive, incapacitating, or blind to become more inclusive and culturally proficient?

   - Culture is a predominant force in society.
   - People are served to varying degrees by the dominant culture.
   - People have individual and group identities.
   - Diversity within cultures is vast and significant.
   - Each cultural group has unique cultural needs.
   - The best of both worlds enhances the capacity of all.
   - The family, as defined by each culture, is the primary system of support in the education of children.
   - School systems must recognize that marginalized populations have to be at least bicultural and that this status creates a distinct set of issues to which the system must be equipped to respond.
   - Inherent in cross-cultural interactions are dynamics that must be acknowledged, adjusted to, and accepted.

6. In what ways do data (i.e., practices and behaviors) from the Cultural Proficiency Continuum provide evidence to support who is thriving in the current system and who is not?

7. What quality indicators or existing data are relevant to current policies and related practices?

(Continued)

FIGURE 12.2 ● (Continued)

8. Briefly describe additional quantitative or qualitative data gathered from surveys, focus groups, interviews, and/or observations.

9. Based on the supporting data, where does the policy fit on the Cultural Proficiency Continuum (R. B. Lindsey et al., 2019)?

CULTURALLY DESTRUCTIVE	CULTURALLY INCAPACITATING	CULTURALLY BLIND	CULTURALLY PRECOMPETENT	CULTURALLY COMPETENT	CULTURALLY PROFICIENT
The language in the policy attempts to eliminate groups of individuals based on cultural identity differences, such as race or social class.	The language in the policy demeans groups of individuals based on cultural identity differences, such as race or social class. The language prompts belief in the superiority of one's culture and disempowers the other group.	The language in the policy intentionally or unintentionally dismisses cultural differences, such as race or social class. The language leads others to believe that cultural differences do not matter or cannot be seen.	The language in the policy inadequately responds to the dynamics of difference between individuals' cultural identities, such as race or social class.	The language in the policy addresses differences between individuals' cultural identities, such as race or social class, and the organization's culture. It takes into consideration value for diversity, managing the dynamics of difference, adapting to diversity, and institutionalizing cultural knowledge.	The language in the policy addresses a commitment to advocating for individuals with varying cultural identities, such as race and social class, who have been underserved by the organization.

10. As you think about changing this policy, what actions will you take using the Essential Elements to:
   - Assess your and your organization's cultural knowledge of the communities you serve?
   - Demonstrate value for the diversity of the community you serve?
   - Manage the dynamics of difference that may arise?
   - Adapt to the diversity of the communities you serve?
   - Institutionalize cultural knowledge about the communities served by your school or district?

Policies and practices that appear on the left side of the Continuum, and are identified by stakeholders as destructive, blind, and incapacitating, can lead educators to engage in reflection and dialogue strategies to produce goals for continuous improvement (Cross et al., 1989; R. B. Lindsey et al., 2019). Once goals are established using the data along the Continuum, educational leaders can determine actionable steps using the Essential Elements. These actions are aimed at achieving the goals and improving student outcomes through continuous learning in various professional learning communities and through parent and community partnerships.

BUILDING-LEVEL CULTURAL PROFICIENCY ANNUAL CYCLE OF CONTINUOUS IMPROVEMENT

The Cultural Proficiency Annual Cycle of Continuous Improvement is a design process for small teams working collectively each month to improve their practice to be more culturally proficient, increase student learning, and promote equity and inclusion within the classroom and/or school. It was developed to help educators in individual school buildings with professional learning communities, grade-level teams, or department-level teams to personalize the work of Cultural Proficiency to meet the needs of the group of students they are currently serving, as well as align with the curriculum and resources used per grade level or department level. Outcomes are based on the level of reflection, dialogue, and action toward change. The first three months of the cycle are focused on setting the purpose, collecting the data, and facilitating reflection and dialogue around the Barriers to Cultural Proficiency. The essential questions used in the *Cultural Proficiency Annual Cycle of Continuous Improvement* guide teams to examine students who are not thriving in their grade levels or departments and to work through the Barriers to acknowledge behaviors, practices, and policies that are unhealthy for students, prevent them from thriving, or are "closing" the door on them. You will notice in Figure 12.3 that the essential questions discussed early in this chapter reflect the same questions from the first three months of this cycle.

In Eaveston School District one of the schools engaged in continuous school improvement efforts using the annual cycle. The building's Cultural Proficiency Committee spent one year building capacity among themselves prior to implementing this work. This included using *Cultural Proficiency: A Manual for School Leaders*, fourth edition, as a guide to learn about the Cultural Proficiency Framework, learning more about their own cultural identities and engaging in culturally proficient learning strategies that they themselves would lead with smaller, grade-level teams. The teams met twice a month during their planning period to focus on helping their students thrive using the Cultural Proficiency Framework. We recommend this model for institutionalizing the work of Cultural Proficiency at the school level.

FIGURE 12.3 ● Cultural Proficiency Annual Cycle of Continuous Improvement

September
Framework

- Who in our grade level/ department is not experiencing success?
- What data do we have to support those students not experiencing success?

October
Problem of
Practice

- To what problem(s) of practice or leverage point do the data relate?
- Given the value we have for "*all* to Learn," what practices are we willing to change?
- What are we willing to do so that the identified students experience success?

November
Barriers

- What are the barriers to culturally proficient educational practice?
- What internal barriers are preventing students from experiencing success related to the problem of practice or leverage point?

December
Guiding
Principles

- What are the Guiding Principles to culturally proficient educational practice?
- What Guiding Principles are informing practices that are causing students to experience success with the problem of practice?

January
Continuum

- What examples of our own behaviors, practices, and policies are being informed by the Barriers and Guiding Principles?

February
Continuum
Essential
Elements

- Given the value we have for "ALL to Learn," how might we adapt our behaviors, practices, and policies to open doors for our students who are "not experiencing success?"

March
Essential
Elements

- What five recommended actions for changing our behaviors, practices, and/or policies do we propose to open doors for our students to experience success?

April
Essential
Elements

- What actions are we implementing for improving our practice related to the identified leverage point?
- To what degree are our students experiencing success?

May
Process
Debrief

- In what ways did we change our practice and/ or policies this year?
- How will this framework help us next year as we plan for student success?

Participants will build knowledge and skills in using the Tools of Cultural Proficiency by engaging in continuous reflection and dialogue to increase culturally proficient educational practice among their teams so that "*all* will learn."

This cycle of continuous improvement is a design process for small teams working collectively each month to improve their practice to be more culturally proficient, increase student learning, and promote equity and inclusion within the classroom and/or school. Outcomes are based on the level of reflection, dialogue, and action toward change.

BUILDING THE CRITICAL MASS

As you continue on your journey of leading your school district or building through transformative, organizational change, we ask you to place the goal of "building the critical mass" at the top of your list. Implementation is one thing you will lead, but sustaining the implementation and institutionalization of the changes will be another. To actualize transformational change in your organization and see true systemic changes that affect student outcomes, you will need to build the critical mass. Merriam Webster Dictionary defines "critical mass" as a size, number, or amount large enough to produce a particular result. The results in Cultural Proficiency are increased equity, access, and inclusion for all students. Build your team; invite stakeholders to engage in reflective and dialogic processes to critically and continuously examine your policies, practices, and behaviors; and ensure equitable outcomes by designing on-ramps for others to join you on this journey.

RACE, SOCIAL CLASS, AND CULTURAL PROFICIENCY: ENSURING EQUITY FOR ALL

We assume, by now, that you are on the highway and have created a plan for your own journey of Cultural Proficiency. Maybe you are moving inch by inch in a traffic jam, or maybe you are cruising smoothly toward your destination. We began this book by talking about the moral imperative of education and leadership. While this book focused your attention on serving students from various racial and social class backgrounds with the Cultural Proficiency Framework, we again call you to focus on all students who are not thriving. We ask you to end with an asset-based reflection on the Intersectionality of cultural identities in your school organization. The diversity of race/ethnicity, national origin, language, gender, sexual orientation, religion/faith, ableness, and social class is vast and significant. Each cultural group has unique needs that must be respected and attended to with our policies, practices, and behaviors. The best of both worlds really does enhance the capacity of all. We, as educators, are called to open doors for all.

One of the most courageous acts as a parent is to leave your child with someone else. To love them, to see them, to hear them as you would. To truly care for them. Parents do this every day. Trusting that we will keep their kids whole.

—Terry Harris (*Twitter*, 2021)

Reflect for a moment on Dr. Harris's quote and on what we, the authors, believe to be the reason we do this work. If you are a parent or have ever had the privilege of being a guardian of a child, this reasoning may resonate with you.

When you have a child and you raise them until they are five years old, you find out what love really is. You take them to a building and drop them off. You say to those people who are greeting you at the door, "Please take them and treat them with the respect they deserve. Please make them smart, take care of them, keep them safe, and give them the basis for what they need to become a successful adult."

Families give us their children, our greatest responsibility, for 12–13 years. We used the terms *leaders*, *educators*, and *teachers* in this book. Teaching is not a profession. It is a calling. There is no parent who would not give up their lives for their child or children, and they are trusting us to keep them safe. So when we think of using the vehicle of the Cultural Proficiency Framework to reach the moral imperative of education, it is to ensure equity, access, and inclusion for each and every child we are entrusted with, regardless of their race/ethnicity, national origin, language, gender, sexual orientation, faith, social class, or ableness. What we do and say matters.

> There is no higher calling!
>
> That is why we need to do this work well for every child.
>
> For whom will you do this work?
>
> What are you willing to do to ensure equity for all?
>
> And how are the children? ("A Tribute to the Maasai"; T. Harris, 2019)

Lead Through the Lens of Cultural Proficiency

Resources

A. **Letters to the Reader**

    Superintendent to Superintendent

    Director of Education to Director of Education

    Principal to Principal

    Teacher to Teacher

B. **Research Articles**

    Welborn, J., & Lindsey, R. (2020). A descriptive study of the case of Eaveston School District: Core values from deficit-based to asset-based. *Journal of Leadership, Equity, and Research, 6*(1), 1–25.

    Welborn, J. (2019). Increasing equity, access, and inclusion through organizational change: A study of implementation and experiences surround a school district's journey toward culturally proficient educational practice. *Educational Leadership Review, 20*(1), 167–189.

    Casey, T., & Welborn, J. (2020, March–April). Cultural proficiency as an advocacy tool to build a diverse workforce. *Association of California School Administrators Leadership Magazine.*

C. **Learning Strategies**

D. **Planning, Graphics, Forms**

    Three- to Five-Year Strategic Planning

    Organizational Chart

    Equity Action Plan Template

    Policy Review

    Culturally Proficient Interview Questions

E. **Book Study**

F. **Cultural Proficiency Books: Essential Questions**

RESOURCE 1A

LETTERS TO THE READER

Dear Superintendent,

For years, our school district took pride in knowing exactly what was working well for our students, as well as our keen ability to identify areas of growth. This was the result of a robust continuous improvement process that was decades old and transcended several superintendents. This cycle of school improvement was the heart of our system and embodied who we were. No one could argue with the results. We achieved high performance on important metrics and were being recognized for our success.

A funny thing happened when we began to implement the Cultural Proficiency Framework and engaged in honest conversations with parents, staff, and students and looked deeper at our data trends. First, we discovered we weren't as good as we thought. Second, everyone in the organization viewed our practices from a different lens.

As you begin this journey, the best piece of advice I can give is to sit back and listen, even if you don't agree with every statement or know you have data to contradict someone's perception. I learned from the onset that listening to how others interpret our intentions was a game changer. It wasn't easy to hear some of the criticism about hiring practices or student performance, but the insight made me a better leader.

As I reflected early on in the cultural proficiency process, I realized we were like most school districts. We did a lot of things very well, but we could always be better. The question was do we fully immerse ourselves in this work to take us further than we've ever been? The answer was simple and we've actually never been in a better place. I've been amazed at the number of staff members who are so passionate about the work. They care so deeply about our students and are willing to do whatever it takes to help them succeed.

Leading this work at the district level can be tricky. We all know the results truly occur when those closest to our students (school staff) fully embrace any school reform. How we frame the work and what language we use as we communicate with our staff are critical. For me, it was pretty straightforward. Our dedication to the Cultural Proficiency Framework is about learning as much as we can about our students and their backgrounds so we can do whatever it takes academically, social emotionally, and relationally to prepare them for life. It's really hard for anyone to argue against that. The other major component is the deep reflection of the organization that serves the community. Are we actually doing the things we say we are? Are our practices supportive or in some cases interfering with our mission?

You must eventually include your entire school community in this work if you're really going to make a difference. Our continuous school improvement model is built around parent, student, and community involvement, so that part was already built in for us. You can learn so much from your community about perceptions and beliefs through conversation. Every parent wants their child to be successful and learning more about how they view school and district practices is critical.

I can state without hesitation that our commitment to the Cultural Proficiency Framework has made me a better leader and our school district an even better place for students and staff. In our profession, you never actually "arrive." It's about consistently moving forward over time. We all get knocked down at some point, but the thought of leading a more cultural proficient organization is the only motivation I need to keep going.

Eaveston's Superintendent of Schools

RESOURCE 2A

LETTERS TO THE READER

DIRECTOR OF EDUCATION TO DIRECTOR OF EDUCATION

Dear District Leader,

The work you are starting—or perhaps resuming—is some of the most important work you will do. All educators have a responsibility to serve all students and help all learn and achieve. Although that was a part of our district mission, we still found students struggled, didn't perform at the levels they should, and did not see themselves as successful learners or feel school was relevant or welcoming to them. When I first joined this district more than a dozen years ago, equity work was taking place, but the efforts were disjointed. While many supported equity work, other educators struggled to see the relevance of this work and how it was affecting students. As we shifted our focus to Cultural Proficiency, we began working with a lens to affect all of our efforts district-wide, improving on disconnected, though well-intentioned, efforts throughout different buildings.

As a district leader supporting Cultural Proficiency, it is important to remember the aim is to change the way all see teaching and learning—and all other supports schools provide to students and their families. To do this, stakeholders from throughout the district and community must have a voice. How can you serve all well if a homogeneous group is making decisions for those who have been disenfranchised? Without representation, structures of power are reinforced, not diversified. Creating tangible goals is also important, but the work must be ongoing, providing a structure to guide continuous improvement. Most districts already have a model for school improvement. Using Cultural Proficiency as a part of that model incorporates equity into school growth and allows a deeper look at the barriers that are blocking change. Continuous growth also includes providing professional development that increases the capacity of a district's staff to serve all.

This work has shaped me as a leader and shifted the way I view my role as an agent of change as well. I've learned this work is of the head and of the heart—if those in your district don't believe all students have a capacity to achieve, difficult conversations must take place to disrupt this thinking. This requires creating places where people can speak openly and will listen with the intent to understand. The benefit is the personal, professional, and leadership development that takes place for all who take part. I have seen passionate teachers become leaders, shaping district- and building-level work. It is the ongoing growth of these stakeholders and the opportunities that evolve for all to lead that brings me much pride. Teachers and administrators rethinking practices, changing behaviors, and seeing challenges as opportunities move us as a district to support all learners who can and will achieve.

Best wishes to you, your administrators and teachers, and to your students— your leadership and vision are vital to their success!

Director of Education

RESOURCE 3A

LETTERS TO THE READER

PRINCIPAL TO PRINCIPAL

Dear Administrator,

In 2012, I walked into a very different environment at Eaveston School than exists today. The student discipline rates were high, and the academic achievement levels were low; both of which were extremely concerning. There also seemed to be a disconnect between staff and students; staff wondered why students couldn't just "act right" and why students weren't growing academically. Our administrative team knew we needed to make changes within our school for the good of our students, and we also knew that to make those changes, teachers would have to understand why those changes were needed.

What we didn't know was exactly how to do that. So we tried our best; we brought in one-day speakers, gave surveys to staff and students and evaluated the results, did book studies on differentiation, sent people to conferences, started instituting positive behavior interventions and supports, instituted an Advisory class to help students make connections, and so on. And all of that was valuable. But the disconnect continued to exist between staff and students. That disconnect became even more apparent during the unrest following the shooting death of another Black male in the local area.

Like most schools nationwide, the staff at Eaveston was predominantly Caucasian and female, many of whom had not been raised in culturally diverse areas and had not had life experiences that allowed them to understand perspectives different from their own; this, in turn, created situations in which teacher-student interactions became tense.

That's when cultural proficiency became crucial to making changes in our school. We learned that to understand and learn from other cultures, we needed to back up all the way to the beginning, to ourselves as individuals. It was important to understand what culture is and how everyone belongs to a culture that is made up of all the experiences that make us who we are: our gender, race, religion, socioeconomic status, where we grew up, when we were born, and so on. Once we had the opportunity to look at ourselves and how our cultures shaped us, we then could begin to recognize that others, those who grew up with different life experiences and in cultures other than our own, may not see the world as we do, may not react to the world as we do, and may not feel about the world as we do. It allowed us to look at our students more objectively, to question the "why" behind student actions, and to listen more intently to both verbal and nonverbal student communications.

From this process, I've learned not only about cultural proficiency but also about leadership. As a leader, it's important to remember that everyone is at a different place on the spectrum of cultural proficiency and will have a different comfort level while moving forward. We have to celebrate the small changes as well as the big. We have to be inclusive and provide opportunities for all comfort levels to learn, reflect, and share. We also have to create an environment in which we can have "oops" and "ouch" moments and still know we'll be okay afterward. I've also learned, and our building now has a collective understanding, that cultural proficiency work is an ongoing process; while we may be in a much better position than we were on embarking on our journey, we are a long way from our destination. I am proud of the staff at Eaveston School for their continuous learning and the changes they have made within themselves and within their classrooms.

Sincerely,

Eaveston's School Principal

RESOURCE 4A

LETTERS TO THE READER

TEACHER TO TEACHER

Dear Teacher,

I entered this journey with the expectation of becoming a better teacher. I have always felt that I was "fair" in my approach to equality and equity. This is not to say that I was well versed in the area of Cultural Proficiency, but I felt I knew enough to help me dismantle barriers that may exist between learning, communication, and the overall understanding between two cultures.

As I reflect on the knowledge and application of the Cultural Proficiency Framework, I quickly become aware of my own biases and areas for growth. I cannot discount what knowledge I have gained from experience, but overall, when teaching, I had a way to go before becoming proficient. Studying the framework has allowed me to become more intentional with teaching and learning.

When considering school improvement and growth, it is essential for all stakeholders to be involved in the process of learning the framework. To fully implement change, those who will operate as change agents must participate in doing the foundational work. It requires us as educators to make a conscious effort to shift our thought process, how we present curriculum, the tools we use when helping students become independent learners and thinkers, as well as being reflective on our personal practices. Many may not recognize or want to acknowledge the impact our personal biases have in our professional judgment. These actions can be both direct and indirect. As districts expand their structures, families and community members should be included. Hearing from family members will help guide the areas of growth and continue to build on strengths.

This work has not been light. Many question their ability to make a change. I always recommend that one start within. Your level of comfortability will guide you to having tough discussions, advocating for students, diverse curriculum, advocacy, and equity. Start small, and build on these tasks. Choose one area to focus on, whether that includes revamping your classroom library, learning about another culture, visiting another country, or simply taking time to connect with students beyond the curriculum; each of these will be beneficial in working with the framework of Cultural Proficiency.

Whatever area you decide to focus on, do not get discouraged. Remember to be reflective, share your experience (regardless of the outcome), and celebrate each attempt.

Kind regards,

An Elementary Teacher

RESOURCE 1B

RESEARCH ARTICLES

Welborn, J., & Lindsey, R. (2020). A descriptive study of the case of Eaveston School District: Core values from deficit-based to asset-based. *Journal of Leadership, Equity, and Research, 6*(1), 1–25. Retrieved from https://journals .sfu.ca/cvj/index.php/cvj/article/view/73/147

A Descriptive Study of the Case of Eaveston School District: Core Values From Deficit-Based to Asset-Based

*Don't tell me what you value, tell me what you do and
I will tell you what you value.*

—Attributed to Malcolm X

Jaime E. Welborn, *Saint Louis University, St. Louis, MO*

Randall B. Lindsey, *Emeritus, California State University, Los Angeles, CA*

ABSTRACT

A growing body of research has linked educational leadership and student achievement; however, the oppression of students of diverse race, ethnicity, and social class has perpetuated inequities and educational gaps for decades across the United States. Some educational leaders who care deeply about equity and social justice are examining their core values, behaviors, and beliefs, as well as their organization's policies and practices to identify and implement knowledge and skills that disrupt the inequities producing educational and opportunity gaps. This article reports findings that are part of a larger qualitative descriptive case study that investigated the implementation and experiences of Eaveston School District's intentional journey to become a culturally proficient school district. For this article, the authors included findings related to (1) how the implementation of the *Cultural Proficiency Framework* influenced change and (2) the challenges educational leaders face while implementing the work of Cultural Proficiency. The findings and conclusions of the study suggest that educators can lead organizational change and increase equity, access, and inclusion for all students by using the *Four Tools of Cultural Proficiency* to cause shifts from deficit-based to asset-based mindsets about students.

Keywords: equity, cultural proficiency, organizational change, core values, school improvement

INTRODUCTION

Parker's quote, "The greatest educational challenge of our time is upon us," as cited in the foreword of *Culturally Proficient Education* (Lindsey, Karns, & Myatt, 2010, p. viii), embodies one of the most pernicious and intractable educational research topics in the United States—inequity and opportunity in educational practice and policy. While many believe that one goal of education is to prepare all students for success in the world, numerous researchers have shown the persistence of inequities within school systems and structures, with emphasis on the depressed educational outcomes among students from lower-social-class and racialized backgrounds (Apple & Beane, 1995; Darling-Hammond, 1995; Freire, 1970; Hammond, 2015; Howard, 2006; Kozol, 2005; Ladson-Billings, 2006; Noguera, 2008).

Some leaders, like those from Eaveston School District, have engaged in a critical examination of their core values and their impact on educational practice. Included here are those *deficit-based core values* associated with negative beliefs and behaviors that focus on what is not working or what is wrong with the students, and *asset-based core values* that inform positive beliefs and behaviors and are focused on how teachers and leaders serve the needs of all students. In Eaveston, school leaders are applying the equity framework of Cultural Proficiency to address inequities and education gaps among student groups. Research related to evidence-based practice is essential for empowering leaders to initiate and sustain actions to change policies and practices that better support school effectiveness and fulfill the moral imperative of education in society (Fullan, 2003; Lindsey, Nuri-Robins, Terrell, & Lindsey, 2019). One approach to investigating and understanding complex social and educational contexts is through case study methodology.

This article reports findings and conclusions from part of a descriptive, qualitative case study that investigated one district's journey of becoming a culturally proficient school district (Welborn, 2019). The methodology focused on using the Tools of Cultural Proficiency as a change initiative. It is important to note the purpose of the study was not to evaluate the Cultural Proficiency Framework, which was codeveloped for education by one of this article's authors, but rather, to investigate the implementation and experiences of Cultural Proficiency work in a suburban, public PK–12 school district in the Midwest United States. In this article, the authors discuss behaviors and practices associated with deficit-based and asset-based core values related to (1) the ways in which implementation of the Cultural Proficiency Framework influenced change and (2) challenges educational leaders faced while implementing the work of Cultural Proficiency. This research calls educational leaders to more closely examine and consider empirical research to inform their efforts in seeking knowledge and skills in designing equitable policies and practices within their districts, schools, and classrooms. Often, educational leaders depend on social justice–conscious inquiry methods to examine inequitable outcomes and failure. Attention to the research outcomes of this study may inform transformative change within organizations. With cultural, social, political, and economic contexts in mind, the urgency around leadership using an equity framework such as Cultural Proficiency to address inequities in education is needed more than ever, and leaders are called to rely on emancipatory methodologies, those that advance equity and transform marginalized communities, for social justice in education.

A DEEPER LOOK: EAVESTON SCHOOL DISTRICT

Eaveston School District, pseudonymous for a suburban, public PK–12 school district in the Midwest United States, was established as "A Place to Live, Learn, and Grow." With almost 6,000 students, Eaveston School District has one high school, two middle schools, one traditional school (PreK–8), five elementary schools, as well as preschool and alternative education settings serving students in grades 6–12. Eaveston School District stands among many businesses, factories, casinos, and an international airport in a metropolitan county of more than one million people. The district receives approximately 90% of funds from local sources, and its student population represents 78 different countries, speaks 48 languages, and demographically is 46% White, 34% African American/Black, 11% Hispanic, 5% multiracial, and 4% Asian. The intersectionality of cultural differences among Eaveston's students is coupled by nearly half of Eaveston School District's students who are living at or below the United States defined poverty line. District officials are proud of its rating as the most diverse school district in the state.

The Eaveston School District operates with a focus on its mission and core values. The mission, "That all will learn," relates to the district's asset-based core values, which guide development and implementation of many practices and policies. Faced with challenges stemming from major geographical and economic changes in the larger community over the last two decades, as well as the diversity of the student body in terms of culture, race, and social class, the district has defined diversity as a positive contribution to the values and assets of the school district. Some district and school-site leaders identify themselves as transformative leaders using the Framework of Cultural Proficiency (Lindsey et al., 2019). Consequently, they believe their leadership actions have influenced the improvement in the district's accreditation status and student achievement indicators on state performance ratings and demographic group achievement. In past years, Eaveston School District has been recognized as one of the best school districts in the state, according to state rankings.

EAVESTON'S WHY FOR CULTURAL PROFICIENCY

A key element of case study methodology is shaping "why" and "how" questions. The researcher collected and examined evidence from both questions: *Why is the work of Cultural Proficiency important, and how is the work being implemented?* Responses to the "why" question were found in documents and other artifacts as well as from interviews. As written in Eaveston's mission, student success for all learners is essential. The district's expressed core values of *Diversity, Knowledge, Commitment, Care, Safety, Learning, Interdependence, Contribution, Strength, Freedom,* and *Success* guide the design, development, implementation, and revision of policies, practices, events, and programs in efforts to achieve the mission. So why did leaders in Eaveston commit to using the Framework for Cultural Proficiency? The rationale for selecting this framework included the need to

1. systemically address opportunity and educational gaps among students in regards to demographics such as race, ethnicity, and social class;

2. manage the dynamics of difference from the high level of cultural, racial/ethnic, and social class diversity;

3. provide stakeholders in the district with tools to examine current implementation and outcomes of practices and policies and to make changes to those adversely affecting student success; and

4. develop a common language around increasing school improvement efforts through opportunity, access, and equity, while building capacity among all district stakeholders to initiate and sustain significant changes.

It is important to note both authors, including the researcher, did not introduce the school district to the Cultural Proficiency Framework. In 2016, the district embarked on a journey to use the Framework, including two days of professional development, led by Corwin consultants, and the formation of the District Cultural Proficiency Committee. In 2017, at the superintendent's request, the researcher began working with a central office administrator and building administrator to plan and implement professional learning using the Cultural Proficiency Framework. The period of data collection for this study was limited from August 2018 to May 2019, but Eaveston School District continues to implement the Cultural Proficiency Framework with plans to continue the work with administrators, support staff, and new teachers for the 2020–2021 school year. No incentives were provided to the school district or its employees aside from the researcher's gratis service to the school district.

LITERATURE REVIEW

Research on educational leadership, school reform, and student achievement is substantive. In fact, since Coleman's *Equality of Educational Opportunity* was published, as well as *A Nation at Risk* (National Commission on Excellence in Education, 1983), many scholars and practitioners have focused on educational reform (Berliner & Biddle, 1995; Byrk & Schneider, 2002; Fullan, 2016; Ladson-Billings, 2009; Sarason, 1990). National, state, and local efforts to reduce educational gaps through initiatives (i.e., Elementary and Secondary Education Act of 1965, No Child Left Behind, 2002, Every Student Succeeds Act, 2015) have led to improvements. However, the commitment to equal opportunity of a quality education has failed to produce the intended outcomes for some groups of students. Many schools in the United States continue with systems, policies, and practices that largely reflect the values and behaviors of the dominant, most powerful groups in society. These practices and behaviors, guided by deficit-based core values, perpetuate inequities and educational achievement deficits for students of color and from lower-social-class communities (Apple & Beane, 1995; Darling-Hammond, 1995; Freire, 1970; Hammond, 2015; Howard, 2006; Kendi, 2019; Kozol, 2005; Ladson-Billings, 2006; Noguera, 2008; Sarason, 1990).

Recently, literature focusing on culturally proficient leadership encourages educators to advocate for increasing educational access and opportunity for those students who have been historically underserved by school systems. Culturally proficient leadership focuses on using an inside-out process to examine individuals' values and behaviors, as well as the organization's policies and practices (Lindsey et al., 2019). Thus, school leaders are called to implement and sustain professional learning using the Cultural Proficiency Framework for serving all students. The following sections address the literature focusing on (1) the conceptual framework of Cultural Proficiency, (2) the importance of school leadership in educational reform, and (3) the role of culturally proficient leadership for organizational change.

Cultural Proficiency. Cultural Proficiency reflects a mindset based on social justice and equity, and the literature supported the development of tools for individuals and organizations to navigate cross-cultural interactions. The mindset is based on the belief that all cultures are important and have assets that drive positive contributions to the school, community, and/or society. Educators whose values and behaviors align with the mindset of Cultural Proficiency are more likely to view cultural differences as assets on which to build educational programs, not as a problem to be solved (Lindsey, Nuri-Robins, & Terrell, 2009).

> Cultural proficiency is a mindset for how we interact with all people, irrespective of their cultural membership. Cultural proficiency is a worldview that carries explicit values, language, and standards for effective personal interaction and professional practices. Cultural proficiency is a 24/7 approach to our personal and professional lives. Most important, cultural proficiency is not a set of independent activities or strategies that you learn to use with your students, colleagues, or community members. (Terrell & Lindsey, 2009, p. 21)

Often, educators and school organizations that use the Framework of Cultural Proficiency intentionally utilize the interrelated set of four tools to increase access to equal educational opportunity and assist in practices related to developing and implementing school board policies, allocating resources, using assessment data, delivering curriculum and instruction, interacting with parents and community members, and planning and delivering professional development. Some authors suggested the use of the four tools may support changes to practices and policies leading to equal opportunity and equitable outcomes. Lindsey et al. (2009) suggested acknowledging deficit-based core values and how they present barriers to culturally proficient practice. Those practices increase understanding of how to overcome oppressive systems and practices, as well as resistance to change in schools that perpetuate inequitable outcomes for students.

Conceptual Framework. In research, a conceptual framework is a tool that aids in explaining the main concepts studied, such as key factors, constructs, and variables (Miles & Huberman, 1994). This qualitative study integrated constructs such as educational leadership, school reform, and student achievement with the Cultural Proficiency Framework. The equity framework of Cultural Proficiency (Figure 1) is an inside-out approach educational leaders can utilize to unpack inequities and educational gaps in student achievement and school improvement as well as to address the responses to diversity that are encountered in educational organizations (Cross, Bazron, Dennis, & Issacs, 1989; Lindsey et al., 2019).

The Cultural Proficiency Framework has four unique Tools: (1) the Barriers, (2) the Guiding Principles, (3) the Continuum, and (4) the Essential Elements. Figure 1 displays how the tools work interdependently. Educational leaders may increase equitable outcomes by examining the Barriers that are guided by deficit-based core values, as indicated on the lower left side of the framework. The Barriers include being resistant to change, being unaware of the need to adapt, not acknowledging systemic oppression, and benefiting from underserved privileges and entitlements based on class, race, or gender. The Barriers inform unhealthy practices, policies, and behaviors that deny or reduce access to quality education for students. The Guiding Principles, as shown on the lower right side of the framework, include nine "values related to issues that emerge in diverse environments and when engaging with people who are not members of the dominant culture" (Lindsey, Nuri-Robins, & Terrell, 2009, p. 61). The Guiding Principles are directed by asset-based core values and inform healthy practices, policies, and behaviors that increase access to quality education for students and create conditions in which all students can thrive. The Barriers and Guiding Principles inform the placement of unhealthy and healthy practices, policies, and behaviors on the Continuum that are discovered through self-examination and case study.

The third tool, the Continuum of Cultural Proficiency, includes six points for recognizing and aligning practices, policies, and behaviors of a school organization. As individuals within the organization rely on their personal and organizational core values, they transform their thinking and practices to those that promote healthy practices, policies, and behaviors and effective cross-cultural interactions (as shown from left to right in Figure 1) (Lindsey, Nuri-Robins, & Terrell, 2009). The fourth tool, the Essential Elements of Cultural Proficiency, is indicated at the top of the framework and provides five actions for increasing equity, access, and inclusion: (1) assessing culture, (2) valuing diversity, (3) managing the dynamics of difference, (4) adapting to diversity, and (5) institutionalizing cultural knowledge. The Essential Elements guide educational leaders to be intentional in their journey of creating goals and action toward increasing equity and access for all students. These standards of action become normal practice in making decisions about policy and practices that align with the core values the individuals in the organization profess, thus leading to increased equity in the organization.

The key strategies for effective utilization of the framework in cross-cultural situations are reflection and dialogue (Lindsey, Terrell, Robins, & Lindsey, 2010). For decades, scholars have written about the importance of self-awareness in the role of educational change agents. As educational leaders implement and sustain systemic, transformative organizational

FIGURE 1 ● Cultural Proficiency Framework.

The Five Essential Elements of Cultural Competence

Serve as standards for personal, professional values and behavior, as well as organizational policies and practices

- **Assessing cultural knowledge**
- **Valuing diversity**
- **Managing the dynamics of difference**
- **Adapting to diversity**
- **Institutionalizing cultural knowledge**

The Cultural Proficiency Continuum portrays people and organizations who possess the knowledge, skills, and moral bearing to distinguish among equitable and inequitable practices as represented by different worldviews:

Informs

Unhealthy, unproductive, and inequitable policies, practices, and behaviors	Differing Worldviews	**Healthy, productive, and equitable policies, practices, and behaviors**
- Cultural destructiveness - Cultural incapacity - Cultural blindness		- Cultural precompetence - Cultural competence - Cultural proficiency

Resolving the tension to do what is socially just within our diverse society leads people and organizations to view selves in terms productive and equitable.

Informs   Informs

Overcoming Barriers to Cultural Proficiency

Serve as personal, professional, and institutional impediments to moral and just service to a diverse society by:

- Being resistant to change,
- Being unaware of the need to adapt,
- Not acknowledging systemic oppression, and
- Benefiting from a sense of privilege and entitlement.

Ethical Tension

Guiding Principles of Cultural Proficiency

Provide a moral framework for conducting one's self and organization in an ethical fashion by believing the following:

- Culture is a predominant force in society.
- People are served in varying degrees by the dominant culture.
- People have individual and group identities.
- Diversity within cultures is vast and significant.
- Each cultural group has unique cultural needs.
- The best of both worlds enhances the capacity of all.
- The family, as defined by each culture, is the primary system of support in the education of children.
- School systems must recognize that marginalized populations have to be at least bicultural and that this status creates a distinct set of issues to which the system must be equipped to respond.
- Inherent in cross-cultural interactions are dynamics that must be acknowledged, adjusted to, and accepted.

Source: Adapted from R. B. Lindsey, Nuri-Robins, and Terrell (2009, p. 60).

change in efforts to improve outcomes and increase equity, they may begin with intentional reflection and personal change before focusing efforts on the system (Dilts, 1990; Fullan, 1997; Gardner, 2004; Lindsey et al., 2019).

The Importance of School Leadership in Educational Reform. **Research** regarding the relationship between school leadership and student achievement is substantive. Many educators rely on the literature to guide their responsibilities and practices regarding effective schools and closing educational gaps (Byrk & Schneider, 2002; Hallinger & Heck, 1996; Leithwood, Seashore-Louis, Anderson, & Wahlstrom, 2004; Lezotte & Snyder, 2011; Marzano, Water, & McNulty, 2005). Often, cultural differences between educators and students influence student achievement outcomes in educational settings because differences in core values, deficit-based and asset-based, lead individuals to develop behaviors and implement practices.

In committing to the moral imperative of educational leadership, it is important to note that despite national, state, and local reform efforts, educational gaps in academic outcomes between African American, Native American, and Latino students, and certain white and Asian American peers, still persist (Hammond, 2015; Howard, 2010; Kendi, 2019; Kozol, 1995; Ladson-Billings, 2006; Noguera, 2008). Fullan (2003) discussed the meaning of the moral imperative for educational leaders, with an emphasis on introducing new elements into the setting that are intended to influence behavior for the better. When introduced into the setting as assets, stakeholders with varying interests, economic situations, cultural origins, religions, ethnicities, and racialized group memberships are essential to educational reform. Since race and social class are complex issues for school leaders, no one approach will close educational and access gaps (Barton & Coley, 2009; Murphy, 2009).

However, Murphy (2009) suggested two ways educators can support or empower students on the lower end of opportunity and educational gaps. Leaders may use programs that target disadvantaged students and use strategies that can provide gains to all, but greater gains for those disadvantaged students. School leaders focused on closing educational gaps through educational reform efforts may engage in reflective practices and collaborative work to create organizational change and influence learning outcomes. Often, principals are those expected to launch initiatives and develop programs that are evidence based to raise student achievement and disproportionately advantage those performing on the lower end of educational gaps (DuFour & Mattos, 2013). Fullan (2003) suggested, "At the school level—the moral imperative of the principal involves leading deep cultural change that mobilizes the passions and commitments of teachers, parents, and others to improve the learning of all students, including closing the achievement gap" (p. 41).

In educational reform efforts, it is necessary for the school leader to acknowledge the "what" of change and the "how" of change. The importance of school leadership in educational reform is the ability to build capacity with a focus on results. In order for large-scale reform to reduce educational outcome gaps, school leaders must develop a shared meaning with a focus on individual and organizational change in the complex social context (Fullan, 2016).

Culturally Proficient Leadership for Organizational Change. Terrell, Terrell, Lindsey, & Lindsey (2018) described culturally proficient leadership as an approach grounded in the belief that leaders who are effective in cross-cultural settings have an understanding of their own assumptions, beliefs, and values regarding people and cultures different from their own. Furthermore, Fullan (2003) defined the moral imperative of school leadership as the individual's responsibility for all students. With the moral imperative, knowledge, and skills, effective educators examine their values, behaviors, and beliefs, as well as their organization's policies and practices (Cross, Bazron, Dennis, & Issacs, 1989).

Culturally proficient leaders utilize the Tools of Cultural Proficiency, to acknowledge behaviors and values, as well as school policies and practices that have performance ramifications related to student demographics (Lindsey et al., 2018). Professional learning focusing on Cultural Proficiency supports leaders dedicated to changing systems that will effectively serve all students. For example, change is expected in education, and school improvement plans help guide organizations toward increased student achievement targets. Dilts's model of nested levels of learning details the importance of professional learning and collaboration necessary for organizational change to occur. The five levels of organizational change identified by Dilts (1990) included identity, belief system, capabilities, behaviors, and environment. Culturally proficient leaders rely on perspectives and ideas of diverse stakeholders to be most effective in developing policies and practices that produce the most equitable outcomes for students (Clark-Louque, Lindsey, Quezada, & Jew, 2020; Fullan, 2016; Lindsey et al., 2019). Overall, professional learning and collaboration are necessary components for educational change, hence the focus on reflection, dialogue, and action toward transforming one's mindset from deficit-based to asset-based in culturally proficient leadership. Literature suggests it is essential educational leaders understand that organizational change begins with self (Dewey, 1938; Dilts, 1990; Gardener, 2004).

RESEARCH METHODOLOGY AND DESIGN

This research study was conducted using a descriptive, qualitative case study methodology to "reveal the multifaceted nature of certain situations, settings, processes, relationships, systems, or people" regarding Eaveston School District's journey to become a culturally proficient district (Leedy & Ormrod, 2013). With the intent to investigate a district's why and how of the application of the Cultural Proficiency Framework, data from interviews, observations, and documents were collected and analyzed to determine findings and conclusions related to the research questions and conceptual framework of this study. The findings present rich descriptions and analyses of a contemporary set of events in a single, bounded system, Eaveston School District (Merriam, 2001; Yin, 2018). Although case study does not allow for replication of a situation, process, or system, it is heuristic in the sense that the case study "illuminates the reader's understanding of the phenomenon under study" and can be used to generalize experiences (Merriam, 2001; Yin, 2018). Eaveston School District was selected for this case study because of (1) the school district's implementation of professional learning using the Cultural Proficiency Framework at the district and building levels; (2) the school district's high level of cultural, racial/ethnic, and social class diversity; (3) its increase in student achievement; and (4) its proximity to a metropolitan city with racial and social class implications on governmental, political, and educational contexts.

PURPOSE AND RESEARCH QUESTIONS

The case study focused on the implementation and experiences of cultural proficiency work in a suburban, public PK–12 school district in the Midwest United States. This article provides findings and conclusions related to two research questions that were used to guide part of a larger case study:

- In what ways do the school district's implementation plans and experiences influence changes associated with culturally proficient practice to serve all students?

- What challenges do educational leaders face during the work of Cultural Proficiency?

POPULATION AND SAMPLE

The population for this case study research consisted of *leaders* in Eaveston School District who were involved in the implementation or experiences of the Cultural Proficiency work and/or participated in quarterly, full-day professional development related to Cultural Proficiency during the 2017–2018 and 2018–2019 school years. The term leaders in this study included teachers, building and district administrators, staff, parents, and community members involved in the work of Cultural Proficiency. The population included three groups. Figure 2 provides details related to each population group. The first population group included 55 leaders involved in the work at the district level. The second population included 110 teachers, administrators, and staff from two middle schools in Eaveston School District. These teachers participated in whole staff Cultural Proficiency professional development during the 2017–2018 school year. The third population was from one middle school and included a group of 70 teachers, staff, and administrators led by members of a building-level Cultural Proficiency Committee. This group formally continued their professional development using the Cultural Proficiency Framework during bimonthly meetings.

FIGURE 2 ● Population and Sample of Eaveston School District Case Study.

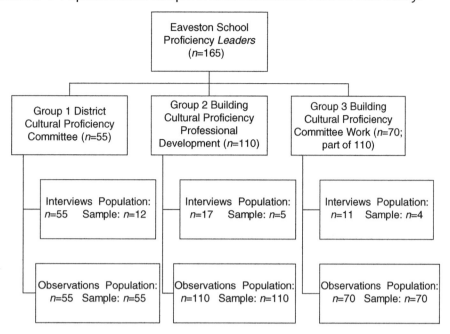

Sampling involves decisions for the researcher related to which people to interview and/or observe, which documents to mine for data, as well as settings, events, and social processes (Miles, Huberman, & Saldana, 2020). Because of the conceptual framework of Cultural Proficiency and the research questions, the researcher set boundaries within the settings, events, documents, and people involved in the work of Cultural Proficiency. The sample in this case study included 14 volunteers from the three population groups. Through purposeful sampling, the researcher selected the sample based on respondents' availability and desire to participate. Merriam (2009) suggested purposeful sampling to maximize findings in a research study. The researcher sampled from individuals who experienced the Cultural Proficiency work as part of one or more of the three groups included in Figure 2 (Creswell, 2013). Fourteen individuals responded to an invitation to participate, and the researcher conducted interviews with the sample group of 14 volunteers. Table 1 displays the interview participants' characteristics, population and group membership, and school level.

INSTRUMENTATION

The researcher developed and utilized three instruments to collect data in this case study to better understand the implementation process: (1) an interview protocol, (2) an observation guide, and (3) a document retrieval form. In order to answer the research questions, an interview protocol was developed with ten questions to ask participants during the interview sessions (Creswell, 2014). The interview questions were designed using a

TABLE 1 ● Interview Participants' Characteristics

ROLE	GENDER	POPULATION MEMBERSHIP	GROUPS*	SCHOOL LEVEL
(1) Principal	Female	Building CPC	2,3	Middle
(2) Principal	Male	District CPC	1	Elementary
(3) Principal	Female	District CPC	1	Elementary
(4) Principal	Male	District CPC	1	Elementary/Middle
(5) Assistant Principal	Female	District /	1,2,3	Middle
(6) Teacher	Female	Building	1,2,3	Middle
(7) Sp. Language Pathologist	Female	District /	1	High
(8) Sp. Education Teacher	Female	Building	2,3	Middle
(9) Teacher	Female	District	1	Elementary
(10) Parent	Male	Building CPC	1	All
(11) Teacher	Female	District CPC	1	Middle
(12) Assistant Superintendent	Female	Building CPC	1	All
(13) Director	Female	District CPC	1	All
(14) Principal	Male	District CPC	1	Middle

Note: Group 1 District Cultural Proficiency Committee (CPC) Work; Group 2 Building Cultural Proficiency Professional Development; and Group 3 Building Cultural Proficiency Committee (CPC) Work.

semi-structured approach and addressed school leadership, educational reform, and culturally proficient practice and policy. The data were used to produce perspectives about facts and feelings related to the work of Cultural Proficiency (Leedy & Ormrod, 2013).

The researcher developed an observation guide to use during Cultural Proficiency events such as planning meetings and work sessions at the district and building levels. The observation guide included a T-chart to separate descriptive notes from reflective notes. Since participant observation can be subjective, the researcher observed in a way to address the research questions related to the application of the Tools of Cultural Proficiency and challenges to produce trustworthy results. In addition, the observation guide included ways to collect data regarding the physical settings, participants, activities and interactions, and the researcher's own behavior (Merriam, 2009).

Similar to the observation guide, the researcher developed a document retrieval form to collect and analyze data mined from various district documents. The document retrieval form was designed as a T-chart to separate descriptive notes from reflective notes (Merriam, 2009). This instrument's purpose was to mine data from various documents in categories of school improvement (planning), description, and communication. To refrain from subjectivity, the researcher collected data in a systematic way to address the research questions, specifically focusing on the Four Tools of Cultural Proficiency.

DATA COLLECTION AND ANALYSES

The researcher collected data throughout this case study to answer the research questions and provide an example of one school district's journey to become a culturally proficient organization by developing and implementing culturally proficient policies and practices. Merriam (2001) and Yin (2018) provided details for the data collection phase in case study methodology. Typically, this process involves interviewing, observing, and analyzing documents. During the 2018–2019 school year, the researcher completed three phases of data collection. The phases do not represent chronological order, rather they focus on the source of collection. Phase I yielded data from 14 interviews to build thick, rich descriptions of school leaders' perceptions and experiences of implementing the equity and access work. In Phase II, the researcher collected field notes on the observation protocol during building- and district-level Cultural Proficiency Committee meetings and professional development events. Descriptive notes were recorded such as descriptions of the activities and participants in the setting. The researcher utilized the T-chart to record behaviors and reflective notes to summarize the meetings and professional development events (Creswell, 2014).

Phase III included a collection of data from document retrieval forms using descriptive and reflective notes. Thomas (2011) explained the importance of finding the right documents in a case study. The researcher focused on documents related to the Cultural Proficiency work and reflected the espoused values and beliefs of the district, as well as the values-in-action. Therefore, data were mined from several available district documents such as vision/mission statements, policies, handbooks, brochures, a book chapter, school improvement plans, climate survey reports, electronic documents available on the district's website, newsletters, and social media posts.

In the final step of conducting this case study, the researcher analyzed and interpreted the collected data to answer the research questions and draw conclusions. The findings and conclusions in this article focus on the school district's use of core values in identifying Barriers, relying on the Guiding Principles, and changing practices and policies identified on the Continuum using the Essential Elements of Cultural Proficiency. The researcher conducted the analysis by preparing and organizing the data, and then reducing it into themes after using an *in vivo* coding process related to the conceptual framework (Creswell, 2014). The themes gathered from the three data collection instruments were triangulated to develop conclusions and implications of the study. Throughout the study and reporting of the school district's journey of Cultural Proficiency, confidentiality, reliability, and validity of the data collection and analysis processes were conducted with the highest integrity. The researcher used prolonged engagement in the field to build trust with the participants, learn the culture, and check for misinformation; as well as triangulation (Figure 3) to provide corroborating evidence from different data sources (Creswell, 2013). The school district and all employees' anonymity were guaranteed and protected to promote transparent responses in interviews and behaviors within observed professional development events.

Limitations. As with any research study, this case study has limitations that affect the findings, conclusions, and implications for practice. The limitations include the sample size, the difficulty in replicating the study across all settings, and the researcher's role. The sample size of this study was small in relation to the number of employees working for the district. Therefore, generalizations made through the findings and conclusions are difficult to transfer across all buildings within the district and beyond.

In addition, the researcher played a role in the meetings and professional learning events by providing content and learning strategies related to the Cultural Proficiency Framework. Yin (2018) posited, researchers using case study methodology must understand the conditions of the case prior to the study. More importantly, the researcher must acknowledge that this knowledge is what can introduce bias and sway the researcher toward supportive or favorable evidence. The researcher avoided this bias by looking at all relevant data and being open to supportive and contrary evidence. Interviews and observations produced data that were both supportive of and contrary to the preconceptions of the researcher. Contrary evidence were supported through discussions about the Barriers and challenges of implementing and sustaining the work of Cultural Proficiency. Leedy and Ormrod (2013) suggested, "Good researchers demonstrate their integrity by admitting, without reservation, that bias is omnipresent and may well have influence on their findings" (p. 219). The researcher was aware that the dual role of professional developer and researcher would influence the research design, thus limiting the findings and conclusions. Reflexivity allowed the researcher to acknowledge interfering biases, speculate effects, and interpret results in order to reduce bias (Leedy & Ormrod, 2013).

FINDINGS RELATED TO THE TOOLS OF CULTURAL PROFICIENCY

The descriptive single case study data were collected from participants through interviews, observations, and relevant documents and analyzed using the lens of the Tools of Cultural Proficiency. Three themes emerged from the triangulation of data that are related to the implementation and experiences of Cultural Proficiency in Eaveston School District: (1) professional learning through various professional learning communities, (2) diverse family and community involvement, and (3) continuous school improvement toward student achievement. Figure 3 provides details about the triangulation of data. The themes are presented in detail throughout the analysis. The report begins with the findings in relation to the conceptual framework (Figure 1) and concludes by answering two research questions, part of the overall study, as displayed in Table 5. The findings are organized with rich descriptive details by the Tools of Cultural Proficiency used by

FIGURE 3 ● Case Findings From Data Collection and Analysis.

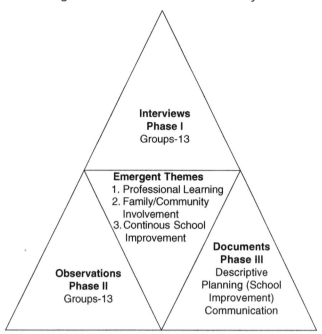

Eaveston School District leaders in implementing this work. Focus is given to how core values, both deficit-based and asset-based, can lead action toward organizational change.

BARRIERS OF CULTURAL PROFICIENCY: IDENTIFYING BEHAVIORS AND PRACTICES INFORMED BY DEFICIT-BASED CORE VALUES

One tool used in the implementation of Cultural Proficiency is the Barriers. During Cultural Proficiency Committee meetings and professional development sessions, the three population groups engaged in a data collection process of using the Continuum of Cultural Proficiency. During the process, participants worked to identify themes among practices and behaviors on the left side of the Continuum, those that are informed by Barriers and function as deficit-laden core values, to set a direction to begin increasing equity and access for students in Eaveston. The emergent findings are displayed in Table 2 to explain ways Eaveston leaders identify and overcome four Barriers to Cultural Proficiency: (1) systemic barriers, (2) unawareness of the need for educators to adapt to the diversity of the community being served, (3) a sense of privilege and entitlement, and (4) resistance to change.

Unfolding the Barriers to Cultural Proficiency as a means to embrace their historical negativity provided Eaveston's stakeholders opportunity to study, embrace, and adapt the inclusive Guiding Principles of Cultural Proficiency and guide the district from being school-centric to being a community-centric district focused on the academic and social needs of Eaveston's diverse community.

TABLE 2 ● Eaveston School District's Application of Cultural Proficiency's Barriers to District Core Values and Actions

Systemic barriers present in Eaveston's policies and prevalent practices to be addressed, minimized, and eliminated include: • Policies that perceived different norms, values, beliefs, behaviors as wrong (e.g., dress code that resulted in disciplinary actions and other negative sanctions against students of color); • A diverse student body in contrast to school administration, faculty, and staff who were White, middle class, and female; • Differing feelings of belonging to the school (i.e., historical implications due to parents' childhood school experiences, teacher/administrator relationships with families, past experiences of families coming to school—discipline, IEP meetings, celebrations, student awards); • Differing levels of support for family engagement (i.e., PTO, family attendance at events); and • Historical effects of stress between African American community and police in the area.
The manner in which Eaveston will overcome the identified barriers is: • Use data, communicate clearly about who is being left out or being denied access, then commit to action; • Review/revise policies using the Framework; • Review hiring practices through engagement with Cultural Proficiency Committee; • Extend and deepen Restorative Practices activities at school sites; • Extend and deepen school and family involvement/engagement; and • Use of Cultural Proficiency learning strategies to promote asset-based approaches to difference (i.e., Managing Conflict With Our Core Values, Guiding Principles Discussion Starters, Listening and Hearing; Source: Lindsey, Nuri-Robins, Terrell, & Lindsey, 2009).
The Barrier—unawareness of the need for Eaveston educators to adapt to the community include: • Well-intentioned adults who desire to do the work, but don't know how to initiate or sustain self-study; • Differences in norms, experiences, behaviors, learning styles among educators and community served give rise to culturally based misunderstandings that too often lead to mistrust; and • Educators' lack of knowledge and experiences related to the community's history and experiences of being oppressed.
The manner in which Eaveston will overcome internalized unawareness of the need to adapt to the community being served is: • Work continuously toward equity and understanding, appreciating, and respecting differences in cultures—targeted resources; • Implement Eaveston's Personalized Learning Initiative; and • Maintain high expectations, assess needs, and focus on communication.
The Barrier—a sense of entitlement or privilege at Eaveston, include: • Rejection of the term "privilege"; • Historical "roles" of teacher vs. student as a power struggle; and • Perspectives become some school members' reality in which community perspectives are often viewed as being wrong.
The manner in which Eaveston will overcome a sense of privilege and entitlement involve: • Encourage family engagement strategies as a means for educators to gain healthy perspectives about communities served by Eaveston District. • Implement personalized learning and competency-based curricula that utilize research-based strategies and scaffolding to support students realizing their full potential. • Maintain high expectations, ensure discipline policies are equitable, expand use of Restorative Practices; and • Honor individual stories of school members as well as community members.

The Barrier—resistance to change at Eaveston include:

- Resistance against mandated Cultural Proficiency professional development;
- Resistance/avoidance by some educators and staff members due to fear, discomfort in addressing issues related to cultural differences; and
- Resistance because some believe there has been little progress, change, or sustainability in prior equity work.

The manner in which Eaveston will overcome resistance to change is:

- Focus change from individuals to our values and behaviors;
- Change the model and methods of professional development to focus on educator needs in responding to a diverse community;
- Utilize professional learning strategies of reflection, dialogue, and action to build trust, empathy, and relationships in professional development programs; and
- Provide opportunities for teachers and students to respond to contentious issues, to express feelings, and to support inclusive change processes.

THE GUIDING PRINCIPLES: EAVESTON'S CORE VALUES FOR SYSTEMIC CHANGE

Eaveston School District leaders used Tool 2, the Guiding Principles, in the implementation of the cultural proficiency work. Participants identified themes among practices and behaviors on the right side of the Continuum, those that are informed by guiding principles and function as asset-based core values. Eaveston School District's Core Values have been summarized as:

Expressed Values—Diversity, Knowledge, Commitment, Care, Safety, Learning, Interdependence, Contribution, Strength, Freedom, Success

Underlying Values—Communication, Creativity, Curiosity, Teamwork, Growth, Hope, Quality, Innovation, Achievement, Service

As a result of the district's Cultural Proficiency journey, Eaveston's expressed and underlying core values have been expanded through thoughtful consideration of the Guiding Principles of Cultural Proficiency. Table 3 displays an analysis of data from interviews, observations, and document reviews regarding Eaveston leaders' adaptations of the Guiding Principles in a manner that deepens the district's expressed and underlying core values.

Relying on the Guiding Principles of Cultural Proficiency as an avenue to organizational change provided Eaveston's stakeholders opportunities to study and embrace the asset-based core values that have led to many policies, practices, and behaviors implemented to meet the academic and social needs of Eaveston's students.

THE CONTINUUM OF CULTURAL PROFICIENCY: EAVESTON'S AWARENESS OF "TELLING STORIES" AND CHANGING THE CONVERSATION

Over several months, administration, faculty, and staff engaged in processes to identify systemic barriers to students' access to equitable educational outcomes and rely on the Guiding Principles using Tool 3 of the Cultural

TABLE 3 ● Eaveston School District's Application of Cultural Proficiency's Guiding Principles to District Core Values and Actions

Culture is a predominant force in society.
1. Eaveston is focused on building the critical mass of educators who are committed to the equity work, but recognizes that due to cultural values and behaviors, some are uncomfortable, some are critical, and some avoid the conversation altogether.
2. Culture will bring in a dynamic of difference. Eaveston School District leaders are committed to continuous conversation and training, both informally and formally to promote growth and development related to cultural knowledge.

People have group identities and personal identities.
1. Eaveston is implementing personalized learning to help each child thrive and succeed in the learning environment.
2. Eaveston School District promotes conversations and deconstruction of assumptions among staff related to perceived group identities and behaviors that follow (i.e., discipline, misunderstood language or behaviors, academics).

Diversity within cultures is important.
1. As a district on the journey to Cultural Proficiency, Eaveston leaders are acutely aware of their recognized diversity in terms of race/ethnicity, socioeconomic status, and language. Data to support knowledge regarding the diversity within those cultures is less apparent.
2. The district is focused on students' individual stories, building relationships, increasing communication, and providing services and support related to those stories is trending.

Each group has unique cultural needs that must be respected.
1. Educators in Eaveston use professional development and professional learning communities to learn about the unique cultural needs that individual students have (i.e., socioeconomic status, disability). These events are subconsciously used to teach members of the dominant group about differences.
2. "Wrap-around" services and support programs are available to help meet those unique cultural needs (i.e., tiered system, food, medical, dental, clothing, etc.).

The best of both worlds enhances capacity of all.
1. Diversity is an attribute to the district, a part of the district that is not looked at as an obstacle.
2. Eaveston provides avenues for continuous growth through reflection and dialogue, where multiple perspectives are included for the purpose of serving each and every child in the district.

The family, as defined by each culture, is the primary system of support in the education of children.
1. Eaveston School District leaders engage families by purposefully reaching out to increase diversity, perspective, and participation among various cultures on committees and events.
2. One of the core values related to family engagement is communication. The district keeps families informed and connected through multiple modalities of communication, including those who are translated and/or interpreted.
3. Eaveston School District connects with and engages families through "community-centric" events/activities that meet the basic needs of children and their family members (i.e., food, school supplies, clothing, glasses or dental care).

Proficiency Framework, the Continuum. Pertinent to the conclusions of this study, leaders in Eaveston ensured parents and community members were involved in professional learning opportunities at the district level. Armed with awareness and understanding the function of core values among the Barriers and Guiding Principles of Cultural Proficiency, group participants, identified in Figure 2, immersed themselves in understanding policies and practices they posted along the six points of the Cultural Proficiency Continuum. Figure 4 includes examples on individual sticky notes that represent each point on the Continuum.

Whereas illustrations along the Continuum provided vivid detail to the manner in which policy and practice examples of *Destructiveness*, *Incapacity*, and *Blindness* supported deficit-based core values, policy and practice examples of *Precompetence*, *Competence*, and *Proficiency* supported asset-based core values. Eaveston leaders' study of the Cultural Proficiency Framework proceeded to the fourth tool, the Essential Elements of Cultural Proficiency. It is at this point that members were prepared to be intentional in devising actionable pathways derived from core values that embraced students' cultures as assets on which to build their educational experiences. For each of the six points, participants were asked to contribute at least one policy or practice of Eaveston School District or individual behavior, meaning something someone has said or done. An example from each point on The Continuum is included in Figure 4.

Using the most powerful themes from the data collected by the District Cultural Proficiency Committee, the members created action plans for the next school year related to (1) disparity in student discipline, (2) diversity among Eaveston's workforce, and (3) continued learning and growth using the Cultural Proficiency Framework. Although each group produced separate themes and action plans, these findings were gathered during the district's cultural proficiency events using observations and document analyses of

FIGURE 4 ● The Continuum of Cultural Proficiency: Examples of Practices, Policies, and/or Behaviors Gathered on Color-Specific Sticky Notes During The Data Collection Process, Both Negative and Positive.

Culturally Destructive Policies Practices Behaviors	Culturally Incapacitating Policies Practices Behaviors	Culturally Blind Policies Practices Behaviors	Culturally Precompetent Policies Practices Behaviors	Culturally Competent Policies Practices Behaviors	Culturally Proficient Policies Practices Behaviors
Example "If they can't understand or read my homework or newsletter, that is their problem."	Example Giving nicknames to students with unfamiliar names, mocking the pronunciation of the name, or negatively commenting on the "uniqueness of the name."	Example "I don't see color; all students are treated fairly in my class."	Example Hosting Diversity Days, International Night, Black History Month, Hispanic Heritage Month, etc.	Example Choosing literature for the classroom and library that represents cultural differences and providing training on using it appropriately.	Example Disaggregating data and changing practice on recruiting and hiring a diverse workforce, and facilitating conversations with stakeholders about current and best practice.

the sticky notes collected during this learning strategy, as well as other documents related to the action plan themes listed above.

THE ESSENTIAL ELEMENTS OF CULTURAL PROFICIENCY: COMMITTING TO STANDARDS OF CHANGE THROUGH IMPROVEMENT AND GROWTH

The five Essential Elements of Cultural Proficiency, Tool 4 of the framework, serve to guide policy development and implementation as well as intentional practices in support of all students achieving high levels through continuous school improvement. The Essential Elements are an overlapping and mutual reinforcing means to inclusive macro–policymaking, as well as guidance for the everyday behaviors of school district members. Table 4 presents illustrations of how the Essential Elements are being used to

TABLE 4 ● Essential Elements Inform Organizations' Policies and Practices and Individuals' Values, and Behaviors

EXAMPLES FROM CASE	DATA SOURCE(S)	EMERGENT THEME(S)
Assessing Culture		
Leaders and educators review, revise, and implement instructional practices based upon cultural knowledge to ensure high expectations and rigorous standards through personalized learning.	Observations Document Analysis	Professional Learning Communities Continuous School Improvement
Valuing Diversity		
Leaders examine how well the school is meeting students' and the community's needs and search for new strategies to engage families. Eaveston involves students, parents, and community members' perspectives in planning special events and celebrations.	Interviews Observations Document Analysis	Family and Community Involvement Continuous School Improvement Professional Learning Communities
Managing the Dynamics of Difference		
The human resource department and administrators in Eaveston are committed to managing the difference in student demographics and teacher demographics by recruiting, hiring, and promoting people who think and act inclusively. Teachers of color are actively involved in the prospective teacher recruitment process.	Interviews Observations Document Analysis	Continuous School Improvement Family and Community Involvement
Adapting to Diversity		
Educators in Eaveston are committed to effective communication; particularly in learning new ways to effectively communicate to families who speak a native language other than English.	Interviews Observations Document Analysis	Family and Community Involvement
Institutionalizing Cultural Knowledge		
Eaveston is building capacity of individuals committed to sustainable equity-based diversity training using the Tools of Cultural Proficiency to identify and overcome barriers to access, achievement, and success.	Interviews Observations	Continuous School Improvement Family and Community Involvement Professional Learning Communities

inform policymaking and practice, as well as educator values and behaviors. The examples represent organizational change to increase equity and access for all students in Eaveston based upon asset-based core values.

Assessing culture relates to the way Eaveston School District leaders are examining their core values and culture, as well as the cultural norms of the school district. These Essential Elements require educators understand how the culture of the organization affects those with different cultures. An example of Eaveston's action toward organizational change is evidenced from data gathered in observations and document analyses. Table 4 includes the practice of leaders and educators reviewing, revising, and implementing instructional practices based upon cultural knowledge to ensure high expectations and rigorous standards through personalized learning. During a District Cultural Proficiency meeting, two district administrators presented a new personalized learning initiative including components such as learner profiles. Similarly, in a document analysis, the personalized learning plan was described as "a competency-based, personalized learning environment in preschool through 12th grades that leads students to be ready for high school course content, and ultimately, success after graduation." In this plan, Eaveston is preparing its employees through professional learning and input from family and the community to customize learning to meet student needs, which includes an in-depth look at student and family culture. Eaveston is committed to embedding Cultural Proficiency in all aspects of the district, especially those related to the personalized learning plan, to maximize efforts toward continuous school improvement.

Valuing diversity is another standard that intentionally guides Eaveston in their journey to become culturally proficient. In this area of organizational change, Eaveston School District leaders are celebrating and encouraging the presence of a wide variety of people in all activities, as well as accepting that each culture finds some values and behaviors more important than others. Data from interviews, observations, and document analyses indicated Eaveston's leaders examine how well the school is meeting students' and the community's needs and how leaders search for new strategies to engage families and include students, parents, and community members' perspectives in planning special events and celebrations.

The standard of Managing the Dynamics of Difference is about responding to conflict. Eaveston leaders are committed to responding appropriately and effectively when issues arise based upon cultural differences. One goal that developed from the district's Cultural Proficiency Committee work with the Continuum was the need to diversify the workforce. As indicated in Table 4, data from interviews, observations, and document analyses concluded that the human resource department and administrators in Eaveston are committed to managing the difference in student and teacher demographics by recruiting, hiring, and promoting people who think and act inclusively. In an interview, the Assistant Superintendent of Human Resources commented on the district's recent changes to who accompanies him at career fairs. In order to manage the dynamics of difference in this situation, these administrators are now adapting to diversity by joining forces and taking teachers of color, both male and female, with them to recruitment fairs and ensuring diversity is represented in interview committees. A document produced by the human resources department from a meeting with the District Cultural Proficiency Committee demonstrated commitment to teachers' of color active involvement in the prospective teacher recruiting process. Ideas on recruitment and hiring were collected from the members on the District Cultural Proficiency Committee.

Adapting to diversity is a standard that Eaveston leaders are using to change practices that acknowledge the differences among students, families, and staff. The data collected from interviews, observations, and document analyses related to this standard concluded some educators in Eaveston are committed to effective communication; particularly in learning new ways to communicate to families who speak a native language other than English. In an interview, a principal commented, "We have Family English Night here where families can come two nights a week to take a formal English class for free." Through observations, members of the District Cultural Proficiency Committee discussed ways in which documents such as handbooks and letters are translated to provide increased access for families who do not speak English.

Eaveston leaders have used the standard of institutionalizing cultural knowledge to drive changes into the organization. In the district committee's work with the Continuum, leaders created a goal for building capacity of individuals committed to sustainable equity-based diversity training. Both district- and building-level leaders sponsored professional learning opportunities related to equity, diversity, and Cultural Proficiency to inform district members and the school as an organization. In an interview a teacher commented, "I am part of the district's Cultural Proficiency Committee, and I feel like we're really digging deeper and doing it in a way that we want to make plans for growth with staff and students." At the building level, observations of planning meetings demonstrate the commitment to institutionalizing cultural knowledge by discussing and incorporating knowledge of how one's own culture, students' cultures, and the school or district's culture affect those with different cultures. A member of the Building Cultural Proficiency Committee commented, "I think that we're headed in the right direction because we have a great group on our committee that is willing to kind of take the reins and do this professional development training that we need with our staff. I think it's going to be much more meaningful coming from their colleagues and not from administrators." In a planning document for the district's Professional Development Committee, one goal is written as, "Exploring means to support and provide leadership for staff development initiatives at both the district level and building level." Overall, the work of Cultural Proficiency is being implemented by using the standards of the Essential Elements to inform action toward organizational change.

CASE STUDY RESEARCH QUESTIONS AND FINDINGS

The case study focused on the implementation and experiences of Cultural Proficiency work in a suburban, public PK–12 school district in the Midwest United States. The two research questions used to guide part of a larger case study included (1) In what ways do the school district's implementation plans and experiences influence changes regarding culturally proficient practice to serve all students? (2) What challenges do educational leaders face during the work of Cultural Proficiency? (Welborn, 2019). Table 5 includes the emergent themes related to the implementation experiences and challenges faced by Eaveston's leaders.

In what ways do the school district's implementation and experiences influence changes regarding culturally proficient practice to serve all students?

This research question was used to investigate the ways in which educational leaders have implemented and experienced the work of Cultural Proficiency to influence change and serve all students. Behavior, practice, and policy changes result from using asset-based core values informed by the Guiding Principles to counter deficit-based core values informed by the Barriers of Cultural Proficiency. Out of the analyses of data from leader interviews, meeting and professional learning event observations, and related document reviews, two themes emerged from the data to support the answer to this research question. The themes include (1) professional development through professional learning communities with subthemes of high expectations, individual students, student achievement, and excellence and (2) dialogue and action planning with family and community involvement.

Eaveston's leaders involved in implementing the Cultural Proficiency Framework focus on increasing equity for all students by providing opportunities for staff members to examine core values and practices through collaboration in professional learning communities. For example, there are many opportunities for staff members to collaborate with others in the district around topics such as restorative practices, trauma-informed care, social-emotional learning, personalized learning, and Cultural Proficiency.

TABLE 5 ● Case Study Research Questions and Findings

RESEARCH QUESTIONS	EMERGENT THEMES
In what ways do the school district's implementation and experiences influence changes regarding culturally proficient practice to serve all students?	(1) Professional development through professional learning communities (PLC) with subthemes of high expectations, individual students, student achievement and excellence and (2) dialogue and action with family and community involvement.
What challenges do educational leaders face during the work of Cultural Proficiency?	(1) Barriers to Cultural Proficiency; (2) availability of time and resources; and (3) building site-specific capacity to implement and sustain the equity work across the district.

This includes sessions for new teachers and support staff. District administrators increased their involvement in events related to implementing the Cultural Proficiency Framework and utilized the tools in their discussions with the board members, families, and community members (Welborn, 2019).

Eaveston School District has experienced change in the organization through reflection and dialogue in using the Four Tools of Cultural Proficiency. The utilization of the Continuum of Cultural Proficiency is instrumental in beginning work to address areas of needed improvement. One key to successful implementation of the framework is involving families and community members in discussions and work related to advancing the goals set out by the committee. District leaders engage community members by bringing in experts to help facilitate conversations about restorative practices and trauma. They also include parents in school improvement planning and as members of the district's Cultural Proficiency Committee. District leaders plan to build capacity among the district's committee by increasing opportunity for reflection and dialogue so that all school buildings in the district gain support in implementing the Tools of Cultural Proficiency to promote equity, access, and inclusion (Welborn, 2019).

WHAT CHALLENGES DO EDUCATIONAL LEADERS FACE DURING THE WORK OF CULTURAL PROFICIENCY?

This research question focused on the challenges educational leaders face as they implemented the work of Cultural Proficiency in Eaveston School District. From the data emerged three themes. The themes include barriers to Cultural Proficiency, availability of time and resources, and building site-specific capacity to implement and sustain the equity work across the district. Eaveston School District leaders acknowledge barriers such as the unawareness of the need to adapt, resistance to change, and mistrust impede the journey of becoming a culturally proficient school district. The historical mistrust that was formed from a previous social justice training plays a role in building capacity for all district employees to engage in the work. Using the tool, Guiding Principles of Cultural Proficiency, and focusing on asset-based core values, district leaders work to build capacity and trust among those involved in the work through reflection, dialogue, and action (Welborn, 2019).

Some leaders in Eaveston feel insufficient time and resources are the greatest challenges in implementing the Cultural Proficiency work across the district. Professional learning sessions require both time and resources, which limits the number of sessions that can involve teachers, administrators, and support staff throughout the school year when students are present. Many school leaders have realized that this work is challenging, and it is a journey. School leaders implement this work by prioritizing the utilization of time and resources to build capacity and embed the work in all aspects of the Eaveston School District. They want to ensure that all who educate Eaveston's youth understand this work is here to stay. Building site-specific capacity to implement and sustain the equity work across the district is a challenge prompting school leaders to balance the urgency of spreading the equity work beyond the district's Cultural Proficiency Committee and throughout the district. School leaders want to ensure the Cultural Proficiency work is implemented with urgency, but not in a way that causes an increase in resistance, protest, and unrest within the larger system (Welborn, 2019).

CONCLUSIONS AND RECOMMENDATIONS

Case study data reveal richness and depth of a single-bounded system. At present, Eaveston School District is on an ascendant trajectory in the manner in which it is addressing policies and practices that impede student access and achievement. Leaders determined it necessary to uncover issues of inequities as an important initial step in the journey to having inclusive policies and educator practices that result in increasing student academic and social success in the Eaveston School District. Eaveston's leaders know the importance of aligning what is expressed as core values with the policies and practices of the district and the behaviors of educators throughout the district. Being deliberate in unpacking and overcoming Barriers to Cultural Proficiency served as an important initial link to being able to consider deeply the Guiding Principles of Cultural Proficiency in shaping district core values. It was in this deep consideration of Barriers and Guiding Principles that district leaders were able to make the Essential Elements actionable in district policy and educator practices. In other words, "aligning what they say with what they do." Viewing students and their cultures as assets is an important step in building and selecting curricular, instructional, and assessment approaches. In doing so, educators view their role as being engaged in their own professional learning. The old deficit-based model of what is wrong with students and their cultures is relegated to the historical bin of our segregated history.

Findings from single case studies can be used to support generalizations for other school district leaders to consider (Yin, 2018). The conceptual framework of Cultural Proficiency has been used and studied within a specific, bounded, contemporary setting. The important point to note is for district leaders to *study the study* as well as the conceptual framework and focus on the "why" and "how" for their context and conditions.

In addition to the examples included within the findings of the case study, three implications are provided for school-district and building administrators as a result of the conclusions of the research. Culturally proficient educators can lead organizational change and may increase equity, access, and inclusion for all students by applying the Four Tools of Cultural Proficiency, causing shifts in core value-related mindsets and actions from deficit-based to asset-based. The implications for practice include:

1. Developing a common language around the Cultural Proficiency Framework, intentionally embedding the work of reflection, dialogue, and change to promote access and equity for all students during professional learning through various professional learning communities;

2. Building the capacity of all stakeholders in the district community by inviting diverse family and community perspectives to help in identifying barriers, focusing on core values, and creating goals and action for changing inequitable practices, policies, and behaviors; and

3. Aligning the district's strategic plan, professional learning, and policy review with the mission and core values of the district. Embed Cultural Proficiency in every aspect of the district while focusing on continuous school improvement toward student achievement.

Thus far, Eaveston's story has revealed that some district leaders understand and appreciate that their journey to becoming a culturally proficient school district has barely begun. They recognize the journey before them embraces the students and their families, along with their multiple cultures, as assets on which successful school programs will be constructed. Some district leaders understand and appreciate that they, just like the students in their classrooms, are learners as they continue to strive for ways to meet the academic and social needs of their diverse community.

REFERENCES

Apple, M., & Beane, J. (1995). *Democratic schools*. Alexandria, VA: Association for Supervision and Curriculum Development.

Barton, P., & Coley, R. (2009). *Parsing the achievement gap II*. Princeton, NJ: Educational Testing Service.

Berliner, D. C., & Biddle, B. J. (1995). *The manufactured crisis: Myth, fraud, and the attack on America's public schools*. Reading, MA: Addison-Wesley.

Byrk, A. S., & Schneider, B. (2002). *Trust in schools: A core resource for improvement*. New York, NY: Russell Sage.

Clark-Louque, A., Lindsey, R., Quezada, R., & Jew, C. (2020). *Equity partnerships: A culturally proficient guide to family, school, and community engagement*. Thousand Oaks, CA: Corwin.

Coleman, J., Campbell, E., Hobson, J., McPartland, J., Mood, A., Weinfeld, F., & York, R. (1966). *Equality of educational opportunity*. Washington, DC: Brookings Institution Press.

Crenshaw, K. (2016). *The urgency of intersectionality* [Video file]. Available from https://www.ted.com/talks/kimberle_crenshaw_the_urgency_of_intersectionality?language=en

Creswell, J. W. (2013). *Qualitative inquiry and research design: Choosing among five approaches*. Los Angeles, CA: Sage.

Creswell, J. W. (2014). *Research design: Qualitative, quantitative, and mixed methods approaches*. Thousand Oaks, CA: Sage.

Cross, T., Bazron, B., Denis, K., & Issacs, M. (1989). *Towards a culturally competent system of care* (Vol. 1). Washington, DC: Georgetown University Child Development Center, CASSP Technical Assistance Center.

Darling-Hammond, L. (1995). Restructuring schools for student success. *Daedalus, 124*, 53–162.

Dilts, R. (1990). *Changing belief systems with NLP*. Capitola, CA: Meta.

DuFour, R., & Mattos, M. (2013). How do principals really improve schools? *Education Leadership, 70*(7), 34–40.

Freire, P. (1970). *Pedagogy of the oppressed*. New York: Herder & Herder.

Fullan, M. (1997). *What's worth fighting for in the principalship*. New York: Teachers College Press.

Fullan, M. (2001). *Leading in a culture of change.* San Francisco, CA: Jossey-Bass.

Fullan, M. (2003). *The moral imperative of school leadership.* Thousand Oaks, CA: Corwin.

Fullan, M. (2016). *The new meaning of educational change* (5th ed.). New York: Teachers College Press.

Gardener, H. (2004). *Changing minds.* Boston, MA: Harvard Business School Press.

Hallinger, P., & Heck, R.H. (1996). Reassessing the principal's role in school effectiveness: A review of empirical research 1980-1995. *Education Administration Quarterly, 32*(1), 5–44.

Hammond, Z. (2015). *Culturally responsive teaching & the brain.* Thousand Oaks, CA: Corwin.

Howard, G. (2006). *We can't teach what we don't know: White teachers, multiracial schools* (2nd ed.). New York: Teachers College Press.

Howard, T. (2010). *Why race and culture matter in schools: Closing the achievement gap in America's classrooms.* New York: Teachers College Press.

Jencks, C. (1972). *Inequality: A reassessment of the effect of family and schooling in America.* New York: Basic Books.

Kendi, I. (2019). *How to be an antiracist.* New York: Penguin Random House.

Kozol, J. (2005). *The shame of the nation: The restoration of apartheid schooling in America.* New York: Three Rivers Press.

Ladson-Billings, G. (2006). From the achievement gap to the education debt: Understanding achievement in U.S. schools. *Educational Researcher, 35*(7), 3–12.

Ladson-Billings, G. (2009). *The dream keepers: Successful teachers of African American students.* San Francisco, CA: John Wiley.

Lambert, L. (1998). *Building leadership capacity in schools.* Alexandria, VA: Association for Supervision and Curriculum Development.

Leedy, P., & Ormrod, J. (2013). *Practical research: Planning and design.* Boston, MA: Pearson Education.

Leithwood, K., Seashore-Louis, K., Anderson S., & Wahlstrom, K. (2004). *Review of research: How leadership influences student learning.* Retrieved from https://www.wallacefoundation.org/knowledge-center/Documents/How-Leadership-Influences-Student-Learning.pdf

Lezotte, L., & Snyder, K. (2011). *What effective schools do: Re-envisioning the correlates.* Bloomington, IN: Solution Tree Press.

Lindsey, R., Karns, M., & Myatt, K. (2010). *Culturally proficient education: An asset-based response to conditions of poverty.* Thousand Oaks, CA: Corwin.

Lindsey, R., Nuri-Robins, K., & Terrell, R. (2009). *Cultural proficiency: A manual for school leaders* (3rd ed.). Thousand Oaks, CA: Corwin.

Lindsey, R., Nuri-Robins, K., Terrell, R., & Lindsey, D. (2019). *Cultural proficiency: A manual for school leaders* (4th ed.). Thousand Oaks, CA: Corwin.

Marzano, R., Water, T., & McNulty, B. (2005). *School leadership that works: From research to results.* Alexandria, VA: ASCD and Aurora, CO: Mid-content Research for Education and Learning.

Merriam, S. (2001). *Qualitative research and case study applications in education.* San Francisco, CA: Jossey-Bass.

Merriam, S. (2009). *Qualitative research: A guide to design and implementation.* San Francisco, CA: Jossey-Bass.

Miles, M., & Huberman, M. (1994). *Qualitative data analysis: An expanded sourcebook.* Thousand Oaks, CA: Sage.

Miles, M., Huberman, M., & Saldana. J. (2020). *Qualitative data analysis: A methods sourcebook.* Thousand Oaks, CA: Sage.

Murphy, J. (2009). Closing the achievement gaps: Lessons from the last 15 years. *Kappan,* 8–12.

Noguera, P. (2008). *The trouble with black boys: And other reflections on race equity, and the future of public education.* San Francisco, CA: John Wiley.

Reeves, D. (2009). *Leading change in your school: How to conquer myths, building commitment, and get results.* Alexandria, VA: Association of Supervision and Curriculum Development.

Sarason, S. (1990). *The predictable failure of educational reform: Can we change before it's too late?* San Francisco, CA: Jossey-Bass.

Stake, R. (2000). *Case studies*. In N. K. Denzin & Y. S. Lincoln (Eds.), *Handbook of qualitative research* (2nd ed., pp. 435–454). Thousand Oaks, CA: Sage.

Stringer, P. (2013). *Capacity building for school improvement*. Rotterdam: Sense.

Terrell, R., Terrell, E., Lindsey, R., & Lindsey, D. (2018). *Culturally proficient leadership: The personal journey begins within*. Thousand Oaks, CA: Corwin.

Thomas, G. (2011). *How to do your case study: A guide for students and researchers*. Thousand Oaks, CA: Sage.

Welborn, J. (2019). Increasing equity, access, and inclusion through organizational change: A study of implementation and experiences surrounding a school district's journey toward culturally proficient educational practice. *Educational Leadership Review, 20*(1), 167–189.

Yin, R. K. (2018). *Case study research design and methods* (6th ed.). Thousand Oaks, CA: Sage.

RESOURCE 2B

RESEARCH ARTICLES

Welborn, J. (2019). Increasing equity, access, and inclusion through organizational change: A study of implementation and experiences surround a school district's journey toward culturally proficient educational practice. *Educational Leadership Review, 20*(1), 167–189. Retrieved from https://www.icpel.org/uploads/1/5/6/2/15622000/elr_volume_20_1__fall_2019.pdf

Increasing Equity, Access, and Inclusion through Organizational Change: A Study of Implementation and Experiences Surrounding a School District's Journey Towards Culturally Proficient Educational Practice

Jaime E. Welborn, Ph.D.

Saint Louis University

A Final Copy Manuscript submitted to the International Council of Professors of Education Leadership for publication in Education Leadership Review

October 2019

ABSTRACT

This qualitative case study investigated the implementation and experiences of access and equity work in a suburban, public K–12 school district in the Midwest United States. While the literature regarding educational leadership, student educational gaps, and school change is prolific, inequities in policy and practice perpetuate predictable failure for some of our nation's youth. Using the lens of the Cultural Proficiency Framework, this study aimed to address the research questions by examining (1) the educational leader's role in school change, (2) policies and practices used in the school district, (3) the ways in which implementation of the Cultural Proficiency Framework influenced change, and (4) challenges educational leaders *face during the work of Cultural Proficiency. The findings of the study revealed consistency among three emergent themes for successful culturally proficient practice and policy implementation including outcomes from professional learning communities, diverse family and community involvement, and continuous school improvement toward student achievement. Implications of this study suggest application of the Four Tools of Cultural Proficiency with contextual usage of the emergent themes for leading organizational change toward increased equity, access, and inclusion.*

Keywords: educational leadership, equity, cultural proficiency, organizational change, family and community engagement, professional learning communities, school improvement

For decades, educational leadership has served as a catalyst for reform efforts across education (Fullan, 2016; Marzano, Waters, & McNulty, 2005; Murphy & Datnow, 2003; Tucker, 2019). Since the *Coleman Report* (1966) was published, access, opportunity, and achievement gaps between and among students of diverse racial, ethnic, and social class backgrounds have been the focus of research and goals of educational reform efforts across the United States (Apple & Beane, 1995; Fullan, 2000; Jencks, 1972; Sarason, 1996). While the roles of educational leaders have undergone fundamental change with increased focus on instruction and learning (Cotton, 2003; Glatthorn, 2000; Smith & Andrews, 1989), it is important to note that culturally proficient educational leaders have led the way through transformative leadership in standing firm against oppressive educational systems by fighting for those students who have historically been underserved due to their racial and ethnic identity and/or social class (Terrell, Terrell, Lindsey, & Lindsey, 2018). The increasing concern regarding inequitable student outcomes, that presage predictable failure for these students, have led educational leaders across the country and those responsible for leadership preparation programs to seek knowledge and skills related to developing equitable policies and practices within their districts, schools, and classrooms.

Research related to evidence-based practice is necessary for our society to disrupt access and educational gap trends and empower leaders to implement and sustain equity work into the everyday practices of their districts and schools. Many, like Eaveston School District leaders, are implementing the equity framework of *Cultural Proficiency* to address inequities found in their service to diverse populations, improve school effectiveness, and fulfill the moral imperative of education (Fullan, 2003; Lindsey, Nuri-Robins, Terrell, & Lindsey, 2019).

CONCEPTUAL FRAMEWORK

Miles and Huberman (1994) described a conceptual framework as a tool for explaining the main concepts studied in research, including key factors, constructs, and variables. The conceptual framework used in this qualitative case study sought to describe the relationship between cultural diversity, economics, power, policy, pedagogy, school improvement, and student achievement outcomes. The research analysis integrates these constructs with the equity framework of Cultural Proficiency (Cross, Bazron, Dennis, & Issacs, 1989).

The *Cultural Proficiency Framework* is an interrelated set of four tools that assist educational leaders in performing tasks such as developing and implementing school board policies, allocating resources, using assessment data, delivering curriculum and instruction, interacting with parents and community members, and planning and delivering professional development (Lindsey et al., 2019). One tool, *the Barriers to Cultural Proficiency*, leads educators to understand how to overcome resistance to change in schools. Another tool, *the Guiding Principles of Cultural Proficiency*, guides the development and implication of positive personal values and organizational practices and policies to counter the systemic nature of the barriers. *The Cultural Proficiency Continuum* is a third tool comprised of six points, three negative and three positive, that depict the range of unhealthy to healthy practices and policies. In using the Continuum and the fourth tool, the *Essential Elements of Cultural Proficiency*, educators identify practices and policies that produce equitable outcomes and those in areas of needed improvement. Ethical decisions and intentional actions lead to organizational change (Cross et al., 1989; Lindsey et al., 2019).

As educational leaders consider systemic, transformative organizational change to improve outcomes and create effective schools (Lezotte & Snyder, 2011; Sergiovanni, 1989), increase equity, and serve all, they must keep constant vigilance of self in their roles as change agents (Gay, 2000; Howard 2006; Nelson & Guerra, 2014). The starting point for long-term, systemic change does not begin with changing the system or others around us. It is commenced by change within ourselves (Dilts, 1990; Fullan, 1997; Gardner, 2004; Lindsey et al., 2019).

PURPOSE STATEMENT AND RESEARCH QUESTIONS

The purpose of this study is to investigate the implementation and experiences of Cultural Proficiency work in a suburban, public K–12 school district in the Midwest United States. The following research questions were used as a guide to fulfill the objectives of this study:

1. How do educational leaders report/describe their role in school change for culturally proficient practice?

2. What policies and practices are used in the school district related to culturally proficient practice?

3. In what ways do the school district's implementation and experiences influence changes regarding culturally proficient practice to serve all students?

4. What challenges do educational leaders face during the work of Cultural Proficiency?

REVIEW OF RELATED LITERATURE

The foundations of education are rooted in a belief that educated children become better citizens. Although diversity holds great importance in democracy, too many schools in this country continue with systems, policies, and practices that largely reflect the values, behaviors, and aspirations of the most powerful groups (Apple & Beane, 1995; Darling-Hammond, 1995; Ravitch, 1985; Sarason, 1990). Systemic oppression, policy impacts on marginalized students, and privilege and entitlement limit educational outcomes and the reality of access and equity for all (Lindsey, Karns, & Myatt, 2010). The continuous oppression of students of diverse race, ethnicity, and social class has perpetuated inequities and educational performance deficits (Banks & Banks, 1995; Freire, 1970; Hammond, 2015; Howard, 2006; Kozol, 2005; Ladson-Billings, 2006; Noguera, 2008).

Recently, scholars indicated culturally proficient educational leaders are advocates for learning with the intent to meet the needs of all students using an inside-out process. With the moral imperative, knowledge, and skills, effective educators examine their values, behaviors, and beliefs, as well as their organization's policies and practices (Lindsey et al., 2019). Thus, professional learning focusing on Cultural Proficiency is essential for educational leaders dedicated to serving all students.

THE IMPORTANCE OF EDUCATIONAL LEADERSHIP IN STUDENT ACHIEVEMENT

Research presents a correlation between school leadership and student achievement (Byrk & Schneider, 2002; DuFour & Mattos, 2013; Hallinger & Heck, 1996; Leithwood, Seashore-Louis, Anderson, & Wahlstrom, 2004; Marks & Printy, 2003; Marzano, Waters, & McNulty, 2005). Fullan (2003) posited the moral imperative of educational leadership is for leaders to introduce new elements into the setting, intended to influence behavior for the better, all while managing different interests, economic situations, cultural origins, religions, ethnicities, and races. Leaders are responsible for fostering social unity in our society of increasingly diverse students, families, and educators. Concurrently, leaders must maintain focus on educational reform through continuous improvement efforts so all children of our nation are afforded the intended outcomes of public school. The correlates of effective schools research (Edmonds & Frederiksen, 1978) identified the primary aim of public schools to reach the intended outcomes as teaching and learning (Lezotte & Snyder, 2011). Educational leaders' focus on teaching and learning is essential.

The moral imperative requires collective efficacy—combined efforts for making a difference in the lives of students, building relationships, and monitoring one's responsibility and contributions in closing educational gaps. Research findings suggest collective efficacy has strong correlative effects on student achievement (Donohoo, 2016; Eells, 2011; Goddard, Hoy, & Woolfolk Hoy, 2004; Hattie, 2012). Defined by Bandura (1997) as "a group's shared belief in its conjoint capability to organize and execute the courses of action required to produce given levels of attainment" (p. 477), collective efficacy influences the personal culture, how one thinks and behaves, and the school culture, which indirectly impacts student achievement (Donohoo, Hattie, & Eells, 2018). Educational leaders play an integral role in building the collective efficacy. Fullan (2001, 2003) suggested, the moral imperative involves leading cultural change that activates passions and commitments of stakeholders, such as teachers and parents, to improve the learning of all students, including closing the achievement gap.

Building relationships is another critical factor in student achievement and school success (Milner, 2013). Educational leaders are expected to take risks toward change by assessing cultural knowledge and learning from each other, thus becoming more aware of the personal lives and interests of teachers, staff, students, and their families (Marzano, Waters, & McNulty, 2005; Wagner & Kegan, 2006). In a meta-analysis, Marzano et al. (2005) identified relationships as a part of school leadership impacting the effectiveness of many other tasks and responsibilities completed at the school. The study identified behaviors and characteristics applicable to relationships between administrators, teachers, and their students and families, all of which influence school effectiveness and student achievement.

Because of the strong correlation between educational leadership and student achievement, educators who monitor their own responsibility and contributions in closing the educational gaps are essential. While the research on the effect size of school and environmental factors, as they relate to student achievement, is ongoing, it is greatly debated because there is not a definitive answer for closing the educational gaps. Barton and Coley (2009) and Murphy (2009) have written extensively about educational gaps and declared the solution is complex and cannot be managed by one focused effort. However, school leaders can contribute by ensuring teaching is disproportionately advantaging students on the lower end of the educational gaps. Race and socioeconomic status are critical issues, and equitable learning outcomes can be actualized as leaders accept responsibility for performance and development of themselves, teachers' performance, and students' achievement and growth (Murphy, 2009). Overall, school leaders are responsible for promoting a collaborative culture and monitoring the collective impact of teaching on student achievement (Donohoo et al., 2018; Lezotte & Snyder, 2011).

EDUCATIONAL LEADERS AND ORGANIZATIONAL CHANGE TOWARD CONTINUOUS IMPROVEMENT

The educational system must change in one way or another, backward to intellectual and moral standards of prescientific age, or forward to the development of the possibilities of growing and expanding experience (Dewey, 1938). Educational leaders acknowledge change is inevitable and necessary for improvement in any school system. Each year school leaders complete school improvement plans, providing a roadmap with goals of increasing student achievement—thus, changing the organization. While well-planned initiatives are paramount, the process of involving stakeholders at the district and building levels, as well as families and community members, is equally valuable in developing a shared meaning in the continuous improvement process (Epstein, 2019; Lezotte & Snyder, 2011; Marks & Pinty, 2003). Fullan (2016) further described stakeholder involvement in the change process as the shaping and reshaping of good ideas, while building capacity and ownership among participants.

Moreover, Dilts's model of *nested levels of learning* provides further awareness of the importance of professional learning and collaboration necessary for organizational change and gains in student achievement. The five levels of organizational change identified by Dilts (1990) are (1) identity, (2) belief system, (3) capabilities, (4) behaviors, and (5) environment. It is vital educational leaders understand change begins with identity, the individual's and/or group's sense of self, and one's own lived experiences, as Dewey noted.

EDUCATIONAL LEADERS AND CULTURE, RACE, AND POVERTY IN STUDENT ACHIEVEMENT

Research on the topic of culture presents ideas and concepts related to race, ethnicity, social class, language, ability, gender, age, and religion. In fact, culture has broadly been defined by a person's identity constructed of the above-mentioned concepts, as well as one's beliefs, norms, customs, traditions, values, and behaviors (Bolman & Deal, 2003; Deal & Peterson, 1999; Fraise & Brooks, 2015). Culture plays an integral part in our society, thus impacting interactions between school leaders, teachers, students, and family members, and consequently, student achievement in all educational settings. Stakeholders in an organization enter into a setting with their individual and shared history, beliefs, values, and patterns of behavior. These differences give rise to cultural-based conflicts in which the educators of the institution respond based upon their experiences, beliefs, and values. Often times, those responses are inadequate in that they unknowingly and unwittingly perpetuate a predictable failure for students who are culturally different from the dominant group (Lindsey et al., 2019). As Murphy (2009) suggested, educational leaders focused on increasing student achievement and closing educational gaps are attentive to racial and socioeconomic status identities of the students the organization serves.

Race. Educational opportunity has been inequitable throughout the history of the United States. For the past century and a quarter, our country's courts and legislators, at all levels, have wrestled with educational equity issues in decisions such as *Plessy v. Ferguson*, *Mendez v. Westminister*, and *Brown v. Board of Education*. While the 1960s and decades since have brought integration movements and federal government-led reform efforts such as the Elementary and Secondary Education Act, the educational inequities and racial segregation in schools persist (Howard, 2010; Kozol, 2005; Ladson-Billings, 2009).

Poverty. Socioeconomic status is a distinct demographic group that intersects with other cultural identifications such as race, ethnicity, language, gender, sexual orientation, and ability. Often students living in poverty have different experiences in the world related to limited access to experiences and opportunities afforded to many of their school-age peers. Kimberle Crenshaw (2016) coined the term *Intersectionality* by the way in which individuals see where power comes, collides, interlocks, and intersects. While Crenshaw directly discerned interlocking social identifiers of race and gender, it is important to note how interlocking systems of power impact historically marginalized groups and focus on the ideology of social identifiers, namely race and social class. Deficit thinking surrounding poverty can give way to asset-based thinking and action when educators examine their own assumptions, beliefs, and behaviors; focus on relationships; and model resilience and promotion of self in the context of society (Lindsey, Karns, & Myatt, 2010).

The aforementioned literature review provided a summary of comprehensive consideration of the literature relative to the object of study. Three themes were included within the review of literature: (1) educational leadership and student achievement, (2) educational leadership and organizational change toward continuous improvement, and (3) educational leadership and culture, race, and social class in student achievement. The purpose of this study and research questions were designed to fill the gaps in literature around outcomes related to implementation and experiences surrounding a school district's journey toward culturally proficient educational practice and student achievement. While extensive literature exists regarding educational leadership, student achievement, and organizational change for school reform, there is little evidence of practical application for utilizing an equity framework at the school district level, namely the Cultural Proficiency Framework, to create organizational change and increase student achievement.

RESEARCH METHODOLOGY AND DESIGN

A descriptive case study was employed in order to investigate the implementation and experiences of Cultural Proficiency work in a suburban, public K–12 school district in the Midwest United States. Merriam (2001) described case study as a design "employed to gain an in-depth understanding of the situation and meaning for those involved" (p. 19). The qualitative study included data collection and analysis of interviews with district stakeholders, who hold leadership roles and are involved in the work of Cultural Proficiency, observations of meetings and professional learning events related to Cultural Proficiency, and associated district documents. Themes and insights emerging from case study data collection and analysis can directly influence policy, practice, and future research for school organizations.

CASE DESCRIPTION

With the intent to investigate the implementation and experiences of Cultural Proficiency work, Eaveston School District, pseudonymous for a suburban, public K–12 school district in the Midwest United States, was selected according to the methodology of the study. Merriam (2001) differentiated case studies from other types of qualitative research in that they present rich descriptions and analyses of a single, bounded system. The rationale for selecting this unique, bounded system to address the research questions includes (1) the school district's history of change among student demographics in regards to race and social class, and its increase in student achievement over the last two decades; (2) the school district's implementation of professional learning using the Cultural Proficiency Framework at the district and building levels; (3) the school district's high level of cultural, racial/ethnic, and social class diversity; and (4) its proximity to a metropolitan city with racial and social class implications on governmental, political, and educational contexts.

Eaveston School District, established in 1879, is "A Place to Live, Learn, and Grow." With almost 6,000 students, Eaveston School District has one high school, two middle schools, one traditional school (PreK–8), five elementary schools, as well as preschool and alternative education settings (6–12). Situated in a metropolitan county of more than one million people, Eaveston School District encompasses 27 square miles and stands among many businesses, factories, casinos, and an international airport, receiving approximately 90% of funds from local sources. With 46% White, 34% African American/Black, 11% Hispanic, 5% multiracial, and 4% Asian, the student population represents 78 different countries and 48 languages and is rated the most diverse school district in the state. With Intersectionality at the heart of the access, opportunity, and achievement gaps, it is important to note 49% of Eaveston School District's students are eligible for free or reduced lunch, hence, living at or below the United States defined poverty line.

The mission, "That all will learn to become responsible citizens in a nurturing environment where diversity means strength, knowledge means freedom, and commitment means success," has proven successful despite the rise of challenges from major geographical and economic changes to the school district in the last two decades. Increased diversity in culture, race, social class, and mobility provided context for challenges, but through adaptive, transformational, and culturally proficient leadership, the district has defined diversity as a contribution to the values and assets of the school district. Gains in the district's performance standards and indicators, including state achievement tests, college entry exams (i.e., ACT, SAT), completion of advanced courses, college placement, graduation rates, attendance rates, and subgroup achievement, have led to Eaveston School District being recognized as the No. 6 best school district in the state and by *U.S. News and World Report* as the *Best High School in the U.S.*

POPULATION AND SAMPLE

The population for this case study research consisted of two groups. The primary population included 55 stakeholders in Eaveston School District, who serve as members on the district Cultural Proficiency Committee. The term *leader*, used throughout this study, refers to district stakeholders who serve in any traditional or nontraditional leadership role. The population and sampling of these leaders do not solely include administrators, but rather stakeholders that are leading the efforts in the work of Cultural Proficiency. These stakeholders, including, but not limited to, teachers, building and district administrators, staff, parents, and community members, participated in quarterly, full-day professional learning events during the 2017–2018 and 2018–2019 school years. The second population included 70 middle school teachers and administrators, who engaged in bimonthly professional learning events related to Cultural Proficiency in the 2017–2018 and 2018–2019 school years.

The sampling of this study was from the population, a total of 72 participants. In qualitative studies, a researcher uses purposeful sampling to investigate with the intent of maximizing findings and learning (Merriam, 2009). The researcher conducted interviews with 14 participants who volunteered. The participants included representatives from the population groups: building and district office administrators, teachers at all school levels, and parents with diversity among race/ethnicity and gender.

INSTRUMENTATION

The researcher developed three instruments and utilized them to collect data in this study: (1) an interview protocol, (2) an observation guide, and (3) a document retrieval form. An interview protocol, with ten questions, was developed and used to ask questions and record answers during the qualitative interviews (Creswell, 2014). The researcher audiotaped the interviews for transcribing, coding, and analysis. Additionally, the researcher developed an observation guide to collect data during Cultural Proficiency professional learning events at the district and building levels. The observation guide included a single page with a dividing line down the middle to separate descriptive notes from reflective notes (Merriam, 2009). Similar to the observation guide, the third instrument used during the case study included a document retrieval form to mine data from various documents such as policies, handbooks, online materials, and brochures.

DATA COLLECTION AND ANALYSIS

Data collection in qualitative research is a complex research process that includes various steps to ensure reliability, validity, and ethical considerations. It includes gaining permissions, having a reliable sampling strategy, developing means of recording information, and storing the data (Creswell, 2013). The data collection phase of this case study was conducted as a series of interrelated activities aimed at gathering information to answer the research questions. According to Merriam (2009), data collection in case study research usually involves three strategies: interviewing, observing, and analyzing documents. During a one-year data collection process, the researcher's purposeful selection of data led to rich, descriptive findings around the conceptual framework, purpose, and research questions of the case study. Data were stored electronically, organized, and protected.

The final step in completing this case study was to analyze and interpret the collected data to answer the research questions and draw conclusions. Creswell (2014) described analysis as preparing and organizing the data, then reducing the data into themes through a process of coding and condensing the codes. An abundance of data and correlative themes were produced from the case study, thus requiring a triangulation of the data to validate the findings. The researcher triangulated the themes from the three sources of data to develop validity in the conclusions and implications for the field (Creswell, 2014).

FINDINGS AND ANALYSIS

The findings of this qualitative study are organized by research question. Table 1 summarizes the themes that emerged from vivo coding and triangulation of the three data sources. The themes are presented in detail throughout the analysis. Educational leaders and educational leadership professors can utilize the concepts presented through these themes to promote equity, access, and inclusion work in their schools, organizations, and institutions by utilizing the Cultural Proficiency Framework.

RESEARCH QUESTION 1

The first research question explored educational leaders' perceptions of their own roles in school change related to culturally proficient educational

TABLE 1 ● Research Questions' Relationship to Themes

RESEARCH QUESTIONS	THEMES
(1) How do educational leaders report/describe their role in school change for culturally proficient practice?	Involvement, Collaboration, Interaction, Communication, Inquiry, Self-Focus, Role Model, Vision and Mission, Growth and Improvement
(2) What policies and practices are used in the school district related to culturally proficient practice?	Professional Learning, Innovative Strategies, Programs, Communication, Family/Community Involvement, Continuous Improvement, Diversity, Student Achievement
(3) In what ways do the school district's implementation and experiences influence changes regarding culturally proficient practice to serve all students?	Professional Learning Communities, Action, Student Achievement, Excellence, Individual Students, High Expectations, Professional Development, Family/Community Involvement, Decision Making
(4) What challenges do educational leaders face during the work of Cultural Proficiency?	Barriers (Resistance, Unawareness), Time and Resources, Building Site-Specific Capacity

practice. The emergent themes include (1) being present and involved in the work; (2) collaborating, interacting, and communicating; (3) serving as a role model by helping and supporting others on the journey; and (4) focusing on the vision and mission of the school for continuous growth and improvement.

Being Present and Involved in the Work. Educational leaders can have a vision of a culturally proficient school or district, but without intentional actions to ensure a presence and involvement in the work, there is little change or measurable progress. In the case of Eaveston School District, leaders have taken a stance on the importance of being present and involved in equity work using the Tools of Cultural Proficiency for building an organization of equity and excellence for its diverse student population. The Assistant Superintendent for Learning and Teaching, who has been involved extensively with the Cultural Proficiency Committee, described her role:

> It's my job to work collaboratively with various components that we have in the teaching and learning department to find out what is it we can do to support administrators and teachers who ultimately support all of our learners. I always feel like it's important for me to be as involved as I can in learning, growing, and developing myself because if I can't talk the talk and understand the equity work using the Tools of Cultural Proficiency, then how can I support it? It's important that I'm there with them learning, especially on topics that maybe I'm not as proficient in myself.

Eaveston School District takes pride in its family involvement. Valuing diversity is essential to the Cultural Proficiency Committee's desired equity outcomes and goals in guiding Eaveston to achieve its vision and mission. One school's PTO President commented about his involvement regarding the vision of serving all students.

> My role is being as active in the work as possible: from the PTO, to my children's academic and extracurricular activities, to the Cultural Proficiency Committee. My general practice in helping any cultural diversity situation is to be present because I feel people lack experience. This is what helps to build really true cross-cultural proficiency. It's an academic process of understanding history, but personal interaction, and actually, presence, is probably where people become most proficient. Being an ethnic minority, I have life experience that isn't necessarily understood by the majority culture, so just being present and being active is a way I feel I can participate.

Those who are present and involved in the work in Eaveston embody the personal nature of the inside-out approach of transformative change. By focusing on core values, they are better able to identify personal and institutional barriers to access and achievement that have perpetuated the inequitable outcomes for many students of color and those living in poverty.

Collaborating, interacting, and communicating. Eaveston School District educators approach the work of Cultural Proficiency with a mentality of "We're in this together." Cultural Proficiency Committee members rely on the Essential Elements for continuous planning and growth towards organizational change for the district. Collaboration and communication are key for interactions that work to promote equitable outcomes for all students of Eaveston. District leaders, including the superintendent, assistant superintendent, and executive directors have noted the collaborative relationships and progress with the Cultural Proficiency Committee. An executive director commented,

> I am very impressed regarding the facilitation of the Cultural Proficiency training. I have observed people's willingness to open up and share their experiences and be willing to have some tough conversations. The district is moving forward with having those tough conversations and wanting to find ways to take that work and expand it to all.

District administrators acknowledge there is a need to move forward with the collaborations and involve all educators and employees in the district; while at the same time, they are trying to balance the varying perspectives and points along individuals' cultural proficiency journeys, which are embodied by the faculty and staff at Eaveston School District. Cultural Proficiency Committee members agree this work be done with urgency and by all employees of the district, but they also acknowledge the challenges present in planning for and sustaining the work in the upcoming years. An executive director reflected, "We have to respect the balance of inviting people in and not forcing it on people all at the same time, which could actually deteriorate the work being done by people who are passionate about it."

One special education teacher, who serves on the district's Cultural Proficiency Committee, relies on collaboration and communication to increase her awareness and understanding of individuals with differing cultures from her own.

> I try to do an even better job of communication in my own work: trying to observe more; trying to learn more; trying to have more conversations with people about difficult issues for me. Some topics are not easy to talk about, and I've had to educate myself on some aspects of culture, thus assessing cultural knowledge. Leaders need to be aware of the fact that what something means in one culture, might not mean the same thing in another culture. Really, we just need to talk with people in a way that we can start to see into somebody else's experience and perspective a little better.

The Board of Education and district officials in Eaveston are committed to providing resources to ensure educators in all departments and across buildings are provided opportunities to collaborate around the equity work.

These collaboration efforts are focused on communication through reflection and dialogue, which allow stakeholders to assess their cultural knowledge and move toward transformative change in practice.

Serving as a role model by helping and supporting others on the journey. Change leadership and learning require modeling. Administrators and teachers in Eaveston School District, who are most involved in the equity and access work, realize their role in modeling culturally proficient educational behaviors and practices, while supporting others on the journey.

An elementary principal described her role:

> I want to be a role model in the Cultural Proficiency work, I want to be that individual that is walking the talk, and my staff, students, families, and community members are able to see that we don't just go around saying, "Diversity is our strength." Honestly, I believe I want to show growth towards Cultural Proficiency in everything I do, in everything I say, every single day.

A teacher at Eaveston believes she has to model continuous learning around culture, diversity, equity, and access.

> I just try to keep learning and talk with people in a way that we can start to see into others' experiences and perspectives a little better. One of the most difficult challenges in this work is the realization that everyone is on a journey of Cultural Proficiency, some much further along on the Continuum than others. I serve as a role model by being a reminder to all that we are all at different points on the Continuum of Cultural Proficiency. My responsibility is to be calm and effective in conversations with others. Serving as a role model and supporting others on their journeys is vital for building the critical mass in Eaveston School District. We need to be cognizant that some staff members are not as comfortable with certain conversations related to culture as others. We have to find a way to try to make them feel comfortable. This work is urgent.

Educational leaders in Eaveston have a defined sense of self, others, and the ability to be supportive by relieving others from being forced to change by modeling behaviors that breakdown the barriers for underserved populations. They model strategies for managing the dynamics of difference and resolving conflict by listening, learning, and changing the way things are done.

Focusing on vision and mission for continuous growth and improvement. Historically, Eaveston School District stakeholders have experienced what many tend to find true about continuous improvement efforts for closing access and achievement gaps. Frustration and anger have followed some sluggish, slow, delayed, and disjointed efforts; however, the Cultural

Proficiency Committee keeps the vision and mission at the forefront of goal setting and action planning. Being in the top 1% of diverse school districts in the state, Eaveston School District administrators and teachers focus efforts on valuing diversity through the mission. A teacher, who serves on the district's Cultural Proficiency Committee, discussed the urgency of relying on the mission of the school district.

> What do we do next? We can take something (Cultural Proficiency training) that has been challenging and insightful and make it work without being overly simplistic or reductionist, or doctrinaire to the point of alienating people instead of inviting them to reconsider some of their assumptions. We go back to our mission and our sense of really trying to understand students as they intersect and collaborate with others of differing cultural and linguistic backgrounds and identities.

While it is difficult to find a school district that doesn't express value toward "educating all," educators in Eaveston, deeply committed to removing barriers for children of color and/or those living with socioeconomic disparities, have focused on one question: *Do the behaviors of individuals and the policies and procedures implemented, executed, or enforced reflect the values and mission of Eaveston School District?*

RESEARCH QUESTION 2

The second research question was used to explore the practices and policies used in the school district related to culturally proficient educational practice. In service of answering this research question, the emergent themes have been divided into policy and practice. The findings under policy cover themes related to student achievement, diversity, high expectations, continuous improvement, and needs-based programming. Similarly, the findings under practice are divided into three themes related to innovative strategies and programs, professional learning, and communication and collective family and community involvement.

School board policies to support cultural proficiency. Eaveston School District, like many public school districts, is guided by policies written by school district stakeholders and adopted, reviewed, and rewritten by the local elected school boards. The board policies are typically adopted or revised according to state guidelines or mandates, state and federal legislative decisions, and sometimes when the district experiences a convergence of differences that requires clear written language for governing the school district. School board members who rely on the Guiding Principles and Essential Elements of Cultural Proficiency set up procedures for reviewing policies to address the needs of all demographic groups of students. The school board policy for developing school board policies is written to include language addressed in core values, the Guiding Principles, and action, the Essential Elements. The text has been italicized to point out the related language.

The Board of Education shall determine the policies to *serve as a basis for the administration of the school district.* The formulation, development, adoption and revision of written policies is a Board function, and adopted policies are among the Board's governing documents.

The district's *policies shall be consistent with the philosophy, goals, and objectives of the district.* In the event of a discrepancy between written materials in the district, Board policy will take precedence.

The Board will *review its policies on a continual basis in an effort to ensure that they are current* and in compliance with the most recent federal and state regulations, statutes and court decisions.

Lindsey, Karns, and Myatt (2010) described culturally proficient policy development with two components for school leaders to consider. First, educational leaders should consider supporting values and policies by deeply considering the Guiding Principles and Essential Elements of Cultural Proficiency. By examining personal and organizational values in this process, stakeholders have improved language in some of their policies to address barriers that may be obstructing the lived mission of the school district. Second, school leaders in Eaveston intentionally engage in reflection and dialogue around policies to ensure the language written is to promote action, monitoring, and continuous improvement.

Throughout the Cultural Proficiency work in the district, educators, families, and community members regularly come to the table to discuss the status and outcomes of policy and measurable plans of action. The creation of goals and action steps is important for ensuring all students in Eaveston learn in a safe and productive environment without barriers to each child realizing their potential and experiencing high levels of achievement and success during their time in the district. Overall, school board members and school leaders in Eaveston School District are committed to prioritizing efforts that focus on the big picture through the comprehensive school improvement plan. As written on the school board's web page:

The Eaveston School District Board of Education is committed to providing exemplary educational opportunities for ALL children. In order to accomplish this goal, partnerships with parents, business leaders, and district patrons must continue to be actively developed in order to engage the entire community as the district strives for educational excellence.

Practices to support culturally proficient educational practice. The researcher encountered an abundance of practices in Eaveston School District related to Cultural Proficiency throughout the study. The following themes emerged among the practices: (1) innovative strategies and programs, (2) professional learning, and (3) communication and collective family and community involvement. School leaders in Eaveston are cognizant of opportunities and experiences afforded to the children that attend their schools. They have an understanding that challenges, caused by differences in social class and other demographic groups, require a mindset to treat each child individually, accurately assess needs, and develop programs accordingly. One elementary principal, who leads in a building that piloted a competency-based learning model for the district, described the mental model his staff holds about individual students:

> The staff I have has a mental model that they're lucky that they get to work with the kids here. Our motto is "think different, learn different, and teach different." They go to where the individual child is instead of an old school, traditional model of fitting a kid into a program that already exists. We need to adapt differently to the product coming into our schools from a public school standpoint. Every child is different and everybody has their own story. We take that and build from that to make our community better.

Additionally, the district has taken the competency-based learning model and expanded it into a personalized learning initiative. In 2018, the district took the comprehensive school improvement plan and updated it to include the following task, "Design a competency-based, personalized learning environment in preschool through 12th grades that leads students to be ready for high school course content and, ultimately, success after graduation." In order to do so, the district outlined innovative strategies and programs in the school improvement plan to meet all students' needs such as a five-year personalized learning plan.

Another theme related to culturally proficient educational practice is the professional learning opportunities that are available to administration, faculty, and staff. There are frequent opportunities for professional learning related to student achievement, trauma-informed responsiveness, restorative practices, social-emotional learning, and equity. For the past two years, the district has made professional learning related to equity a priority by allocating time and resources to build capacity and embed the work of Cultural Proficiency in all aspects of the district. Specifically, school leaders at all levels are working to increase learning and skills in utilizing the Tools of Cultural Proficiency to increase the effectiveness of the school district. Professional learning related to Cultural Proficiency occurs regularly among the district's Cultural Proficiency Committee, in individual schools among groups of administrators, teachers, staff, and parents, in new teacher trainings, and in integrated, district-hosted events such as the Fall Professional Development Day and Spring Rally, where edcamp-style professional development is available to all employees of the school district. Although the process has varied in each of these settings, the district's Cultural Proficiency Committee committed to learning the Tools of Cultural Proficiency and created an action plan with three targets: (1) impact disparities in discipline, (2) promote and support further Cultural Proficiency training, and (3) support and grow staff diversity. The focus of this culturally proficient educational practice is to continue the work, build capacity and the "critical mass," and focus on accountability and sustainability of the work.

The third emergent theme of practices examined in this study is communication and involvement with families and community members. Educational leaders in Eaveston recognize the importance of having families, students, and community members participate as much as possible on committees that impact student learning. Stakeholders from across these categories are regularly invited to participate on committees such as the Strategic Planning Committee and the Cultural Proficiency Committee. While involvement does not look the same for all families in Eaveston, school leaders are attentive to the needs of families and try to get to know them so they can forge toward greater understanding and better partnerships.

RESEARCH QUESTION 3

The third research question was used to investigate the ways in which educational leaders have implemented and experienced the work of Cultural Proficiency to influence change and serve all students. In reviewing the participants' responses, observing meetings and professional learning events, and mining documents for data for changes in policies and practices, two themes emerged from the data. The themes include (1) professional development through professional learning communities (PLC) with subthemes of high expectations, individual students, student achievement and excellence; and (2) dialogue and action with family and community involvement.

Professional development through PLC. Educational leaders in Eaveston are focused on increasing equity, inclusion, and access for its students in the district by providing opportunities to all staff members and encouraging collaboration through professional learning communities. From interviews, observations, and documents, there are many opportunities for staff members to collaborate with others in the district around topics such as restorative practices, trauma-informed care, social-emotional learning, personalized learning, and Cultural Proficiency. While some trainings are required, Eaveston grants autonomy in working toward Cultural Proficiency through choice in professional learning and topics of discussion in professional learning communities. New teachers and staff to Eaveston engage in reflection and dialogue in an introductory session related to the Tools of Cultural Proficiency. There are opportunities presented through the year in which they attempt to build capacity to use the framework through introductory sessions for those who have not been able to be a part of the district's Cultural Proficiency Committee or in buildings where it is being implemented. One middle school teacher reflected on her professional learning at Eaveston:

> We engage in professional development on students of trauma, understanding Cultural Proficiency, and how that affects your discipline and how it affects how you communicate with students. We have professional development on making sure that what's present

in our literature and books is reflective of a variety of cultures. We get Cultural Proficiency training from a lot of different angles. We have speakers and small groups. We have someone come in and talk to us about it, and we've tried to have staff members talk to staff members about it. We've had it district-wide and building-wide. We have it every year, and multiple times it's offered.

Additionally, district administrators have realized the importance of being involved in the district-level professional learning events and utilizing the tools in their discussions with the Board, families, and community members.

Dialogue and action planning with family and community involvement. **Reflection** and dialogue are key components of equity work. Eaveston School District has experienced change in the organization through reflection and dialogue in using the Four Tools of Cultural Proficiency. Members of the district's Cultural Proficiency Committee utilized the Continuum of Cultural Proficiency to address areas of needed improvement in the district that are most urgent. The key to success in working toward achieving the goals of the committee is involving families and community members in these discussions and work. An example of utilizing the community includes bringing in experts to facilitate conversations about restorative practices and strategies for managing students facing trauma. These are two ways the district is making gains in one of the goals related to discipline disparities. A middle school assistant principal reflected:

> We have identified our black students, particularly our black boys, being disciplined at a greater number than any other race and gender. I take a lot of pride in our staff for learning how to change with our students. Just the other day, we had a situation where lots of things were going wrong with behavior and discipline. All of a sudden, I had four students in my office. Each one of the four sat down with the teacher(s) and talked with them; it was a one-on-one conversation using restorative practices, where there was respect coming from both parties. What could have turned into this teacher writing four referrals, turned into repairing relationships and everyone walking away happy and ready to start again the next day in class.

As for promoting and supporting further Cultural Proficiency training, the district is making plans to build capacity among the district's committee by increasing opportunity for reflection and dialogue so that all school buildings in the district gain support in implementing the Tools of Cultural Proficiency to promote equity, access, and inclusion.

RESEARCH QUESTION 4

The final research question of this qualitative study focused on the challenges educational leaders face during their work of Cultural Proficiency. Participants throughout the district discussed three themes, and observational data illuminated similar contexts within meetings and professional learning events. The themes include (1) Barriers to Cultural Proficiency, (2) availability of time and resources, and (3) building site-specific capacity to implement and sustain the equity work across the district.

Barriers to cultural proficiency. Educational leaders and stakeholders in Eaveston School District acknowledged the barriers to becoming culturally proficient. Participants discussed four barriers they encountered including the unawareness of the need to adapt, resistance to change, historical mistrust formed from a previous social justice training, and historical, social, and racial segregation contexts in Eaveston's metropolitan area. By relying on the Guiding Principles and core values, district leaders have built trust and empowerment of all voices on the Cultural Proficiency Committee through reflection, dialogue, and action.

Availability of time and resources. Time and resources are always a factor in society, education, and organizational change. Some participants interviewed felt time and resources have been a challenge for implementing this work in a way that would lead to the most impactful changes. The district committee utilized four, full-day professional learning experiences during each of the last two years, which required approximately 30 substitute teachers in classrooms each session. Consequently, individual schools were also left shorthanded by administrators being gone during these days. The school-site committees utilized grade-level time twice a month for professional learning and dialogue related to equity, access, inclusion, and student achievement. The reality has set in for many of the educators that this work is challenging, and it is a journey. With the right people in leadership positions, the priority will remain in utilizing time and resources to build capacity and embed the work in all aspects of Eaveston School District. Leaders want to ensure that there is an understanding that this work is here to stay, and Cultural Proficiency is not going to be a place in which the district arrives, but the journey of educating Eaveston's youth.

Building site-specific capacity to **implement** *and sustain the equity work across the district.* Research (Lambert, 1998; Reeves, 2009; Stringer, 2013) claims building capacity among those in a system is vital in implementing change and sustaining the work for continuous improvement. Participants in the study discussed the challenge of balancing the urgency of spreading the equity work beyond the district's Cultural Proficiency Committee and throughout the district. We know many decisions of schools are made at the site level, which means different cultures, people, practices, values, and beliefs, and behaviors. The district's progress is challenged by implementing professional learning with urgency, but not in a way that causes an increase in resistance, protest, and unrest within the larger system. Participants held views that a "top-down" or a "one size fits all" decision on the logistics of implementation would lead to no progress, and maybe even destruction of the progress gained over the last two years.

CONCLUSIONS

The findings of this study are important to the field of education because of the long-standing opportunity, access, and achievement gaps that have been perpetuated by inequitable policies and practices in our systems, the increase in student diversity, barriers to equity and access such as systemic oppression and resistance to change, and the need for the continuation and strengthening fight for social justice. This study investigated (1) the educational leader's role in school change, (2) policies and practices used in the school district, (3) the ways in which implementation of the Cultural Proficiency Framework influenced change, and (4) challenges educational leaders face during the work of Cultural Proficiency. The analysis of data from interviews, observations, and documents provided explanations that can be insightful to educational leaders and educational leadership professors preparing educators to lead change for increasing equity, access, and inclusion.

The main ideas and explanations of the findings, which are related to factors and emergent themes of the study include professional learning communities, family and community involvement, and continuous school improvement toward student achievement. These explanations are discussed in four conclusions corresponding to the research study's conceptual framework: (1) overcoming the Barriers to Cultural Proficiency, (2) relying on core values using the Guiding Principles of Cultural Proficiency for organizational change, (3) telling our stories and changing the conversation with the Continuum of Cultural Proficiency, and (4) Committing to standards of change through improvement and growth through the Essential Elements of Cultural Proficiency. Figure 1 represents the emerging themes discussed in the conclusions drawn from the case study findings in Eaveston School District.

FIGURE 1 ● Emergent Themes Discussed in the Conclusions From the Eaveston Case Study

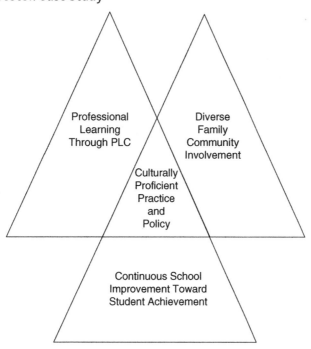

Figure 1 is a triangulated diagram representing the power of emergent themes from the data collection and analysis. The conclusions drawn from the case study that investigated implementation and experiences surrounding a school district's journey toward culturally proficient educational practice and organizational change included emphasis on professional learning through professional learning communities, diverse family and community involvement, and continuous school improvement toward student achievement. School leaders focused on these areas of emphasis while utilizing the Cultural Proficiency Framework are able to experience effective organizational change toward increasing culturally proficient practices and policies.

The first conclusion regarding successful implementation and experiences of Cultural Proficiency work is acknowledgment of systemic barriers and challenges. Resistance to change, unawareness of the need to adapt, a sense of privilege and entitlement, and systems of oppression are the identified Barriers to Cultural Proficiency. These Barriers push against the historic ideals in most school districts across the country and lead to denied access for some students through inequitable policies and practices (Cross et al., 1989; Lindsey et al., 2019).

Educational leaders' success in implementing the work of Cultural Proficiency, and creating organizational change that provides equitable outcomes, depends on honoring individual stories through continued learning in varied professional learning communities. A collaborative culture and sense of collective responsibility in professional learning communities (DuFour, DuFour, Eaker, Many, & Mattos, 2016) can support school leaders in effective dialogue and reflection of their own behaviors and practices that may be perpetuating unintended outcomes. Culturally proficient learning communities deepen commitment and provide clarity through intentionality in acknowledging systemic barriers and challenges (Lindsey, Jungwirth, Jarvis, & Lindsey, 2009). Furthermore, educational leaders encourage family and community partnerships in professional learning and decision-making (Epstein, 2019; Lezotte & Snyder, 2011) to ensure a diverse group of stakeholders are present and involved in the work. Valuing diversity brings in varying perspectives for decision-making purposes, thus increasing the ability to engage in dialogue that may acknowledge the Barriers to culturally proficient practice and policy. Embedding the work in all aspects of the district and building capacity for continuous school improvement through a collaborative culture focused on student achievement allows educational leaders to overcome the Barriers and increase equitable outcomes (Lezotte & Snyder, 2011; Lindsey et al., 2019).

Another conclusion of implementing and experiencing the work of Cultural Proficiency is to rely on the core values of the organization and use the Guiding Principles of Cultural Proficiency to promote transformational changes to the organization (Arriaga & Lindsey, 2016; Lindsey et al., 2019). The vision, mission, core values, and comprehensive school improvement plan are integral parts in the implementation of the work of Cultural Proficiency. It is imperative that all involved, including family and community members, know the mission and core values of the district and are able to offer diverse ideas and reactions toward setting goals and changing policies and practices that will increase student outcomes and improve their schools (Darling-Hammond, 1995; Epstein et al., 2019).

Diversity, knowledge, commitment, care, learning, freedom, and success are overt core values of Eaveston School District, but more important than stating them is creating accountability measures around them for continuous improvement through the mission and vision (Allen 2001; Lezotte & Snyder, 2011). Culturally proficient educational leaders committed to building knowledge around the diversity of its students rely on the Guiding Principles to promote equitable and inclusive practices and policies to increase learning outcomes (Lindsey et al., 2019). As educators lead efforts to examine the current policies and practices through professional learning communities, comprised of school and community partners, the Guiding Principles can aid in the actualization of the deep work necessary to promote changes to policies and practices that make educational outcomes more equitable, accessible, and inclusionary.

The third suggested conclusion in effective implementation of the work of Cultural Proficiency is continuous improvement efforts toward increasingly culturally proficient educational practices and policy development using the Continuum. The focus for educational leaders should be to create opportunities where all have a voice, the ability to tell their personal stories or lived experiences, come to new understandings, and change the conversation. The Continuum of Cultural Proficiency is a way for all stakeholders to have a voice in what is most needed for all students to learn and achieve at high levels (Lindsey et al., 2019). Those practices, policies, behaviors, values, and beliefs that appear on the left side of the Continuum and are identified by stakeholders as destructive, blind, and incapacitating can lead educators to further their reflection and dialogue to produce goals for continuous improvement (Cross et al., 1989; Lindsey et al., 2019). Once goals are established using this data along the Continuum, educational leaders have the ability to form actionable steps aimed at achieving the goals and increasing student outcomes through learning in various professional learning communities and through parent and community partnerships.

Lastly, a suggested conclusion based upon the findings of this study is that successful implementation of the work of Cultural Proficiency requires an understanding of the Essential Elements of Cultural Proficiency and a commitment to standards of change through improvement and growth. The Essential Elements of Cultural Proficiency include assessing cultural knowledge, valuing diversity, managing the dynamics of difference, adapting to diversity, and institutionalizing cultural knowledge (Cross et al., 1989; Lindsey et al., 2019). It is important educational leaders know these actions are not necessarily linear but cyclical, because the work of Cultural Proficiency is never over, and student and staff diversity is constantly evolving. To truly achieve the moral imperative of education in which all students achieve at high levels in our society, it is critical we use these actions in our everyday practices (Lindsey et al., 2019). Professional learning opportunities and professional learning communities, with family and community involvement, bring together sources of knowledge, power, and experiences that can formulate and fulfill actions to help educate all students, especially those who have been historically underserved by our systems. DuFour et al. (2016) identified results orientation, a focus on student learning, and collaborative culture as key ideas that drive the work in professional learning communities. Educational leaders and professors preparing educational leaders are vital in sustaining the work through continuous improvement action plans, partnerships, and capacity building.

IMPLICATIONS FOR EDUCATIONAL LEADERS AND PREPARATION PROGRAMS

Based upon the findings and conclusions from this case study in Eaveston School District, the following are implications for educational leaders and educational leadership professors responsible for fulfilling the moral imperative of education. These implications suggest using the Tools of Cultural Proficiency can directly impact the ways in which students experience education. There should be an intentional alignment of the school district's strategic plan, professional learning design, and policy review. The use of the Tools of Cultural Proficiency should not be separate from the long-term planning for the district, nor the day-to-day operations. In order for educational leaders to build capacity in their districts and schools, there must be a common language around the Framework and use of data to drive the change. In building capacity, all must be invited to change the lives of students through academic, social, emotional, and physical development programs, practice, and policies, but most importantly, educational leaders and educational leadership professors must be active role models and change agents in using the Cultural Proficiency Framework. The creation of opportunities for faculty and staff to come together with families and community partners serves as the collective commitment to equity, access, and inclusion for all.

Superintendent and principal preparation programs should also embed formal training related to the understanding and utilization of the Tools of Cultural Proficiency throughout the program. Experience with reflection and dialogue with others in cross-cultural situations can only improve efforts to manage the dynamics of different cultures and increase efforts to achieve the moral imperative of education in that all students will learn. It is further suggested that preparation program faculty and staff reflect on their own cultures in preparing those who will lead efforts of adapting to diversity and institutionalizing that change in our schools. As our schools grow more diverse, the moral imperative for educational leaders is to change the context; change the mindset; and engage stakeholders in an embedded, continuous effort to change practices and policies that have historically underserved groups of students in the organization.

REFERENCES

Allen, L. (2001). From plaques to practice: How schools can breathe life into their guiding beliefs. *Phi Delta Kappan, 12*(2), 289–293.

Apple, M., & Beane, J. (1995). *Democratic schools*. Alexandria, VA: Association for Supervision and Curriculum Development.

Arriaga, T., & Lindsey, R. (2016). *Opening doors: An implementation template for Cultural Proficiency*. Thousand Oaks, CA: Corwin.

Bandura, A. (1977). Self-efficacy: Toward a unifying theory of behavioral change. *Psychological Review, 84*(2), 191–215.

Banks, C., & Banks, J. (1995). Equity pedagogy: An essential component of multicultural education. *Theory in Practice, 34*(3), 152–157.

Barton, P., & Coley, R. (2009). *Parsing the achievement gap II*. Princeton, NJ: Educational Testing Service.

Bolman, L., & Deal, T. (2003). *Reframing organization: Artistry, choice, and leadership*. San Francisco, CA: Jossey-Bass.

Byrk, A. S., & Schneider, B. (2002). *Trust in schools: A core resource for improvement*. New York, NY: Russell Sage.

Cotton, K. (2003). *Principals and student achievement: What the research says*. Alexandria, VA: Association for Supervision and Curriculum Development.

Crenshaw, K. (2016). *The urgency of intersectionality* [Video file]. Available from https://www.ted.com/talks/kimberle_crenshaw_the_urgency_of_intersectionality?language=en

Creswell, J. W. (2013). *Qualitative inquiry and research design: Choosing among five Approaches*. Thousand Oaks, CA: Sage.

Creswell, J. W. (2014). *Research design: Qualitative, quantitative, and mixed methods approaches*. Thousand Oaks, CA: Sage.

Cross, T., Bazron, B., Denis, K., & Issacs, M. (1989). *Towards a culturally competent system of care* (Vol. 1). Washington, DC: Georgetown University Child Development Center, CASSP Technical Assistance Center.

Darling-Hammond, L. (1995). Restructuring schools for student success. *Daedalus, 124*, 53–162.

Deal, T., & Peterson, K. (1999). *Shaping school culture: The heart of leadership*. San Francisco, CA: Jossey-Bass.

Dewey, J. (1938). *Experience and education*. New York, NY: Simon & Schuster.

Dilts, R. (1990). *Changing belief systems with NLP*. Capitola, CA: Meta.

Donohoo, J. (2016). *Collective efficacy: How educators' beliefs impact student learning*. Thousand Oaks, CA: Corwin.

Donohoo, J., Hattie, J., & Eells, R. (2018). The power of collective efficacy. *Educational Leadership, 75*(6), 40–44.

DuFour, R., DuFour, R., Eaker, R., Many, T., & Mattos, M. (2016). *Learning by doing: A handbook for professional learning communities at work*. Bloomington, IN: Solution Tree Press.

DuFour, R., & Mattos, M. (2013). How do principal really improve schools? *Education Leadership, 70*(7), 34–40.

Edmonds, R., & Frederiksen, J. R. (1978). *Search for effective schools: The identification and analysis of city schools that are instructionally effective for poor children*. Cambridge, MA: Harvard University Center for Urban Studies.

Eells, R. (2011). *Meta-analysis of the relationship between collective efficacy and student achievement*. Unpublished doctoral dissertation. Loyola University of Chicago.

Epstein, J., & Associates. (2019). *School, family, and community partnerships: Your handbook for action*. Thousand Oaks, CA: Sage.

Fraise, N., & Brooks, J. (2015). Toward a theory of culturally relevant leadership for school community culture. *International Journal of Multicultural Education, 17*(1), 6–21.

Freire, P. (1970). *Pedagogy of the oppressed*. New York: Herder & Herder.

Fullan, M. (1997). *What's worth fighting for in the principalship*. New York: Teachers College Press.

Fullan, M. (2001). *Leading in a culture of change.* San Francisco, CA: Jossey-Bass.

Fullan, M. (2003). *The moral imperative of school leadership.* Thousand Oaks, CA: Corwin.

Fullan, M. (2016). *The new meaning of educational change* (5th ed.). New York: Teachers College Press.

Gardener, H. (2004). *Changing minds.* Boston, MA: Harvard Business School Press.

Gay, G. (2000). *Culturally responsive teaching: Theory, research, and practice.* New York: Teachers College Press.

Glatthorn, A. (2000). *The principal as curriculum leader: Shaping what is taught and tested.* (2nd ed.). Thousand Oaks, CA: Corwin.

Goddard, R. D., Hoy, W. K., & Woolfolk Hoy, A. (2004). Collective efficacy beliefs: Theoretical developments, empirical evidence, and future directions. *Educational Researcher, 33*(3), 3–13.

Hallinger, P., & Heck, R. H. (1996). Reassessing the principal's role in school effectiveness: A review of empirical research 1980-1995. *Education Administration Quarterly, 32*(1), 5–44.

Hammond, Z. (2015). *Culturally responsive teaching & the brain.* Thousand Oaks, CA: Corwin.

Hattie, J. (2012). *Visible learning for teachers: Maximizing impact on learning.* New York, NY: Routledge.

Howard, G. (2006). *We can't teach what we don't know: White teachers, multiracial schools* (2nd ed.). New York, NY: Teachers College Press.

Howard, T. (2010). *Why race and culture matter in schools: Closing the achievement gap in America's classrooms.* New York, NY: Teachers College Press.

Jencks, C. (1972). *Inequality: A reassessment of the effect of family and schooling in America.* New York, NY: Basic Books.

Jossey-Bass Publishers. (2001). *The Jossey-Bass reader on school reform.* San Francisco, CA: Jossey-Bass.

Kozol, J. (2005). *The shame of the nation: The restoration of apartheid schooling in America.* New York: Three Rivers Press.

Ladson-Billings, G. (2006). From the achievement gap to the education debt: Understanding achievement in U.S. schools. *Educational Researcher, 35*(7), 3–12.

Ladson-Billings, G. (2009). *The dream keepers: Successful teachers of African American students.* San Francisco, CA: John Wiley.

Lambert, L. (1998). *Building leadership capacity in schools.* Alexandria, VA: Association for Supervision and Curriculum Development.

Leithwood, K., Seashore-Louis, K., Anderson, S., & Wahlstrom, K. (2004). *Review of research: How leadership influences student learning.* Retrieved from https://www.wallacefoundation.org/knowledge-center/Documents/How-Leadership-Influences-Student-Learning.pdf

Lezotte, L., & Snyder, K. (2011). *What effective schools do: Re-envisioning the correlates.* Bloomington, IN: Solution Tree Press.

Lindsey, D., Jungwirth, L., Jarvis, P., & Lindsey, R. (2009). *Culturally proficient learning communities: Confronting inequities through collaborative curiosity.* Thousand Oaks, CA: Corwin.

Lindsey, R., Karns, M., & Myatt, K. (2010). *Culturally proficient education: An asset-based response to conditions of poverty.* Thousand Oaks, CA: Corwin.

Lindsey, R., Nuri-Robins, K., Terrell, R., & Lindsey, D. (2019). *Cultural proficiency: A manual for school leaders* (4th ed.). Thousand Oaks, CA: Corwin.

Marks, H. M., & Printy, S. M. (2003). Principal leadership and school performance: An integration of transformational and instructional leadership. *Educational Administration Quarterly, 39*(3), 370–397.

Marzano, R., Water, T., & McNulty, B. (2005). *School leadership that works: From research to results.* Alexandria, VA: ASCD and Aurora, CO: Mid-content Research for Education and Learning.

Merriam, S. (2001). *Qualitative research and case study applications in education.* San Francisco, CA: Jossey-Bass.

Merriam, S. (2009). *Qualitative research: A guide to design and implementation.* San Francisco, CA: Jossey-Bass.

Miles, M., & Huberman, M. (1994). *Qualitative data analysis: An expanded sourcebook.* Thousand Oaks, CA: Sage.

Milner, R., IV. (2013). *Start where you are, but don't stay there: Understanding diversity, opportunity gaps, and teaching in today's classroom.* Cambridge, MA: Harvard Education Press.

Murphy, J. (2009). Closing the achievement gaps: Lessons from the last 15 years. *Kappan,* 8–12.

Murphy, J., & Datnow, A. (2003). *Leadership lessons from comprehensive school reforms.* Thousand Oaks, CA: Corwin.

Nelson, S., & Guerra, P. (2014). Educator beliefs and cultural knowledge: Implications for school improvement efforts. *Education Administration Quarterly, 50*(1), 67–95.

Noguera, P. (2008). *The trouble with black boys: And other reflections on race equity, and the future of public education.* San Francisco, CA: John Wiley.

Ravitch, D. (1985). *The schools we deserve: Reflections on the educational crisis of our time.* New York, NY: Basic Books.

Reeves, D. (2009). *Leading change in your school: How to conquer myths, building commitment, and get results.* Alexandria, VA: Association of Supervision and Curriculum Development.

Sarason, S. (1990). *The predictable failure of educational reform: Can we change before it's too late?* San Francisco, CA: Jossey-Bass.

Sarason, S. B. (1996). *Revisiting "the culture of the school and the problem of change."* New York, NY: Teachers College Press.

Seashore Louis, K., & Miles, M. (1990). *Improving the urban high school: What works and why.* New York, NY: Teachers College Press.

Sergiovanni, T. (1989). The leadership needed for quality schools. In T. J. Sergiovanni & J. H. Moore (Eds.), *Schooling for tomorrow: Directing reforms to issues that count* (pp. 213–226). Boston, MA: Allyn & Bacon.

Smith, W., & Andrews, R. (1989). *Instructional leadership: How principals make a difference.* Alexandria, VA: Association for Supervision and Curriculum Development.

Stringer, P. (2013). *Capacity building for school improvement.* Rotterdam: Sense Publishers.

Terrell, R., Terrell, E., Lindsey, R., & Lindsey, D. (2018). *Culturally proficient leadership: The personal journey begins within.* Thousand Oaks, CA: Corwin.

Tucker, M. (2019). *Leading high performance school systems: Lessons room the world's best.* Alexandria, VA: Association for Supervision and Curriculum Development.

Wagner, T., & Kegan, R. (2006). *Change leadership: A practical guide to transforming our schools.* San Francisco, CA: Jossey-Bass.

RESOURCE 3B

RESEARCH ARTICLES

Casey, T., & Welborn, J. (2020, March–April). Cultural proficiency as an advocacy tool to build a diverse workforce. *Association of California School Administrators Leadership Magazine.* Retrieved from https://leadership.acsa.org/cultural-proficiency-as-an-advocacy-tool-to-build-exclusively in support aff

By Tamika Casey and Jaime Welborn | March | April 2020

Who has the most impact on student achievement and overall student success? Clearly, classroom teachers are well-positioned to impact students' overall success in school. However, not all students perform at the same level, which indicates that not all teachers approach student relations, assessments, and instruction in the same way (Hattie, 2009; Jankowski, 2017; Kuh, 2008). Some educators are still asking the question, "Do we believe all students can learn?" even while the data are clear that all students are learning irrespective of their circumstances (Comer, Joyner, & Ben-Avie, 2004; Edmonds & Fredericksen, 1978; Lezotte & Snyder, 2011). Perhaps the more appropriate question for teachers and administrators is, "Do we believe we can educate all students?" The purpose of this article is to examine the current teacher workforce and ask what can be done to reach and teach more students than ever before. Using a case study format, the authors present a model for close examination of increasing diversity of the workforce in our schools. Since the publication of the Coleman Report in 1966, educational leadership has served as a catalyst for educational reform efforts across the United States with a focus on continuous school improvement and student achievement. With findings that continue to identify access, opportunity, and other educational gaps between and among students of diverse racial and ethnic backgrounds, as well as social classes, we must refocus our attention on educators in the workforce who have the most contact with our students. A report from the Learning Policy Institute claims teacher diversity in California public K–12 schools has increased since the turn of the 21st century (Carver-Thomas, 2018). Therefore, districts are moving in the right direction. However, more effort must be made to increase our diverse workforce in classrooms. A model for systemic change is needed to move forward. Students must see themselves in their teachers and administrators, not exclusively in support staff. But how do we go about this advocacy or change? The gaps relate to inequities in society with strong implications in our school organizations. Advocacy for equitable recruitment, hiring, and retention practices—removing barriers and providing resources and actions for change—can provide avenues to increase the diversity among the workforce. The Cultural Proficiency Framework provides a clear model for advocacy and organizational change by using four interrelated tools toward increasing equity and access through educational practice and policy.

EQUITY FRAMEWORK FOR A DIVERSE WORKFORCE ADVOCACY

The conceptual framework used in a recent qualitative case study in Eaveston School District (pseudonym) sought to describe the relationship between cultural diversity, economics, power, policy, pedagogy, school improvement, and student achievement outcomes (Welborn, 2019). The research analysis integrated these constructs with the equity framework of cultural proficiency, an inside-out approach that provides tools for addressing the responses to diversity that we encounter in our schools (Cross, Bazron, Dennis, & Issacs, 1989; Lindsey, 2019). Like Eaveston, San Bernardino City Unified School District has also engaged in the work of Cultural Proficiency, using the interrelated tools for increasing equitable outcomes. SBCUSD, in collaboration with their community partners, is embarking on an ambitious journey to develop interorganizational systems, which will allow them to identify, develop, recruit, hire, and retain teachers of color. Educators who are advocates for increasing the diversity of the workforce can utilize the conceptual framework for continuous improvement by beginning at the bottom of the framework with the barriers that guide unhealthy practices and the guiding principles that guide healthy practices. The third tool of the framework is the Continuum, in which practices and policies related to recruitment, hiring, and retention can be analyzed from most destructive to most proficient, and then the fourth tool, the Essential Elements, provides actions for increasing equity, access, and inclusion. Cultural proficiency utilizes dialogue and reflection in cross-cultural situations related to personal values and behaviors of individuals and the organization's policies and practices. As educational leaders consider systemic, transformative organizational change to improve outcomes of recruiting, hiring, and retaining teachers and administrators of color, as well as increase equity, and serve all students, they must keep constant vigilance of self in their roles as change agents. The starting point for sustainable, systemic change in human resources practices related to a diverse workforce does not begin with changing the system or others around ourselves, but rather it is a personal mindset of individual practice based on social justice and equity of viewing cultural differences as assets on which to build educational programs.

ACKNOWLEDGING SYSTEMIC BARRIERS AND CHALLENGES

Barriers and challenges in any organization can often stop progress right in its tracks. When it comes to recruiting, hiring, and retaining teachers of color, delays in the journey of increasing cultural proficiency within these practices can be detrimental and lead to further perpetuation of inequitable outcomes for students. The reality for approximately 25 million students of color in U.S. schools is that they are not educated by teachers of color (Pew Research Center, 2018), and it is important to note research provides evidence of reading and math achievement increases for students of color who are assigned a teacher of the same race. School districts across the U.S. are looking to their human resources departments for guidance in helping to better educate students of color by creating a value for diversity and sense of belonging for all. The first step for human resource departments is to be able to acknowledge the systemic barriers and challenges present for recruiting, hiring, and retaining teachers of color in the district. The barriers to culturally proficient practice include (1) systemic oppression, (2) a sense of privilege or entitlement, (3) unawareness of the need to adapt, and (4) resistance to change. Knowing about how to use the barriers to cultural proficiency leads to recognizing aspects of human resource–related practice and policy and understanding how to overcome resistance to increasing the diversity of the workforce in schools. Eaveston's assistant superintendent of Human Resources suggests school districts make intentional efforts to disaggregate data by race and gender related to recruiting, hiring, and retaining practices. Taking it one step further, barriers such as bias-related oppression or unawareness of the need to adapt can be removed if school administrators are transparent and intentional in their communications and human resource efforts. Confronting the challenges to recruiting, hiring, and retaining teachers of color is also a priority in Eaveston and SBCUSD. While external challenges such as the systemic structures of teacher preparation programs and outcomes influence the disproportionality in race—White versus non-White—of the number of applicants that are eligible to apply for certified teacher vacancies, using the Cultural Proficiency Framework requires human resource administrators to look for change from within. While human resources administrators in Eaveston work with state and local universities to explore the barriers that may be preventing some candidates of color from getting their certification, there are great efforts around growing Eaveston's own.

> We are working on an educational assistance program for our support staff who wants to get a teacher certification. We also realize the importance of educating our high school students about the career path for becoming a teacher. There's so much talk about the problem and the challenges, but how do we get from talking about it action? We have to talk to kids about their experiences here in Eaveston. (Assistant superintendent of Human Resources, Eaveston School District)

RELYING ON CORE VALUES AND USING THE GUIDING PRINCIPLES OF CULTURAL PROFICIENCY

To address the pernicious effect of the barriers and challenges encountered by human resources departments in recruiting, hiring, and retaining teachers of color, personnel must rely on the core values of the school organization and use the Guiding Principles of Cultural Proficiency. The school district's expressed core values promote a foundational component of practice—what they actually do. Use of the Guiding Principles of Cultural Proficiency provides human resource personnel a tool for aligning their practices in recruiting, hiring, and retaining teachers of color to the core values, often expressed in the vision, mission, and goals of the school district. The intentional choice to align the core values with behaviors and practice around recruiting, hiring, and retaining teachers of color in the district sends the message to the school community—including families, students, and community members—that you have a keen sense of cultural knowledge related to student needs and value diversity of the workforce in educating those students. The mission of Eaveston school district is that "all will learn." In order to reach the mission of the school district, the human resources department keeps the core values of care, safety, learning, and interdependence at the heart of the work. Building a community where unity among students, families, patrons, and staff fosters learning, responsibility, and appreciation of the diverse individual, the assistant superintendent believes his role in the Cultural Proficiency work is to identify and recommend to the board of education the very best employees in the district who will help students achieve and meet their goals.

> For every role, I want to hire the best bus drivers, custodians, music teachers, chemistry teachers, and so on. We would like our work force to represent the exact student demographics we have, but we have to work within the job applicants holding appropriate certifications to get the very best job done.

Reliance on one guiding principle in particular, "people are served in varying degrees by the dominant culture," has led Eaveston human resources department to change one of its recruitment practices. For all recruiting trips, both to local fairs and to Historically Black College and Universities, the assistant superintendent and director of human resources take teachers of color because they acknowledge that people are served by varying degrees of their own cultures and diversity at the table will lead to diversity in those prospective teacher candidates who visit the table. Overall, the Guiding Principles equips culturally proficient educators with the ability to implement practices and policies that express the culture and worldview that is backed by actions that value diversity.

USING THE CONTINUUM FOR INCREASING CULTURALLY PROFICIENT EDUCATIONAL PRACTICES AND POLICY DEVELOPMENT

Human resources administrators involve themselves in best practice and identify areas in which they can improve the practices related to teacher recruitment, hiring, and retention. The intention is to hire for talent in order to create effective classrooms that drive student achievement. The Continuum of Cultural Proficiency is a tool that contains six points with which human resource personnel's practices and behaviors align with from most culturally destructive to most culturally proficient. The Barriers to Cultural Proficiency produce behaviors, practices, and policies on the three points on the left side of the Continuum that are unhealthy for recruiting, hiring, and retaining teachers of color, and consequently perpetuate the inequitable outcomes for students in our schools. The Guiding Principles of Cultural Proficiency produce behaviors, practices, and policies on the three points on the right side of the Continuum that are healthy for recruiting, hiring, and retaining teachers of color, which can increase access and equity for students in our schools.

School districts across the United States are looking to their human resources departments for guidance in helping to better educate students of color by creating a value for diversity and sense of belonging for all.

Human Resources personnel in Eaveston School District work closely with the Cultural Proficiency Committee in the district to monitor their behaviors and practices related to recruiting, hiring, and retaining their teachers of color. Identifying numerous behaviors and practices within the district on the left side of the Continuum led the Cultural Proficiency Committee to choose increasing workforce diversity as one of the top three goals for the district for opening access for students in Eaveston School District.

COMMITTING TO STANDARDS OF CHANGE WITH THE ESSENTIAL ELEMENTS

The fourth tool of Cultural Proficiency is the Essential Elements, which provide five action verbs for committing to standards of organizational change. Human resources departments focused on recruiting, hiring, and retaining teachers of color use these action verbs to take the identified behaviors, practices, and policies and rely on the Guiding Principles to initiate change. This change in behavior, practice, or policy opens doors for students by increasing diversity in the workforce, which research concludes is educationally beneficial for students of color. The Essential Elements of Cultural Proficiency include (1) assessing cultural knowledge, (2) valuing diversity, (3) managing the dynamics of difference, (4) adapting to diversity, and (5) institutionalizing cultural knowledge. In Eaveston, human resources personnel have worked closely with the Cultural Proficiency Committee to examine some of the current recruiting, hiring, and retaining practices in the district and make changes through action to improve the outcomes. As part of assessing cultural knowledge, the human resources department worked to identify the culture of themselves as individuals and recognize how that culture might affect others. As previously mentioned, a cultural norm of the organization has been to send two administrators to job fairs. Part of valuing diversity has been to have conversations about the culture of teachers that two White males might attract to Eaveston's recruitment table compared to teachers of color and understand the effect that historical contexts may have on these present-day interactions, thus impacting the recruitment and hiring efforts and outcomes. In order to manage the dynamics of difference in this situation, these administrators are now adapting to diversity by joining forces and taking teachers of color, both male and female, with them to recruitment fairs and ensuring that diversity is represented in interview committees. As for San Bernardino, the formation of the Teachers of Color Campaign is one example of adapting to diversity. Pre-hiring teachers of color at the district's recruitment fair and then sending the candidates to sites for interviews, creating a guest teacher pipeline where district substitutes go through an onboarding process and extensive training in hopes of recruiting them to become future classroom teachers, university partnerships, and the district's Grow Your Own initiative have doubled the efforts for increasing teachers of color. The work has helped to begin institutionalizing cultural knowledge and the attempts to increase diversity in the workforce in Eaveston and San

Bernardino. Overall, best practice of advocacy indicates an intentional commitment to increasing workforce, namely certified teachers, including commitments of funding, staff, time, and a culturally proficient lens of practice. The purpose of this article was to demonstrate the need for a more diverse teacher workforce, supported by a districtwide change initiative for equity and access. The Cultural Proficiency Framework provides a systematic model school district leaders can utilize for advocacy and organizational change toward culturally proficient practices and policies. Given an effective classroom teacher has the most impact on student achievement and overall success, the time is now to advocate in school districts across California and beyond to increase diversity of the workforce in our schools again. This mission is about social justice.

REFERENCES

Carver-Thomas, D. (2018). *Diversifying the teaching profession: How to recruit and retain teachers of color.* Learning Policy Institute. Retrieved from https://learningpolicy-institute.org/sites/default/files/product-files/Diversifying_Teaching_Profession_REPORT_0.pdf

Cross, T., Bazron, B., Denis, K., & Issacs, M. (1989). *Towards a culturally competent system of care* (Vol. 1). Washington, DC: Georgetown University Child Development Center, CASSP Technical Assistance Center.

Edmonds, R., & Frederiksen, J. R. (1978). *Search for effective schools: The identification and analysis of city schools that are instructionally effective for poor children.* Cambridge, MA: Harvard University Center for Urban Studies.

Geiger, A. W. (2018, August 27). *America's public school teachers are far less racially and ethnically diverse than their students.* Pew Research Center.

Hattie, J. (2009). *Visible learning: A synthesis of over 800 meta-analyses relating to achievement.* New York: Routledge.

Jankowski, N. (2017). Unpacking relationships, instruction, and student outcomes. Retrieved from https://www.acenet.edu/Documents/Unpacking-Relationships-Instruction-and-Student-Outcomes.pdf

Kuh, G. (2008). *High-impact educational practices: What they are, who has access to them, and why they matter.* Washington, DC: Association of American Colleges and Universities.

Lezotte, L., & Snyder, K. (2011). *What effective schools do: Re-envisioning the correlates.* Bloomington, IN: Solution Tree Press.

Lindsey, R., Nuri-Robins, K., Terrell, R., & Lindsey, D. (2019). *Cultural proficiency: A manual for school leaders* (4th ed.). Thousand Oaks, CA: Corwin.

Welborn, J. (2019). Increasing equity, access, and inclusion through organizational change: A study of implementation and experiences surrounding a school district's journey towards culturally proficient educational practice. *Education Leadership Review, 20*(1), 167–189.

Tamika Casey serves as Program Specialist-Equity and Targeted Student Achievement for the San Bernardino City Unified School District and Jaime Welborn is an assistant professor at Saint Louis University.

RESOURCE C: LEARNING STRATEGIES

LEARNING STRATEGY 1: BARRIERS TO CULTURAL PROFICIENCY (R. B. LINDSEY ET AL., 2019, P. 245)

Purpose

To identify aspects of the school or district culture that may be Barriers to Cultural Proficiency

Time Needed

Sixty minutes

Materials

Response Sheet: Barriers to Cultural Proficiency

Briefing

Let's see if we can identify some of the Barriers to Cultural Proficiency in our school (or district).

Process

1. Distribute Response Sheet: Barriers to Cultural Proficiency.
2. Review the meaning of the terms to be sure that people understand them.
3. Organize participants into groups of three to five.
4. Ask each group to brainstorm examples for each term.
5. Invite each small group to share with the larger group.

Debriefing

1. What did you think, feel, or wonder as you completed this exercise?
2. What surprises you?
3. What made this activity difficult or easy?
4. What conclusions can you draw from the answers of the group?
5. What would you like to do with this information?

RESPONSE SHEET: BARRIERS TO CULTURAL PROFICIENCY

In your small groups, list examples within your organization of these Barriers to Cultural Proficiency.

- Systemic Oppression
  - Distributing power and privilege (consciously or unintentionally) only to members of dominant groups
  - Abusing power accrued through rules and roles within the organization

- The Presumption of Entitlement and Unearned Privilege
  - Not recognizing that members of certain groups receive more privileges because of their position or because of the groups to which they belong
  - Assuming that you accrued all of your personal achievements and societal or organizational benefits because of your competence or your character and do not need to share or redistribute what you have or help others to acquire what you have

- Unawareness of the Need to Adapt
  - Not recognizing the need to make personal and organizational changes in response to the diversity of the people with whom you and your organization interact
  - Believing instead that only the others need to change and adapt to you

- Resistance to Change
  - Believing that the changes need to be made externally, by others, not within self.
  - Not recognizing that the journey to Cultural Proficiency is a change process, not an event.

Throughout most organizations are systems of institutionalized racism, sexism, heterosexism, ageism, and ableism. Moreover, these systems are often supported and sustained without the permission of and at times without the knowledge of the people whom they benefit. These systems perpetuate domination and victimization of individuals and groups.

LEARNING STRATEGY 2: DIVERSITY LIFELINE (R. B. LINDSEY ET AL., 2019, P. 199)

Purpose

To have participants analyze and share the significant events in their lives that have affected their perception of diversity

To aid participants in understanding that diversity is a dynamic that has been and will be ever present in their lives

To expand participants' understanding of the concept of diversity

Time Needed

Ninety minutes

Materials

Chart paper for each participant

Markers for each participant

Masking tape

Tables or floor space for participants to draw their lifelines

Enough wall space for all participants to hang their lifelines and discuss them in small groups

Briefing

Think about your life: How have you been affected by your diversity? When did you become aware of the diversity around you? How has your understanding of diversity changed? On the chart paper, draw a graph of your life marking the significant points that reflect your awareness of diversity.

Process

1. Distribute markers and chart paper to each person.

2. Organize the participants into groups of two or three people. Encourage the participants to diversify their small groups. It is important to keep the groups small so that each person can share extensively. It is also important that people in the small groups are comfortable with each other.

3. Allow about twenty minutes for participants to draw and post their lifelines.

4. Allow about fifteen minutes per person to describe his or her lifeline.

5. Reorganize the small groups into one large group, allowing time for participants to view all of the lifelines.

Debriefing

1. What did you feel, think, or wonder as you started the assignment?

2. What did you notice about yourself as you drew?

3. What did you learn about yourself from this process?

4. What did you notice about your group members as they spoke or listened to the other members in the group?

5. What did you learn about your group members?

6. What did you learn about diversity? What is the relationship of diversity to inclusion or to equity?

7. How might this inform your work?

8. How will you use what you have learned?

Variations

1. Use the lifeline process to have participants tell their stories without emphasizing any particular aspect of their lives.

2. Cover the wall with chart paper. As a group, draw a lifeline for the organization.

3. Allow participants to draw their personal lines to indicate where their lives intersect with the life of the school.

LEARNING STRATEGY 3: NAME FIVE THINGS (R. B. LINDSEY ET AL., 2019, P. 201)

Purpose

To help participants clarify how they define themselves

(This activity will also demonstrate the effects of Cultural Blindness.)

Time Needed

Fifteen minutes

Materials

Blank paper

Briefing

Think about who you are and how you describe yourself.

Process

1. Write five words or short phrases that describe the essence of who you are. These should be things that if they were taken away from you, you would not be the same person (five minutes).

2. Rank the list, and cross off one of the items.

3. Now cross off another. Note with some drama how people may be feeling about crossing items off of their lists.

4. Now cross two more items off of your list so that only the purest essence of who you are remains.

5. Participants may try to cooperate, but they will definitely struggle.

The point of this activity is to help you to see that when you seek to engage with only one aspect of someone, you are asking them to erase or deny the essence of who they are. It may be more difficult and take more time in a diverse environment, but if you don't engage fully, you won't be experiencing all of who each person is.

Debriefing

1. What did you notice as you wrote your list?

2. What did you notice as you shared your list?

3. How did it feel to have to cross items off of your list?

4. Where in life does this happen?

5. How does it affect the people we encounter to see only one aspect of them?

6. What conclusions can you draw about the members of this group?

7. Do we ever ask, directly or indirectly, our students to leave part of who they are when they come to school? Do we ask their parents to abandon their culture while on campus?

Variation

With a partner, share your list (fifteen minutes).

After the participants have written their lists, ask them to cross off one item, then another, until only two are left.

Consider not allowing the participants to share what was crossed off of their lists. This will demonstrate for them what it feels like to be in a group where they are only allowed to show a portion of themselves.

LEARNING STRATEGY 4: CLARIFYING OUR VALUES (P. X)

This learning strategy is widely used and adapted by many educators and scholars. We adapted it to relate to the Cultural Proficiency Framework.

Purpose

To clarify your values as you seek to understand how those core values influence your behaviors as an educator. Participants will reflect on the ways in which students are asked to "give up part of who they are at the door" when they enter the school system.

Time Needed

Twenty to thirty minutes

Materials

A list of 50 core values, separated onto individual cards or paper

Envelope for the cards

Paper

Writing utensils for participants

Briefing

Give each participant an envelope with a set of 50 core values, and ask that they have a piece of paper and something to write with available.

Process

1. Participants take cards out of the envelope.

2. Ask them to sort their cards, on first looking at the core value, into three piles.

   a. "Most important to you"

   b. "Somewhat important to you"

   c. "Not important to you"

3. Participants should place the "not important pile" and the "somewhat important pile" back into the envelope.

4. Ask participants to sort their cards again, trying to achieve the same three different piles of importance.

5. Again, participants should place the "not important pile" and the "somewhat important pile" back into the envelope.

6. Ask participants to take the "most important pile," select five top values, and commit them to writing on the piece of paper.

7. Participants reflect on their behaviors as educators who are influenced by those five top values. Once time has been given for reflection, participants get in triads (groups of three) to dialogue about their core values and associated behaviors.

8. Participants will debrief as a group.

9. Ask participants to take the list of five top values and cross out one of the top values; then another; then another.

10. Participants should identify feelings associated with crossing off the values. Ask participants to reflect on the degree to which students must give up who they are at the "door" to enter their district, school, or classroom.

Debriefing

1. What did you learn about yourself?

2. What are you learning about others?

3. How did you experience this activity?

4. How does this activity relate to our students?

5. Do our students have to give up part of who they are at the door because their core values differ from the core values of our school or from me as an individual?

6. How might we use this information about our core values?

Template

MOST IMPORTANT	SOMEWHAT IMPORTANT	NOT IMPORTANT

LEARNING STRATEGY 5: YOUR NAME—YOUR STORY (P. 96)

Purpose

To help people get acquainted with each other, building on differences and similarities of other people in the room.

Time Needed

Ten to twenty minutes for activity; then an additional one to two minutes per person to introduce themselves to the group.

Materials

Chart paper on walls of room

Markers for participants

Masking tape

Briefing

As participants come in, ask them to draw words or pictures to represent their name on a piece of chart paper.

Process

1. Write or draw words, pictures, or symbols for each of the following:
   a. Your name
   b. Name(s) others call you
   c. One of your core values
   d. A person who was instrumental in your decision to become an educator
   e. A symbol that represents you
   f. Someone you would like to spend the day with
2. Hang chart papers on walls.
3. Participants introduce themselves to the group.

Debriefing

1. What did you learn about yourself?
2. What did you learn about others?
3. What do we have in common?
4. What are some differences we have?
5. What conclusions can you draw from the stories of our names?
6. What questions do you have for group members?

Template

One of your core values	Name	A person you would like to spend the day with
A person who was instrumental in your decision to become a teacher	What name others call you	A symbol that represents you

LEARNING STRATEGY 6: INTRODUCTORY GRID (R. B. LINDSEY ET AL., 2019, P. 223)

Purpose

To help people get acquainted with each other

(This "sponge" activity orients participants to the differences and similarities of the other people in the room. As an opener or closer, a sponge activity soaks up extra people and extra time. People do not have to start at the same time to benefit from the activity.)

Time Needed

Because this is a sponge activity to be used at the beginning of a session, ten to twenty minutes for the activity and the debriefing are sufficient.

Materials

Chart paper on walls of room

Markers for participants

Masking tape

Briefing

As participants come in, ask them to fill in the blanks on the chart paper.

Process

1. Place a category at the top of each piece of chart paper:
   a. Name
   b. City of birth
   c. Astrological sign
   d. City of residence
   e. Favorite restaurant or type of food
   f. Hobby or leisure activity
   g. Expectation for the session
   h. Preferred type of pet
   i. Other creative categories that will get people thinking and talking

2. Number the lines of Chart A with the number of participants.

3. Participants select a number on Chart A and then complete each chart using the same number so that their answers can be identified.

Debriefing

1. What do we have in common?
2. What are some differences we have?
3. What conclusions can you draw from the answers on the charts?
4. What questions do you have for group members?

Variation 1

Have members stand and introduce themselves by adding to the information on the charts, such as where they work and why they are participating.

Variation 2

Divide the participants into random groups of four or five people.

Have each group list the following:

a. What everyone in the group has in common.

b. Something unique about each member.

c. What they hope to achieve by the end of the program.

d. A name for the group.

Each small group makes a brief presentation to the larger group.

Variation 3

Add to the last page of the grid the category "Significant Family Value." Discuss the differences and similarities of family values and how, even when all the values appear to be positive and laudatory in a common workplace, those values may conflict with one another or cause conflicts within the individual. For example, the values for honesty and courtesy often conflict, because sometimes it is impossible to be honest and not hurt someone's feelings, which is considered discourteous.

LEARNING STRATEGY 7: STRENGTH BOMBARDMENT (R. B. LINDSEY ET AL., 2019, P. 221)

Purpose

To build a sense of team among participants through sharing personal stories and discovering similarities and differences

(This is a good activity for team building. We have had success with it as an opening activity with a group whose members know one another well. We also have had success with it as a culminating activity for groups that have been working together on a project. This activity provides for a personal focus, allows for individual expression, and uses positive feedback as a communication tool.)

Time Needed

Sixty to ninety minutes, depending on the size of the subgroups

Materials

Small adhesive labels, preferably colored circles about the size of a quarter (if large colored dots are not available, get labels that are large enough for writing one word; each participant should have about twenty to fifty labels, depending on the size of the small group)

Briefing

In your small groups, you will be sharing stories about important aspects of your life.

Process

1. Distribute a plain sheet of 8 × 11½ inch paper to each participant.

2. Ask participants to write their names in the middle of the page.

3. Ask participants to turn the paper over. Divide your life into ten- or fifteen-year increments. For each of these periods, identify things that you have done that you are proud of. This does not necessarily mean achievements from the perspective of society but accomplishments as you define them. Participants can make notes on the page.

4. Organize participants into groups of three to six. A group of three people will need about thirty minutes. Add ten minutes of processing time for each additional member of the group.

5. In the small group, each person will take five minutes to share his or her accomplishments. The person is not to be interrupted during the telling of the story.

6. While the first person is telling his or her story, other group members are writing one-word adjectives on the labels that describe their assessment of his or her character in light of the accomplishments. In five minutes, each group member will write on several of the labels.

7. When the first person has completed his or her story, during which time colleagues have been recording their adjectives on the labels, he or she listens to the feedback from colleagues.

8. In turn, each colleague looks the storyteller in the eye and tells him or her what is written on each dot and alternately affixes it to the reverse side of the speaker's strength bombardment sheet—for example, "Mary, I see you as courageous because you stood up to your brother." In just a few minutes, Mary has many labels on her sheet that describe her character.

9. Repeat the process for each participant.

Debriefing

1. What did you think, feel, or wonder while assessing your life?

2. What did you think, feel, or wonder while telling your story?

3. What was your reaction to the feedback you received in the two forms of communication: the verbal message with direct eye contact from your colleagues and the label dots affixed to the reverse side of your sheet?

4. (It never varies with this activity that someone will minimize the feedback from his or her colleagues. Some will indicate that their colleagues were generous. If this should occur, remind them that it was that person's story; the colleagues were only feeding back to that person what they were hearing.)

5. Let participants know that, yes, life is not always expressed in terms of positive feedback, but it sure does feel good when it occurs. Then continue with the following questions.

6. What did you think, feel, or wonder as you heard the stories of your group members?

7. What implications does this have for our work with students? With parents? With one another?

8. Invite participants to keep this sheet in a safe place so that someday in the future, they can pull it out and remind themselves of what people had to say to them on this day.

LEARNING STRATEGY 8: WHAT'S IN A NAME (R. B. LINDSEY ET AL., 2019, P. 227)

Purpose

To demonstrate that people have strong feelings and interesting stories about their names

To underscore that learning and pronouncing a name correctly is one of the first and easiest ways to connect to another person

Time Needed

Twenty minutes

Materials

Copies of Response Sheet: What's in a Name?

Briefing

This activity will give you a chance to get to know something new about your colleagues.

Process

Ask participants to sit in pairs (or small groups if you have the time) and share their responses to the questions in the response sheet.

Debriefing

1. What did you learn about yourself in the process of telling your story?

2. What did you learn about your colleagues as you listened to their stories?

3. Why is it important to acknowledge someone's name?

4. How have you experienced an individual or a person's culture being disrespected by the way someone in authority used or misused their name?

5. What stories do you think your clients would tell about how their names are used (or not) in this school?

6. What customer service standards might you set relating to the names of the students, their families, and others who visit this school?

Variation

Tell a story about your name.

This activity can be done in fifteen minutes or can take as long as an hour depending on how you focus the conversation during the debriefing.

RESPONSE SHEET: WHAT'S IN A NAME?

1. What is your name?

2. Have you had any other names?

3. What is the story of how you acquired your name?

4. What does your name mean?

5. How does your name reflect your culture?

6. How do people respond when they see or hear your name for the first time?

7. If you changed your name, what would it be?

LEARNING STRATEGY 9: EXAMINING YOUR ORGANIZATIONAL VALUES (R. B. LINDSEY ET AL., 2019, P. 271)

Purpose

To identify the Barriers to Cultural Proficiency that are evidenced in the covert values of your school or district

Time Needed

90–120 minutes

Materials

Copies of Response Sheet: Examining Your Organizational Values

Copies of the school's core values or shared values for diversity

Chart paper and marking pens or overhead projector and transparency markers

Briefing

This activity will provide you with the opportunity to apply your understanding of (a) the sense of entitlement concept and (b) unawareness of the need to adapt. You will also examine the relationship between our stated and unarticulated values and the implication that this has for creating change in our school. The activity will be a mix of personal and group viewpoints and experiences.

Process

1. Distribute the school's shared values, or core values, for diversity.
2. Review the meaning of covert value or unarticulated value. Remind participants that it is the hidden curriculum.
3. Add your school's core values in the first column. You may do this ahead of time.
4. Ask each person to spend fifteen minutes making notes on the response sheet that reflect his or her individual views and perspectives.
5. Have participants form into diverse groups of four to six.
6. Give participants thirty to sixty minutes to discuss each core value and complete the response sheet.
7. Request that participants post their work on a chart or onto transparencies.
8. Encourage critical review of and reflection on the responses.

Debriefing

1. What were your feelings when you first received the response sheet?
2. What did you think, feel, or wonder about the discussion in your small group?
3. How do you feel about the levels of congruence between the stated and unarticulated values?
4. What observations do you have about the columns "Consequences" and "Implications for Change"?
5. What did you learn about your school? Your colleagues? Yourself?
6. What is the implication of this activity for you in your role at school?
7. What information or skills do you believe you need to do an even better job?
8. How will you use this information?

Variations

Divide the participants into culturally specific small groups.

LEARNING STRATEGY 10: THE WORLD CAFÉ: GUIDING PRINCIPLES (P. 117)

The World Café (http://www.theworldcafe.com) is a popular collaborative learning strategy for structuring dialogue of a large group. We have adapted it here to facilitate learning about the Guiding Principles of Cultural Proficiency.

Purpose

To reinforce the Guiding Principles of Cultural Proficiency by seeking an understanding of what each principle means and how it relates to examples in a school system.

Time Needed

Sixty minutes

Materials

Chart paper on walls of room

Markers for participants

Masking tape

Briefing

Place nine pieces of chart paper, one for each Guiding Principle on tables or walls. Write one Guiding Principle on each sheet.

Process

1. Divide participants into nine equal groups.

2. Each group will rotate the room from poster to poster using nine rounds.

3. Facilitator will keep time for each group, asking a different question per round.

    a. Facilitator asks question.

    b. Participants spend two minutes, silently answering the question on the poster.

    c. Participants spend three minutes discussing the meaning with members of the group.

    d. Facilitator asks participants to rotate to the next poster.

    e. Participants spend two minutes reading what has been written on the poster.

    f. Facilitator asks new question (repeat a–f).

        Round 1: What does this guiding principle mean to you as an educator?

        Round 2: What is resonating with you about this guiding principle?

Round 3: What thoughts does this guiding principle evoke for you?

Round 4: What would be strategies/practices for responding to this principle?

Round 5: How does this guiding principle relate to your role as an educator?

Round 6: In what ways are you relating this guiding principle to your organization?

Round 7: What are your feelings related to this guiding principle?

Round 8: What are examples that illustrate our understanding of this principle?

Round 9: What issues might arise if this principle is not acknowledged?

Debriefing

1. How did you experience this learning strategy?

2. What happened in your small groups? What did you learn?

3. What are you wondering?

4. How might we use this information?

Template

This template can be used to further the discussion around each guiding principle or can be used virtually to facilitate this learning strategy.

GUIDING PRINCIPLE	WHAT DOES THIS GUIDING PRINCIPLE MEAN TO US AS EDUCATORS?	HOW DOES THIS GUIDING PRINCIPLE RELATE TO WHAT WE ARE TRYING TO DO IN OPENING DOORS FOR ALL OF OUR STUDENTS AND STAFF?
Culture is a predominant force in society.		
People are served to varying degrees by the dominant culture.		
People have individual and group identities.		
Diversity within cultures is vast and significant.		
Each cultural group has unique cultural needs.		
The best of both worlds enhances the capacity of all.		
The family, as defined by each culture, is the primary system of support in the education of children.		
School systems must recognize that marginalized populations have to be at least bicultural and that this status creates a distinct set of issues to which the system must be equipped to respond.		
Inherent in cross-cultural interactions are dynamics that must be acknowledged, adjusted to, and accepted.		

LEARNING STRATEGY 11: GUIDING PRINCIPLES DISCUSSION STARTERS (R. B. LINDSEY ET AL., 2019, P. 263)

Purpose

To reinforce the Guiding Principles of Cultural Proficiency

To identify how the Guiding Principles of Cultural Proficiency can be translated into school behavior

Time Needed

Sixty minutes

Materials

Response Sheet: Guiding Principles of Cultural Proficiency

Briefing

Let's look at the Guiding Principles of Cultural Proficiency to make sure we know what they mean in relationship to how we do things at this school.

Process

1. Distribute Response Sheet: Guiding Principles of Cultural Proficiency. Divide the group into small groups, assigning one question to each group.

2. Ask the small groups to discuss the principle and to make meaning for their group discussion. What does it mean? How does it relate to my life? How does it relate to my work? How does it relate to what we are trying to do as a professional community? What examples might we cite to illustrate this principle?

3. Reconvene the large group and share the responses, encouraging critical reflection and review.

Debriefing

1. What happened in your small groups? How easy or difficult was it to answer the questions?

2. How do you feel about your responses?

3. Have you ever thought of parents, community, students, or one another as customers?

4. How does thinking in terms of customer or client relations alter the way you respond to these groups?

5. What are the implications for your responses?

6. How will you use this information?

Variations

Examine the principles from the perspective of a classroom or the district.

Conduct this activity with one large group, inviting discussion and responses of everyone to all the questions. Answer these questions for each of the principles:

1. What would your classroom look like if this principle were acknowledged?

2. What would be strategies for responding to this principle in your classroom?

3. What issues might arise when this principle is not acknowledged?

4. Give examples of the types of conflict that might arise.

RESPONSE SHEET: GUIDING PRINCIPLES OF CULTURAL PROFICIENCY

Culture Is a Predominant Force.

Acknowledge culture as a predominant force in shaping behaviors, values, and institutions. Although you may be inclined to take offense at behaviors that differ from yours, remind yourself that they may not be personal; they may be cultural.

People Are Served in Varying Degrees by the Dominant Culture.

What works well in organizations and in the community for you and others who are like you may work against members of other cultural groups. Failure to make such an acknowledgment puts the burden for change on one group.

The Group Identity of Individuals Is as Important as Their Individual Identities.

Although it is important to treat all people as individuals, it is also important to acknowledge their group identity. Actions must be taken with the awareness that the dignity of a person is not guaranteed unless the dignity of his or her people is also preserved.

Diversity Within Cultures Is Vast and Significant.

Since diversity within cultures is as important as diversity between cultures, it is important to learn about cultural groups not as monoliths—for example, Asians, Hispanics, Gay men, and Women—but as the complex and diverse groups that they are. Often, because of the class differences in the United States, people have more in common across cultural lines than within them.

Each Group Has Unique Cultural Needs.

Each cultural group has unique needs that cannot be met within the boundaries of the dominant culture. Expressions of one group's cultural identity do not imply disrespect for yours. Make room in your organization for several paths that lead to the same goal.

(Continued)

(Continued)

The Family, as Defined by Each Culture, Is the Primary System of Support in the Education of Children.

The traditional relationship between home and school is to place most of the responsibility for involvement directly with parents. While that holds true for most cultural groups, Cultural Proficiency provides a different frame by which teachers, parents, and education leaders assume greater responsibility for finding authentic ways to engage in culturally proficient practices to support student achievement.

People Who Are Not a Part of the Dominant Culture Have to Be at Least Bicultural.

Parents have to be fluent in the communication patterns of the school, as well as the communication patterns that exist in their communities. They also have to know the cultural norms and expectations of schools, which may conflict with or be different from those in their communities, their countries of origin, or their cultural groups. In ideal conditions, their children are developing bicultural skills, learning to code switch appropriately as the cultural expectations of their environments change, yet parents may not have these skills. They are then penalized because they do not respond as expected to the norms set by educators, nor do they negotiate well the educational systems of the public schools.

Inherent in Cross-Cultural Interactions Are Social and Communication Dynamics That Must Be Acknowledged, Adjusted to, and Accepted.

People who belong to groups that have histories of systemic oppression have heightened sensitivities regarding the societal privileges they do not receive and to the many unacknowledged slights and putdowns that they receive daily. These microaggressions are usually unnoticed by dominant group members and, when brought to their attention, are often dismissed as inconsequential.

The School System Must Incorporate Cultural Knowledge Into Practice and Policymaking.

Culturally proficient educators are self-consciously aware of their own cultures and the culture of their schools. This is crucial knowledge, because in addition to the cognitive curriculum, the cultural norms and expectations of the school must be taught as well. First, culturally proficient educators must assess and raise consciousness about their own individual and organizational cultures. Then, as they teach the cultural expectations of the school and classroom to all students and their families, educators must learn about the cultures of their students.

LEARNING STRATEGY 12: GOING DEEPER WITH THE CONTINUUM (R. B. LINDSEY ET AL., 2019, P. 275); GALLERY WALK; LISTENING TRIADS

Purpose

To identify examples of the points on the Cultural Proficiency Continuum

Time Needed

Thirty minutes

Materials

Response Sheet: Cultural Proficiency Continuum

Chart paper

Marking pens

Masking tape

Briefing

Let's look at the Cultural Proficiency Continuum presented in this chapter and on Response Sheet: Cultural Proficiency Continuum to see what meaning it has in our lives. We are going to develop some examples of the points on the Cultural Proficiency Continuum.

Process

1. Label six pieces of chart paper with the six points on the continuum. Put one point at the top of each chart. Hang the chart paper on the wall.

2. Distribute a marker and about ten sheets of 4 × 6 inch sticky notes to each participant.

3. Ask the groups to generate examples for the points along the continuum. Think about negative and positive comments about students that you have heard from other educators. Write one comment on each of your sticky notes.

4. After people have written comments on their sticky notes, invite them to place the notes on the appropriate charts.

5. As you, the facilitator, read the comments, you may need to move some of the sticky notes to more appropriate charts. Participants tend to place their comments higher on the continuum than they deserve to be.

6. Encourage participants to mill around, reading all of the comments.

Debriefing

1. What did you notice as you wrote the comments?

2. What did you notice as you read the other comments?

3. What did you feel, think, or wonder about the comments or the process?

4. What does this say about you?

5. What does this say about your school or district?

Variation

Focus the discussion on classroom behavior instead of on district or school behavior.

RESPONSE SHEET: CULTURAL PROFICIENCY CONTINUUM

Looking at Differences

Cultural Proficiency is a set of values and behaviors in an individual or the set of policies and practices in an organization that creates the appropriate mindset and approach to respond effectively to the issues caused by diversity. A culturally proficient organization interacts effectively with its employees, its clients, and its community. Culturally proficient people may not know all there is to know about others who are different from them, but they know how to take advantage of teachable moments, how to ask questions without offending, and how to create an environment that is welcoming to diversity and to change. There are six points along the continuum.

Cultural ▼ Destruction		Cultural ▼ Blindness		Cultural ▼ Competence	
	▲ Cultural Incapacity		▲ Cultural Precompetence		▲ Cultural Proficiency

Cultural Destructiveness: See the Difference; Stomp It Out

Cultural Destructiveness comprises any policy, practice, or behavior that effectively eliminates all vestiges of other people's cultures. It may be manifested through an organization's policies and practices or through an individual's values and behaviors. Sometimes these destructive actions occur intentionally:

- Social reproduction wherein one group re-creates itself, resulting in the exclusion of most other groups

- Discrimination against observable manifestations of ethnicity (e.g., accent, hair, and adornments)

- No institutional support for people whose socioeconomic class affects their work

Cultural Incapacity: See the Difference; Make It Wrong

Members of dominated groups receive treatment based on stereotypes and the belief that the dominant group is inherently superior. Cultural Incapacity includes any policy, practice, or behavior that disempowers people who differ from the dominant group. Examples include the disproportionate allocation of resources, discrimination against people on the basis of whether they "know their place," and belief in the supremacy of the dominant culture. Other examples are discriminatory hiring practices, subtle messages to people who are not members of the dominant group that they are not valued or welcome, and generally lower expectations of performance for minority group members. Yet more examples include the following:

- Questioning the qualifications of people of color

- Assuming that affirmative action appointees are not proficient

- Not perceiving people of color as successful unless they are bicultural

- Establishing committees for compliance with, not for commitment to, a goal

Cultural Blindness: See the Difference; Act Like You Don't

Failure to see or to acknowledge differences among and between groups often do make a difference to the groups and the individuals who are members of those groups. This is the belief that color and culture make no difference and that all people are the same. Values and behaviors of the dominant culture are presumed to be universally applicable and beneficial. It is also assumed that members of minority cultures do not meet the cultural expectations of the dominant group because of some cultural deficiency or lack of desire to achieve, rather than the fact that the system works only for the most assimilated of the minority groups. Following are some examples:

- Using the behavior of a "model minority" as the criteria for judging all minority groups

- Using management training that does not address diversity

- Not articulating the cultural expectations of the organization to all of its members

Cultural Precompetence: See the Difference; Respond Inappropriately

People and organizations that are culturally precompetent recognize that their skills and practices are limited when interacting with other cultural groups. They may have

(*Continued*)

(Continued)

made some changes in their approaches to the issues arising from diversity, but they are aware that they need assistance and more information. They may also do the following:

- Recruit people who are not part of the mainstream culture but not provide them with any support or make any adaptation to their differences.

- Show discomfort and unwillingness to confront or hold accountable people from dominated groups who are not performing well.

- Make rules instead of teaching appropriate behavior (e.g., rules against hate speech).

Cultural Competence: See the Difference; Understand the Difference That Difference Makes

Cultural Competence involves the use of the essential elements as the standards for individual behavior and organizational practice. This includes acceptance and respect for difference; continuing self-assessment regarding culture; careful attention to the dynamics of difference; continuous expansion of cultural knowledge and resources; and a variety of adaptations to belief systems, policies, and practices. Other forms of cultural competence are as follows:

- Performance standards for culturally appropriate behavior

- Modeling appropriate behaviors

- Risk-taking (e.g., speaking against injustice, even when doing so may cause tension and conflict)

Cultural Proficiency: See the Difference; Respond Positively and Affirmingly

Cultural Proficiency involves knowing how to learn and teach about different groups; having the capacity to teach and to learn about differences in ways that acknowledge and honor all the people and the groups they represent; holding culture in high esteem; and seeking to add to the knowledge base of culturally proficient practice by conducting research, developing new approaches based on culture, and increasing the knowledge of others about culture and the dynamics of difference.

THE CULTURAL PROFICIENCY CONTINUUM

CULTURAL DESTRUCTION	CULTURAL INCAPACITY	CULTURAL BLINDNESS	CULTURAL PRECOM-PETENCE	CULTURAL COMPETENCE	CULTURAL PROFICIENCY
Reactive >>>>>>>>>>>>>>>>>> Tolerance			Proactive >>>>>>>>>>>>> Transformative		

LEARNING STRATEGY 13: JIGSAW OF THE ESSENTIAL ELEMENTS OF CULTURAL PROFICIENCY (P. 167)

Purpose

To create a team of experts on each Essential Element that examines various strategic, transformative leverage points (i.e., curriculum, instruction, programs, professional development) in the district as addressed in the goals identified in the "Choosing Our Goals" learning strategy.

Time Needed

Sixty Minutes

Materials

Three goals

Response sheet

Articles, books, handouts about the Essential Elements

Briefing

Now that we have identified equity goals, let's use the Essential Elements of Cultural Proficiency to discuss what actions (practices and behaviors) we could use to become more culturally proficient and increase equity and access for our students.

Process

1. Divide participants into groups of five.
2. Each participant in the group selects one of the Essential Elements of which to focus.
3. Participants read articles, books, and handouts, focusing on the chosen Essential Element.
4. Participants record three to four most important points (MIPs) and possible actions for the Essential Element to meet the identified goal.
5. Individual participants then share their responses with the small group and facilitate a discussion to advance learning and plan for increasing equity and access for students.
6. After sufficient time has passed, ask each group to share its responses with the larger group.
7. Further learning can occur if you wish to group all educators by Essential Element.

Debriefing

1. What are the MIPs for each Essential Element?
2. What similarities and differences exist between and among the MIPs from the "expert groups"?
3. How might we use the actions we identified to meet our equity goals?

Template

GOAL		
ESSENTIAL ELEMENTS	**MOST IMPORTANT POINTS**	**WHAT ACTIONS SHOULD WE TAKE TO MEET THE IDENTIFIED GOAL?**
Assessing cultural knowledge		
Valuing diversity		
Managing the dynamics of difference		
Adapting to diversity		
Institutionalizing cultural knowledge		

LEARNING STRATEGY 14: USING THE ESSENTIAL ELEMENTS (P. 169)

Purpose

To reinforce and deepen efficacy with the Essential Elements and begin the process of translating the concepts into individual behaviors and organizational practice.

Time Needed

Sixty minutes

Materials

Response sheet: Guiding Questions to Deepening Efficacy with the Essential Elements

Briefing

Prepare participants to take a deeper look at the Essential Elements.

Process

1. Divide participants equally into groups.

2. Participants use the questions on the response sheet as they reflect and dialogue with each other.

3. Participants relate each Essential Element to examples of practice or behaviors in their organization.

4. After sufficient time has passed, ask each group to share its response with the entire group, and have the other participants add to their list of practices or behaviors.

Debriefing

1. How did you experience this learning strategy?

2. What did you learn as you identified examples of practices or behaviors in your organization?

3. How might we use this information?

Template

ESSENTIAL ELEMENT	QUESTIONS	EXAMPLES OF PRACTICES OR BEHAVIORS IN YOUR ORGANIZATION
Assessing cultural knowledge	What are the unwritten rules in your school? How do you describe your own culture? How does your school provide for a variety of learning styles?	

(Continued)

Valuing diversity	How would you describe the diversity in your current professional setting? How do you react to the term *valuing diversity*? How do you and your colleagues frame conversation about the learners?	
Managing the dynamics of difference	How do you handle conflict in the classroom? In the school? Among the adults? What skills do you possess to handle conflict? Describe situations of cross-cultural conflict that may be based on historic distrust.	
Adapting to diversity	How have you recently adapted to the needs of a new member? How has your organization recently adapted to the needs of new members? Describe examples of inclusive language and inclusive materials. How do you teach your clients about the organization's need to adapt to cultures?	
Institutionalizing cultural knowledge	What do you currently know about the cultural groups in your organization and among your clients? What more would you like to know about those cultures? How do you and your colleagues learn about these cultural groups?	

LEARNING STRATEGY 15: CULTURAL COMPETENCE SELF-ASSESSMENT (R. B. LINDSEY ET AL., 2019, PP. 289–292)

Purpose

To provide a baseline of information and a starting point for conversation about becoming culturally proficient

(This checklist will not certify anyone. It simply provides some key questions for exploration.)

Expertise of Facilitator

Moderate

Readiness of Group

Intermediate

Time Needed

Twenty minutes to complete the assessment and an additional twenty to forty minutes to discuss the results

Materials Needed

Response Sheet: Cultural Competence Self-Assessment

Briefing

This instrument will ask you questions that will help you to determine where to start as you develop your Cultural Competence.

Process

1. Distribute Response Sheet: Cultural Competence Self-Assessment.
2. Encourage participants to be candid in their responses.

Debriefing

1. How do you think you did?
2. Was there any pattern to your responses?
3. What would you like to know, do, and learn as a result of your answers?
4. What additional questions would you add to this self-assessment?
5. Where shall we go as a group?

Variations

1. Organize the participants into cohort groups. Have them share their responses with one another, and decide as a group what they would like to do next.
2. Organize the participants into five groups, one for each element. Have each group brainstorm ideas for developing skills and knowledge that will increase their competence for that particular element.

CULTURAL COMPETENCE SELF-ASSESSMENT

Circle the numbers that best reflect your responses to the questions:

rarely = 1, seldom = 2, sometimes = 3, often = 4, usually = 5

ASSESSES CULTURE						
1.	I am aware of my own culture and ethnicity.	1	2	3	4	5
2.	I am comfortable talking about my privilege and entitlements.	1	2	3	4	5
3.	I know the effect that my culture and ethnicity may have on the people in my work setting.	1	2	3	4	5
4.	I recognize microaggressions when they occur and how they affect individuals and the organization's culture	1	2	3	4	5
5.	I recognize when current cultural norms do not serve well everyone in the organization.	1	2	3	4	5
6.	I seek to learn about the cultures of this organization's clients.	1	2	3	4	5
7.	I anticipate how this organization's clients and employees will interact with, conflict with, and enhance one another.	1	2	3	4	5

(Continued)

(Continued)

	VALUES DIVERSITY					
8.	I welcome a diverse group of clients and colleagues into the work setting.	1	2	3	4	5
9.	I recognize that diversity is more than gender, ethnicity, and gender orientation.	1	2	3	4	5
10.	I learn from both the challenges and opportunities that diversity brings.	1	2	3	4	5
11.	I share my appreciation of diversity with my coworkers.	1	2	3	4	5
12.	I share my appreciation of diversity with other clients.	1	2	3	4	5
13.	I work to develop a learning community with the clients (internal or external) I serve.	1	2	3	4	5
14.	I teach the cultural expectations of my organization or department to those who are new or who may be unfamiliar with the organization's culture.	1	2	3	4	5
15.	I proactively seek to interact with people whose backgrounds are different from mine.	1	2	3	4	5
	MANAGES THE DYNAMICS OF DIFFERENCE					
16.	I recognize that conflict is a normal part of life.	1	2	3	4	5
17.	I work to develop skills to manage conflict in productive ways.	1	2	3	4	5
18.	I help my colleagues to understand that what appear to be clashes in personalities may in fact be conflicts in culture.	1	2	3	4	5
19.	I help the clients I serve to understand that what appear to be clashes in personalities may in fact be conflicts in personal or organizational culture.	1	2	3	4	5
20.	I check myself to see if an assumption I am making about a person is based upon facts or upon stereotypes about a group.	1	2	3	4	5
21.	I accept that the more diverse our group becomes, the more we will change and grow.	1	2	3	4	5
	ADAPTS TO DIVERSITY					
22.	I realize that once I embrace the Principles of Cultural Proficiency, I, too, must change.	1	2	3	4	5
23.	I am committed to the continuous learning that is necessary to deal with the issues caused by differences.	1	2	3	4	5
24.	I seek to enhance the substance and structure of the work I do so that it is informed by the Guiding Principles of Cultural Proficiency.	1	2	3	4	5
25.	I recognize that I may need to share the resources or power that come from the unearned privileges I currently enjoy.	1	2	3	4	5
26.	I know how to learn about people and cultures unfamiliar to me without giving offense.	1	2	3	4	5
	INSTITUTIONALIZES CULTURAL KNOWLEDGE					
27.	I work to influence the culture of this organization so that its policies and practices are informed by the Guiding Principles of Cultural Proficiency.	1	2	3	4	5
28.	I speak up if I notice that a policy or practice unintentionally discriminates against or causes an unnecessary hardship for a particular group in this organization's community.	1	2	3	4	5

29.	I take advantage of teachable moments to share cultural knowledge or to learn from my colleagues.	1	2	3	4	5
30.	I advocate for the marginalized and voiceless in my school/ district among my colleagues, the students, and their communities.	1	2	3	4	5
31.	I seek to create opportunities for my colleagues, managers, clients, and the communities we serve to learn about one another.	1	2	3	4	5

RESOURCE 1D

THREE- TO FIVE-YEAR STRATEGIC PLANNING

Implementing, Evaluating, and Sustaining the Work of Cultural Proficiency
School District Level

Expected Outcmes for School Implementation Teams

- View Cultural Proficiency as a shared journey for educating the youth in our schools
- Experience Cultural Proficiency as personal and professional work
- Use the Cultural Proficiency Framework as a guide in addressing equity and access gap issues
- Use the Tools of Cultural Proficiency to build professional capital for changing conversations
- Increase equity, access, and inclusion for all students in our schools

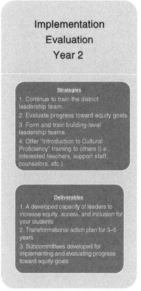
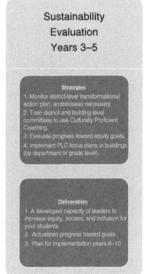

GOALS AND STRATEGIES: Implementing, evaluating, and sustaining the Cultural Proficiency Framework

GOAL 1	GOAL 2	GOAL 3	GOAL 4	GOAL 5
Learning	Professional development	Continuous school improvement and data-based decisions	Family and community engagement	Equity, access, and inclusion
View Cultural Proficiency as a shared journey for educating the youth in our schools	Experience Cultural Proficiency as personal and professional work	Use the Cultural Proficiency Framework as a guide in addressing equity and access gap issues	Use the Tools of Cultural Proficiency to build professional capital for changing conversations	Increase equity, access, and inclusion for all students in our schools
Key performance measures will be established for all goals and strategies to monitor and report progress				
Strategies aligned to Goal 1	Strategies aligned to Goal 2	Strategies aligned to Goal 3	Strategies aligned to Goal 4	Strategies aligned to Goal 5

DISTRICTWIDE MODEL FOR EQUITY IN ALL ASPECTS OF THE ORGANIZATION

District-Wide Model for Raising Equity by Embedding Cultural Proficiency in ALL Aspects of the Organization

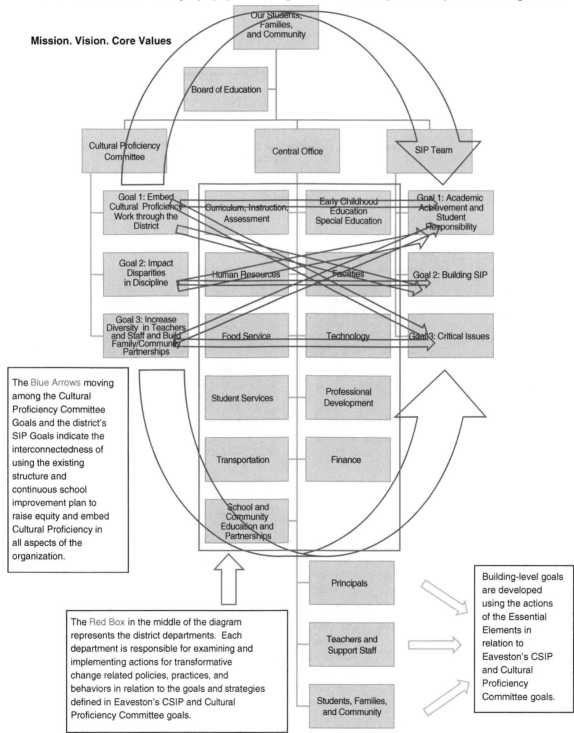

The Blue Arrows moving among the Cultural Proficiency Committee Goals and the district's SIP Goals indicate the interconnectedness of using the existing structure and continuous school improvement plan to raise equity and embed Cultural Proficiency in all aspects of the organization.

The Red Box in the middle of the diagram represents the district departments. Each department is responsible for examining and implementing actions for transformative change related policies, practices, and behaviors in relation to the goals and strategies defined in Eaveston's CSIP and Cultural Proficiency Committee goals.

Building-level goals are developed using the actions of the Essential Elements in relation to Eaveston's CSIP and Cultural Proficiency Committee goals.

RESOURCE 3D

CULTURALLY PROFICIENT INEQUIRY FOR ACTION PLAN

SCHOOL/DISTRICT: _____

OUR DISTRICT/SCHOOL VISION:
OUR DISTRICT/SCHOOL MISSION:

Goals	Culturally Proficient Actions	Success Measure(s) "We will know we are successful if/when . . ." • What is measured? • Who will measure? • When do we measure?	Person(s) Responsible	Date by Which to Be Achieved	Actual Outcomes

• What goals do we need to address to achieve outcome?
 	
• Is the goal written using SMART criteria (see below)?
 	
• To what extent does the goal align with current vision and mission statements? Do the vision and/or mission statements need to be revisited or revised to better align with culturally proficient values?
	• List actions chronologically.
	
	• Include preparation (e.g., funding) and implementation actions.
	
	• Include actions for the following:
	  ○ Assessing cultural knowledge and the current reality
	  ○ Valuing diversity
	  ○ Managing the dynamics of diversity
	  ○ Adapting to diversity
	  ○ Institutionalizing cultural knowledge				

OUTCOME: CRITICAL QUESTION FOR INQUIRY: What do we want to know that will address gaps of inequity? What data will we need?

Goal One:	Actions to Achieve Goal One:	Success Measure(s):	Person(s) Responsible:	Date:	Outcomes:
Goal Two:	Actions to Achieve Goal Two:	Success Measure(s):	Person(s) Responsible:	Date:	Outcomes:

OUTCOME: SKILLS: What skills and capacity will we need for culturally proficient inquiry?

Goal One:	Actions to Achieve Goal One:	Success Measure(s):	Person(s) Responsible:	Date:	Outcomes:
Goal Two:	Actions to Achieve Goal Two:	Success Measure(s):	Person(s) Responsible:	Date:	Outcomes:

(Continued)

(Continued)

SCHOOL/DISTRICT:

OUR DISTRICT/SCHOOL VISION:
OUR DISTRICT/SCHOOL MISSION:

OUTCOME: INCENTIVES: What incentives might we use to engage people in culturally proficient inquiry and practice?

What goals do we need to reach this outcome?

	Actions to Achieve	Success Measure(s)	Person(s) Responsible	Date	Outcomes
Goal One:	Actions to Achieve Goal One:	Success Measure(s):	Person(s) Responsible:	Date:	Outcomes:
Goal Two:	Actions to Achieve Goal Two:	Success Measure(s):	Person(s) Responsible:	Date:	Outcomes:

OUTCOME: RESOURCES: How might we orchestrate technical, material, organizational, and human resources for culturally proficient practice?

What goals do we need to reach this outcome?

	Actions to Achieve	Success Measure(s)	Person(s) Responsible	Date	Outcomes
Goal One:	Actions to Achieve Goal One:	Success Measure(s):	Person(s) Responsible:	Date:	Outcomes:
Goal Two:	Actions to Achieve Goal Two:	Success Measure(s):	Person(s) Responsible:	Date:	Outcomes:

SMART Goals:

Specific = Who, what, when, where, which, why?

Measurable = Concrete criteria for measuring success: How much, how many, how will we know?

Attainable = What do we need to be successful? What knowledge, skills, attitudes, and/or resources do we need to develop to attain the goal?

Realistic = Is our goal high enough, and are we willing to work hard enough to reach it?

Timely & **T**angible = What is our sense of urgency? Do we have a timeline with short- and long-term actions to achieve the goal? Can we picture the outcome? Do we know when we have reached the outcome?

RESOURCE 4D

CULTURALLY PROFICIENT POLICY AND PRACTICE REVIEW

Policy	
Procedure cross-references	
Law cross-references	
District-level application	

CULTURALLY DESTRUCTIVE	CULTURALLY INCAPACITATING	CULTURALLY BLIND	CULTURALLY PRECOMPETENT	CULTURALLY COMPETENT	CULTURALLY PROFICIENT
The practices and/or behaviors attempt to eliminate groups of individuals based on cultural identity differences, such as race or social class.	The practices and/or behaviors demean groups of individuals based on cultural identity differences such as race or social class. The practices and/or behaviors prompt belief in the superiority of one's culture and disempower the other group.	The practices and/or behaviors intentionally or unintentionally dismiss cultural differences, such as race or social class. The practices and/or behaviors lead others to believe that cultural differences do not matter or cannot be seen.	The practices and/or behaviors inadequately respond to the dynamics of difference between individuals' cultural identities, such as race or social class.	The practices and/or behaviors address differences between individuals' cultural identities, such as race or social class, and the organization's culture. They take into consideration value for diversity, managing the dynamics of difference, adapting to diversity, and institutionalizing cultural knowledge.	The practices and/or behaviors address a commitment to advocating for individuals with varying cultural identities, such as race and social class, who have been underserved by the organization.

Using the professional learning strategies of personal reflection and dialogue with colleagues, use the space below to record your feelings and thoughts about continuous school improvement.

1. What practices and behaviors are related to the named policy?

2. What practices and behaviors align with the descriptions of precompetent, competent, and proficient?

(Continued)

3. What practices and behaviors align with the descriptions of destructive, incapacitating, and blind?

4. For the policies, practices, and behaviors aligned with the descriptions of destructive, incapacitating, or blind, what barriers (R. B. Lindsey et al., 2019) are overtly or covertly present?

   - Presumption of privilege or entitlement
   - Unawareness of the need to adapt
   - Systemic oppression—racism, sexism, classism
   - Resistance to change

5. In what ways must the Guiding Principles (R. B. Lindsey et al., 2019) as core beliefs be internalized for the policies, practices, and behaviors rated destructive, incapacitating, or blind to become more inclusive and culturally proficient?

   - Culture is a predominant force in society.
   - People are served to varying degrees by the dominant culture.
   - People have individual and group identities.
   - Diversity within cultures is vast and significant.
   - Each cultural group has unique cultural needs.
   - The best of both worlds enhances the capacity of all.
   - The family, as defined by each culture, is the primary system of support in the education of children.
   - School systems must recognize that marginalized populations have to be at least bicultural and that this status creates a distinct set of issues to which the system must be equipped to respond.
   - Inherent in cross-cultural interactions are dynamics that must be acknowledged, adjusted to, and accepted.

6. In what ways do data (i.e., practices and behaviors) from the Cultural Proficiency Continuum provide evidence to support who is thriving in the current system and who is not?

7. What quality indicators or existing data are relevant to current policies and related practices?

8. Briefly describe additional quantitative or qualitative data gathered from surveys, focus groups, interviews, and/or observations.

9. Based on the supporting data, where does the policy fit on the Cultural Proficiency Continuum (R. B. Lindsey et al., 2019)?

CULTURALLY DESTRUCTIVE	CULTURALLY INCAPACITATING	CULTURALLY BLIND	CULTURALLY PRECOMPETENT	CULTURALLY COMPETENT	CULTURALLY PROFICIENT
The language in the policy attempts to eliminate groups of individuals based on cultural identity differences, such as race or social class.	The language in the policy demeans groups of individuals based on cultural identity differences, such as race or social class. The language prompts belief in the superiority of one's culture and disempowers the other group.	The language in the policy intentionally or unintentionally dismisses cultural differences, such as race or social class. The language leads others to believe that cultural differences do not matter or cannot be seen.	The language in the policy inadequately responds to the dynamics of difference between individuals' cultural identities, such as race or social class.	The language in the policy addresses differences between individuals' cultural identities, such as race or social class, and the organization's culture. It takes into consideration value for diversity, managing the dynamics of difference, adapting to diversity, and institutionalizing cultural knowledge.	The language in the policy addresses a commitment to advocating for individuals with varying cultural identities, such as race and social class, who have been underserved by the organization.

10. As you think about changing this policy, what actions will you take using the Essential Elements to:
   - Assess your and your organization's cultural knowledge of the communities you serve?
   - Demonstrate value for the diversity of the community you serve?
   - Manage the dynamics of difference that may arise?
   - Adapt to the diversity of the communities you serve?
   - Institutionalize cultural knowledge about the communities served by your school or district?

REOURCE 5D

CULTURALLY PROFICIENT INTERVIEW QUESTIONS

Assessing Culture

1. Tell us about your understanding of cultural diversity and what that would mean in your classroom.

2. What cultural experiences will you bring that will have a positive impact on all of our learners?

Valuing Diversity

1. What are your core values as an educator?

2. How will you make all of your students feel not just invited, but like they belong, in your classroom?

3. Tell us about a time you have valued diversity in the classroom or in your personal life that would support equity, access, and/or inclusion.

4. How might you recognize and celebrate diversity in your classroom?

Managing the Dynamics of Difference

1. How would you respond to an upset parent of a child in your classroom who claims you treat him/her differently based on a cultural difference such as race, gender, social class, or ability?

2. In what ways will you manage and support differences/diversity in school?

Adapting to Diversity

1. Tell us about a time you worked with someone different from you and what you did to solve the problem together.

2. How might you adapt your instructional or assessment practices to meet the needs of your students?

Institutionalizing Cultural Knowledge

1. How will you help us to increase equitable outcomes for students in our district?

2. How will you teach students about diversity and how to advocate for others who are oppressed, underserved, or underprivileged?

RESOURCE E

LEADING CHANGE THROUGH THE LENS OF CULTURAL PROFICIENCY

CHAPTER BOOK STUDY GUIDE

The Essential Elements and Inquiry-Based Approaches to Change

Book Study Guide

Leading Change Through the Lens of Cultural Proficiency:

An Equitable Approach to Race and Social Class in Our Schools

Jaime E. Welborn, Tamika Casey, Keith T. Myatt, Randall B. Lindsey

Corwin, 2021

Reflection and Dialogue are essential processes for individuals and organizations engaged in a journey toward Cultural Proficiency.

• Reflection is the discussion we have with ourselves to understand our values and behaviors.

- Dialogue is the discussion we have with others to understand their values and behaviors.

The following sets of questions are devised to support your learning. The questions are designed for your personal use as well as for professional use with colleagues.

CHAPTER 1. LEADING EQUITY STARTS WITH "WHY"

CONTENT QUESTIONS TO CONSIDER

- What do you understand to be the significance of the "why" question?
- What is the "personal journey" as discussed in the chapter?

PERSONAL REACTION QUESTIONS TO CONSIDER

- In what ways might cultural proficiency be a personal journey for you?
- As you think about your school or district, in what ways might cultural proficiency foster systemic change?
- What were your reactions to the "Names, Events, Trends" section of the chapter?

CHAPTER 2. THE CULTURAL PROFICIENCY FRAMEWORK: RESEARCH AND PLANNING

CONTENT QUESTIONS TO CONSIDER

- How do you define and describe Critical Race Theory?
- In what ways would you define and describe Intersectionality?
- What are some of the educational inequities described in this chapter?
- What do you understand to be the importance of addressing community and school issues of children and adolescents from low income environments?
- In what ways are Barriers and Guiding Principles in juxtaposition to one another?
- What do you see to be the function of the Essential Elements of Cultural Proficiency?
- As you examine the Framework, in what ways are the Tools of Cultural Proficiency interrelated?
- What are some ways in which Eaveston's leaders addressed the "why" question?
- What are some benefits of a researcher and school district developing a partnership? What do you see as the significance of Table 2.1, The Essential Elements and Inquiry-Based Approaches to Change?

- On reading the first part of the chapter, what thoughts and reactions did you have on reading about Critical Race Theory and Intersectionality?

- What is your reaction, personally and professionally, as you read about and understand the tools?

- What more do you want to know or learn about Cultural Proficiency?

CHAPTER 3. THE INTERSECTIONALITY OF RACE AND SOCIAL CLASS

CONTENT QUESTIONS TO CONSIDER

- In what ways did Kimberle Crenshaw contribute to our understanding of where topics and issues of race intersect with social class in our school and the communities we serve?

- What is your understanding of race as a social construct?

- What meaning do you make of the section "Opportunity, Access, and Educational Gaps"?

- What are some "takeaways" when reading the section on opportunity, achievement, and success?

- What is your understanding of educational debt being asset-based?

- Please summarize two or three important points in Dr. Ladson-Billings article.

PERSONAL REACTION QUESTIONS TO CONSIDER

When reading about race as a social construct, what thoughts and reactions do you have?

- What are your thoughts or reactions when considering the extent might opportunity be given or withheld in your school or district?

- What would it be for you and your school or district if you and your colleagues start using phrases such as "achievement gap" or "lost learning"?

CHAPTER 4. INDIVIDUAL AND ORGANIZATIONAL CHANGE LEADERSHIP

CONTENT QUESTIONS TO CONSIDER

- How might you describe Eaveston's Action Plan to a leadership group in your school or district?

PERSONAL REACTION QUESTIONS TO CONSIDER

- What are some of your personal thoughts or reactions as the Eaveston story is being introduced?

CHAPTER 5. OVERCOMING BARRIERS TO CULTURAL PROFICIENCY

- In what ways might barriers serve as core values in our beliefs as educators?

- In what ways might barriers serve as core values informing policies and practices for our schools and districts?

- In what way might you summarize "Acknowledging and Overcoming Barriers" from the Eaveston Case Story?

- What is the most important point from the Eaveston Vignette?

- What reactions do you have to descriptions of barriers in educator and school values and practice?

- What was your initial reaction when reading our invitation, "Your Turn: Acknowledging Barriers of Cultural Proficiency"?

CHAPTER 6. RELYING ON OUR INCLUSIVE CORE VALUES: THE GUIDING PRINCIPLES OF CULTURAL PROFICIENCY FOR ORGANIZATIONAL CHANGE

1. In what ways do the Guiding Principles inform vision and mission statements for schools and school districts?

2. How would you describe "The Zone of Ethical Tension" in the Cultural Proficiency Framework?

3. How would you describe learning or insights gained from the Eaveston vignettes?

4. In considering the learning strategies in this chapter, which might work to extend and deepen professional learning in your school or district? What might be some reasons for your thinking?

5. In what ways do you distinguish between Eaveston's overt and covert values? Why might any distinctions be important for today's "schooling."

6. What are you learning from our colleagues in the Eaveston district? Why might these learnings be important for you and your practice?

1. As you consider the Guiding Principles, in what way do they inform your core values as an educator?

2. In what ways do the Guiding Principles inform your assessment of your school or district's mission and vision statements?

3. What is your reaction to the phrase, "Do you do what you say you do?"

CHAPTER 7. TELLING OUR STORIES AND CHANGING THE CONVERSATIONS: THE CULTURAL PROFICIENCY CONTINUUM

CONTENT QUESTIONS TO CONSIDER

- In what ways do the Barriers inform the Continuum?

- In what ways do the Guiding Principles inform the Continuum?

- In reflecting on Eaveston's "Post-it Activity" and the Continuum, how might you describe the data generated? What value do you see in gathering and analyzing such data?

- How might themes used from data analyses be used to inform educator practice? School or district policies and practices?

PERSONAL REACTION QUESTIONS TO CONSIDER

- What observations do you have when reading Eaveston's findings with the Post-it Activity and Continuum?

- What questions would you want to ask members of the Eaveston Cultural Proficiency Committee?

CHAPTER 8. COMMITTING TO STANDARDS OF EQUITY-FOCUSED CHANGE THROUGH IMPROVEMENT AND GROWTH WITH THE ESSENTIAL ELEMENTS

CONTENT QUESTIONS TO CONSIDER

- Describe how the Guiding Principles inform and support the Essential Elements.

- The Essential Elements are driven by the five powerful verbs? In what ways are the five verbs powerful for individual educators? For schools and districts?

- In what ways do the Essential Elements support the notion of planned change?

- In what ways does the practice of dialogic conversation about the Essential Elements inform and support planned change in schools and districts?

- In what ways do you understand Breakthrough Questions?

- What is your "takeaway" from reading Table 8.9 Eaveston's Strategic Plan?

- Describe how our colleagues at Eaveston used the Essential Elements to monitor progress toward equity goals.

- What are you learning about yourself and equity-focused planned change? For yourself? For your school or district?

- In reflecting on your responses to Table 8.2, what are your learnings about self? About your school or district?

- To develop facility in use of Breakthrough Questions, what are you willing to do to develop facility in posing such questions?

- Where are you with your own growth and learning relative to the Cultural Proficiency Framework with particular emphasis on the Essential Elements?

CHAPTER 9. IMPLEMENTATION: PLANNING FOR CHALLENGES ALONG THE JOURNEY

CONTENT QUESTIONS TO CONSIDER

- List key points in preparing for the challenges of your Cultural Proficiency journey:

  o Barriers

  o Meaningful Leadership

  o Professional Learning Structures

  o Assessment

  o Culture of Collaboration

  o Teams

  o Sustainability

PERSONAL REACTION QUESTIONS TO CONSIDER

- In reading this book and engaging in reflection and dialogue processes, what are three things you have learned or affirmed about yourself as a leader?

- Briefly describe your feelings and reactions to engaging in this equity-focused work.

CHAPTER 10. LESSONS LEARNED AND RECOMMENDATIONS FOR SCHOOL LEADERS

CONTENT QUESTIONS TO CONSIDER

- List key points in Recommendations for Implementation

  o Diverse Family and Community Engagement

  o Professional Learning Communities

  o Continuous School Improvement

- Take a few moments to describe the commitments being requested of you in this chapter.

- Whether you are a novice or a seasoned veteran on the equity journey, what strengths or assets do you take forward in doing this work?

- What more do you want to learn about your school or district?

CHAPTER 11. IMPLEMENTATION AND SUSTAINABILITY: COMMITMENT TO ACTION PLANNING

CONTENT QUESTIONS TO CONSIDER

- In talking about this chapter with an educator from another school district, how might you describe transformational action planning?

- How are you making sense of the differences between strategic planning and transformational action planning? How will you help others with the differences?

PERSONAL REACTION QUESTIONS TO CONSIDER

- What are your personal hopes and fears of creating a strategic plan and transformational plan?

CHAPTER 12. SUSTAINABILITY: COMMITMENT TO ENSURING EQUITABLE OUTCOMES

CONTENT QUESTIONS TO CONSIDER

- In what ways will you embed the work of Cultural Proficiency in all aspects of your district or school using the organizational chart or already existing school improvement plan in your district or school? How might you use a model similar to the *Districtwide Model for Raising Equity*?

- How will you use the *Culturally Proficient Policy and Practice Review* to sustain the implementation of applying the Tools of Cultural Proficiency in examining the impact of policies and practices on your students and staff?

- How might you use the *Cultural Proficiency Annual Cycle of Continuous Improvement* to help teams embed the work of Cultural Proficiency in their everyday classroom practices?

PERSONAL REACTION QUESTIONS TO CONSIDER

- What more do you want to learn about your students' communities?

- What assets will you rely on as you lead the work to build capacity among stakeholders in your organization?

CULTURAL PROFICIENCY BOOKS' ESSENTIAL QUESTIONS

CORWIN CULTURAL PROFICIENCY BOOKS	AUTHORS AND EDITORS	FOCUS AND ESSENTIAL QUESTIONS
Cultural Proficiency: A Manual for School Leaders, 4th ed., 2019	Randall B. Lindsey, Kikanza Nuri-Robins, Raymond D. Terrell, and Delores B. Lindsey	This book is an introduction to Cultural Proficiency. The book provides readers with extended discussion of each of the tools and the historical framework for diversity work. • What is Cultural Proficiency? How does Cultural Proficiency differ from other responses to diversity? • In what ways do I incorporate the Tools of Cultural Proficiency into my practice? • How do I use the resources and activities to support professional learning? • How do I identify barriers to student learning? • How do the Guiding Principles and Essential Elements support better education for students? • What does the "inside-out" process mean for me as an educator? • How do I foster challenging conversations with colleagues? • How do I extend my own learning?
Culturally Proficient Instruction: A Guide for People Who Teach, 3rd ed., 2012	Kikanza Nuri-Robins, Delores B. Lindsey, Randall B. Lindsey, and Raymond D. Terrell	This book focuses on the five Essential Elements and can be helpful to anyone in an instructional role. This book can be used as a workbook for a study group. • What does it mean to be a culturally proficient instructor? • How do I incorporate Cultural Proficiency into a school's learning community processes? • How do we move from "mindset" or "mental model" to a set of practices in our school? • How does my "cultural story" support being effective as an educator with my students? • In what ways might we apply the Maple View Story to our learning community? • In what ways can I integrate the Guiding Principles of Cultural Proficiency with my own values about learning and learners? • In what ways do the Essential Elements as standards inform and support our work with the Common Core Standards? • How do I foster challenging conversations with colleagues? • How do I extend my own learning?
The Culturally Proficient School: An Implementation Guide for School Leaders, 2nd ed., 2013	Randall B. Lindsey, Laraine M. Roberts, and Franklin CampbellJones	This book guides the reader to examine their school as a cultural organization and to design and implement approaches to dialogue and inquiry. • In what ways do "Cultural Proficiency" and "school leadership" help me close achievement gaps? • What are the communication skills I need to master to support my colleagues when focusing on achievement gap topics?

(Continued)

CORWIN CULTURAL PROFICIENCY BOOKS	AUTHORS AND EDITORS	FOCUS AND ESSENTIAL QUESTIONS
		• How do "transactional" and "transformational" changes differ and inform closing achievement gaps in my school/district?
		• How do I foster challenging conversations with colleagues?
		• How do I extend my own learning?
Culturally Proficient Coaching: Supporting Educators to Create Equitable Schools, 2nd ed., 2020	Delores B. Lindsey, Richard S. Martinez, Randall B. Lindsey, and Keith T. Myatt	This updated edition aligns the Essential Elements with Costa and Garmston's Cognitive Coaching model. The book provides coaches, teachers, and administrators a personal guidebook with protocols and maps for conducting conversations that shift thinking in support of all students achieving at levels higher than ever before.
		• What are the coaching skills I need in working with diverse student populations?
		• In what ways do the Tools of Cultural Proficiency and Cognitive Coaching's States of Mind support my addressing achievement issues in my school?
		• How do I foster challenging conversations with colleagues?
		• How do I extend my own learning?
Culturally Proficient Inquiry: A Lens for Identifying and Examining Educational Gaps, 2008	Randall B. Lindsey, Stephanie M. Graham, R. Chris Westphal Jr., and Cynthia L. Jew	This book uses protocols for gathering and analyzing student achievement and access data. Rubrics for gathering and analyzing data about educator practices are also presented.
		• How do we move from the "will" to educate all children to actually developing our "skills" of doing so?
		• In what ways do we use the various forms of student achievement data to inform educator practice?
		• In what ways do we use access data (e.g., suspensions, absences, enrollment in special education or gifted classes) to inform schoolwide practices?
		• How do we use the four rubrics to inform educator professional learning?
		• How do I foster challenging conversations with colleagues?
		• How do I extend my own learning?
Culturally Proficient Leadership: The Personal Journey Begins Within, 2nd ed., 2018	Raymond D. Terrell, Eloise K. Terrell, Delores B. Lindsey, and Randall B. Lindsey	This book guides the reader through the development of a cultural autobiography as a means to becoming an increasingly effective leader in our diverse society. The book is an effective tool for use by leadership teams.
		• How did I develop my attitudes about others' cultures?
		• When I engage in intentional cross-cultural communication, how can I use those experiences to heighten my effectiveness?
		• In what ways can I grow into being a culturally proficient leader?
		• How do I foster challenging conversations with colleagues?
		• How do I extend my own learning?

Culturally Proficient Learning Communities: Confronting Inequity Through Collaborative Curiosity, 2009	Delores B. Lindsey, Linda D. Jungwirth, Jarvis V. N. C. Pahl, and Randall B. Lindsey	This book provides readers a lens through which to examine the purpose, the intentions, and the progress of learning communities to which they belong or wish to develop. School and district leaders are provided protocols, activities, and rubrics to engage in actions focused on the intersection of race, ethnicity, gender, social class, sexual orientation and identity, faith, and ableness with the disparities in student achievement. • What is necessary for a learning community to become a "culturally proficient learning community?" • What is organizational culture and how do I describe my school's culture in support of equity and access? • What are "curiosity" and "collaborative curiosity," and how do I foster them at my school/district? • How will "breakthrough questions" enhance my work as a learning community member and leader? • How do I foster challenging conversations with colleagues? • How do I extend my own learning?
The Cultural Proficiency Journey: Moving Beyond Ethical Barriers Toward Profound School Change, 2010	Franklin CampbellJones, Brenda CampbellJones, and Randall B. Lindsey	This book explores cultural proficiency as an ethical construct. It makes transparent the connection between values, assumptions, and beliefs, and observable behavior, making change possible and sustainable. The book is appropriate for book study teams. • In what ways does "moral consciousness" inform and support my role as an educator? • How does a school's "core values" become reflected in assumptions held about students? • What steps do I take to ensure that my school and I understand any low expectations we might have? • How do we recognize that our low expectations serve as ethical barriers? • How do I foster challenging conversations with colleagues? • How do I extend my own learning?
Culturally Proficient Education: An Assets-Based Response to Conditions of Poverty, 2010	Randall B. Lindsey, Michelle S. Karns, and Keith Myatt	This book is written for educators to learn how to identify and develop the strengths of students from low-income backgrounds. It is an effective learning community resource to promote reflection and dialogue. • What are "assets" that students bring to school? • How do we operate from an "assets-based" perspective? • What are my and my school's expectations about students from low-income and impoverished backgrounds? • How do I foster challenging conversations with colleagues? • How do I extend my own learning?
Culturally Proficient Collaboration: Use and Misuse of School Counselors, 2011	Diana L. Stephens and Randall B. Lindsey	This book uses the lens of Cultural Proficiency to frame the American Association of School Counselor's performance standards and the Education Trust's Transforming School Counseling Initiative as means for addressing issues of access and equity in schools in collaborative school leadership teams. • How do counselors fit into achievement-related conversations with administrators and teachers? • What is the "new role" for counselors?

(Continued)

(Continued)

CORWIN CULTURAL PROFICIENCY BOOKS	AUTHORS AND EDITORS	FOCUS AND ESSENTIAL QUESTIONS
		• How does this "new role" differ from existing views of school counselor?
		• What is the role of site administrators in this new role of school counselor?
		• How do I foster challenging conversations with colleagues?
		• How do I extend my own learning?
A Culturally Proficient Society Begins in School: Leadership for Equity, 2011	Carmella S. Franco, Maria G. Ott, and Darline P. Robles	This book frames the life stories of three superintendents through the lens of Cultural Proficiency. The reader is provided the opportunity to design or modify his or her own leadership for equity plan.
		• In what ways is the role of school superintendent related to equity issues?
		• Why is this topic important to me as a superintendent or aspiring superintendent?
		• What are the leadership characteristics of a culturally proficient school superintendent?
		• How do I foster challenging conversations with colleagues?
		• How do I extend my own learning?
The Best of Corwin: Equity, 2012	Randall B. Lindsey (Ed.)	This edited book provides a range of perspectives of published chapters from prominent authors on topics of equity, access, and diversity. It is designed for use by school study groups.
		• In what ways do these readings support our professional learning?
		• How might I use these readings to engage others in learning conversations to support all students learning and all educators educating all students?
Culturally Proficient Practice: Supporting Educators of English Learning Students, 2012	Reyes L. Quezada, Delores B. Lindsey, and Randall B. Lindsey	This book guides readers to apply the five Essential Elements of Cultural Competence to their individual practice and their school's approaches to equity. The book works well for school study groups.
		• In what ways do I foster support for the education of English learning students?
		• How can I use action research strategies to inform my practice with English learning students?
		• In what ways might this book support all educators in our district/school?
		• How do I foster challenging conversations with colleagues?
		• How do I extend my own learning?
A Cultural Proficient Response to LGBT Communities: A Guide for Educators, 2013	Randall B. Lindsey, Richard M. Diaz, Kikanza Nuri-Robins, Raymond D. Terrell, and Delores B. Lindsey	This book guides the reader to understand sexual orientation in a way that provides for the educational needs of all students. The reader explores values, behaviors, policies, and practices that impact lesbian, gay, bisexual, and transgender (LGBT) students, educators, and parents/guardians.
		• How do I foster support for LGBT colleagues, students, and parents/guardians?
		• In what ways does our school represent a value for LGBT members?

		• How can I create a safe environment for all students to learn?
		• To what extent is my school an environment where it is safe for the adults to be open about their sexual orientation?
		• How do I reconcile my attitudes toward religion and sexuality with my responsibilities as a preK–12 educator?
		• How do I foster challenging conversations with colleagues?
		• How do I extend my own learning?
Fish Out of Water: Mentoring, Managing, and Self-Monitoring People Who Don't Fit In, 2016	Kikanza Nuri-Robins and Lewis Bundy	This book helps the reader manage the dynamics of difference by focusing on sustaining a healthy organizational culture using the Cultural Proficiency Continuum as a template. Strategies based on the Guiding Principles and the Essential Elements are provided for supporting both children and adults who are struggling to understand or use the cultural norms of a particular environment. A Study Guide is provided in the Resources so that the book can easily be used for professional development or a small-group book study. 1. How do I determine the nature of diversity in this environment? 2. How might I understand who is thriving in this setting and who is not? 3. Are there any groups that are being targeted? 4. Are the rules of the environment oppressive to any individuals or groups in the environment? 5. Why are certain groups making the organizational rules for everyone? 6. How might I address systems to make the environment healthier? 7. What strategies are available to my colleagues and me as we seek to sustain a healthy, inclusive environment for all? 8. What strategies are available to an individual who is trying to succeed in a toxic environment? 9. How do I extend my own learning?
Guiding Teams to Excellence With Equity: Culturally Proficient Facilitation, 2017	John Krownapple	This book provides mental models and information for educators to develop as facilitators of professional learning and organizational change for equity in education. It also supports experienced professional development professionals with tools for doing their work in a culturally competent and proficient manner. This book is for organizations working to build internal capacity and sustainability for Cultural Proficiency. Essential Questions: 1. Assuming we value excellence and equity in education, why do we need Cultural Proficiency and culturally proficient facilitators of the process? 2. How can we use Cultural Proficiency as content (framework) and process (journey) to achieve excellence with equity? 3. What do facilitators do in order to work with teams in a culturally proficient manner?

(Continued)

(Continued)

CORWIN CULTURAL PROFICIENCY BOOKS	AUTHORS AND EDITORS	FOCUS AND ESSENTIAL QUESTIONS
Culturally Proficient Response to the Common Core: Ensuring Equity Through Professional Learning, 2015	Delores B. Lindsey, Karen M. Kearney, Delia Estrada, Raymond D. Terrell, and Randall B. Lindsey	This book guides the reader to view and use the Common Core State Standards (CCSS) as a vehicle for ensuring all demographic groups of students are fully prepared for college and careers. • In what ways do I use this book to deepen my learning about equity? • In what ways do I use this book to deepen my learning about CCSS? • In what ways do I use this book with colleagues to deepen our work on equity and on the CCSS? • How can I and we use the Action Planning guide as an overlay for our current school planning?
Culturally Proficient Inclusive Schools: When All Means All, 2018	Delores B. Lindsey, Jacqueline S. Thousand, Cynthia L. Jew, and Lori R. Piowlski	This book provides responses and applications of the four Tools of Cultural Proficiency for educators who desire to create and support classrooms and schools that are inclusive and designed intentionally to educate all learners. General educators and Special Educators will benefit from using the five Essential Elements and the tenets of Inclusive Schooling to create and sustain educational environments so that when we say *all* students, we truly mean *all* students will achieve at levels higher than ever before. Essential Questions: 1. What might be some ways general and special educators can work collaboratively to create conditions for all students to be successful? 2. In what ways does this book address issues of equity and access for all students? 3. How do the four Tools of Cultural Proficiency inform the work of Inclusive Schooling? What's here for you? 4. In what ways does the Action Plan template offer opportunities for you and your colleagues? 5. For what are you waiting to help narrow and close equity gaps in your classroom and schools? 6. How do I foster challenging conversations about inclusive education with colleagues? 7. How do I extend my own learning about ways in which to facilitate inclusive learning environments?
The Cultural Proficiency Manifesto: Finding Clarity Amidst the Noise, 2017	Randall B. Lindsey	This book is a call to action for educators to ensure we are creating culturally inclusive and responsive environments for our students. Essential Questions: 1. What are the Lessons Learned, the answers to which equip educators to address issues of inequity? 2. In what ways do educators use the Tools of Cultural Proficiency in listening for clarity while living amid turmoil? 3. What are behaviors of commitment in moving from practices of inequity to practices of equity?

Equity Partnerships: A Culturally Proficient Guide to Family, School and Community Engagement, 2019	Angela Clark-Louque, Randall B. Lindsey, Reyes L. Quezada, and Cynthia L. Jew	This book provides guidance to educators intent on making culturally inclusive family and community engagement central to their professional practice as well as to the policies and practices. Essential Questions: 1. What are the historical, social, and educational foundations for community engagement being a moral imperative for today's schools? 2. In what ways do the Cultural Proficiency Framework build on and inform the work of Epstein, Constantino, and Mapp and Kuttner? 3. How do we develop, initiate, monitor, and assess community engagement action plans? 4. How might I engage others to create a capacity building culture for partnering? 5. How might we intentionally execute an inclusive and equitable plan for family, school, and community engagement?
Leading While Female: A Culturally Proficient Response for Gender Equity in Schools, 2020	Trudy T. Arriaga, Stacie L. Stanley, and Delores B. Lindsey	This book is a call to action for women, men, hiring managers, mentors, and sponsors to ensure we are creating gender-inclusive work environments that foster pipelines and pathways to executive leadership for women. • What key factors in educational systems must shift to ensure women/females are equitably prepared to serve in executive leadership? • In what ways might the Tools of Cultural Proficiency be used to support pipelines and pathways for women in executive leadership? • How might the Continuum of Cultural Proficiency support long-term systems change? • What are the opportunities and actions for men to support opening doors for women? • What is my role as mentor and sponsor toward ensuring hiring disparities for women in executive leadership are eliminated?
Leading Change Through the Lens of Cultural Proficiency: An Equitable Approach to Race and Social Class in Our Schools	Jaime E. Welborn, Tamika Casey, Keith T. Myatt, and Randall B. Lindsey	This book presents the Cultural Proficiency Framework as documented in a narrative case study conducted with the Eaveston School District. The design of the book focuses alternately on individual leaders' and on a systemic approach for facing disparities as with respect to racial and socioeconomic membership. 1. What is the Cultural Proficiency Framework? 2. What are the Cultural Proficiency tools that are embedded in the Framework? 3. In what ways did leaders in the Eaveston District implement each of the Tools of Cultural Proficiency? 4. What were Eaveston's systemic lessons learned in implementation of the Tools? 5. In what ways do I engage my own "inside-out" learning journey focused on my values and beliefs? 6. In what ways do I engage others throughout the school/district to engage in a systemic approach to "inside-out" journey focused on policies and practices? 7. Now that I know what I know, to what am I willing to commit?

References

Abrams, Laura S., & Moio, Jene A. (2009). Critical race theory and the cultural competence dilemma in social work education. *Journal of Social Work Education, 45*(2), 245–261. https://doi.org/10.5175/JSWE.2009.200700109

Anderson, Kim L., & Davis, Bonnie M. (2012). *Creating culturally considerate schools.* Thousand Oaks, CA: Corwin. https://doi.org/10.4135/9781483387550

Apple, Michael W., & Beane, James A. (1995). *Democratic schools.* Alexandria, VA: Association for Supervision and Curriculum Development.

Arriaga, Trudy T., & Lindsey, Randall B. (2016). *Opening doors: An implementation template for cultural proficiency.* Thousand Oaks, CA: Corwin.

Arriaga, Trudy T., Stanley, Stacie L., & Lindsey, Delores B. (2020). *Leading while female: A culturally proficient response to gender equity.* Thousand Oaks, CA: Corwin.

Augustine-Shaw, Donna. (2015). Leadership and learning: Identifying and effective design for mentoring new building leaders. *The Delta Kappa Gamma Bulletin, Winter,* 21–29.

Bambrick-Santoyo, Paul. (2018). *Leverage leadership 2.0: A practical guide to building exceptional schools.* San Francisco, CA: Jossey-Bass. https://doi.org/10.1002/9781119548539

Bandura, Albert. (1997). *Self-efficacy: The exercise of control.* New York, NY: W. H. Freeman.

Banks, Cherry A. McGee, & Banks, James A. (1995). Equity pedagogy: An essential component of multicultural education. *Theory in Practice, 34*(3), 152–157. https://doi.org/10.1080/00405849509543674

Barton, Paul E., & Coley, Richard J. (2009). *Parsing the achievement gap II.* Princeton, NJ: Educational Testing Service.

Bell, Derrick. (1992). *Faces at the bottom of the well.* New York, NY: Basic Books.

Block, James H., Everson, Susan T., & Guskey, Thomas, R. (1995). *School improvement programs: A handbook for school leaders.* New York, NY: Scholastic.

Bolman, Lee G., & Deal, Terrence E. (1997). *Reframing organizations: Artistry, choice, and leadership* (2nd ed.). San Francisco, CA: Jossey-Bass.

Brannon, Tiffany N., Higginbotham, Gerald D., & Henderson, Kyshia. (2017). Class advantages and disadvantages are not so Black and White: Intersectionality impacts rank and selves. *Current Opinion in Psychology, 18,* 117–122. https://doi.org/10.1016/j.copsyc.2017.08.029

Brown, Brene. (2012). *Daring greatly: How the courage to be vulnerable transforms the way we live.* New York, NY: Avery.

Brown v. Board of Education of Topeka, 354 U.S. 483 (1954). 347 U.S. 483 (more) 74 S. Ct. 686; 98 L. Ed. 873; 1954 U.S. LEXIS 2094; 53 Ohio Op. 326; 38 A.L.R.2d 1180

Burrell-Craft, Kala. (2020). Are (we) going deep enough? A narrative literature review addressing critical race theory, racial space theory, and Black identity development. *Taboo: The Journal of Culture and Education, 19*(4). Retrieved from https://digitalscholarship.unlv.edu/taboo/vol19/iss4/2

Bybee, Roger. (1997). *Achieving scientific literacy: From purposes to practices.* Portsmouth, NH: Heinemann.

Bybee, Roger W., & Landes, Nancy. (1990). Science for life and living: An elementary school science program from Biological Sciences Improvement Study (BSCS). *The American Biology Teacher, 52*(2), 92–98. https://doi.org/10.2307/4449042

Byrk, Anthony S., & Schneider, Barbara. (2002). *Trust in schools: A core resource for improvement.* New York, NY: Russell Sage.

CampbellJones, Franklin, CampbellJones, Brenda, & Lindsey, Randall B. (2010). *The Cultural Proficiency journey: Moving beyond ethical barriers toward profound school change.* Thousand Oaks, CA: Corwin.

Casey, Tamika, & Welborn, Jaime E. (2020). Cultural proficiency as an advocacy tool to build a diverse workforce. *Association of California School Administrators Leadership Magazine* (March–April 2020). Retrieved from https://leadership.acsa.org/cultural-proficiency-as-an-advocacy-tool-to-build-

Children's Defense Fund. (2018). *Child Poverty in America 2018: National analysis.* Washington, DC: Author.

Chism, Monique M. (2020, May 15). *Isolated from opportunity: Reflections on Brown v. Board of Education 66 years later.* https://www.air.org/resource/field/isolated-opportunity-reflections-brown-v-board-education-66-years-later

Chubb, John E., & Loveless, Tom. (2002). *Bridging the achievement gap.* Washington, DC: Brookings Institution Press.

Clark-Louque, Angela R., Lindsey, Randall B., Quezada, Reyes L., & Jew, Cynthia L. (2019). *Equity partnerships: A culturally proficient guide to family, school, and community engagement.* Thousand Oaks, CA: Corwin.

Coburn, Cynthia E., Penuel, William R., & Geil, Kimberly E. (2013). *Research practice Partnerships: A strategy for leveraging for educational improvement in school districts.* New York, NY: William T. Grant Foundation.

Coleman, James S., Campbell, Ernest Q., Hobson, Carol J., McPartland, James, Mood, Alexander M., Weinfeld, Frederick D., & York, Robert L. (1966). *Equality of educational opportunity* (No. FS 5.238:38001). Washington, DC: National Center for Educational Statistics, Office of Education, U.S. Department of Health, Education, and Welfare.

Conley, David T., & Darling-Hammond, Linda. (2013). *Creating systems of assessment for deeper learning.* Stanford, CA: Stanford Center for Opportunity Policy in Education.

Conroy, Patrick. (1986). *The prince of tides.* Boston, MA: Houghton Mifflin Harcourt.

Cooperrider. David L., & Whitney, Diana (2005). *Appreciative inquiry.* San Francisco: Berrett-Koehler.

Costa, Arthur L., & Garmston, Robert J. (2015). *Developing self-directed leaders and learners.* Norwood, MA: Christopher-Gordon.

Covey, Stephen R. (1989). *The 7 habits of highly effective people.* New York, NY: Free Press.

Crenshaw, Kimberle. (1988). Race, reform and retrenchment: Transformation and legitimation in anti-discrimination law. *Harvard Law Review, 101*(7), 1331–1387. https://doi.org/10.2307/1341398

Crenshaw, Kimberle. (1989). *Feminism in the law: Theory, practice, and criticism.* Chicago, IL: University of Chicago Legal Forum.

Crenshaw, Kimberle. (1991). Mapping the margins: Intersectionality, identity politics, and violence against women of color. *Stanford Law Review, 43*(6), 1241–1299. https://doi.org/10.2307/1229039

Crenshaw, Kimberle. (2016). *The urgency of intersectionality* [Video file]. Retrieved from https://www.ted.com/talks/kimberle_crenshaw_the_urgency_of_intersectionality?language=en

Creswell, John W. (2014). *Research design: Qualitative, quantitative, and mixed methods approaches.* Thousand Oaks, CA: Sage.

Cross, Terry L., Bazron, Barbara J., Dennis, Karl W., & Isaacs, Mareasa R. (1989). *Towards a culturally competent system of care.* Washington, DC: Georgetown University Child Development Center, CASSP Technical Assistance Center.

Cross, Terry L., Bazron, Barbara J., Dennis, Karl W., & Isaacs, Mareasa R. (1993). *Toward a culturally competent system of care* (Vol. 2). Washington, DC: Georgetown University Child Development Program, Child and Adolescent Service System Development Program.

Darling-Hammond, Linda. (1995). Restructuring schools for student success. *Daedalus, 124,* 53–162.

Deal, Terrence E., & Kennedy, Allan A. (2000). *Corporate cultures: The rites and rituals of corporate life.* Boston, MA: Addison-Wesley.

Deal, Terrence E., & Peterson, Kent D. (1991). *The principal's role in shaping school culture.* U.S. Department of Education, Office of Educational Research and Improvement, Programs for the Improvement of Practice.

Delgado, Richard. (1989). Storytelling for oppositionists and others: A plea for narrative. *Michigan Law Review, 87*(8). https://doi.org/10.2307/1289308

Delgado, Richard. (2017). *Critical race theory* (3rd ed.). New York, NY: New York University Press.

Delpit, Lisa. (2006). *Other people's children.* New York, NY: New Press.

Deming, W. Edwards. (n.d.). *Every system is perfectly designed to get the results it gets.* Quote Deming. Retrieved from https://deming.org/quotes/10141/

Dewey, John. (1934). Individual psychology and education. *The Philosopher, 12*(1), 1–6.

Dewey, John. (1938). *Experience and education.* New York, NY: Simon & Schuster.

Dilts, Robert B. (1990). *Changing belief systems with NLP.* Capitola, CA: Meta.

Donohoo, Jenni. (2016). *Collective efficacy: How educators' beliefs impact student learning.* Thousand Oaks, CA: Corwin.

Donohoo, Jenni, Hattie, John, & Eells, Rachel. (2018). The power of collective efficacy. *Educational Leadership, 75*(6), 40–44.

Donohoo, Jenni, & Velasco, Moses. (2016). *The transformative power of collaborative inquiry: Realizing change in schools and classrooms.* Thousand Oaks, CA: Corwin.

DuFour, Rick, DuFour, Rebecca, Eaker, Robert, Many, Thomas W., & Mattos, Mike. (2016). *Learning by doing: A handbook for professional learning communities at work.* Bloomington, IN: Solution Tree Press.

DuFour, Rick, & Mattos, Mike. (2013). How do principal really improve schools? *Education Leadership, 70*(7), 34–40.

Edmonds, R., & Frederiksen, J. R. (1978). *Search for effective schools: The identification and analysis of city schools that are instructionally effective for poor children.* Cambridge, MA: Harvard University Center for Urban Studies.

Eells, Rachel J. (2011). *Meta-analysis of the relationship between collective efficacy and student achievement*

[Unpublished doctoral dissertation]. Loyola University Chicago, Chicago, IL.

Elementary and Secondary Education Act of 1965. www2.ed.gov/documents/essa-act-of-1965.pdf

Ellison, Jane, & Hayes, Carolee. (2003). *Cognitive coaching: Weaving threads of learning and change into the culture of an organization.* Norwood, MA: Christopher-Gordon.

Epstein, J., & Associates (2019). *School, family, and community partnerships: Your handbook for action.* Thousand Oaks, CA: Sage.

Everson, Susan T. (1995). Selecting school improvement programs. In James H. Block, Susan T. Everson, & Thomas R. Guskey (Eds.), *School improvement programs: A handbook for educational leaders* (pp. 433–452). New York, NY: Scholastic.

Every Student Succeeds Act. (2015). https://www.ed.gov/ESEA

Ferguson, Ronald F. (2008). *Towards excellence with equity: An emerging vision for closing the achievement gap.* Cambridge, MA: Harvard Education Press.

Fields, Howard E., III. (2021). *How to achieve educational equity.* Author.

Fisher, Douglas, Frey, Nancy, & Pumpian, Ian. (2012). *How to create a culture of achievement in your school and classroom.* Alexandria, VA: Association for Supervision and Curriculum Development.

Fixen, Dean L., Blasé, Karen A., Van Dyke, Melissa. (2019). *Implementation practice and science.* Chapel Hill, NC: Implementation Practice and Science Network.

Fraise, Nicole J., & Brooks, Jeffery S. (2015). Toward a theory of culturally relevant leadership for school-community culture. *International Journal for Multicultural Education, 17*(1), 6–21. https://doi.org/10.18251/ijme.v17i1.983

Franco, Carmella S., Ott, Maria G., & Robles, Darline P. (2011). *A culturally proficient society begins in school: Leadership for equity.* Thousand Oaks, CA: Corwin.

Freire, Paulo. (1970). *Pedagogy of the oppressed.* New York, NY: Herder & Herder.

Fullan, Michael. (1997). *What's worth fighting for in the principalship.* New York, NY: Teacher's College Press.

Fullan, Michael. (2000). The return of large-scale reform. *Journal of Educational Change, 1*(1), 5–28. https://doi.org/10.1023/A:1010068703786

Fullan, Michael. (2001). *Leading in a culture of change.* San Francisco, CA: Jossey-Bass.

Fullan, Michael. (2003). *The moral imperative of school leadership.* Thousand Oaks, CA: Corwin.

Fullan, Michael. (2004). *Leadership and sustainability: System thinkers in action.* Thousand Oaks, CA: Corwin.

Fullan, Michael. (2016). *The new meaning of educational change* (5th ed.). New York, NY: Teachers College Press.

Gardener, Howard. (2004). *Changing minds.* Cambridge, MA: Harvard Business School Press.

Garmston, Robert J., & Wellman, Bruce M. (1999). *The adaptive school: A sourcebook for developing collaborative groups.* Norwood, MA: Christopher-Gordon.

Garmston, Robert J., & Wellman, Bruce M. (2016). *The adaptive school: A source book for developing collaborative groups* (3rd ed.). Norwood, MA: Christopher-Gordon.

Gay, Geneva. (2000). *Culturally responsive teaching: Theory, research, and practice.* New York, NY: Teachers College Press.

Goddard, Roger D., Hoy, Wayne K., & Hoy, Anita W. (2004). Collective efficacy beliefs: Theoretical developments, empirical evidence, and future directions. *Educational Researcher, 33*(3), 3–13. https://doi.org/10.3102/0013189X033003003

Gotanda, Neil. (1991). A critique of "Our Constitution Is Color-Blind." *Stanford Law Review, 44*(1), 1–68. https://doi.org/10.2307/1228940

Griffith, Priscilla L., Ruan, Jiening, Stepp, Jennifer, & Kimmel, Susan J. (2014). The design and implementation of effective professional development in elementary and early childhood settings. In Linda E. Martin, Sherry Kragler, Diana J. Quatroche, & Kathryn L. Bauserman (Eds.), *Handbook of professional development in education* (pp. 189–204). New York, NY: Guilford Press.

Hallinger, Philip, & Heck, Ronald H. (1996). Reassessing the principal's role in school effectiveness: A review of empirical research 1980–1995. *Education Administration Quarterly, 32*(1), 5–44. https://doi.org/10.1177/0013161X96032001002

Hammond, Zaretta. (2015). *Culturally responsive teaching & the brain.* Thousand Oaks, CA: Corwin.

Hargreaves, Andy, & Fink, Dean. (2004). The seven principles of sustainable leadership. *Educational Leadership, 61*(7), 8–13.

Hargreaves, Andy, & Fullan, Michael. (2012). *Professional capital: Transforming teaching in every school.* New York, NY: Teacher's College Press.

Harris, Cheryl. (1993, June). Whiteness as property. *Harvard Law Review, 106*(8), 1707–1791. https://doi.org/10.2307/1341787

Harris, Terry. (2019). And, how are the children? Mindfully preparing all children to thrive. *TEDxDelmarLoopED.*

Harris, Terry. (2021). Twitter communication.

Hattie, John. (2012). *Visible learning for teachers: Maximizing impact on learning.* New York, NY: Routledge. https://doi.org/10.4324/9780203181522

Heifetz, Ronald, & Linsky, Marty. (2017). *Leadership on the line: Staying alive through the dangers of change.* Boston, MA: Harvard Business Review Press.

Horsford, Sonya D., Grosland, Tanetha, & Gunn, Kelly M. (2011). Pedagogy of the personal and professional: Toward a framework for culturally relevant leadership. *Journal of School Leadership, 21,* 582–606. https://doi .org/10.1177/105268461102100404

Howard, Gary. (2006). *We can't teach what we don't know: White teachers, multiracial schools* (2nd ed.). New York, NY: Teachers College Press.

Howard, Gary. (2014). *We can't lead where we won't go: An educator's guide to equity.* Thousand Oaks, CA: Corwin.

Howard, Tyrone. (2010). *Why race and culture matter in schools: Closing the achievement gap in America's classrooms.* New York, NY: Teachers College Press.

Ighodaro, Erhabor, & Wiggan, Greg. (2010). *Curriculum violence: America's New Civil Rights Issue.* Hauppauge, NY: Nova Science.

Jencks, Christopher, Smith, Marshall A., Henry, Bane, Mary Jo, Cohen, David, Gintis, Herbert, Heyns, Barbara, & Michelson, Stephanie. (1972). *Inequality: A reassessment of the effect of family and schooling in America.* New York, NY: Basic Books.

Jussim, Lee, Coleman, Lerita M., & Lerch, Lauren. (1987). The nature of stereotypes: A comparison and integration of three theories. *Journal of Personality and Social Psychology, 52*(3), 536–546. https://doi.org/10.1037/0022-3514.52.3.536

Kendi, Ibram. (2019). *How to be an antiracist.* New York, NY: Penguin Random House.

Kennedy, Robert. (1966). *Ripple of Hope Speech.* http:// www.rfksafilm.org/html/speeches/speechrfk.php

Kozol, Jonathan. (1991). *Savage inequalities: Children in America's schools.* New York, NY: Crown.

Kozol, Jonathan. (2005). *The shame of the nation: The restoration of apartheid schooling in America.* New York, NY: Three Rivers Press.

Krownapple, John. (2017). *Guiding teams to excellence with equity: Culturally proficient facilitation.* Thousand Oaks, CA: Corwin.

Ladson-Billings, Gloria. (2006). From the achievement gap to the education debt: Understanding achievement in U.S. schools. *Educational Researcher, 35*(7), 3–12. https://doi.org/10.3102/0013189X035007003

Ladson-Billings, Gloria. (2009). *The dreamkeepers: Successful teachers of African American students.* San Francisco, CA: Wiley.

Ladson-Billings, Gloria. (2013). Critical race theory: What it is not! Teachers College Record. In Marvin Lynn & Adrienne D. Dixson (Eds.), *The handbook of critical race theory in education* (pp. 34–37). New York, NY: Routledge.

Lambert, Linda. (1998). *Building leadership capacity in schools.* Alexandria, VA: Association for Supervision and Curriculum Development.

Lawson, Michael A. (2003). School-family relations in context: Parent and teacher perceptions of parent involvement. *Urban Education, 38*(1), 77–133. https://doi.org/10.1177/0042085902238687

Leithwood, Keith, Seashore-Louis, Karen, Anderson, Stephen, & Wahlstrom, Kyra. (2004). *Review of research: How leadership influences student learning.* Retrieved from http://www.wallacefoundation.org/knowledge-center/school-leadership/key-research/documents/how-leadership-influences-student-learning.pdf

Lezotte, Lawrence W., & Snyder, Kathleen McKee. (2011). *What effective schools do: Re-envisioning the correlates.* Bloomington, IN: Solution Tree Press.

Lindsey, Delores B., Jungwirth, Linda D., Pahl, Jarvis V. N. C., & Lindsey, Randall B. (2009). *Culturally proficient learning communities: Confronting inequities through collaborative curiosity.* Thousand Oaks, CA: Corwin.

Lindsey, Delores B., Kearney, Karen M., Estrada, Delia, Terrell, Raymond D., & Lindsey, Randall B. (2015). *Culturally proficient response to the common core: Ensuring equity through professional learning.* Thousand Oaks, CA: Corwin.

Lindsey, Delores B., Martinez, Richard S., Lindsey, Randall B., & Myatt, Keith T. (2020). *Culturally proficient coaching: Supporting educators to create equitable schools.* Thousand Oaks, CA: Corwin.

Lindsey, Delores B., Thousand, Jacqueline S., Jew, Cynthia L., & Piowlski, Lori R. (2018). *Culturally proficient inclusive schools: All means ALL!* Thousand Oaks, CA: Corwin. https://doi.org/10.4135/9781506356259

Lindsey, Randall B. (Ed.). (2012). *The best of Corwin: Equity.* Thousand Oaks, CA: Corwin.

Lindsey, Randall B. (2017). *The cultural proficiency manifesto: Finding clarity amidst the noise.* Thousand Oaks, CA: Corwin. https://doi.org/10.4135/9781071801093

Lindsey, Randall B., Diaz, Richard M., Nuri-Robins, Kikanza, Terrell, Raymond D., & Lindsey, Delores B. (2013). *A cultural proficient response to LGBT communities: A guide for educators.* Thousand Oaks, CA: Corwin. https://doi.org/10.4135/9781483304281

Lindsey, Randall B., Graham, Stephanie M., Westphal, R. Chris, Jr., & Jew, Cynthia L. (2008). *Culturally proficient inquiry: A lens for identifying and examining educational gaps.* Thousand Oaks, CA: Corwin.

Lindsey, Randall B., Karns, Michelle S, & Myatt, Keith. (2010). *Culturally proficient education: An asset-based response to conditions of poverty.* Thousand Oaks, CA: Corwin.

Lindsey, Randall B., Nuri-Robins, Kikanza, & Terrell, Raymond D. (2009). *Cultural proficiency: A manual* for school leaders (3rd ed.). Thousand Oaks, CA: Corwin.

Lindsey, Randall B., Nuri-Robins, Kikanza, Terrell, Raymond D., & Lindsey, Delores B. (2019). *Cultural proficiency: A manual for school leaders* (4th ed.). Thousand Oaks, CA: Corwin.

Lindsey, Randall B., Roberts, Laraine M., & Campbell Jones, Franklin. (2005). *The culturally proficient school: An implementation guide for educator.* Thousand Oaks, CA: Sage.

Lindsey, Randall B., Roberts, Laraine M., & Campbell Jones, Franklin. (2013). *The culturally proficient school: An implementation guide for school leaders* (2nd ed.). Thousand Oaks, CA: Corwin.

Love, Barbara J. (2004). Brown plus 50 counterstorytelling: A critical race theory analysis of the "majoritarian achievement gap" story. *Equity & Excellence in Education, 37*(3), 227–247. https://doi.org/10.1080/10665680490491597

Love, Bettina L. (2019). *We want to do more than just survive: Abolitionist teaching and the pursuit of educational freedom.* Boston, MA: Beacon Press.

Marks, Helen M., & Printy, Susan M. (2003). Principal leadership and school performance: An integration of transformational and instructional leadership. *Educational Administration Quarterly, 39*(3), 370–397. https://doi.org/10.1177/0013161X03253412

Marzano, Robert J., Waters, Timothy, & McNulty, Brian A. (2005). *School leadership that works: From research to results.* Alexandria, VA: ASCD and Aurora, CO: Mid-content Research for Education and Learning.

Mattan, Bradley T., Kubota, Jennifer K. & Cloutier, Jasmin. (2017). How social status shapes person perception and evaluation: A social neuroscience perspective. *Perspectives on Psychological Science, 12*(3), 468–507. https://doi.org/10.1177/1745691616677828

Maxwell, John C. (2015, October 19). John C. Maxwell on Twitter. *Twitter.* https://twitter.com/johncmaxwell/status/656115194129707008?lang=en

Maxwell, John C. (2021). John C. Maxwell quotes. *Goodreads.Com.* https://www.goodreads.com/quotes/282092-a-great-leader-s-courage-to-fulfill-his-vision-comes-from

McLaughlin, Milbrey W., & Talbert, Joan A. (1993). *Contexts that matter for teaching and learning.* Palo Alto, CA: Stanford Center for Research on the Context of Secondary School Teaching.

Melville, Herman. (2009). *The globe and mail.* Toronto, Ontario, Canada: CTVglobemedia.

Mendez v. Westminster School District of Orange County et al. (1946). https://law.justia.com/cases/federal/district-courts/FSupp/64/544/1952972/

Mertens, Donna M. (2010). *Research and evaluation in education and psychology: Integrating diversity with quantitative, qualitative and mixed methods* (3rd ed.). Thousand Oaks, CA: Sage.

Milner, H. Richard, IV. (2013). *Start where you are, but don't stay there: Understanding diversity opportunity gaps, and teaching in today's classroom.* Cambridge, MA: Harvard Education Press.

Moore-Berg, Samantha L., & Karpinski, Andrew. (2018). An intersectional approach to understanding how race and class affect intergroup processes. *Social and Personality Psychology Compass, 13*(1), e12426. https://doi.org/10.1111/spc3.12426

Murphy, Joseph. (2009). *The educator's handbook for understanding and closing achievement gaps.* Thousand Oaks, CA: Corwin.

Murphy, Joseph, & Datnow, Amanda. (2003). *Leadership lessons from comprehensive school reforms.* Thousand Oaks, CA: Corwin.

Nelson, Sarah, & Guerra, Patricia. (2014). Educator beliefs and cultural knowledge: Implications for school improvement efforts. *Education Administration Quarterly, 50*(1), 67–95. https://doi.org/10.1177/0013161X13488595

Noguera, P. (2008). *The trouble with Black boys: And other reflections on race, equity, and the future of public education.* San Francisco, CA: Wiley.

Nuri-Robins, Kikanza, & Bundy, Lewis. (2016). *Fish out of water: Mentoring, managing, and self-monitoring people who don't fit in.* Thousand Oaks, CA: Corwin. https://doi.org/10.4135/9781506341224

Nuri-Robins, Kikanza, Lindsey, Delores B., Lindsey, Randall B., & Terrell, Raymond D. (2012). *Culturally proficient instruction: A guide for people who teach* (3rd ed.). Thousand Oaks, CA: Corwin.

Obama, Barack. (2008, February 5). Barack Obama's Feb 5 speech. *The New York Times.* https://www.nytimes.com/2008/02/05/us/politics/05text-obama.html

Paige, Rod, & Witty, Elaine. (2010). *The black-white achievement gap: Why closing it is the greatest civil rights issue of our time.* New York, NY: Amacom American Management Association.

Penuel, William R., Allen, Anna-Ruth, Coburn, Cynthia E., & Farrell, Caitlin, (2015). Conceptualizing research-practice partnerships as joint work at boundaries, *Journal of Education for Students Placed at Risk (JESPAR), 20,* 1–2, 182–197. https://doi.org/10.1080/10824669.2014.988334

Pierson, Rita. (May, 2013). Every kid needs a champion. *TedTalk.* Retrieved from https://www.ted.com/talks/rita_pierson_every_kid_needs_a_champion

Plessy v. Ferguson, 63 U.S. 537 (1896). caselaw.findlaw.com/us-supreme-court/163/537.html

Plous, Scott L., & Williams, Tyrone. (1995). Racial stereotypes from the days of slavery: The continuing legacy. *Journal of Applied Social Psychology, 25*(9), 795–817. https://doi.org/10.1111/j.1559-1816.1995.tb01776.x

Quezada, Reyes L., Lindsey, Delores B., & Lindsey, Randall B. (2012). *Culturally proficient practice: Supporting educators of English learning students*. Thousand Oaks, CA: Corwin. https://doi.org/10.4135/9781506335742

Ravitch, Diane. (1985). *The schools we deserve: Reflections on the educational crisis of our time*. New York, NY: Basic Books.

Reeves, Douglas. (2009). *Leading change in your school: How to conquer myths, building commitment, and get results*. Alexandria, VA: Association of Supervision and Curriculum Development.

Richeson, Jennifer A., & Sommers, Samuel R. (2016). Toward a social psychology of race and race relations for the twenty-first century. *Annual Review of Psychology, 67*, 439–463. https://doi.org/10.1146/annurev-psych-010213-115115

Roberts, Terrence. (2018). *Teaching the Little Rock Nine to students in Chicago* [Video file]. PBS: Chicago Tonight. https://news.wttw.com/2018/12/11/teaching-little-rock-nine-students-chicago

Sarason, Seymour B. (1990). *The predictable failure of educational reform: Can we change before it's too late?* San Francisco, CA: Jossey-Bass.

Sarason, Seymour B. (1996). *Revisiting "the culture of the school and the problem of change."* New York, NY: Teachers College Press.

Schwab, Joseph J. (1960). Inquiry, the science, and the educator. *The School Review, 68*(2), 176–195. https://doi.org/10.1086/442536

Scollay, Susan J., & Everson, Susan T. (1985). Measuring school improvement: A few experientially based words of caution. *Urban Review, 17*(3), 201–209. https://doi.org/10.1007/BF01142466

Sergiovanni, Thomas J. (1989). The leadership needed for quality schools. In Thomas J. Sergiovanni & John H. Moore (Eds.), *Schooling for tomorrow: Directing reforms to issues that count* (pp. 213–226). Boston, MA: Allyn & Bacon.

Shields, Carolyn M. (2010). *Transformative leadership: Working for equity in diverse contexts*. Educational Administration Quarterly, 46, 558–589. https://doi.org/10.1177/0013161X10375609

Sinek, Simon. (2009). *Start with why*. New York, NY: Penguin Books.

Singh, Candace. (2018). *Role model: 4 tips on how to be the best one for your students' lives*. https://www.leaderinme.org/blog/role-model/

Singleton, Glenn. (2018). Beyond random acts of equity. *Learning Forward Journal, 39*(5), 28–33.

Smith, Lew. (2008). *Schools that change: Evidence-based improvement and effective change leadership*. Thousand Oaks, CA: Corwin. https://doi.org/10.4135/9781483329680

Smith-Maddox, R., & Solórzano, D. G. (2002). Using critical race theory, Paulo Freire's problem-posing method, and case study research to confront race and racism in Education. *Qualitative Inquiry, 8*(1), 66–84. https://doi.org/10.1177/107780040200800105

Solorzano, Daniel G., & Yosso, Tara J. (2002). Critical race methodology: Counter-storytelling as an analytical framework for education research. *Qualitative Inquiry, 8*(1). https://doi.org/10.1177/107780040200800103

Stephens, Diana L., & Lindsey, Randall B. (2011). *Culturally proficient collaboration: Use and misuse of school counselors*. Thousand Oaks, CA: Corwin. https://doi.org/10.4135/9781483387406

Stringer, Patricia. (2013). *Capacity building for school improvement*. Rotterdam, Netherlands: Sense. https://doi.org/10.1007/978-94-6209-329-4

Taliaferro, A. (2011). It is simple, but not easy—culturally responsive leadership and social capital: A framework for closing the opportunity gap. *Academic Leadership, 9*(4), 1–7.

Tapia, Michael. (2010). Untangling race and class effects on juvenile arrests. *Journal of Criminal Justice, 38*(3), 255–265. https://doi.org/10.1016/j.jcrimjus.2010.03.002

Terrell, Raymond D., Terrell, Eloise K., Lindsey, Delores B., & Lindsey, Randall B. (2018). *Culturally proficient leadership: The personal journey begins within* (2nd ed.). Thousand Oaks, CA: Corwin

Thomas, D., & Fry, R. (2020, November 30). Prior to COVID-19, child poverty rates had reached record lows in U.S. Retrieved from https://www.pewresearch.org/fact-tank/2020/11/30/prior-to-covid-19-child-poverty-rates-had-reached-record-lows-in-u-s/

Tucker, M. (2019). *Leading high performance school systems: Lessons from the world's best*. Alexandria, VA: Association for Supervision and Curriculum Development.

U.S. Department of Education. (2009). *Achievement gaps: How Black and White students in public schools perform on mathematics and reading on the National Assessment of Educational Statistics*. Retrieved from http://nces.ed.gov/nationsreportcard/pdfd/studies/2009455.pdf

Vagianos, Allana. (2015, June 2). The *Huffington Post* features Justice Ginsburg's remarks at the Radcliffe Institute. https://www.radcliffe.harvard.edu/news-and-ideas/ruth-bader-ginsburg-tells-young-women-fight-for-the-things-you-care-about

Wagner, Tony, Kegan, Robert, Lahey, Lisa L., Lemons, Richard W., Garnier, Jude, Helsing, Deborah, Howell, Annie, Rasmussen, Harriette T. (2006). *Change leadership: A practical guide to transforming our schools*. San Francisco, CA: Wiley.

Washington, Booker T. (1963). *Up from slavery: An autobiography*. Garden City, NY: Doubleday.

Welborn, Jaime E. (2019). Increasing equity, access, and inclusion through organizational change: A study of implementation and experiences surrounding a school district's journey towards culturally proficient educational practice. *Educational Leadership Review, 20*(1), 167–189.

Welborn, Jaime E., & Lindsey, Randall B. (2020). A descriptive study of the case of Eaveston School District: Core values from deficit-based to asset-based. *Journal of Leadership, Equity, and Research, 6*(1), 1–25.

Wheatley, M. (2002). Turning to one another: Simple conversations to restore hope to the future. *Journal for Quality and Participation, 25*(2), 8–19.

Yin, Robert. (2018). *Applications of case study research.* Thousand Oaks, CA: Corwin.

Index

culture of collaboration, 67, 190, 200, 345
cultures, 8–10, 17–20, 102–7, 109–11, 118–22, 124–26,
    140–42, 165–66, 168–69, 180–81, 232–34, 243–44,
    249–51, 262–63, 265–66, 277–79, 283–84, 321–22,
    329–32, 337–39
  district's, 89, 266
  organizational, 6, 111, 114, 142, 198, 322, 332, 349
  organization's, 120, 331–32
  school's, 177, 349
cultures of students of color, 141
curiosity, 116, 171, 174, 261, 349
Curriculum Development, 270–71, 295–97
curriculum violence, 42–43, 54

data, 50–51, 60, 64–65, 80, 136–37, 139, 146–47, 150–52,
    157–58, 160, 174–76, 202, 214, 221–22, 235–36,
    255–58, 261–63, 265–68, 280–81, 348
  climate survey, 174–75
  collected, 150, 256–57, 281
  observational, 191, 290
  organization's, 142
  out-of-school suspension, 176
  supporting, 234, 338
data collection, 150, 152, 155, 248, 257, 280–81, 292
data collection process, 144, 171, 259, 263, 281
data of staff and students, 175
data samples, 147–48
Data to support knowledge, 262
Dear District Leader, 241
Debriefing, 304, 306, 308–9, 311–12, 314–17, 319–20,
    324, 328–29, 331
deficit, 45–46, 54, 107
deficit-based core values, 102, 246, 248, 250, 259, 267
deficit thinking, 45, 278
definition race and social class, 54
Delgado, 40–41
Deliverables, 219, 333
Delores, 347–50, 352–53
Democratic schools, 270, 295
demographic changes, 12, 180
demographic groups, 45, 48, 52–53, 100, 175–76, 184–
    85, 287
demographic groups of students, 20–22, 45, 52, 63, 88,
    285, 352
demographic groups of students in Eaveston School
    District, 88
departments, human resource, 106, 264–65, 299
descriptions, 137, 141, 164, 168, 176, 209, 233, 254,
    256–57, 338, 343
descriptions of barriers in educator and school
    values, 343
descriptive study, 27, 239, 244–45
design, 28, 35, 247, 253, 271, 278, 287, 297, 347, 350, 353
designing equitable policies and practices, 246
developed capacity of leaders, 219
developing equitable policies and practices, 273

developing mission, 108
development, 22–23, 75, 108–9, 116, 120, 163, 215, 218,
    220–21, 247, 249, 274, 276
development and implementation of healthy poli-
    cies, 108
development of educator actions, 22
development of inclusive core values, 163
development of inclusive educator core values, 109
development of inclusive educator values and
    behaviors, 22
development of tools for individuals and organiza-
    tions, 249
Dewey, 75–76, 253, 276–77, 295
dialogic conversations, 115, 138, 344
dialogic processes, 7, 68, 237
dialogue, 14, 29–30, 56, 77, 87, 90–91, 101–3, 117–18,
    131–33, 158, 169–70, 185–86, 194–95, 198–200,
    206–12, 224, 233–36, 267–69, 288–90, 292–94
dialogue practices, 206
dialogue processes, 35, 99, 117, 171, 345
difference in student and teacher demographics by
    recruiting, 265
differences, 92–94, 96–98, 100–101, 140–43, 145–46,
    160–61, 165–66, 168–72, 175, 177–78, 182–83,
    185–86, 232, 234, 260, 262–66, 310–13, 324–26,
    337, 339–40
differences in core values, 252
Differences in norms, 92, 260
dignity, 111, 168, 321
Dilts, 69, 76–77, 252–53, 270, 274, 277, 295
Dilts's Nested Levels, 58, 69–70
disability, 21, 33, 48, 51, 91, 139, 148, 176, 178, 262
disadvantaged students, 46–47, 252
Disaggregated student achievement data, 2
discipline, 5–6, 88, 92, 130–31, 152–53, 174–78, 180,
    206, 209, 229–30, 260, 262, 287–89
discipline data, 123, 146, 171, 174–76
discipline policies, 93, 172, 177, 260
disparities, 47, 50–51, 134, 152, 174, 176, 192, 209,
    229–30, 349, 353
disparity in student discipline data, 176
dispersion patterns, 197, 199–200, 228
Distribute Response Sheet, 304, 320, 331
distributes, 65, 313, 317, 323
district, 22–27, 61–64, 67–71, 88–91, 106–9, 115–29,
    131–37, 154–58, 174–83, 191–96, 203–11, 215–18,
    228–31, 246–48, 255–59, 261–63, 265–70, 285–90,
    298–302, 339–46
  community-centric, 91, 259
  proficient, 191, 253
  school/, 353
  train, 333
district administrators, 71, 123, 125, 180, 209, 254,
    265, 268, 280, 283, 289
District administrators and teachers focus
    efforts, 285

As you read **Leading Change through the Lens of Cultural Proficiency**, we invite you to connect with other school leaders on social media using the hashtags below. Let us know how you are implementing the Cultural Proficiency Framework and applying the Tools in your organization.

#LEADINGTHRUEQUITY

#CULTURALLYPROFICIENTLEADERSHIP

@midwestccps   @leadthruequity

To download templates and other resources found in this book, use the QR codes below.

Keep Learning...

AVAILABLE CONSULTING

The Center for the Culturally Proficient Educational Practice (CCPEP)

Our vision is to provide and support educators with an equity-based professional learning framework that ensures high-quality teaching and learning experiences exist for all learners. CCPEP offers professional learning opportunities, including a three-phase professional learning certification process, and a host of various resources to help support the vision.

For more information, visit CCPEP.org.

CES
CASEY EDUCATIONAL SOLUTIONS

Casey Educational Solutions (CES)

Casey Educational Solutions offers consulting, coaching, facilitating, planning, and support to build the capacity of teams. Through an experiential approach, participants will utilize the Tools for Cultural Proficiency and learn culturally responsive practices, helping to transform organizations from the inside out.

Midwest Collaborative for Cultural Proficiency in Schools (MCCPS)

MCCPS offers highly personalized in-person and virtual professional learning opportunities for educators, including district-level and school-level teams, who wish to embed the work of Cultural Proficiency in all aspects of the school organization. Participants apply the Tools of Cultural Proficiency for addressing equity, access, and inclusion issues in schools and opening doors so all students can thrive.

For more information, visit www.midwestccps.org or contact Jaime E. Welborn at info@midwestccps.org.

A SAGE Publishing Company

Helping educators make the greatest impact

CORWIN HAS ONE MISSION: to enhance education through intentional professional learning.

We build long-term relationships with our authors, educators, clients, and associations who partner with us to develop and continuously improve the best evidence-based practices that establish and support lifelong learning.